Contents

Foreword vii
Introduction ix
Map 1 : South Eastern Australia xvi
Map 2 : Hobart To Bruny Island xvii

Chapter 1   St Columba's Seminary, Springwood
                  Letters 1–10 1
                  Reflection by Kate Fogarty 35

Chapter 2   St Columba's Seminary, Springwood
                  Letters 11 – 20 37
                  Reflection by Austin Cooper OMI 75

Chapter 3   St Patrick's Seminary, Manly
                  Letters 21 – 30 77
                  Reflection by Edmund Campion 110

Chapter 4   Ordination Year
                  Letters 31 – 42 113
                  Reflection by Corrie van den Bosch 143

Photos I 145

Chapter 5   Launceston & Hobart
                  Letters 43 – 53 151
                  Reflection by Graeme Howard 197

Chapter 6   Tasmania
                  Letters 54 – 64 199
                  Reflection by Bobby Court 235

Chapter 7   Priesthood and Columbans
                  Letters 65 – 79 239
                  Reflection by Gabrielle McMullen 282

Chapter 8	Tasmania	
	Letters 80 – 88	285
	Reflection by Adrian L. Doyle	314
Photos II		316
Chapter 9	Tasmania	
	Letters 89 – 95	327
	Reflection by Angela Hazebroek	356
Chapter 10	Letters To Brian	
	Letters 96 – 100	359
	Reflection by David Ranson	383
Epilogue		385
	Reflection by Stancea Vichie	385
Acknowledgments		391
Chart of John Corcoran Wallis' Letters		392
Time Line of Events		396
Index of Names		398
Index of Topics		407
John Corcoran Wallis 1910 to 2001		410
	Reflection by Fay Woodhouse	410

*I acknowledge the traditional and original peoples
of the land in Australia.
I pay my deep respects to them,
especially to the peoples of the areas referred to in this book.*

*For
My two sisters, Carmel and Margaret
and nineteen cousins
Mary, John (dec.), Jane, Frances, Kathleen, Annie,
Gerard (dec.), Moira, Peter, Marie, Brian,
Christopher, Bernard, Gabrielle, Gerard, Pauline, Karen, David and
Loretta –
nieces and nephews of Father John Wallis
and grandchildren of Emily (Emma) Wallis and Abraham Wallis*

Proceeds of this book will go to
The Missionary Sisters of Service and
Highways and Byways – A Community of Service
(formerly the John Wallis Foundation)
www.missionarysisters.org.au
www.highwaysandbyways.org.au

Dear Mother Dear Father

John Corcoran Wallis'
Letters Home 1927-1949

Bernadette T. Wallis

COVENTRY
PRESS

Published in Australia by
Coventry Press
33 Scoresby Road
Bayswater Vic. 3153
Australia

ISBN 9780648360179

Copyright © Missionary Sisters of Service 2019

All rights reserved. Other than for the purposes and subject to the conditions prescribed under the *Copyright Act*, no part of this publication may be reproduced, stored in a retrieval system, or transmitted in any form or by any means, electronic, mechanical, photocopying, recording or otherwise, without the prior permission of the publisher.

Cataloguing-in-Publication is available from the National Library of Australia
http://catalogue.nla.gov.au

Cover image by Michael Rebbechi
Cover design by Ian James – www.jgd.com.au
Text design by Megan Low, Filmshot Graphics (FSG)

Photos from family collections, the archives of the Missionary Sisters of Service and other acknowledged sources.

Foreword

Bernadette Wallis is a niece of John Wallis who wrote these letters. She is a grand-daughter of Abraham and Emily, the principal recipients of these letters. The compilation is a labour of love, thoroughly and painstakingly undertaken to reflect the character of the priest John Wallis who founded the Missionary Sisters of Service of which Bernadette is a member. Bernadette is certainly the person best qualified to order and draw fruit from these 100 letters. She has grouped letters with a common theme and time in each chapter. Each chapter is commenced with a loving reflection by Bernadette on the emerging character of the writer John as he moves through his years of seminary training, discerning his vocation to the founding of the religious congregation.

Bernadette deftly offers insights into John's priestly ministry for those on the margins and those in the bush. His three deaf siblings provided daily experience of those who can be so easily overlooked. Early in his priestly ministry, he was pulled up short by the parishioner on Bruny Island who wanted the assurance that her family would enjoy the same priestly ministry as those in Hobart.

With a brilliant flourish, Bernadette has invited prominent Catholics to write a brief reflection on the letters at the end of each chapter. These reflections allow the reader to apply the spiritual insights and journeying of the letters to the contemporary church scene. And it's not all sweetness and light. Reflecting on John's later ministry to the Australian church teaching the documents of Vatican II, Bernadette observes: "While many, especially women, did adopt changes, there were others, including priests, both diocesan and religious, who did not and some refused, with dire consequences for the presently imploding clericalised Church."

Fr Ed. Campion reflecting on the letters written during John's early seminary days from 1929 to 1931, looks forward to the day in 1968 when the president of Manly Seminary came to breakfast, unfolded his napkin and was startled to find a revolutionary slogan printed there: WE WANT MATURITY, NOT MAXIMUM SECURITY. Campion observes, "It was time to change. By then, however, Father John Wallis had already written many of the chapters of his remarkable life".

As a young Jesuit, I was privileged to know John when he came to do a course on Ignatian spirituality. He had already given a lifetime of priestly service, grounded in the daily pastoral ministry in the Archdiocese of Hobart, inspired to proclaim the spirit of Vatican II the length and breadth of Australia, and having founded a dynamic congregation of sisters able to emulate his vision. He was humble, ordered, and always focused on future ministry. In recent years, I have been further privileged to deliver some of the John Wallis Memorial Lectures in Tasmania and in Toowoomba where I went to school. I have encountered the spirit of John Wallis still alive and active.

Bernadette Wallis has provided the contemporary reader with a lovingly familiar insight into the development and vision of one of Australia's great pioneer priests, opening the *Paschalls Westward Ho! Toffee Assortment* tin and providing a rich array of spiritual sweets for all palates seeking the taste of the Reign of God breaking in here and now.

Fr Frank Brennan SJ AO
CEO
Catholic Social Services Australia

Introduction

This book makes public a hundred hand-written letters sent by Father John Wallis to his family from 1927 to 1949, a period of twenty-two years. One could ask the question, why publish old letters? Why publish John Corcoran Wallis' old letters – they only tell the story of John's younger life? Such questions were indeed considered in the gestation of this book. With others, I pondered, could they shed light on another time in Australia and in the Australian Church of the reality of how life was lived, what people believed, and the ways they expressed their faith in the context of the Australian society? Today, aspects of the letters may seem inconceivable. Change has been rapid in our world at all levels of society, including in our understanding of ourselves living our faith in a global context, with an awareness of the universe never known prior to this time in history. History, then, is a gift from which to understand and attempt to make sense of our past and our present, often to make resolutions and decisions, even unconsciously, moving into a hope-filled future.

The majority of John's letters are to his mother and father, beginning from when he was sixteen years of age and had just entered the seminary at St Columba's College, Springwood, at the base of the Blue Mountains in New South Wales. Two years later, he went from there to the seminary at St Patrick's College, Manly in Sydney. In 1932, John was ordained as a priest for the Archdiocese of Hobart, Tasmania, and in 1944 he founded the Missionary Sisters of Service (MSS), a Catholic religious order.

The Mystery of the Letters

The personal letters were found in a highly decorated rectangular tin – *Westward Ho! Assorted Toffee Tin* that came to the light of day in 2014, when I was working for a few weeks in the Missionary Sisters of Service archives at the Wallis Centre in Hobart. The faithful and astute archivist, Sister Carmel Hall MSS, had been entrusted with them. As the MSS archives were moved from place to place, Carmel had them protected and well hidden. John's brother, Father Brian Wallis, who had a strong sense of history, brought the letters from Melbourne to Hobart in 1966, eleven years after his mother's death in West Brunswick, Melbourne. As one of the executors of her will, he presumably took responsibility for her personal papers plus the *Assorted Toffee Tin* of letters to deal with them appropriately.

Brian sought a meeting with Sister Teresa Morse, the MSS Congregational Leader in Hobart at the time. Brian then made enquiries as to whether the Congregation could, firstly, care for the private collection of letters and, secondly, that their existence not be disclosed to anyone until after John Wallis and his siblings had died. He feared that John would not see the letters as important and that they would be destroyed. Realising their significance, Carmel Hall assured Brian they would be appropriately cared for – and they were.

John died in 2001. Carmel was busily engaged in her work as the Archivist for the Archdiocese of Hobart, so it was not until she retired from the diocesan work that she gave the letters some attention and revealed them to me. As a niece of John and grand-daughter of his parents, I am privileged to have worked with the letters and now to make them available to all his nieces and nephews and a wider audience.

The *Assorted Toffee Tin*

Embossed on the base of the *Assorted Toffee Tin* are the words *Paschalls, Claremont, Tasmania*. The English Cadbury Organisation developed its first overseas factory at Claremont in 1920, which opened in 1921. The firm operated as a subsidiary having joined with Fry and Paschall to become Cadbury-Fry-Paschall.[1] How the *Westward Ho! Assorted Toffee Tin* found its way to Yea and then West Brunswick is unknown. Maybe the *Assorted Toffee Tin* came into Emma's possession when she and Abe visited Tasmania. They had already been to Tasmania on their honeymoon in 1908, not realising how Tasmania would become a significant place in their lives and a familiar topic in their family conversation.

About the Wallis Family

John's parents, Abraham Knight Wallis and Emily Kathleen Corcoran, were married on 22nd January 1908 at St Brigid's Church, Fitzroy. Abe came from Seymour, Emma, as she was known, came from Yea, Victoria. They eventually made their home on a farm *Wirrabong* at Homewood, Yea, north east of Melbourne. Their children were Marie Corcoran (1908), John Corcoran (1910), Donald Corcoran (1912), Thomas Chester (1916), Brian Emmett (1920) and Charles Patrick (1923). Three of the children were profoundly deaf – Marie, Don and Charlie.

---

1   See Rogers, T.B., *A Century of Progress 1831-1931*, p. 83

Marie Wallis attended the Dominican school for Deaf children at Waratah near Newcastle, New South Wales, from 1916–1926, so had left school when John went to the seminary at Springwood. Don Wallis also attended Waratah from 1918, and then in 1923 moved to the newly opened St Gabriel's School for Deaf Boys at Castle Hill, west of Sydney and across the valley from Springwood. Charlie Wallis was also a student at St Gabriel's from 1930–1939. This explains the familiarity of John's Deaf siblings with Sydney and being away from home. The other two children, Chester and Brian Wallis, attended the Homewood State School, St Mary's School conducted by the Sisters of Mercy at Seymour and then the Marist Brothers' Assumption College, Kilmore. Brian also attended St Virgil's College, Hobart for one year after John was ordained and living in Tasmania. This background information assists in contextualising aspects of the letters.

From 1927 to approximately 1936, Emma established a business in Seymour, Wallis' Café, Motorist Tea Rooms, Sydney Road on the Old Hume Highway, in order to partly finance John's seminary education and the education of the other children. She lived and worked in Seymour, her daughter, Marie, assisting in the café cooking pastries and pies. John's father, Abe, stayed on the farm, and at weekends came to Seymour bringing produce and to assist at the café. After the café was sold, Emma returned to the farm at Homewood.

In 1945, Abraham died at home. Soon after the farm was sold, Emma and her son, Chester, bought a property near Broadford. Eventually, Emma settled in West Brunswick, where the letters in the *Assorted Toffee Tin* found a home until her death in 1955.

Schooling

John began his schooling at the local public school at Homewood, riding his horse, Bonnie. After one year at Sacred Heart Primary School with the Sisters of St Joseph in Yea, he attended Assumption College Kilmore (ACK) conducted by the Marist Brothers for his secondary education. Being an independent and stubborn child, and used to the freedom of the bush, he was a challenge to contain at school because of his buoyant energy. Thus, he had his ups and downs, at one time close to being expelled. These problems did not deter him from his dream to serve as a missionary and pastoral priest, even when he was not accepted by some dioceses and religious orders on health grounds. It seems he was diagnosed with a 'murmur of the heart'.

Training for the Priesthood

On 15th April 1927, John Corcoran Wallis arrived at St Columba's College, Springwood seminary, where the students took a two-year program of philosophy. If they succeeded in their studies, they moved to the seminary at St Patrick's College, Manly, for four years of theology in preparation for ordination. A student had to be at least twenty-two and a half before he could be ordained. In John's case, he was too young after his six years of study and was required to wait a further six months for ordination. While his peers were ordained in July, his ordination took place on 18th December 1932.

Ordination

John was ordained at St Patrick's Church, Kilmore, Victoria. While not wanting any fuss or aggrandisement at his ordination, the reality was different. Even a special train catered for all the visitors from Melbourne, including a number of dignitaries and, in particular, Archbishop William Hayden of Hobart, who ordained him for his Archdiocese.

Archdiocese of Hobart

In 1933, John began his ministry as a priest in Tasmania. Initially, he was in Launceston for ten weeks before going to the St Mary's Cathedral parish in Hobart as an Assistant Priest. Mid-year, he was introduced to Bruny Island, south of Hobart, an isolated part of the parish that received very little attention from the Church. It became of great significance to John in the context of his life.

On his first visit to Bruny Island in his first year in Tasmania, John met the young mother, Kit Hawkins, who challenged him with such questions: What about our children? Doesn't the Church care about us and our faith? Don't our children matter? What about us? Out of sight, out of mind? These questions plagued John's mind for ten years before he established a group of women, that later became a religious order, to go into the *highways and byways* of rural Australia, so that the Church could minister to those in remote and isolated areas, just like Bruny Island.

John's life was characterised by his pastoral ministry. He established different ministries in the Archdiocese. He was a man before his time – so when Vatican II was announced, he rejoiced that the *windows* of the institutional Church could be opened and the freshness of the Spirit could flow. In Tasmania with the liturgical Archbishop Guilford Young, deeply involved in the activity and discussions at Vatican II and who carried the enthusiasm of the theology emanating from Vatican II nourished the spirituality of the people of Tasmania educating them in theological thinking from the Vatican Council II. John was part of this and knocked on Archbishop Young's door as soon as he had returned from each Vatican Council II session to collect copies of the most recent documents released.

John then travelled to many parts of Australia to give lectures and retreats mostly to religious and priests to inform, and impress upon them the call to change. In the 1960s and 1970s, many, and perhaps most Sisters in Australia, especially those influenced by John, had their own copy of the Vatican II documents and were reading them. While many, especially women did adopt changes, there were others, including priests, both diocesan and religious, who did not and some refused with dire consequences for the presently imploding clericalised Church.

The Letters

John wrote separate letters to his mother and father addressing them 'Dear Mother' and 'Dear Father'. While this book is not a full biography of Father John Wallis, its main purpose is to share in nine chapters the ninety-five surviving letters written by John to his mother and father (and two to siblings when they were young) and to put them into context. A tenth chapter has been added with five letters from John his brother, Brian, written between 1944 and 1947, and were included in the private collection. They are most significant and fill out the picture even more.

There are gaps of information between the letters. Some letters may have been lost or deliberately destroyed, so there are significant events in the family that do not get a mention, the reason being that John would have been present at family events, for example, when he is celebrant for Don and Chester's weddings. A description of his father's death is another major occasion that is not found in this collection of letters, because John was present. He had already shared the experience with his family. The reader of the letters assumes the death of John's father, because he writes of his concern and worry about his mother's welfare and future.

From each of the letters I have drawn quotes that are sometimes slightly modified for clarity. These quotes are used at the top of each letter. They can draw attention to how John is thinking and feeling – and can inspire us.

In the original letters, it seems John is often writing in haste and he also compromises on the use of stationery. Thus, he leaves minor words out, for example 'the'. Often I have added words with [] brackets; other places the letters have been left as they were written, if the meaning was still clear. He used the symbol '&' throughout his letters, which was tedious when reading them. Because, for the purpose of this book I am looking at the content of the letters, I have replaced '&' with 'and'. I have added commas in sentences to make more sense of the meaning. Quite often John uses upper case for the initial letter in such words as 'gold', 'printing office', 'altar' where it is unnecessary and interrupts the flow of the letter. I have changed this to lower case for most such words. John sometimes misspells or uses the wrong name for fellow students or others, for example, Morgan instead of Morganti, Kenny instead of Kennedy. Sometimes he calls 'Ted' as 'Ed', etc. I have noted it when this is obvious or known. I have also made paragraphs where in the original letters John uses every line to the end to use every bit of space on the pages. Often he added a sentence around the side or on top of the stationery.

As I worked with each letter, my hope was to find a gem or gems that energised the life of the young man, Jack. Of particular note is the relationship John had with his mother, which surely enabled him to live his priesthood with such a pastoral approach to people in the context of the reality of our world.

I trust that this collection of John's letters will be read intelligently and with sensitivity to the prevailing spirituality and the Australian milieu in which they were written.

My hope is that by publishing these letters as a book, it may be a resource or pave the way for any future research that may be done in relation to John's other writings.

Introduction

Emma and Abe Wallis kept John's letters in The Paschalls *Westward Ho! Toffee Assortment Tin*, which was manufactured at Cadbury's, Claremont, Tasmania.

MAP 1 : SOUTH EASTERN AUSTRALIA

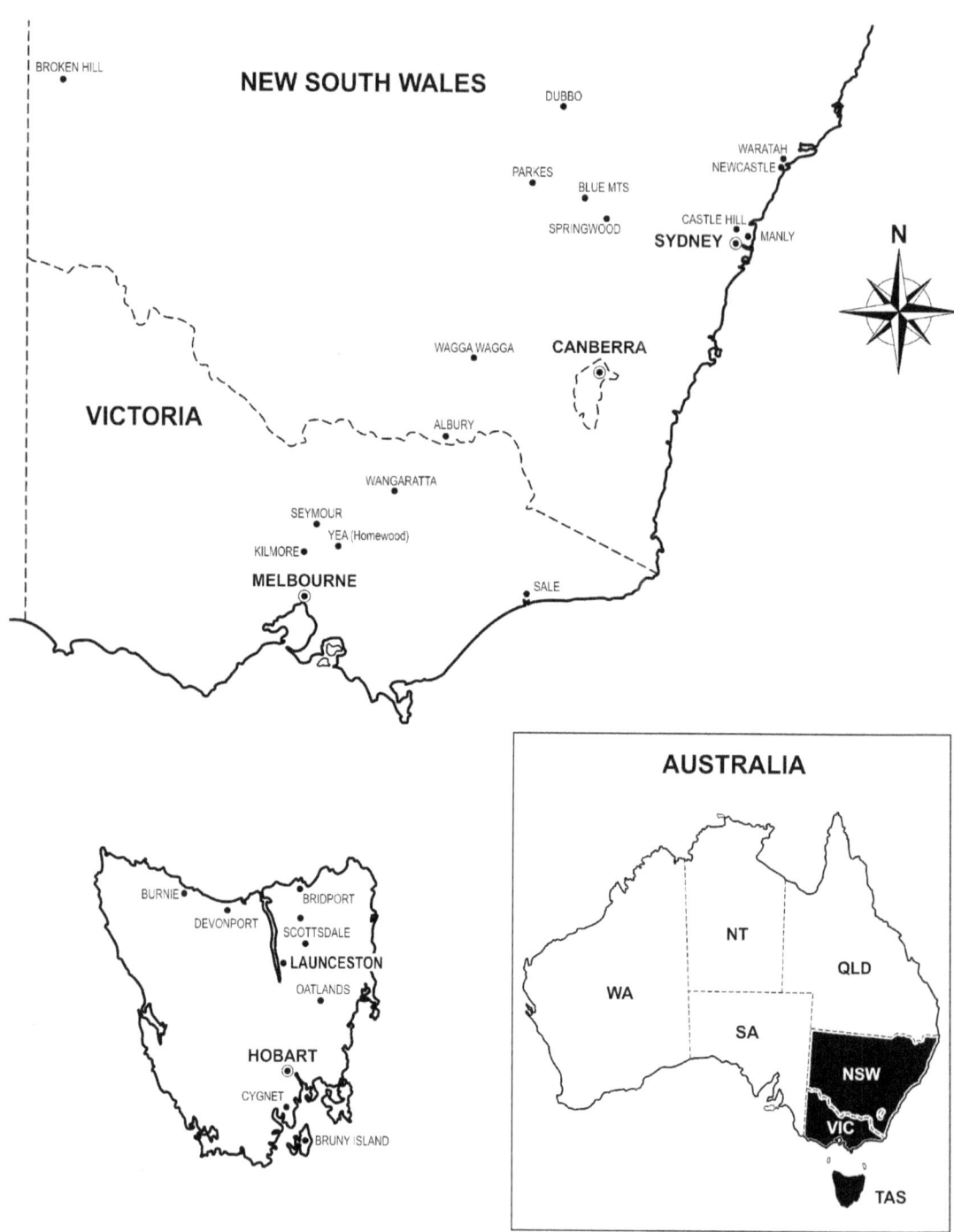

Introduction

MAP 2 : HOBART TO BRUNY ISLAND

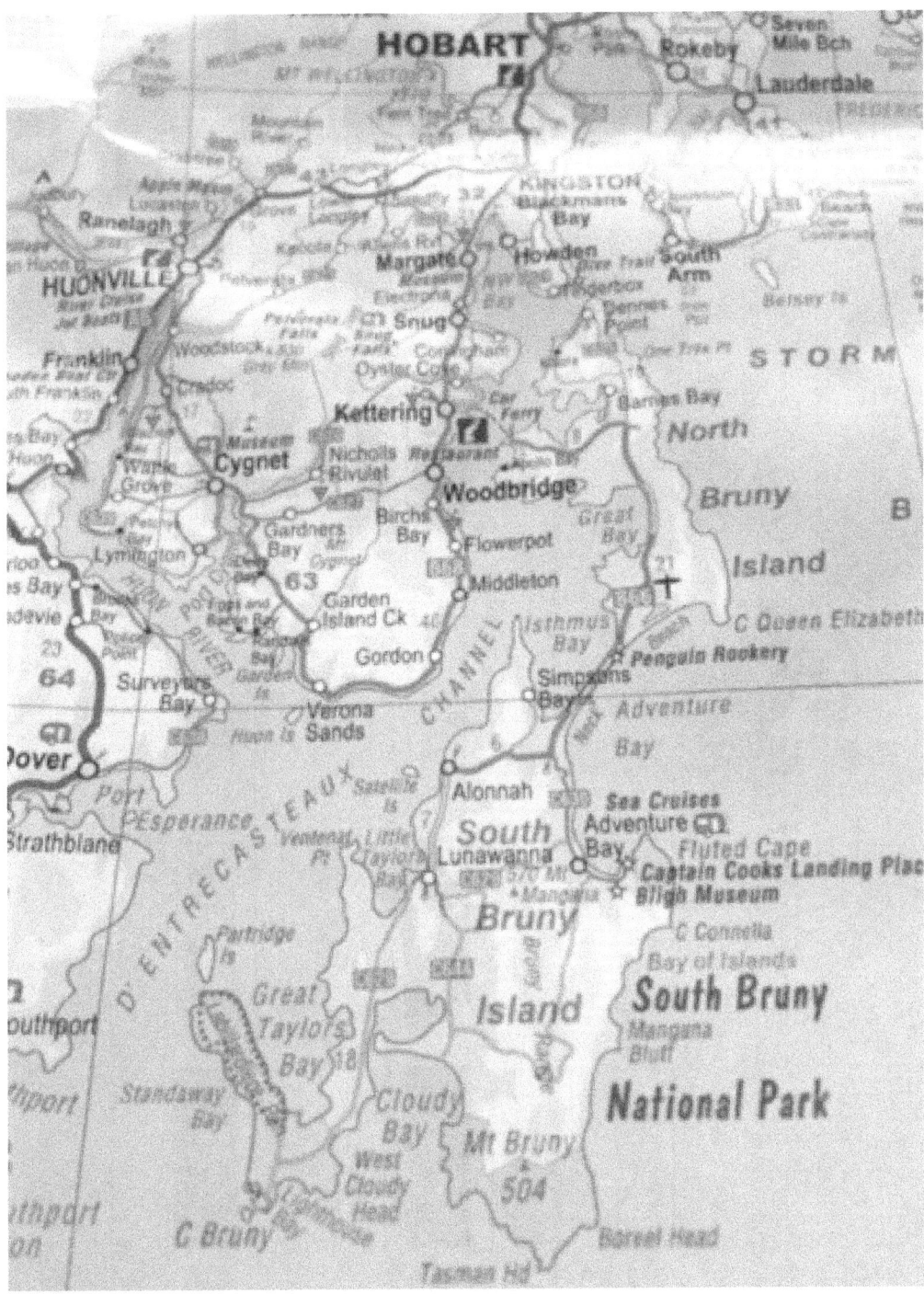

Image of Map, produced in 2012, photographed and used with permission by Carto Plus.

Dear Mother Dear Father

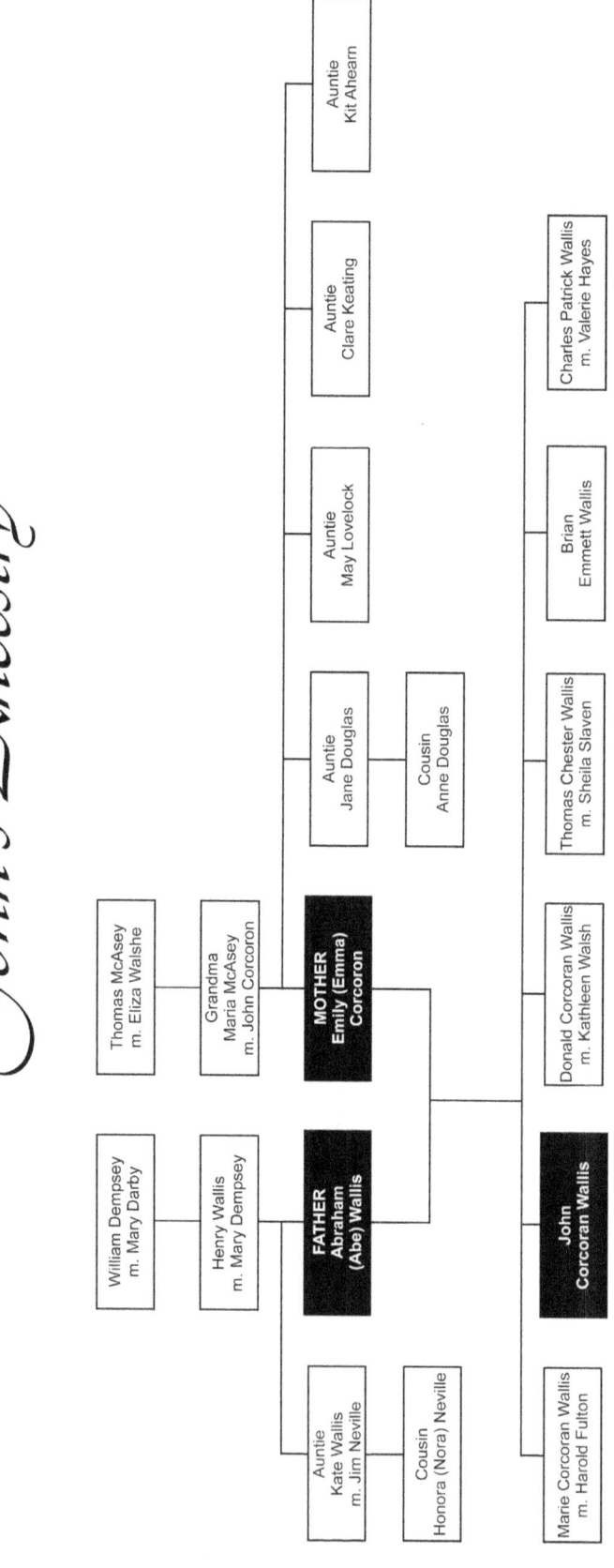

J. C. WALLIS, Yea,
who entered St. Columba's College, Springwood, N.S.W., on March 1st, to study for the priesthood.

Photo 1927, Assumption College, Kilmore Yearbook.

St Columba's Seminary, Springwood 1927
Letters 1–10

INTRODUCTION

On 15th April 1927 John Corcoran Wallis arrived to fulfil his dream and begin studies for the priesthood at St Columba's Seminary, Springwood, which is situated at the base of the beautiful Blue Mountains west of Sydney, New South Wales. Built as a seminary for the training of Catholic priests in 1909, its European monastic architecture was in vast contrast to the surrounding Australian bush.

The first chapter consists of ten letters home from John, six are written to his mother and four to his father in Victoria between April and August 1927, giving insight into John's initial months at St Columba's College. John was known as Jack in the family.

Above: The seminary at St Columba's College, Springwood, NSW. John studied at St Columba's 1927 – 1928.
Photo: Blue Mountains Library, Local Studies collection.

Letter 1 to Mother

*I am in Philosophy. Mother, you do not know
how hard it is going to be for me to get through.*

In this letter of two pages (2nd May 1927), the first known letter, John Wallis writes to his mother at Homewood near Yea, Victoria, for her birthday on 5th May. He is sixteen years old and now at St Columba's College, Springwood. Already finding study hard, especially philosophy and Greek, he writes, *I am a long way behind.* He tells his mother that a letter came from the Irish-born Archbishop William Barry in Hobart, formalising his initial acceptance for the Archdiocese of Hobart. John also reports that he has written to his mentor, Brother William Molloy, a Marist Brother at Assumption College Kilmore, where he did his secondary schooling.

This letter refers to his brother, Don at St Gabriel's School for Deaf Boys, Castle Hill, and that Fred Reilly, originally from Yea district, had been to see John and would bring Don with him next time. He also writes about having plenty of food. Other topics covered money, books, socks and his teeth, leaving his mother with a comforting thought: *Well, Mother, I am getting on alright. I am feeling goodoh!*

* * *

Letter 1. Written 2nd May 1927 from St Columba's College, Springwood

St Columba's College,
Springwood.
Monday [2nd May 1927]

Dear Mother,

I received your most welcome letter on Saturday. I was very glad to get it. I am writing this one to wish you very happy returns of the day on your birthday next Thursday. I suppose Father would get my letter after yours had gone. You did not mention it in your letter. Well Mother I am getting on alright I am feeling goodo. I eat well. There is always plenty to eat.

Fred Reilly was up here on Saturday last. They have property near Springwood. He came out here and brought his Cinema Camera with which he took a number of photos of the College and grounds. He is a very nice man to talk to. He is very young in appearance. He said he will bring Don up one weekend. It is very good of him. I liked him very much.

I have written to Brother William [Molloy][1] re the missal. I also wrote to Fr. Egan. The letter from the Archbishop was about the acceptance for Hobart. I wrote to him thanking him for the offer. I will send the letter home. Will you please keep it, as I may need it later. I wrote to Marie and told her all the news I could think of. I will write to her often.

I am in the Philosophy. Mother, you don't know how hard it is going to be for me to get through. I have about a hundred pages of notes to copy up and learn. A lot of them are in Latin. I am a long way behind. I have to make use of every spare minute I can get.

I arranged about my soutane. I think I will get it next week. It will cost £5/17/6. This is a very high price but there is no other way out of the difficulty. The soprano[2] will be about 50/-. I think I have enough money to pay for it but I do not yet know what the books I had to get will cost. I had to get a number of books all of which are fairly dear. I will be very pleased to get the sox, etc. I wash them myself as they are not washed very well here. My teeth[3] don't seem any better now. I tried them again.

I was sorry to hear about the fire. I hope and pray that all will be well. Has it rained there yet? We don't see any papers here. Fancy one of the priests, Fr. Wallace having stayed out with Fr. Willis during his vacations and knowing Lil and Flo Brown, the Siers and Quinlans.[4] He is only ordained a short time.

---

1   Brother William Molloy is mentioned 24 times in this collection of letters. He was principal at Assumption College, Kilmore 1922–1927, 1931–1936, then returned as a teacher 1943.
2   Soprano, a clergy black shirt.
3   John has a denture that obviously is not fitting properly. His mother sends some adhesive powder to assist him.
4   The people are locals from Yea district, John's home-town. In 1885 the Quinlans bought the property owned by John's great-grandfather, Thomas McAsey.

Well, Mother, I will write again soon. I must first try and get up to the class in Philos and Greek. Goodbye and love to all. Your fond Son.
Remember Month of May is month of Mary.
Jack

Letter 2 to Father

*On the finest night
There are great flashes of lightning
That seem brighter than I have ever seen before*

This is John's first known letter to his Father (early May 1927), consisting of four pages written on the front and back of the St Columba's College stationery. He attempts to take turns to write to each of his parents, but this does not eventuate. The majority of the letters are to his mother.

John is prepared to discuss personal details with both parents as is seen in the saga with his dentures and the *plate powder*! In this letter he is anxious to know what was happening on the farm and with the neighbours – he thinks there is not much news for him to tell. He also realises the challenges with finances at home and the limitations of what his parents can provide. Concerned with a fire on the leased Wentworth's paddock and wondering about the *weaners*, John knows the perils of farming life. He notes the stormy weather they have had at Springwood.

As the 481st student at Springwood, John settles into his studies especially Philosophy which he fears. While he writes about sport and is interested in it, he does not see himself as a sportsman. Other matters he writes about are books, study and exams, laying bricks, rugby, the weather, fees and the lecturers – the concerns of the sixteen year old.

* * *

*S.C.C.
Springwood
Friday*

Dear Father,

Just a note to let you know how I am getting on. I received Mother's letter a couple of days ago and also the parcel of books. I was glad to get them. They are quite alright. I also got the 'Plate Powder' but have not tried it yet. I will try it this evening after school. I am quite well as I hope you and all at home are.

I was sorry to hear of your bad luck with Wentworth's Paddock. Was there a big fire? I hope you will manage to come out of the weaners all right yet. How is the water there? Here we have had a few showers of rain from time to time. I suppose you realise the value of the bore now. I am always

St. Columba's College,
Springwood.
Friday [May 1927]

Dear Father,

Just a note to let you know how I am getting on. I received Mother's letter a couple of days ago and also the parcel of books. I was glad to get them. They are quite alright. I also got the 'Plate Powder' but have not tried it yet. I will try it this evening after school. I am quite well as I hope you and all at home are.

I was sorry to hear of your bad luck with the Wentworth's Paddock.[5] Was there a big fire? I hope you will manage to come out of the weaners all right yet. How is the water there? Here we have had a few showers of rain from time to time. I suppose you realise the value of the bore now. I am always thinking of you. How is Mr. Coonan getting on with his lot?

Things have been going on quite well here. I have finished writing up my Philosophy Notes. I will now have to learn them. This is the hardest part. Last Wednesday we had what is known as "Blue" Wednesday. All the students come together into the one big study. In front are the Professors (7). The Rector is at a table and has two boxes with numbers in them. Nearby is a Rostrum or raised platform. The Professors draw two numbers out of the boxes. Then the pupils whose numbers they are have to come out on the platform in turn and spend 5 minutes answering various questions about a certain subject. Thus there are two students from each class for each subject. I think the reason for having these exams is to make the pupils study. If they don't know the work they are in a very awkward position. Then after the Exam we had a small retreat from 11 o'clock in the Morning till breakfast time next morning. These 'Blue Wednesdays' come every month being the first Wednesday. The next big exam will be in the last week of June when the Mid-winter exams take place.

Operations on the Recreation hall have been going rather slowly. There is only a limited supply of cement. I go and give a hand every evening. It is useful to know how to do these little jobs. The bricks are being made from sand and cement (4 to 1). There is some beautiful sand about here. All the country is of a sandy nature.

Football has been going on for a couple of weeks. The Rugby team is practicing to play Manly. This day they say is the best day of the year. The Aussie Rulers have had about 4 games. In the last two games a few Rugbyites joined and were well pleased with the Game. Last week we had a Handball Comp. I entered but my partner got a sore hip during the game and pulled out.

---

5   The undulating Wentworth's paddock on King Parrot Creek is off Wentworth Road, which rises into the Tallarook State Forest.

I was very poor. I was out of practice. There are still a couple of games to be played before the Comp. ends. There are some good players here.

It has been fairly cold here for the last couple of days. I believe it is extremely cold here in winter. There are the winds called the 'Westerlies' which are very cold. When the sun is shining it is generally warm. On fine days this is a fine place and even on rainy days it is not very cold. It is on those days, which are betwixt and between that it is cold. There is always a lot of lightning here at night. Even on the finest nights there are great flashes of lightning that seem brighter than I have seen before.

The tailor came up and measured me for my soutane and Soprano. He charges fairly high. The soutane is £5.17.6 and the Soprano is about 45/-. He will come up again to fit me. I have enough money to pay for them and for most of my books. But I have yet to get books that I think will cost about 22/6 all told. Would you please send me some money for them? I will try to spend as little as possible. There are really no other big things to be considered but little things, which I got when home on holidays from Kilmore[6] I will have to get here. I asked Msgr. Brauer about the fees. He said it is customary to pay quarterly or half yearly. The full fee is £60.0.0. I think the half yearly way would be best.

Did Mother tell you about Fr. Wallace knowing Fr. Willis. He is only a young priest and is a fine man. He went to Manly to see his old mates and saw Vin Cochrane and Gus Lacey. They wished to be remembered to me. He was said to be the Best Sport in Manly at his time and seeing that he is a Professor so young we can conclude that he is clever too.

We do not see very much of the priests. They keep to themselves. After giving their lectures they go out to their own rooms. They go out in their cars. I have not seen any of them at games of any kind. The Rector comes over to the building sometimes and gives a hand at laying the bricks.

Friday Night. I tried the teeth again, the stuff holds them for a while and then it lets them go again. I have been sucking them and trying to make them keep up. Next time I write I will let you know how they are. Last week M. Brauer put my name on the Roll. I am the 481st student to enroll. All these however have not gone through. Some of them have left off when half way through their course. I am the Second Junior man of the house.

Well, Father, I think news is scarcer here than it would be at home, so I will now close with fondest love from Your loving Son,

Jack

PS. I am enclosing two snaps taken at Blackheath. One is of the fall, Govetts Leap, the other is of the fall after it reaches the valley below.

---

6   Assumption College, Kilmore, John's secondary college.

The fall is about 500 feet. A bush-ranger Govett is supposed to have ridden a horse over here in order to escape the Police. There is a path down the side to the bottom

Govett's Leap, Blue Mountains NSW

Letter 3 to Father

I could not describe the majestic beauty of the place.

In this short two-page letter to his father (mid-late May 1927), John is grateful for the money sent to him and assures his father that he will be careful with money. The children he speaks of are his young brothers at home, Chester, Brian and Charlie. Earlier this month (5th May), Don, his brother at St Gabriel's School for Deaf Boys, writes to his parents: "*I often look at the Blue Mountains and think of Jack. We can see Springwood from here ... I wrote to Jack last week ...*"[7] Don, conscious of Jack across the valley and the hills, looks forward to Fred Reilly taking him to see his brother and where he is actually living.

John's interest in Assumption College Kilmore continues. The older Brother William Molloy mentored many students who joined the priesthood or religious life. He follows them with encouragement and interest.

In this letter the Melbourne-Sydney, Australian Rules and Rugby rivalry is evident with a delightful description of a Rugby match. Also note the hot topic of the British Empire, especially within an Irish Catholic milieu.

The added incomplete letter is to John's mother and describes the *majestic beauty* of a particular part of the Blue Mountains and one of the epic and memorable bush-walking treks and picnics that the young men from the seminary undertook.

* * *

1

ST. COLUMBA'S COLLEGE,
SPRINGWOOD.
BLUE MOUNTAINS, N.S.W.

Sunday Night.

Dear Father,

Just a note to thank you for your cheque which I caved yesterday. I thank you very much for it. I thank

---

7   Letter held by Bernadette Wallis

Sunday Night. [May 1927]

Dear Father,

Just a note to thank you for your cheque which I received yesterday. I thank you very much for it. I thank you also for the £3.50 extra. I think now I can get on with what I had as I found that when the books arrived they were cheaper than I expected. However I can put that away. I will do my best to save as much as possible.

I was sorry to hear about your hard times. I am glad the rain has come. You ought to take a rest now. I am always thinking of you and Mother and the children. I am always interested to know how you are getting along and about everything around the farm.

Well, Xavier got beaten again and the Marist Bros. school up here St. Joseph's[8] *got beaten in the Public School boat race both in the 4's and the 8's. We have been playing a few games of football here. The Aussie Rulers had about 3 games. The Rugby League players had a game today. A few Aussie Rulers including Alf Schmude joined in. They all vowed after that it was their last game. It is a very rough game. If a man has the ball all the others chase him – get him around the neck or up end him by the legs or bring him down to the ground any way. There is no respect for one another. Instead of trying to kick goals they kick out of bounds, and then have a place kick for goal.*

From now till after the Manly match Aussie Rulers will not get a look in. The hand-ball Comp which was started some time ago is over. The tennis court here is very rough. I have not had a game. There are not many players here. We do not hear any news of the Sports outside. The Professors do not tell us any news.

Fancy Kilmore being so dry. I bet the boys will be hard up. We found it rather hard last year for water. It will be very bad this year. I have not heard from Brother William since I came. One of the boys who knew Brother Will got a photo of all those who he taught. There were five of us. I have not seen it yet but he said he would show it to me. We have had very little rain here. The football oval is very hard. The water here comes from a weir of the College about half a mile away. It is pumped up here.

We had a Debate last night the Subject being, "Is it Australia's best policy to remain in the Br. [British] Empire?" The Government argued in the Affirmative. It was a very heated debate, both sides becoming excited. There is to be a Mock Trial next Saturday night.

Well Father I am short of news so I will now close, thanking you once again for your kindness to me in the past and at present. I remain,

Your loving Son,

Jack.

PS. How does the yellow hair look now that it has grown?[9]

---

8   St Joseph's College, Hunters Hill.
9   This may refer to an in-house joke at home or in a conversation with his father.

This part letter is to John's mother that appears to have been written soon after the above letter. The rest of the letter is missing.

...down the bed of a creek – crawling, scrambling over rocks and jumping from point to point. We came at last to a big cave. Here we left nearly all our clothes but singlets, trousers and boots. After going down a rough hill – rougher than any at home, we came to the Springwood Creek. This was in a kind of ravine or gorge between two rows of huge mountains. There were great walls on either side rising up over a hundred feet. I could not describe this majestic beauty of the place. Besides a few patches of maiden hair and a few older berry trees, there was not much vegetation other than the usual bush. But the beautiful shapes of the rocks and the quaint appearance of the walls were worth all the walking. After going for about three miles along this, we came to the Grose. It is not a big river – somewhat about the size of the King Parrot (Creek). But as it came tumbling over rocks it was truly beautiful. In one place there was a kind of lake, which was as calm as the water in a wash dish. It was caused by the mountains melting in the form of a triangle as is easiest shown by illustration. Grose to Springwood Creek.

We stayed there for an hour or so while we had dinner and rested a bit. Then we went up the Springwood Creek. It took us nearly 2 hours to go 3 miles and we were going as quickly as possible as we wanted to break the record for the trip to the Grose. It is very easy to get lost here. All the mountains are so alike and there are so many gullies with walls alike that one forgets his bearings. For every year till this, there had been a party lost but this time all arrived back safely. One of the students killed a Carpet snake 8 feet long. It was the biggest snake I have seen. We got home about half past five having taken 4½ hours to do eight miles. I was very tired. We went to bed half an hour earlier than usual.

When I got home that night I found a letter from Bro. William waiting me. I am sending it on to you. We were given a sleep in on Thursday morning and allowed to have all the morning free. We usually have one lecture on Thursdays so we did not miss much. I have not yet recovered but am feeling very sleepy. I went to sleep in school today. I enjoyed the day thoroughly. The rector was very good. He made himself as one of the students and when they offered him a little extra dinner he became quite indignant. On Thursday morning we had a sleep in till 6.30. We also missed the one lecture we usually have on Thursday. So we all had Thursday off. Of course we had study as usual in the afternoon. I wrote to Bro. William that evening as did Alf also. Alf got a letter from Pat Shanly at ACK[10] in which he gives a detailed account of the St. Kevin's match.

On Saturday last we had our Manuscript night. There were some good pieces of poetry handed in but they were very few. After the MSS (manuscripts) were read, the account of the 2nd trip to the Grose was read. The first party from here got there in 1911. Since then no party succeeded till 1920. There were about 50 in that party. They arrived at the Grose after a very long trip. They then followed it for some miles away in the wrong direction. They all had to camp out for the night – on pretty short rations too. They had gone about 16 miles out of their way. You see how easy it is to get lost. There were two students in that party who were reckoned as the two best bushmen that ever went through this College.

I got my Photo taken today. I could only get the one. It is very hard to get films here and then we have not the same amount of spare time in which to get them taken. However I will try to get more. In the meantime I will send on the one I got taken as soon as possible.

We have not had any rain here yet. It has been very dusty. Whenever there is wind here there is always a lot of sand about. On the desks and on the seats in the chapel. It is marvelous how it comes.

Is Father trying to get any place to make up for Ahearns?[11] No doubt he will miss it. In Bro. Will's letter you will see about M. Coonan. I was indeed surprised to hear about the Co-op.[12] It is just as well you did not have too many shares. What was the cause? What is Grace Bett going to do? I suppose they will be having a clearing out sale there. Mr. Alex Drysdale[13] will be hit hard. So also the trustees.

---

10   Assumption College, Kilmore.
11   Ahearn's paddock on Coonan Road and close to Wallis' farm was leased. It seems the lease on the paddock finished. Ahearn's were original identities in the district.
12   It seems that the Dairy Co-operative in Yea went through a recession with Abe and others losing shares and for some people their livelihood.
13   Drysdales were strong local identities in Homewood.

Letter 4 to Mother

*Every day the sky is cloudless
and the sunrise and sunset are sights to be admired.*

This is a five-page letter from John to his mother (May 1927). He has been concerned about the serious drought in Victoria and many other parts of Australia were also suffering. Poor Bonnie, the horse he rode to school at Homewood, dies during the drought. By the middle of June, the drought breaks.

Challenges are now facing John – he tells his mother about the order of day and the silence that is required. The students hope for visitors on Sundays, but he will not have any, unless his younger brother is brought across from Castle Hill. *Everything is done by the bell,* but John adds that this suits him. He knows what he has to do.

The Manly Rugby League team refers to the senior students at St Patrick's College. From time to time, John mentions Cyril Cochrane and Gus Lacey, both ex-Assumption College students and known to his parents. John's mother typically concerned has asked a question about balance in his life. She knows he can be serious and focus overly on reading and study. *No, I do not cut into recreation!* He is beginning to make friends and tells his mother of two of the students, an Irishman Pat Flarty and Jack McDonald.

From a young student's perspective, John presents an insightful description of a number of the *Pros*, the professors. He adds a little humour – *we were doing Latin at the time the key of the [new Canberra parliament] was being turned* in 1927– an event that was of national interest.

John's maternal Grandma died eighteen months earlier, his mother still grieving her death. Auntie Kate is his father's sister in Seymour. John's sister, Marie, is not well, and has not written to him – she is one who writes with interesting news.

* * *

ST. COLUMBA'S COLLEGE,
SPRINGWOOD,
BLUE MOUNTAINS, N.S.W.

Sunday

Dear Mother,

I have received your most welcome letter yesterday

Sunday. [May 1927]

Dear Mother,

I received your most welcome letter yesterday and also the cheque enclosed for which I thank you and Father. I have not given it to the Rector yet but will give it to him tomorrow morning. I was glad to hear from you. I am well. I hope you and Father and Chester will be able to have a rest now that the rain has come. I am glad the spell is broken. How much did you have? We have had very little here. It has been glorious weather. Every day the sky is cloudless and the Sunrise and sunset are sights to be admired. The air is always nice and fresh.

Every morning after I get up I go for a walk round the oval. We are not allowed to talk at this time. The hours of silence are – at meals except on certain days such as holidays, Sundays and when there are visitors here for meals. At night after prayers till next morning after Breakfast and at study we keep as silent as possible. (We are allowed to talk then but not above a whisper.) I do my Physical Exercise at night. I have not weighed myself. There are no scales here. I might weigh at Mid-winter if we get a Picnic to Wentworth Falls. Mid-Winter is coming on now. It is about 6 weeks till then. The Manly Rugby League Team will be up here then. It is a Picnic day for them. Cyril Cochrane and Gus Laccy will be up then.

I am catching up in Philos a bit now. If I can get a pass at Mid Winter, I will have a chance of getting through. If I do not, I will more than likely have to do another year here in 1st Philos. However I think I will pass as I am getting into the swing of things – No, I do not cut into Recreation. In the evenings I go over to the "Works" on the Recreation hall. Sometimes I do a little Greek in the half hour in the Morning but this is not much. We do not have the long studies we used to have at Assumption College Kilmore. We have four lectures in the morning by the Professors (priests).

By the way it might interest you to know a bit about the Pros as they are called. Monsignor Brauer teaches Physics. He is very clever. He was the head prefect of Manly in his time. He went to Rome 1920 and saw the Canonisation of Joan D'Arc. He comes and helps at the "Works". Father Simonds is the Vice Rector and Bursar. He has charge of the money, looks after food, etc. He is very clever and was also Head Prefect in Manly. He is supposed to be the mug of the family as far as learning goes but yet he can read a book in Greek, Hebrew, Latin and has studied Evolution extensively. He once broadcasted a speech on Darwinism. He also delivered Catholic Credence lectures. He teaches us Latin. He is by far the best teacher here. He is clear and easy to understand.

The next is Father Bowers. He was an All Hallows student and carried off 1st Prize of his school. He is an Irishman. He gives a lecture at times to the students instead of a debate. He is very good. He has a great dislike to Americans and is very good at imitating them. He also imitates the English Cockney people. He is really funny.

Father Nolan is another Irishman. He is hard to understand in his speech. He teaches Philos. He says "weet" for wit, "terum" for term. He is very nice and is rather humourous. Father Downey is a new priest here. He is a Greek teacher. Father O'Brien is rather clever. He is a good singer and musician. He has composed a Mass, which is commonly sung in the Churches. He has a fine library here and studies very hard. He is a teacher of English in which he excels. Father Wallace has only been ordained a short time. He teaches Mathematics.

In the afternoon we have Private study. After this we have Recreation and then Rosary and spiritual Reading. We then have study – tea – study and Recreation. We then have Night Prayers and Meditation.

I am glad you got the snaps. I am enclosing 2 more of the same place, Blackheath. I will get some snaps when I get my new soutane, which is due any day now.

I did not go to Canberra either. We did not hear anything of it except that Mr. Bruce made a very fine speech. Father O'Brien told us that the Prince read his speech. Where is he now? Father Simonds who is rather witty (and often sarcastic) said that when anybody speaks of the opening of Canberra, we were doing Latin at the time the key of Parl House was being turned.

I wrote to Fred Reilly thanking him for his kindness both to myself and to Don. I also wrote to Don. Yes I think it is so nice of him. He is so unassuming in nature. I liked him very much. I have not made any special friend yet. I get on all right with Pat Flarty (Irish boy) and Jack McDonald, who gave me his soutane till I got mine. He is very nice.

Is Rod any good? He must have been rather quiet about it. I did not know of the engagement. Has he had any renovations in the House? I was sorry to hear about poor Bonnie. It was better I think to do that than to let him die of starvation. Has Father got that one [horse] from Mr Coonan?[15] Tell Chester I like to hear all those little things about the place. I am always interested to know how things are going. How many cows are you milking now? They get most of the milk here from a Milkman and make a lot from powder. You can tell the Powdered milk. They get Bread and Meat from the local suppliers. Springwood does well out of the College.

It does seem sad about poor auntie Kate.[16] She was looking forward to being attended to in a few weeks.

---

15   Michael Coonan lived at Homewood on Dairy Road at 'Tara' – they were close neighbours.
16   Auntie Kate is married to Jim Neville.

In your letter you asked if I were happy or not. Well, Mother, I can say that I am really happy. I enjoy myself outside and like the life. The Rule is very easy to follow. It is very beneficial to be under a Rule. All the day is mapped out and there is no time to lag on your hands. Everything is done to a bell. Prayers, meal, study and Recreation.

I sent away to Foys for a few things I wanted. There is a monthly order from here. They are supposed to be able to supply anything from an Anchor to a pin. There are different students to see to different necessities of the students. One looks after the Books. Another has the Boots. This is Frank Massey who is the third of 4 to go for the Priesthood. He has 2 brothers out. Do you remember a Deacon getting the dispensation to give H. Communion to his Father before he died. It was one of his brothers. He has another brother here who entered with him. They will be ordained on the same day. He gets up boots and all kinds of materials for repairs. Another sends away for glasses – another for repairs to Watches. There is a club here now to send films away to be developed. They are trying to get a special discount on all photos printed. Most of the big firms allow discount on goods purchased by Students from here.

Yes, Mother, I will remember Grandma. I will ask the Students to pray for her soul. I always think of her but I will think of her in particular this month. Well, Mother, I have little news here so I will now close with fond love from
Your loving Son
Jack.

PS. I will put a note in for Father here. I will write to him next time. Did Auntie Kate come up? I was sorry to know that Marie was ill. I have not received any letter from her. I will write to her but will not mention anything about her being sick. She is evidently not very well or she would have written me before this.

I cannot get the photos in the envelope. They are too big. I will keep them and show them to you when I go home.

We are to have two holidays this month. Our Lady Help of Christians (The Patroness of Australia) and the feast of the Ascension, two days later. We will also have what is known as Rogation then. That is, we will go in procession to the Grotto of our Lady and around the College.

Well, Mother, Goodnight for the present, I will write again to let you know about the money.

Life was disciplined and spartan for the young seminarians as these later photos of the dining room, classroom and dormitory show. Photos: St Columba's College, Springwood, N.S.W.

Letter 5 to Mother

I am writing this letter in the Bush.
It is beautiful – not a cloud in the sky.

In this two-page letter (25th June 1927), John, after his 17th birthday, again thanks his parents for money and tells his mother he is feeling very much at peace. There is great concern in the family that Chester is ill with a major infection after having his finger accidently chopped off by a mate while yabbying. No antibiotics were available for a quick recovery at that time.

John's language is becoming more religious and theological, mentioning the Guardian Angel, the feast days of the month, (St John the Baptist, Sts Peter and Paul), then a *Missa Cantata* (a sung Tridentine Mass), the high altar, exposition, ecclesiastical subjects and Latin as well. His ideals are high and he takes to heart the meaning of *Tu es sacerdos in aeternum* – *you are a priest forever*. Some studies are less desirable – what about his trigonometry?

* * *

Saturday night. [25th June 1927]

Dear Mother,

I received your registered letter and money (30/-). I also received your book. I thank you for it. I was very pleased to get it. I will write to Father to thank him for the £1.00. I thank you very much for your Birthday present. As I was sending to Pellegrini's for your beads I also ordered a few things I wanted there. I ordered some Olegraphs – those pictures like the ones in Our Rooms of the Guardian Angel. They are only about 6d. each and are truly beautiful. They ought to be here in a few days. I will get the beads blessed. I will send them on as soon as I get them.

Indeed I was very sorry to hear about poor old Chester. It was indeed a very unfortunate affair. I do hope he gets over it. You may be sure I pray for his recovery. I will put in a note for him and also for Brian. Has he to keep his hand in a sling? It will be very painful for him. It was certainly lucky that it did not get any others.

I am writing this letter in the Bush. We have a holiday so I came down to sit on a log and write to you. It is beautiful – there is not a cloud in the sky. We have glorious weather here. It is like a Spring day down south.

We had a picnic yesterday in honour of St. John the Baptist. I went for a walk down to the Gully where the river for the College water is. We had a good day. Today we are having a holiday for the Sacred Heart. On Wednesday we will have one for S.S. Peter and Paul. Today we are having exposition of the Blessed Sacrament. We had a Missa Cantata yesterday and again today. I have been serving lately and served before each of these. I will be on the High Altar tomorrow. Today after the Cantata we had exposition and now we take it in turns to go on adoration. I do not go on till the afternoon but I will go up soon.

We will be starting the exams on Thursday. We have already had a written exam on Trigonometry and in Philos. I do not think I will get many marks in Trig. As it is not an "ecclesiastical" Subject I did not pay particular attention to it. I think I got near a pass in Philosophy. They will be oral exams on Thursday. An "Ecclesiastical" Subject is one, which a student must do and get. The others are merely side lines.

Well Mother I will now close this short note. I have to write to Father (his turn). You will excuse my brevity. Thanking you again for your kind prayers and Birthday present. I am,

Your loving Son,
Jack

PS. I think those were very nice letters. I hope I will as Brother William says here "Tu es sacerdos in aeternum". I think I have chosen rightly because I feel much happier here than at ACK. It is an inward feeling of peace. How is little Charlie? I forgot him while writing to the others.

Letter 6 to Mother

Read books about both sides of the question.
I have done this.

This part of an obviously longer letter to John's mother (1927) may be out of sequence (page 7.) Significantly, while John, in a previous letter, says he is at peace, restlessness is seeping in. Previous verbal discussions, maybe before he left home, appear to have taken place with his parents on an important issue. Will he be a diocesan priest or a religious order priest where he would belong to a community? He needs to discern his course of action. Father Kincella has advised that he will be given the grace he needs to persevere. However, John does not feel he has a confidante who knows him well at the seminary, but he does know he can rely on the trusted Brother William. He will see him during the holidays at Christmas time.

John also writes of humiliating punishment at the seminary – he thinks the practice is stupid and rebels against it, but he does admit that self-control is important.

* * *

Letter 6. Page 7.

(Opening paragraphs are missing)

[1927]

For example, when the person who happens to be reading in the Refectory makes a mistake he has to kneel down before all and say the word correctly three times. It is humiliation such as this makes oneself control himself. I think I could, if I had my mind firmly made up. As Fr. Kincella said, if I have a Vocation to this life God will give me all the grace necessary to persevere.

As you say however I would not like to risk my chances for the Secular priesthood on the mere chance that I had one to the religious life. There is something about the life, which appeals to me. No one more than I knows how it would affect me, Mother and also Father. But even if I were a secular I might be still further away in Tasmania. If I were in the order I would be in either Vic or NSW. Of course, while at the Novitiate I could not see you or write to you, but after that I could.

Bro Will said he had a letter from Marty Brannigan.[17] *I would not have to leave Australia for study. The House of Studies is at Pennant Hills, Sydney – Marty is there now. As for the ordination it would most likely take place in Ballarat. I have read that book again. And really, Mother, would I not be nearer to you than if I were a secular and were in Victoria. What with Parish affairs etc., I would not have as much time as a Religious. As for the solitude I think I would be accustomed to it. No doubt, it would be a struggle but Christ said, "If any man will come after Me, let him take up his cross, deny himself and follow me." As regards to you and Father, I will quote these lines "And when old age comes upon you, when silver crowns your locks, and the world loses it attractions, then it will be consoling.*

And now I, like you, will wind up my letter on the subject of an Order. Since I wrote to you, I wrote to Fr. Kelly CSsR who gave the retreat at Kilmore. He said that the fact that I was in an ecclesiastical College was a "prima facie" argument or very strong one that I should stay here. However he said to give the matter serious thought. Fr. Kincella said to wait for about 2 months and then put the matter before him again. He said to read books about both sides of the question. I have done this. I still feel a desire to go. As you and Father say, it would be a good idea to stay another year. But if I stayed here as adopted by the Bishop of Hobart and then left him, it would not be a very fair thing to him.

---

17   Martin Brannigan became a Redemptorist priest. The Redemptorists were at Pennant Hills, NSW and Ballarat, Victoria.

As you said I could see Bro. William. I can have a good talk to him when I go home. He would know better than even the priest in this case. Of course here we can't put these matters before the Rector. As Rector he is not allowed to hear our confessions, etc. As to wanting to see the Eucharistic Congress, I think Mother, it would be risking a Vocation – And after all, is not the same God or Jesus Christ in the Blessed Sacrament in even the humblest of Chapels. With regard to controlling my desires, etc. one has this much to help him, the fact that all are trying to obey is a great help. There, too, I have I think learnt to go a fair degree to control my self. What is hard there, is having to submit without any protest to whatever is asked of you, to think you give back your child to Our Lord. This is from a little book on Vocations by a Priest of the Order of Preachers.

I hope, Mother, you will not be hurt by anything I have said in here. I am just stating my question. However, I will be very careful and will look forward to Bro. William's advice. I know you will pray for me. It is truly a lovely life, if I have a real vocation. Remember Our Lady of Perpetual Succour.

Good night, dear Mother,
    With love to you Father and All.
        Jack.

Letter 7 to Mother

I will think of you all tomorrow before the Blessed Sacrament.

This is a two-page letter from John to his mother is written after his birthday (11th June 1927.) The food is good like you would *get at a restaurant*, but the sweets are not – maybe not as good as his mother's fare. He has his own soutane now after borrowing one earlier from another student. He has also bought a *soprano*, a clergy black shirt – quite expensive.

St Columba is an Irish missionary saint and the patron of the seminary. On his feast day in June the Springwood students celebrate by playing Rugby against the seminary students from St Patrick's College, Manly, in an annual event.

John's sister Marie is a great source of information from home and she is going to see Harry Neville, an uncle who had been in a train accident. The Brothers from his old school faithfully write to him as trusted mentors. Treasuring their letters he wants to keep them safe.

* * *

St. Columba's College,
Springwood,
Blue Mountains. N.S.W.
Wednesday Night. [June 1927]

Dear Mother,

I received your most welcome letter last Saturday. Thanks very much for your kind wishes on my Birthday. I had a good day. I also received a letter from Marie on Monday. I hope that this letter will find you well again after your illness. I hope all at home are in good health. I frequently think of you all.

Since I wrote to you last we have had a holiday in honour of St. Columba. It came on Monday. We did not have a picnic but stayed here. In the morning there was a Rugby match. The team to play against Manly was selected after this Match. I can understand it a little now but it still seems to be a mere matter [of] which team has the 'Brute' strength and stupidity. These two things seem necessary to a good Rugby player. In the afternoon we had a game of Aussie Rules. We could only get about 13 a side and most of these were not real Aussie rulers. However, we enjoyed ourselves so I suppose that was all we could expect.

We had a special dinner on Sunday in honour of St. Columba. We had fowl and bacon and then jellies and drinks. It did not come up to our banquets at ACK but was very acceptable. I must say that the meals are very good considering the number of students. We have a 3-course meal. We have mutton, vegetables and potatoes, practically the same as at a restaurant. The dessert is not very good but we don't mind this. We get butter for Breakfast and Butter and Jam for tea, plenty of Milk etc. Then on Sunday night we each got a piece of a cake called St. Columba's Birthday cake. The next holiday will be tomorrow (Thursday) for Corpus Christi. We will have a procession around the College and grounds.

I got my soprano a few days ago. I paid the tailor for the soutane, etc. It came to £8.3.0. This seems a very dear price. The soutane was £5.18.6. The soprano £1.19.6 and slip sleeves 5/-. They are to put over the sleeves of the soutane to prevent the elbow wearing a hole in them. I would be very pleased if you would send me ten shillings as I have to pay for some books and then I will want some for my fare if we go to Wentworth Falls for the Mid-Winter holidays. I try to be as easy as possible on my money but it is surprising how many things crop up, levies for football Gernsies for the team and things like this. We each have to give 1/- towards the gernseys for the team.

It will not be long till the Mid Winter exams now – a little over a week. I hope I pass in Philosophy. There are yet six months till the Xmas holidays. We will have a week's holiday for Mid Winter.

Father Kincella came here today to hear confessions. We always have a strange priest to hear confessions usually a Vincentian. Father Slattery is the one who usually comes, as he is sick Father Kincella came.

I was glad to hear that Brian is doing so well at school. I do hope that Chester will get on better. I always think of him. I will write to him one of these days. Fancy Rod with a car – I suppose Father does not hear him cantering home at late hours now – he has got a bike at last.[18] *I received a letter from Marie. She was telling me what pictures she saw. I hope she enjoys herself. She said she thought she would go to see Harry Neville.*

I was surprised to hear about Brother Timothy's departure from Kilmore. A few days later I received a letter from Bro. William, which I enclose, in which he told me about his leaving. Today I received one from Br Michael. They are very nice letters and I would be pleased, Mother, if you would preserve them for me. There are two new students here, one from Queensland and the other from Lismore. The latter is on for Hobart.

Well, Mother, I will now close with fond love to you, Father, and all at home

From Your loving Son
Jack

PS. I will think of you tomorrow before the Blessed Sacrament.

---

18   It is suspected that Rod has a motor-bike with a side-car.

Letter 8 to Father

I think I have chosen the right course in life — and again I thank you.

In writing a two-page letter to his father (July 1927), John fondly expresses his gratitude for the kindness and generosity towards him, especially in regard to financing his education. John again mentions Assumption College Kilmore and compares it with his situation now. Frosts are heavier than at Kilmore and time goes more quickly here. He tells his father about the order of day and about the important job of the *bell man*!

Most of the energy in this letter surrounds Rugby and how it is played. Being from Victoria he continues to be amazed by the game and enjoys telling his father.

* * *

St Columba's College,
Springwood,
Blue Mountains. NSW.
Sunday. [July 1927]

Dear Father,

I suppose you have been expecting a letter from me. Well I had not very much spare time – seeing that the exams will start in a few days. I received the Pound Note in Mother's letter. I thank you very much for it. It's very kind of you to send it.

We have been having glorious weather here. It was only tonight that the sky has clouded up. We have not had any Aussie Rule games since I wrote the last, but the Rugby has been going on. The team which is to play Manly has been picked. They say it is a good team – I don't know. (The College) the rest of the house picked a team to play them. They are supposed to be as good as the 1st team and almost beat them in a match. It was very exciting. Everyone was going for his life and some were nearly killed. They pick a man up by his legs – one on each leg and pulling opposite ways. Others they catch by the neck and screw his head off. It is a good game for blokes that can stand being dumped on the ground, kicked in the face or having about 6 others sitting on the top. Two Aussie rulers played very well, but both came off in a rather bad condition – one with his leg knocked about and one with a stiff neck. They were both in bed for a day. It is only a week till Manly day.

We start the Mid Winter holidays on Friday or Saturday. We will have our oral exams beforehand. Tomorrow we are going to have a Hermeneutics exam. I had a good few kicks today when the Rugbyites were not playing.

I wrote to Nora a few days ago. Has Aunty Kate been operated on yet? Well I have been here somewhere about twelve weeks. It does not seem so long to me. When I was at Kilmore 12 or 13 weeks were very slow in going but time here flies. We rise at six, Mass at 7 and Breakfast at 8. It seems no time then till dinner and then again for Spiritual Reading at 5 o'clock. After this we have about ¾ `hours study and then Benediction and then tea. Everything is done to the second and if the bell man is a second or two out of time he is "squashed" or reprimanded by the head John (Prefect.)

I am very glad I came here and I now wish to thank you for your generosity in allowing me to come and in providing for my education. I think I have chosen the right course in life – and again I thank you. I will now close with fondest love from

Your Loving Son

John C Wallis

PS. Has it been cold down there? We have had some very heavy frosts. They were better than some I saw at Kilmore.

Letter 9 to Mother

I realised how like the Little Irish Mother you are.
I always add that "trimmin'" to the Rosary for all of you
And particularly if God wills I should go through with the priesthood.

His mother's letter has just arrived (July 1927) and John immediately replies in a two-page response, concerned about the sickness of his young brother Chester and his Father's *troubles*. His intimate relationship with his intelligent mother is evident as he expresses his concern for her too. His youthful hopes are shared and he can discuss anything with her.

John appreciates poetry. First published in 1921, the book of poems, *Around the Boree Log* by John O'Brien, (Monsignor Joseph Hartigan of the Diocese of Wagga Wagga New South Wales), reflects the life and faith of so many ordinary Irish families of the era. One poem John has alighted on is *The Trimmin's on the Rosary*. Like the little Irish mother of the poem, Emma also had a special prayer in her heart unknown to others, that her son Jack would be a priest. The other poem of particular relevance is *The Parting Rosary* which speaks of the Irish mother's son who has to go away – and *it is all for the best*.

In his letters John is using more Latin now with Aves and Paters named Hail Marys and Our Fathers.

John is pleased to meet up again with Cyril and Gus at Manly – the common bond being ex-students of Assumption College. His Auntie Jane Douglas lives in Northcote and has three children the youngest, Anne, is John's age. John had frequently visited the family in Victoria.

* * *

Friday Night. [July 1927]

Dear Mother,
I received your letter today. I was indeed sorry to hear about poor little Chester. It came as a shock to me to know that blood poisoning set in. Poor

little child, he must be suffering agony. I do hope he recovers quickly. It was very kind of Father Egan to come down to see him. He is very nice like that. You may be sure I will not forget him in my prayers. By the way I am sending on those beads and I hope that you will be able to say many a "trimmin'" on them. Remember Our Lady took care of Jesus in all his tribulations as a child and I am sure she will take Chester under her care. I have been offering my Communions for him.

I was also sorry to hear about poor Father. He has many troubles indeed. It is wonderful how he bears up under them all. And you also Mother, it was only today when I was reading "Around the Boree Log" that I realised how like the Little Irish Mother you are. I always add that "trimmin'" to the Rosary for all of you and particularly that if God wills I should go through, you and Father will be the first to receive my blessing. Isn't it nice the ideas that are expressed in that book? Despite the rough language they all have a significant meaning. "The Parting Rosary" was also nice. I will get a copy of this book as a keepsake some time perhaps at Xmas.

Well Mother Manly day arrived. We had a most enjoyable time. The Manly team beat our team. Everyone was excited – even Father Simonds who is usually as somber as can be. Gus Lacey and Cyril invited me to their table. We had a great spread. I enjoyed it. About 4 o'clock we had Benediction. There were two deacons assisting. There are about 9 deacons at Manly so that there will be nine priests out next year. We had a fine talk about old days at Kilmore. We are to have a Bushy tomorrow and a Picnic to Wentworth on Tuesday.

I wrote to Marie, Don and Auntie Jane [Douglas]. I got those beads blessed. They are not as good as I expected but I think you will like them. I hope you will say many an Ave and Pater on them. The other pair were sent with them. (I suppose just to thank me for the order.) I got them blessed. They will be suitable for the children.

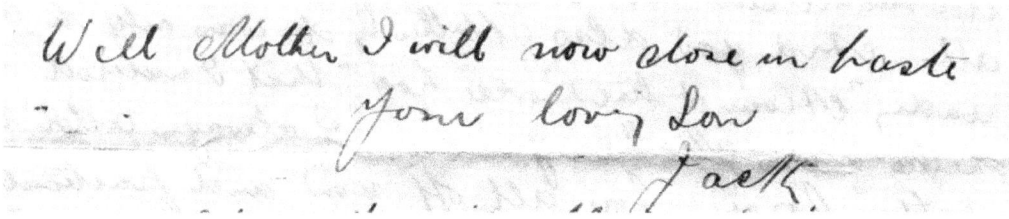

PS. Tonight there are cold west winds blowing. These are supposed to be very cold. They howl through the bush with a mournful sound. They had a sweep here on the Manly match. The winner in our room was Jack Donaldson.[19] My man got a try but not till the last. There were four other sweeps here but I don't know who won them. Well, Goodbye Mother. I am dead tired after yesterday's excitement.

---

19 This may be the Jack McDonald in an earlier letter.

Letter 10 to Father

*Over the whole of the valley
there is always a blue haze very like smoke.
It is no wonder they are called Blue Mountains.*

In this six-page letter to his father (August 1927), John reveals more of his thoughts about the restrictions on his life at Springwood. The Rector, Father Bauers, refuses to allow the students a return football match with Manly, this bothering John. On their bush experience they cannot leave the picnic camp without the prefect. They spend their Sundays around the grounds at the seminary, not able to go out.

The hierarchy of the seminary life, the distance between the professors and students becomes evident – they *merely came in and told us what we would do during the next half and then went out*. John is then surprised that the 23-year-old Father Wallace, one of the *professors*, mixes so easily with them and seems to attempt to change the attitude when he insists he receive the same treatment as the students, rather than being put on a pedestal as a professor.

Revelling in nature and absorbed into his surroundings, John describes the magnificence of the bush of the Blue Mountains, more particularly around Wentworth Falls, the Weeping Rock, the Cascades, the Valley of Waters and the Empress. Those who have traversed these areas will read this 1927 account of the experience of a seventeen-year-old-young man with great interest.

Because of John's background with three Deaf siblings, Sister Martina Carrigan, a Dominican sister at Waratah near Newcastle, takes the opportunity to encourage John's understanding of Deaf ministry and sends him the Catholic Deaf-related magazine, *Ephpheta*. Both his sister Marie and brother Don had attended the Deaf school at Waratah.

Experiencing the half year meeting run on Parliamentary lines with its election of committees is a great learning tool for John. Because the library is of great interest to him, John suggests that a committee be formed for the care of the library, because he sees it as *ill-treated*. He volunteers for the job, the library theme accompanying him throughout his life.

At the end of the letter he refers to the dark mornings when they rise – and how the moon is bright! And he is now used to *hopping out of bed*.

* * *

Tuesday. [August 1927]

Dear Father,

I suppose you have been wondering what has happened to me in not writing. I have not had much time of late. We began work again on Thursday last and I have been pretty busy. I have been going to write to you every night but there always seem to be some work to prepare for next day. I am quite well as I hope you are. I have been told by a number of students I am looking better than when I arrived. How are all at home? Did Chester get on alright? I have been watching for a letter from home to let me know how he is. I do hope he is better.

We had great holidays. They are over now. They went all too quick. In my last letter home I told you about the Manly match. Last Saturday night someone suggested at the meeting of the society that the Head Prefect ask the Rector to try for a return match. He did so but was refused. The rector was in favour of it on one side but said that as a number of the students were still boys they would "muck up".

On the Saturday after we had a Bush picnic, I went to a place called Yellow Rock, which is about 7 miles away on the Nepean or Upper Hawkesbury. We had a fine time. However the bush picnics here are not like the ones at Kilmore. We cannot leave the camp unless the prefect who is head of the party comes with us. There are some fine places around here for Bush Picnics. I will go to Bungaree next time. I believe it is a very nice place.

On the Sunday we spent our time about the grounds. There is always something to do. We had an Australian Rules game on the Sunday. On Tuesday we had a picnic to Wentworth falls, which is higher up in the Mountains. On Monday afternoon we got our clothes washed up.

On Tuesday morning we were up at 10 to 5, in the Chapel for Morning prayers at 5.15. At 5.45 we had Mass and Rosary. Then we had a quick breakfast and walked into Springwood to catch the train, which left at 8 o'clock. It is about three miles to Springwood. As we went higher up, the air got very chilly. It was quite fresh up there. We arrived there about 9.30. I ran on and *got one of the many tables, which are provided for the picnics. There were nine in our party being those who sit at our table in the refectory. We invited Father Wallace to our party. He is more like a student than a "pro". He is only about 23. We left a couple to get dinner ready while we had a look round.*

At the top there was a big bluff and stretching away for miles at the foot of this cliff there was a big valley which is estimated to be 1000 feet below the level of the top. There are supposed to be 118 falls around the district. Over the whole of the valley there was a blue haze very like smoke. It is no wonder they are called Blue Mountains. There is always a blue haze hanging over them.

Near our camp there was a stream, which first of all flowed over a big flat rock and then fell on all sides of it for a distance of about ten feet. It was a very nice sight and is known as the Weeping Rock. From here the water rushed over a number of rocks fully all the way along. This was known as the Cascades. Near here there was a lot of beautiful ferns growing in a kind of cave under the cliff. From here the water went over the Wentworth Fall, which is about three hundred feet deep. There is a continual spray rising. It seemed very much like steam and even if we were 20 or thirty yards away it would dampen our clothes.

After this we went back for dinner. Father Wallace was very nice. He would not take anything without seeing that we all had a share. He is very much of a student yet. The head Prefect and Frank Massey (senior student) came along. They took our photos. Then we all went along a track cut in the side of [the] cliff and about half way up. It was a good long walk along here to the next lot of falls. We got some fine views from it down into the valley.

At last we came to another stream, which had a number of falls. It was called the Valley of Waters because it was made up of a number [of] streams which all met at a place called the Meeting of the Waters which was a big pool where they all flowed into one. The finest of all the falls there was the Empress. It was about 80 feet deep and there was a good volume of water coming over. This water came down through a cleft in the cliff about 30 feet wide. It fell over great rocks for some hundreds of yards and then took the final leap of about 80 feet before it came to the meeting of the waters. There were some nice ferns there also. On the whole there are very few ferns here, there are very few tree ferns but a few big leafy ones, which I have never seen before.

Father Wallace got a student from another party to come with us. He had a camera. When we came to one of the falls he got us all to get up on some rocks right at the foot and get our photos taken. He was leading us all over the place, up and down, away along tracks over grown with scrub. We had a fine time.

At about two o'clock we had afternoon tea and then he lead us off in another way. We walked for two miles along a steep mountainside until we came to the end of the track we were following. We had a longer walk than any other party. I enjoyed myself more there than at Blackheath where we had our last picnic. I would like you and Mother to be able to come up and see these sights for yourselves. Then we walked back to the town of Wentworth Falls. We got home about 7 o'clock. I was indeed glad to go to bed.

On the following day tired and stiff we hobbled into the studies to start the new half. However the Professors merely came in and told us what we would do during the next half and then went out. We had Wednesday to get over it.

On the Tuesday I got an Ephpheta [newsletter] from Waratah. I think Sr. Martina sent it.

On Thursday Morning we had our first lesson – Hermeneutics, that is the Study of Scripture. On the previous Saturday night we had a half yearly meeting (All these are run on Parliamentary principles.) There were a number of offices to be filled for this half. We elected a new president, Secretary, Vice President and Sub Vice President. Then we elected a Sports Committee, Grounds Committee (to do little odd jobs around the grounds for the general convenience), then concert committee and several other offices. I moved that two men should be appointed to look after library. This is a fine library but has been very ill-treated. The motion was passed. Jordan Ross and I were appointed to do it. We are going to have a general clean up.

On each of the above Committees there are 6 men. I was one of the Concert Committee. We have to help get up concerts and to select the items etc. There will be three during this half. We have selected a comedy for the first one, which comes off in about 5 weeks time. We also have Debates on the Society. Then there is the Thesis night. On that night one student picks on a subject and shows that that opinion is the true one. It is merely the defending of a question. Then others criticise him and ask him to give answers for certain opinions or arguments they may put forward. It is more in the line of Philosophy. Then again there is the Manuscript night on which each student sends in some poem or article and then the pick of these are read out.

I have not had any letters of late. It is a long time since I got one from Don. I think Marie owes me one also. I got a nice one from Auntie Jane. I have not written to Father Egan yet. I will write sometime this week. How are all the people of Yea going? I hope you are having better luck now with your sheep. Up here we are having glorious weather – never a cloud in the sky. I think that we will soon have rain as there are clouds starting to come up now.

Well, Father, I will always pray for you. Remember, that, "They that sow in tears shall reap in joy".[20] I will write to poor little Chester. I am sure he would be pleased to get a letter. How are Brian and (Baby) Charlie going? I often think of you when I hear the bell go in the morning to get up. The dorm is pitch dark when first we hear the Prefect's alarm clock and then a little later the bell. When I get down from the Dormitory to go to the Chapel (I am generally 3rd) it is dark and the Moon is shining bright. There is always a nip in the air too. We sometimes have to wait outside in the quadrangle for about 5 minutes before the doors into the lower story are opened. However I am getting fairly used to hopping out [of bed] now.

Well, Father, I am about out of news now so I will close with fondest love from

Your loving Son,
Jack

---

20   From Psalm 126.

THE YOUTHFUL STUDENT AND SON
St Columba's College, Springwood 1927
Letters 1 – 10

Kate Fogarty

Who would have thought that there was so much fun to be had in reading a teenage boy's reflections on his first year in the seminary? John's wry sense of humour and keen observations are a delight. We get the sense that during his boarding years at Assumption College, the warm flow of conversation via letter had already been well established between parents and son. These early seminary letters have such a lovely light touch, and seem to respond diligently to questions or comments that must have been raised by his parents or a sibling. We can easily imagine the heads of various Wallis' siblings poking over mum or dad's shoulders as each new missive arrived from John, and there can be no doubting the great familial affection that existed between the immediate and extended Wallis clan.

Unsurprisingly, the tone and language of the letters are very much of their era. I do not think any of us can imagine a sixteen year-old youth in this day and age casually reminding his mum that *May is the month of Mary,* however the themes that occupy John do not seem that different from the concerns of today's teens: family matters, money woes, food, sport and, of course, his studies! Perhaps not surprisingly, the adolescent fixation of discord between followers of rugby and those of AFL seems to be so deeply rooted in the Australian psyche that it played out at the seminary of 1927 equally as much as it does in the social media of today!

The records at Assumption College show that in John's final year at the school he studied English, Latin, French, Geometry and History. With that background, it is no wonder that philosophy and trigonometry set him quaking, and that subsequently, a number of the letters appear to attempt to '*soften the ground*' for what will possibly be some less than stellar results in the future. Many will also recognise his casual distain for these '*non-ecclesial*' classes as eerily similar to the attitude of today's students to the subjects that will not make up their final university entrance score!

The oft-mentioned Brother William Molloy is a legend of Assumption College and other Marist Brothers schools throughout Australia. He was John's Principal and was renowned as an inspirer and supporter of vocations to both the priesthood and the brothers. Indeed, Archbishop Mannix once noted that *the Church in Victoria has no need of a minor seminary while we have Br William in Kilmore!* Brother William's relationship with John would continue throughout his life, and there are affectionate letters from John to his mentor from as late as the 1960s.

John's surprise at the professional distance between his teachers and the students at the seminary would have been in stark contrast to his experience of the Brothers at Kilmore. In those days, the Brothers were teachers and sports coaches and had a very influential daily presence in the lives of the students. The famous Kilmore 'Bushies' (day holidays) that John compares to his seminary experiences appear in the College Annuals of the time as amazing and daring adventures for the boarders. The lack of freedom he experienced in the seminary, however, seems more than offset by the terrific food and interesting studies and pursuits that fill John's time there. How reassuring that the teenage fixation with good food has ever been, and continues to be, a hallmark of boarding students!

Kate Fogarty

In 2015, Kate Fogarty was appointed as the first female Principal of Assumption College. Marist educated herself, she currently serves on the Marist Association National Council, and also the Caritas Australia National Council. Throughout her education career, Kate has predominantly worked in rural education, and now also in overseeing a boarding College, particularly appreciates and champions the role Catholic education has played, and will continue to play, in the development of rural Australia. In 2018, Father John Wallis was inducted into the Assumption College Hall of Excellence.

St Columba's Seminary, Springwood 1927 – 1928
Letters 11 – 20

INTRODUCTION

The second chapter consists of ten letters from John spanning the period from September 1927 to the end of 1928 completing his seminary studies at St Columba's College, Springwood. Two letters are written to his father and the remainder to his mother.

Letter 11 to Mother

> *Today I went to a rocky point, about three quarters of a mile away. I lay on one of the rocks and had a quiet read.*

In his three-page letter to his mother (September 1927), John gives an account of his life from his diary. He is in good spirits and pleased with his philosophy results after his earnest work in the first part of the year. It has paid dividends. John's study of the Scriptures in Hermeneutics would have been from the Vulgate translation in Latin. *Keeping the rule* is important to John as well as to *study harder*, his resolution from the retreat given by Father Kincella. Special meditations during the retreat were on *Death* and examining one's conscience.

Another bush picnic takes place but with a different purpose – to build a place in the bush on the property for the statue of St Joseph. In John's previous letter he uses the phrase *mucking up* and this time there is a greater sense of what *mucking up* means.

John comments on the interesting *lecturettes*: one about a priest's library resonating with his developing thoughts about the benefits of libraries and his desire to build up his own.

Lastly, the issue of his priestly vocation rises again. Is it to be to a religious order rather than diocesan priesthood? He speaks with Father Kincella about joining the Redemptorist order. It is suggested to him that he lets the dilemma go for the time being and concentrate on his life now with the focus on being *a good priest*. It is resolved for the moment. Father Kincella is known for using the term *to be a good priest*, so among the students he is nicknamed *Good Priest!*

* * *

> St. Columba's College,
> Springwood.
> Sunday [September 1927]

Dear Mother,

I hope this letter finds you and all in good health as I am, thank God. I have been feeling good oh lately.

Well, I will first give an account as from the Diary of the last week. On Monday, I had my first read in the refectory for this half. I also read on Tuesday and Wednesday. The Philosophy marks came out. I got 70. There were two others I think who got above this. Bill Quinn getting 80 and Arthur Booker getting 75. There were two others with me. Alf got 45. I did not expect as many as this.

On Wednesday we had our usual Blue Wednesday. I got a call in Hermeneutics. The question to be treated was the Deluge mentioned in the Bible. I had to show whether it covered the whole earth, or only the civilised world or only a portion inhabited by the Jews. I got on fairly well I think. We do not get any marks allotted in these exams.

We had our usual retreat after this. The special meditation was Death and the secondary one, a General examination of Conscience every night before going to bed is the best means of preparing for Death. Fr. Kincella conducted it. These retreats are very beneficial. They enable one to see how he has been keeping the Rule etc. during the last month. We usually make some special resolution for the ensuing month. Mine for September is to study harder.

Last Tuesday was the feast of the Nativity of the Blessed Virgin we had a Missa Cantata instead of the ordinary Mass. This allowed us to go away earlier for our Picnics than if we had had it after the Community Mass. After

Breakfast we set out immediately for our place. I went out to Joey's Bower (i.e. St. Joseph's), which is about 4 miles away. We took out a kind of canopy made of tin and wood to put in a kind of niche in a rock out there. In it we will put a statue of St. Joseph.

There were 9 in our party. We took it in turns to carry the tools and canopy. It was a very hard job as we had to go through the bush. We arrived there after about two and a half hours stumbling and struggling. The thing was set in place and then we had the rest of the time for "mucking up". After dinner they began to wrestle. Then some students from another party came over and challenged those of our party. We spent the whole afternoon in wrestling and cock fighting as well as a number of other games. I had a splendid day and was glad to tumble into bed that night.

We had special Vespers in honour of Our Lady. This Month is specially devoted to the Joys and Sorrows of Our Lady. I know you will be under her patronage in all your trials and you may be sure I often ask her to be a true Mother to all especially to the three children who have not yet passed their boyhood days. It is only now, Mother that I realise how many dangers one encounters and they are to be found here also. I would like you Mother to say one "Hail Mary" to Our Lady of Perpetual Succour for me each day and I will say this special one for you and all at home in return. On Thursday next we will celebrate the feast of Our Mother of Sorrows.

We have now finished Logic and have started in Meta-physics. This deals with the spirit, the soul, etc. It is divided into Natural Theology and Psychology. I think it should be rather interesting. I notice that the Philosophy is much more interesting now than it was before. We had a couple of "Benos" on Friday. This means "Benedicamus Domino" (Let us bless the Lord). When this is said we are allowed to talk at table. Was given for a visiting priest.

On Saturday there was a good game of tennis played between representatives of 1st Philosophy and of Humanity. The latter team won easily. However it was a very good game.

That evening the general business of the Society was "Lecturettes". The first was on "An Australian Sheep Station" by Brian Doherty. He gave a description of a well to do station "out West". But he gave only the prosperous side as characteristic of all such places, but I don't think he was right. He was merely making it an ideal place. He described the electric power house, etc. and said these were common on sheep runs. He was picked up by many of the students on this score.

The next was "Libraries" delivered by Bill McMahon (Ballarat). It was a fine speech in which he showed the necessity of a priest's having a good literary knowledge and a library of his own and also of establishing a Parish library. This I thought was a good point. Some people find books, which they may or may not read and it is for a priest to decide. If there were a library this difficulty would be avoided and at the same time the people are provided with good wholesome reading.

Mr. Henry gave a lecturette on Physical Culture. It was very good as well as being very instructive. I have been taking my exercise each night before going to bed. Tom Gard gave a speech on Cardinal Vaughan. This also was very instructive.

Today I went to Boronia Point a place about three quarters of a mile away. It is a rocky point. I went and lay on one of the rocks and had a quiet read. It was fairly warm this afternoon. During the rest of the week it has been cool and has been trying hard to rain. However I think the rain has passed again.

We have not heard from Kilmore of late but I think Bro William [Molloy] will write to Alf [Schmude] soon. The boys are now on holidays. The time is slipping by. It is somewhere about 14 weeks till Christmas holidays.

On Wednesday last I had a talk to Fr. Kincella about the Redemptorists. He said just to go on as I am and try and not think about the matter but to observe the rule and act as if I were preparing to be a "good" priest. He is very fond of this phrase, "Good priest", so much so that he is known by no other name among the students. I have often had this thought coming up and really I do think I have a vocation. However I think it would be advisable to continue on here say for another year. If it still comes after this space, it must be a true vocation. I will try to get a book entitled "Religious and Monastic Life Explained" by Rev. J. Vette, O.S.B. price 4/2. It should be useful.

Well Mother I must now write to Chester, so I will now close with fondest love to you, Father, Brian and Charlie.

From Your loving Son,
Jack

Letter 12 to Father

> *Let us hope and pray*
> *that the priests of Australia will in the future*
> *have the interest of the people at heart.*

In this four-page letter to his father (late September 1927), John relates graphically and in detail the story of his accident, any parents' nightmare. John notes and appreciates the kindness of his fellow students in the way they cared about him when he felt unwell. He explains to his father that the soutane he wears is cooler in the warmer weather than having to wear *a heavy coat*. A practical matter!

Then he tells of the *Catholic Paper night* – his father would be interested in the students' presentations. Pat Carmine from New Zealand, a little older than John, gives the paper on the Conversion of Australia, which engages the students in a world fearful of communism and intent on increasing the influence of Christianity and more especially Catholicism. One student responded to this paper with a proposal to campaign against *mixed marriages*, a marriage between a Catholic and a person of another religion. This aroused his fellow students' mirth, writes John.

The second paper on evolution interests John knowing the Church is suspicious of such scientific developments. John seems open to hear more and know more of these new ideas – and sharing them.

An important clue to later events in this letter is that an ex-Kilmore student, Eddie Morganti, has written to him from the Columban Society in Essendon. Eddie has told John about his desire to train for the Irish mission in China – perhaps John is alerted to this possibility for himself.

A strong pastoral approach to the priesthood is developing in this young student. The motto of each priest from Manly is: *For God and Australia*. John pleads in prayer that the priests of Australia have the interest of people at the heart of their priesthood.

* * *

St. Columba's College
Springwood.
SUNDAY. [September 1927]

Dear Father,

It is your turn this week. I hope you and all at home are quite well as I am, thank God. I have a little incident to relate of an occasion on which I was unconscious but I am now quite well. I will tell you this further over.

We have been having fairly cool weather here of late. Sometimes it has looked like rain but it soon goes again. There has been a lot of dust about. It is now about 24 weeks since the last rain. The people of Springwood are getting water carted to them. I have noticed that the priests have been saying a special prayer for rain in their Masses. We have plenty of water here, but the ground is very dry and hard. On one or two occasions we have had some hot days. The soutanes are good for hot weather. They are not as heavy as a coat and are also comfortable. Under a soutane we need only wear a singlet. In fact, I was told that last year some students did not have even a singlet on. The clerical collars are also much cooler than the ordinary ones.

Well, about my accident. I told you in a previous letter that I had helped put up a horizontal bar. On Monday last I went down and had a good few swings on it. One of the students used to teach gymnastics before he came here. He showed me a few turns on the bar. I managed them alright. Then on the following evening (Tuesday) I went down again. After a few swings I had a fall. I remembered someone rubbing me. Then I remembered having a wash and going down to the Chapel. I could not remember what I had done that evening. I was in total oblivion. During Rosary I felt sick and had to go out. Then I went into study. I still felt sick and went to lie down on one of the seats in the back of the study room. The Prefect told me to go to bed. I had a good tea and then went to sleep. I had a very bad headache. At half past nine, the students came up for bed. A number came and asked how I was and what they could do for me.

By the way it is wonderful how they look after a sick student here. Each one comes along to do something. At Kilmore it was only one or two who bothered but here all come to do something – always ready with a helping hand. I did not get to sleep till very late but I slept well after that. When I woke I had a headache but got up for Mass. After a while I got quite right again. I was told that when I fell I closed my eyes and lay on the ground for sometime. The bar is about 10 feet off the ground. I will be more careful in the future.

On Wednesday I got three letters, one from Don, one from Eddie Morganti and one from Nick Morrissey at ACK. Morganti is at St. Columban's College, Essendon and is training for the Irish mission to China. He is the only student there at present and is doing well.

On Friday we got word that Mr. Kerr, the father of Tom Kerr, one of the students had died. This is the fourth father who has died in a little over a month. We also heard that Pat Carmine's mother was sick. He is a New Zealand student. I think she is now out of danger. We had a Requiem Mass on Saturday for Mr. Kerr.

We are losing one of our professors, Father Eris M. O'Brien. He and another priest have been asked by the Archbishop to organise a choir for the Eucharistic Congress. He is a lovely singer and has composed some fine music. He also writes a number of books. He is writing two more books for the congress and also a Play. He has a wonderful library, said to be worth thousands of pounds. We do not know who the new Pro will be.

Last night (Saturday) we had Catholic Paper night. There were two papers read "The Conversion of Australia" and "Evolution." By Catholic papers are meant articles by certain students and read at the meeting of the Society. Mr. Carmine delivered the first one namely the "Conversion of Australia." He brought various schemes, which would be very suitable for making Australia a Catholic nation. Amongst these he mentioned, Books, Catholic papers both daily and periodic, Broadcasting, Catholic Evidence lectures, as well as campaigns against the frivolity of the young people of today. It was a splendid paper. I may be able to get a copy of it from him. A number of students commented on it and added their suggestions.

One student announced that he was going to make a special campaign against Mixed Marriages. This remark brought a hoy from the house and a great deal of laughter. Another said he would make it his business to foster vocations. All proclaimed what they were going to do. Some of course said it was merely first fervor. Let us hope and pray that also the priests of Australia will in the future have the interest of the people at heart. The motto of each priest from Manly is "Pro Deo et Australia" i.e. "For God and Australia."

The other paper on evolution was good. Mr. Thomas delivered it. However he used so big jaw breaking words from Greek and Latin, which could not be understood at least by the younger members of the house. It was very interesting. He showed how Evolution does not conflict with the teaching of the Church. We are allowed to hold the theory that man developed from an ape; but that his soul came from the ape is false. On the whole the Church does not favour Evolution and is very suspicious of much of the literature produced concerning this question.

We had a High Mass today. We heard today that one of the Manly students "threw the job in". He started here in Humanity. After 4 years here he went to Manly where he has been for four years. He was to be ordained next December. He was 'clipped' for his orders. Being clipped means he was not allowed to receive the orders of Deacon, Subdeacon, etc. By rights he should have got the tonsure, the first of the seven orders two years ago. It seems hard to have to quit after 8 years study. This is the second student who has left Manly. God grant that I may be able to complete my course and come out successfully.

We will have a Bush Picnic next Thursday in honor of St. Michael. Alf and I will write to Bro. Michael at Kilmore. On Sunday next there will be exposition of the Blessed Sacrament. Perhaps you will have it at home. It would be grand if you could spend a few minutes at least in the Church while the Sacred Host is exposed. Well, Father, I have no more news at present, so I will close with love to you, Mother and all at home.

Your loving Son,
Jack.

PS. Is Auntie Jane at home yet? I forgot to mention your new scheme. Well, Father, I think you have earned a rest and I am glad that you will have an opportunity to have it. I hope it will be a success. Did you sell the farm? I am looking forward to seeing you all again – only 11 weeks. You may find the time long but it flies here. Remind Mother that October is coming, the month of the Rosary. Perhaps you too Father would join in saying the Rosary especially during the month.

Letter 13 to Father and Mother

Spring is showing up everywhere –
New leaves on the fruit trees.
I have not seen any Waratah flowers yet.

Brought together here are parts of two different letters, one to John's Father (October 1927), and the second seems to be a response to a letter from his Mother written either late September or October. Some pages have disappeared in the ether of time. Mentioned are neighbours from Yea and well known to the family, Dennis and Annie Slavin. Annie had died in August, two months previously. Twenty years later John's brother Chester marries into the Slavin family.

For the upcoming 1928 Eucharistic Congress, the bishops from different parts of Australia and New Zealand have met in Sydney – and there are meetings held at Springwood by the organisers. John notes something of interest, that Father Hurley from Surry Hills in Sydney is described as a powerful influence in an area where there is violence and crime.

An understanding of Deaf ministry is spreading among the students. Bill McMahon has read the Deaf magazine and it ignites his interest to initiate a collection. John directs the donation to St Gabriel's School for Deaf Boys where he knows the need.

John is enthusiastic and zealous for what he is learning and experiencing. He wants everyone, especially his family, to know what he is discovering. Regularly he takes the opportunity to share his pious or devotional thoughts. In an earlier letter he wants his parents to experience what he has seen – including the wonder of the Blue Mountains.

* * *

St. Columba's
Springwood.
Sunday. [October 1927]

Dear Father,

No doubt you and Mother have been wondering what has happened to me in not writing. Well I will tell you as I go on why I have not. I am quite well as I hope you and all at home are.

I will write from my diary. Since I last wrote there have been a few important personages here. There was [a] meeting of the various bishops from the different States and from New Zealand. Bishop Whyte from Dunedin paid us a visit. He stayed only for a day. However we got a "Beno" for him. This means we could talk at the dinner table. This meeting of bishops was called to arrange about the Eucharistic Congress which will take place in about 12 months time.

There were also a number of priests there. Fr. Hack was up. He is the Secretary of the Manly Reunion Society. He was collecting the fees for last year's Manly Annuals. There have been a number of priests up here. Most of them are organisers of the Congress. There has been a Father Hurley up here for a few days. He is supposed to be a fine singer and does most of the chanting in St. Mary's Cathedral. He gave some nice articles of brass to the College Chapel. He has charge of the Surrey [sic] Hills parish in Sydney. This is said to be Sydney's Fitzroy.[1] They said that sometimes the "crooks" get on to him but he generally cleans them up. He has a wonderful influence over these people.

Cricket is now started – Football is over. Cricket is not taking very well. There are a few enthusiasts but the majority are not inclined to it. The pitch is not very good. There have been a few Tennis Competitions so the tennis court here is very rough. Nevertheless there have been some very good games. There are some fine tennis players here.

I had a letter a few days ago from Don. He is quite well, but has been expecting a letter for some time. I wrote to him a few days ago. I have one of those books from Waratah – the Ephpheta. One of the students, Bill McMahon from Ballarat, read it. He then suggested that we take up a collection for it. I suggested that we take it up for Castle Hill since they need it more. So far he has got about £3.0.0 from about 40 students. This is very good.

For the most part the weather has been very warm. A few days ago however it was very cold and there were signs of rain. But the rain passed and since then it has been warm. Summer is coming. A number of students are having two and three cold showers a day. They take their soutanes off in study and some are in their bare singlets. I believe it is very hot here in the real Summer. How are you getting on there? I suppose you are still having ... [pages are missing here]

(Early October, 1927) to Mother

I will ask the prayers of the students for Mrs. Slavin's soul. They say a special Rosary for deceased relatives, friends etc.

Yes I wear my glasses always and find I can't do without them even for a short time at recreation. I feel a great benefit from them. I have an eye shade

---

1   A suburb of Melbourne, then with a similar demographic to Surry Hills in Sydney.

for studying under the electric light. In fact every student here has an eye shade. They are a great boon. I have not been wearing the teeth but I will make another effort to wear them. I have been told by two or three that they will be all right after a while.

I got a letter from Marie. I have had one from Don also. None from Father Egan. And one I will mention later. No, I have not seen any Waratah flowers yet. I have seen plenty of Waratah trees. They are very numerous here.

I am sending you a little parcel containing 2 Prayer books for Brian and Chester (3d each) and a book with prayers to St. Rita. She is the patron of mothers with families and the book was given to me by a student: (Eddie O'Bryan, a Ballarat CBS student, who comes from Terang) and who is trying to spread devotion to her. I think you will like it. We are coming near the end of another month.

The Spring is showing up everywhere – new leaves on the fruit trees, the wattle (it is now finished) and numberless other things. The sun is risen at 6.30 now whereas it used not to rise till seven at times. When we get up now it is fairly bright but we are still using the light. I have been feeling very well lately. Football is now over. We had our sports; they were a great event. I did not win any events but Alf Schmude jumped 5 ft. 3½ ins. This was good considering the nature of the ground. It is very hard from lack of rain …

Letter 14 to Mother

*Let us always lift our hearts up from things of this earth,
From sorrows and trials and think of God.*

This three-page letter (October 1927) is written to John's mother over three or four days. Many themes emerge. John's love for books is growing. This letter tells how he is impressed with Father O'Bryan's[2] library and that it takes up a whole wall! John's own library will take up more walls in the future. He comes to believe they are a great source of education and especially faith education for all people.[3]

John is living in a pious and devotional milieu and era. The practice of celebrating feast days was common – offering relief amid the mundane and regular lifestyle of the institution. For those whose names had an association with a saint or angel, for example, Michael the Archangel on 29th September, their feast days would be celebrated as well. Saying many aspirations to God or Our Lady was a devotional practice to bring to mind the presence of God in one's life. However, it developed in exaggerated ways with people believing that quantity of prayers and aspirations made them more acceptable to God, receiving special dispensations and indulgences.

Other pious acts mentioned are the *Forty Hours' devotion*, an exercise in which continuous prayer is offered for forty hours before the Blessed Sacrament. John undertakes to do this.[4] Another is the act of consecration to the Sacred Heart, a prayer offering one's life to honour and glorify God inspired by St Margaret Mary Alacoque, a 17th century French nun and mystic.[5]

Besides writing about these Catholic practices, John tells of the discussions among the students on contemporary social issues. For example, Prohibition of alcohol, which in America took place between 1920 and 1933, the world-wide Temperance Movement being the major push behind it. A *noble experiment,* it was established to solve social problems. In Australia Prohibition was never enacted nationally and, while a number of State referenda took place, it was in South Australia in 1916 that a 6.00pm early

---

2   Fr O'Bryan is the same Fr O'Brien mentioned in Letter 12.
3   Ten years later in 1938 John began the Catholic Library in Hobart and encouraged the establishment of other Catholic libraries that would be available in parishes. He developed his own library, the remains of which are housed in the Missionary Sisters of Service archives in Hobart. He also encouraged the Missionary Sisters of Service to help others with good reading, thus Catholic Bookshops were established under their care.
4   www.catholiceducation.org.au.
5   http://catholicism.org/saint-margaret-mary-and-the-sacred-heart.html

closing time for pubs and hotels was introduced. Subsequently, Victoria and Tasmania followed suit.[6]

Capital punishment was another issue discussed. Note a surprising outcome of a debate by the students on its abolishment. Capital punishment had already been abolished in Queensland (1922) and, while it was abolished for murder in New South Wales in 1955, it was not until 1985 that it was completely abolished. The other states and territories abolished capital punishment as follows: Tasmania (1968), Australian Capital Territory and Northern Territory, 1973, Victoria (1975), South Australia (1976), and Western Australia (1984).

John asks when his mother will leave for the new home; this reflects the establishment of the new business, Wallis' Cafe, in Seymour. It is now 10 weeks till holidays home.

* * *

St Columba's College,
Springwood.
Sunday [October 1927]

Dear Mother,

Another week has gone. It has not been very eventful but I will give you all the news I have. I am feeling extra well of late. I hope you and all at home are quite well.

On Monday last there was a young Vincentian here. He is a Doctor of Divinity. He went through here for a year and then left for the Vincentian Fathers. He went to Ireland to complete his course. He has only been out a short time. I thought he was just out by the manner in which he said Mass. I do not know his name.

Father O'Bryan's books were being shifted on Monday. There were a great number. He had a fairly big room and I was told that there are book shelves covering the whole of the wall.

On Tuesday, we were told we would have an exam for next Monday in

---

6   https://en.wikipedia.org/wiki/Six_o%27clock_swill

Philosophy. Since then the students have been fairly quiet, as they have a lot to learn up. I think I have a fair idea of the work this time. Father O'Bryan left. He came out and said goodbye to the students. They gave him a great hoy as he left. I believe he was very well liked in the parish of Springwood. He used to have great talks with the young people. Most of the other professors are rather shy in this respect, although I believe Fr. Wallace is well liked.

On Tuesday I wrote to Brother Michael to congratulate him on his feast day, which occurred on Thursday.

I believe the townspeople of Springwood have been very "hard up" for water. They had had no rain for 25 weeks (It is 25 since I came). In the prayers that day we were asked to pray for it. That evening the rain came. It continued all that night and next day, so that on Wednesday we were confined to our study hall for recreation. I took this opportunity of writing to Don.

Fr. Delaney is our new "pro" in Fr. O'Bryan's place. When we saw him we thought he looked a funny fellow but results showed that he was not.

We had our last Greek class at night. I have now caught up to the class. Those who were going to this extra class at night (about 12) decided to give Father Downey some little present in recognition for the time he spent in helping us. It was a voluntary help. They have sent for B... pencil which will cost about 12/-.

The lecture by the Spiritual Director was given on the "Presence of God". That is that we should remember God is working with us and is helping. He told us about a priest who asked a little boy "Is God everywhere?" The boy said, No. The priest said yes, he is in your pocket. The child replied, No he isn't, I ain't got no pocket.

I was reminded by this thought of a couple of words in the Mass, namely "Sursum Corda" which means, "Let us lift up our hearts". When we are in trouble we can always lift our hearts up from things of this earth, from sorrows and trials and think of God. I often think of you, Mother, and I think if you sometimes repeated the words "All for thee, Oh Heart of Jesus", it would help you. We have just been reading about a priest, who was indeed a Saint, Fr. William Doyle. He used to make 100,000 aspirations or acts of love each day.

Do not think this a sermon, Mother, but it is just a thought that struck me in passing. I know you like to hear all these thoughts.

On Thursday we had a Bush picnic. The prayer for Rain was said that morning but I think there were a number of students who had mental reservations. They wanted rain "but not today." At first it was dull but after the High Mass it was fined up.

I went to Joey's Bower. We had a "sports" meeting there. Our party challenged the other two parties out there to produce their wrestlers and cock fighters. We had a contest in our camp first to see who was the Champion. In the wrestling I was thrown on my back before I knew where I was. However in the Cock fight, Charlie Fiscalini and I won. We had a go with some from the other camp and beat them easily. We had a splendid day. Just before we left the camp the rain began but it stopped after a while and we ran most of the way home. The holiday was for St. Michael's day.

I saw a number of Waratah buds. There were none out. However I saw some on one of the altars the next day. They were not out properly but I think they would look very pretty. We are not allowed to pull them except for the Chapel. I may be able to get a plant to take home. That day the new Professor Father Delaney said the Community Mass.

Friday – I wrote to Eddie Morganti. It rained most of the day. It is great to see the rain again. I miss it very much. I suppose it was often so much at ACK. That night we had a good deal of thunder and lightning. There is always a lot of lightning here. Even on a clear night there are very frequent flashes. I gave the Sacristan a hand with the Polishing of the candle sticks etc. in preparation for Exposition today. I frequently help at these little jobs.

Saturday – The Month of the Rosary began. It is a month of special devotion here. We will have Benediction every night. Instead of prayers at the usual time 5 o'clock to 5.30, we go into study. This is in order to save lights. When we go into study early we do not need the electric light and then at prayers we do not need it either. During Benediction we have the Rosary.

Fr. Delaney gave us his first Class. He is an Irishman, going by his speech. He was educated in Ireland. He seems as though he will be a good teacher. He has been in America. He got onto the subject of Prohibition in the course of his lecture. He said that personally he had never tasted drink but did not believe in prohibition. He said that when a youth goes to College he is considered as a 'prude' if he cannot produce his flask of rum. Men, he said, who never before thought of drink were producing it just to break a law. He said that when we get out on the mission that we should not stop a practice but stop its abuse.

We had "Parliamentary Debate" last night, the question being "Should Capital Punishment be Abolished." The Prime Minister said it should. The rest of the house represented Parliament. There were some good arguments brought forward. At the end a vote of the house was taken, and it resulted in a decisive victory for the opposition. It should not be abolished.

Sunday. Fr. Delaney sang High Mass. He has a very sweet voice and sang beautifully. We had exposition of the Blessed Sacrament for the Congress. Joe Bugden one of the students got word that his sister went under a serious operation and was given up by the doctors. He has not heard any more since. A number of students went away learning up Philosophy for tomorrow's exam. At present it is raining fairly heavily. We cannot hear the rain here on the roof as we could at Kilmore.

Next Wednesday will be Blue Wednesday. On Friday, Saturday and Sunday we will have the forty hours adoration. On Friday (1st of the month) I will renew the Act of Consecration to the Sacred Heart before the B.S. (Blessed Sacrament). Perhaps you would all renew it at home as well. I have not heard from Marie of late. I think she must be expecting a letter from me. Is Auntie Jane still with you? How is Chester? When will you be leaving for your new home? It is ten weeks now.

Well Mother I have no more news so I will now close with love,

From your loving Son,
Jack

Letter 15 to Mother

*I wish and pray that my life may be one big sacrifice
made from the small and trivial sacrifices of everyday life.
Sacrifice for love is true happiness.*

This is a four-page letter (11th March 1928) from John to his mother. It is his second year at the seminary, after a long holiday at home in Yea and Seymour, where he worked at Wallis' Café. John is student number 24, out of 80 students. The professors and students sit in order of seniority in the refectory and chapel. John finds the antics of some professors quite humourous as reflected in his colourful descriptions of their idiosyncrasies, which his parents will enjoy. Father Bower's class is *as good as a circus*! Thinking about obedience, John notes that he should not obey out of fear, but to obey for love of God.

Father Justin Simonds has been appointed vice-rector and professor of philosophy. Earlier he had been the Dean and professor of Scripture at the Manly seminary. There is a new Archbishop of Hobart, William Hayden. John asks what was happening about his acceptance for that Archdiocese. He is told by Father Simonds that the last year's report on him had been sent to the Archbishop, so now he must formally apply to be accepted there. Nine years later in 1937 John meets Father Simonds in other circumstances – when he becomes the Archbishop of Hobart.[7]

Again John is aware that money is scarce, and in the latter part of the letter he writes cautiously about his need to buy books. Not surprisingly, John uses his spare time for reading.

* * *

*St Columba's College,
Springwood.
Sunday 11.3.28*

Dear Mother,
I have not told you much about SCC since I came back. The two letters I wrote were fairly scanty. But really there is not much news. Things are very quiet here. But I will tell you all I can. I am feeling splendid as I hope you and all at home are.

---

7   Subsequently, in 1942 Archbishop Simonds was appointed coadjutor Archbishop of Melbourne, with the right of succeeding Archbishop Daniel Mannix, who died in November 1963. Archbishop Simonds died four years after him in 1967.

On Thursday last we began the school year. The first class we had was Hermeneutics. We will be studying the New Testament this year. It should be very interesting. Fr. Simonds did not waste any time in preliminary speeches. Some of the professors do. However this was the class we had for the day. I went for a swim then. In the afternoon we had study and again at night. Besides writing up our notes there was little else to do but read.

On Friday we had a full day. However, as Fr. Brauer is away we had no Physics and could give this hour to something else. Fr. Bowers, the Philos teacher is as good as a circus. He runs all over the room. I can't stop laughing at his antics. I hope he does not go on like this all the year.

We also got fixed up for our new positions in the chapel and at the tables. I am Junior man of our class. The positions in the ref. [refectory] and the chapel are allotted according to seniority. I am 24 of the House out of about 80. I am on one of the tables facing the Professors. It is a very embarrassing place. We can't look at the Pros or can't look round at the others. All we can do is look sideways out of the window and at each other. We are continually laughing as a result of our sad predicament. I suppose we will get used to it after a while.

On Friday Jack Donaldson one of my fellow students, (2nd Philos) got sick. He said he had a cold and went to bed. On Saturday it got worse and he went to Lewisham Hospital. That night we were told that he was very low and were asked to pray for him. The doctor said that owing to his youth and strong constitution he ought to pull through. He is only sixteen but is exceptionally clever.

On Friday night I asked Fr. Simonds about the Bishop's arrangements for me. He said the report had gone in for last year and told me to write and make formal application. This I did tonight.

On Saturday night we had the first Debating Society meeting of the year. There was a heated argument about where we should go on St. Patrick's Day – to Sassafras or to Hawkesbury. I have not been to Sassafras, but I believe there is so much to be seen. I have been to the other place and there is at least a good swim on the river. The Hawkesbury side won after a long discussion. Whether Fr. Simonds (acting Rector) will let us go there or not is another thing. Most likely we will have to go to Sassafras.

Then there was the election of the various committees – Sports grounds, photographs and Concert. I am included in the last one. After this business was over we had impromptu speeches. I got called for one. None of them were about anything serious, but merely for their telling of yarns.

We had our first Solemn Mass today. The students have not yet got into the way of singing. No doubt the choir will be good when they have more practice. Fr. Simonds spent about an hour expounding to us – chiefly for the benefit of new boys and also the old ones – the rules of the college. He asked us to obey them not for fear of him but for the Love of God. When given in one lump they appear pretty formidable and one would think the life pretty hard but put into practice they are easier. He let us know that without looking for it he had particularly seen a student on the way for a smoko. He is very keen – like Bro. William, in his knowledge of character.

I went for a swim in the afternoon. It was fairly cool out but the water was fairly warm. I am afraid the swimming season is coming to a close. It was one form of exercise which I like very much. I have taken up the Physical jerks again. I will do them in the afternoon in future as Fr. Simonds said that if done at night they interfered with the keeping of the great silence – the silence from night prayers till breakfast next day when we are not to talk under [any] pretext at all.

I have not written to Marie yet. I might do so tonight if time allows. I think I left my razor and shaving soap (tube) at home when I was leaving. I also left a red prayer book "Ecce Homo". I would be pleased mother if you would please send them on. I did not see a prospectus for this year but I learnt on arrival here that a towel would be no longer supplied to students. This was due to the misuse of them by certain students last year. I have two here but I want 2 more. If you can spare them at home Mother, would you send me 2 – coloured [towels.]

With regard to books I have only bought one yet – a big Latin Dictionary. It cost 9/-. I do not know yet just what the books will be but certainly they will not amount to more than £1.0.0. I have some and others I can dispense with. If you do not mind, Mother, would you please send me that sum. I don't think I will want any more for some time. Of course you know I try to go as easy as possible and I thank you now, Mother, for your unstinting kindness in the past. If I can't repay it in the hard cash, Mother, you know that I can pay as much by prayers. I am sure Jesus sees the sacrifice you are making and after all the life of each and every one of us must be a sacrifice if [we] wish to gain eternal life. I wish and pray that my life may be one big sacrifice made from the small and trivial sacrifices of everyday life. Sacrifice for love is true happiness.

I began the Novena today. I hope to be able to make a good one and I am sure that St. Joseph will turn every one of us to the Sacred Heart that through it we may be all united in the bonds of true Christian Love. I would also ask you, Mother, if you do not mind to lend me the "Lives of the Saints" which you have.

I will close for the present, dear Mother. Good night and may God bless you.

With love,
From your Son,
Jack

Letter 16 to Mother

The right intention was there and God sees the spirit rather than the actual deed.

In this long six-page letter (25th March 1928) to his mother John covers many topics. While he asked for £1.0.0 in his previous letter, he receives £2.0.0, double the amount. Again, he is grateful for his parents' generosity.

The Concert Committee had been busy organising the entertainment for St Patrick's evening, but a lack of communication amongst the staff on a petty matter has marred the preparations and led to a lecture from Father Simonds. While John is known not to be able to sing in tune, he appreciated others' voices and musical talent. There were gifted students, items for the concert including a tenor voice singing Irish songs and a violinist playing music from an opera – *he seemed to be one with his violin and held the house in suspense.* John's item had been to dress up and act out a skit.

The nuns lived in another building on the property and they were responsible for the domestic work – cooking, washing and cleaning. It seems the students did not see very much of them. While there had been a High Mass for St Patrick's Day, it did not suit them to organise the food for a bush picnic on that Saturday, so the students went on the Monday, St Joseph's feast day. They had had to dress formally and yet went to *a pretty wild place*, Sassafras, for a *glorified bush picnic*. John appreciates the beauty of the mountains and tells of *a wealth of wild undergrowth on both sides of the stream.*

In his last letter John had spoken of one of his peers who was ill. This time the seminarians visit the grave of another student, Tom Hegney, who died while still at the College. Significantly, they all contribute to put up a memorial on his grave. This event surely makes an impression on the young men – one of their own has died. John writes of his sadness that another student, the twelfth of his group from *the old brigade*, had decided not to continue in his studies for the priesthood.

* * *

Feast of Annunciation
St Columba's College,
Springwood.
25.3.28

Dear Mother,

I received your most welcome letter on Friday last. I was very pleased to get it. I received the £2.0.0 enclosed for which I thank you very much. I am pleased to know that you are feeling better and also that Father is well. I am feeling very well thank God.

I see that the last time I wrote was Friday week. I will try to give you all I know from my diary. On Saturday 17th we had a holiday for St. Patrick's Day. Usually there is a picnic on that day but as it was a Saturday it was inconvenient for the Nuns, so that was postponed to Monday. We had our first High Mass. Afterwards we were free. The new students played us old students but were beaten badly. Fr. Hayes (ACK) was the boy's captain.

As there was a concert that night the committee set to work to get things in order early in the day. We intended to go out in the afternoon. Together with three others I was helping to set the scenes when Fr. Simonds came in and asked what we were doing. We told him. He gave us a little lecture and said we should have asked him. It was not our work to do that but the President. He told us to go on but to present the programme. He was quite satisfied on seeing the programme. I think he did not know that Monsignor Brauer let us get ready first.

In the afternoon I went with about 30 others to the cemetery to see Tom Hegney's grave. It looked quite well and had not changed since we fixed it up at the end of the year. We said the rosary there. The students and professors are going to put a cross over the grave and get it fixed up properly. They intend to put just a plain marble cross over it. This is the usual thing for a student. It is estimated to cost £33.0.0. This will mean 2/6 each. The Manly students will also contribute.

After tea the concert came. There were a number of Irish songs. One student J. Fitzgerald has an excellent tenor voice. He sang Molly Branagan. He is wonderful. He sang at Mass today and was simply splendid. Then a new student named Samuels played the violin. He played some music from an opera. He seemed to be one with his violin and held the house in suspense for over quarter of an hour. He is the best I have ever heard on any instrument. From the lowest notes to the highest he went with the utmost ease. Bob Kennedy and I gave an item. We dressed up in old coats and funny hats. I pretended to be a sailor. We gave a few jokes and then had a fight. He ran away and left me alone. It was pretty slow but the house seemed to be satisfied and that is the main thing.

On Sunday we cleaned up the hall. I went to the Grotto for the 1st time this year. In the afternoon I went to the weir for a swim. Monday was St. Joseph's day. We had two Masses.

Then we went for our picnic to Sassafras. This is a "glorified Bush Picnic". We had to dress up. After walking to Springwood we proceeded to Sassafras, which is about 3 miles past the town. It was a pretty wild place. Our party camped on the top. It was a long way down to the bottom where a creek was flowing. After dinner we went down there. It was typical of the Mountains. There was a wealth of wild undergrowth on either side of the stream. A track wound along this stream for nearly two miles. I went with another student to the end of the track. Sometimes there was a noise in the leaves, which sounded like a quail makes. A man on the track told us they were pheasants. There was a big swimming pool at the end of the track. A great number of students went in. I had a dip. Fr. Simonds got a loan of some tights and went in also. We had a fine day and returned home worn out.

We had vespers before tea. One sad feature of the day was that we lost another of our students. Frank Elliott left. He had been here for four years. He just said that he did not think he could go on. I thought from the beginning of the year that he was going to go. This has brought the class down to 22 – 12 of the old brigade missing.

I finished the Novena. I tried to do it as well as possible. I am sure Mother that your Novena was as good if not a great deal better than mine. It does not matter if you could not go to Mass etc. The right intention was there and God sees the spirit rather than the actual deed. However Mother let us not stop there but keep on praying day by day. St. Monica prayed for 17 years without ceasing for her son Augustine who was one of the most notorious of sinners. He is now numbered among the greatest saints of the Church.

Tuesday 20th: I felt very tired after the previous day's exertions. Fr. Slattery, Spiritual Director, was up and spoke on the love we should have of the Passion and Cross.

Wednesday: Study as usual. We had our 1st lecture on Social Science which deals with the organisation of society in general, ie. the rights of a man, his duties and mutual relationships. It is very interesting. Fr. Toal, the Professor is just new. He is very nice and teaches in an interesting fashion. Went for a swim.

Thursday: After the lecture (1) I went to the weir for a dip. The water was great.

Friday: Warm, I went for swim.

Saturday: It was fairly warm, I went to the weir. In the evening we had our usual meeting. The particular business was lecturettes. There were 5.

The 1st (Roy Brown) was on Bishop Kettler a great social reformer of Germany. The next on Napoleon by Tom Gard. I intended to say a few words on this but time would not permit. Jack Garvey (new student) delivered his maiden speech on China. It was very interesting dealing as it did with the people in general. Keith Bush came next, his subject being the "Infant Jesus of Prague". This "Infant Jesus" was a little statute of the child dressed as a Prince and holding in his hand the world. There were many miracles performed through the prayers offered in honour of the Infant. He also stated that there were four cases here last year which received help from this source – one being the very sudden and speedy recovery of the sister of one of the students from a serious illness. He is getting a supply of the beads. I will send you one when they come. The last was delivered by Allen Tullins on the steel works at Newcastle. There was a considerable amount of fun as a result of interjections from the house. This is the one night of the week in which we can have a bit of a free time. I am looking forward to next Saturday night, which is Joke and Story Night. I will have to think of some joke or story to tell.

Today I went to the Grotto and in the afternoon to the Weir. Tomorrow we will celebrate the feast of the Annunciation which has been moved up a day owing to the fact that today is Passion Sunday. I had an Antiphon at Vespers tonight. In the morning we will make a pilgrimage to the Grotto and say the Rosary. Fr. Simonds will bless a new statute of Bernadette, which has been placed there. The Archbishop is coming up in the afternoon. He will stay for three days. I think he is coming for a rest. He has been working hard for the Congress. Have you become a Member?

I am glad to know that business is going on well. I often think of you and I miss being in the shop. Steve Ford asked how you were going. He takes a keen interest in these things. He has travelled nearly all NSW and Queensland. He is the student who goes on walking tours. Last holidays he and his mate covered 300 miles on foot and 250 by lifts in cars. Next Xmas they are coming south. His brother was in the *Lutluan* club which the Indian Club which passed through Seymour. He was a day behind the big party. Steve asked did I see him. I did not know. He may have been in [the Café.]

I was very sorry to hear about Auntie Kate. I must write again to her ... About the towels, Mother, the roller towel is just the thing and thank you very much for it.

I have not got the parcel yet but presume that you have not had time to spare. I am sorry to cause you the trouble of hunting up books etc. I should have done that. I think the "Ecce Homo" had a brown paper cover on it. I sent the money to the Far East tonight. I registered it.

I have not heard yet from Bishop Barry. It is a fortnight since I wrote. I suppose he has a lot of correspondence. I wrote to Fr. O'Connor[8] tonight for a letter of recommendation, which is required after each holiday to give an account of the student's conduct etc. That other student has not yet come back. He cannot get on with the Sydney diocese now. He has written to a number of the students. I feel sorry for him and pray daily for him. However God will help him to do his will. I know you pray for me Mother but pray

---

8   Fr. P.B. O'Connor

especially that I may become more holy. I often think how little I do to make me worthy of that dignity. Remember that that responsibility is so much greater than any other.

Well now Mother, I will close wishing you and all at home God's choicest blessing.   With love from

Your loving Son
Jack

PS. Monday. It was wet this morning. After the second Mass we were free to do what we liked since it was too wet for a formal visit to the Grotto. However a party of us went down in our old togs and did a bit of work there – cleaning out blackberries and also making a cement wall across a creek there to make the Grotto prettier. We went again this afternoon. The rain became fairly heavy later on. The Archbishop came just before tea. He is staying over night perhaps for some time. Well, now Good-bye for the present.

Jack

PPS. I got a note from Auntie Kate today.

Letter 17 to Mother

Turn to the Cross ... and above all never give up hope.
Asking God in his love, kindness and mercy to bless you and guard you.

This short two-page letter to his mother (2nd May 1928) leaves the question as to the situation to which John is responding. Calling his mother *his queen* gives a picture of his admiration and love of her. What were Emma's thoughts, worries and sufferings shared with him in 1928? His father's expression of faith appears not to be as strong as his mother's. While many of the letters show that John's mother had been a spiritual guide to him, there is a reversal of roles in this letter. John as the tender spiritual director or all-knowing young son, beckons his mother to *Turn to the Cross* in her sorrows and *learn to love the Cross. Take up the crucifix that is on your dressing table,* he also encourages her, and *I am sure Mary will fill your heart with grace.* And he exhorts her never to *give up hope.*

The letter also reveals John's growing understanding of the responsibility he will accept in his life as a priest, including the expectations he has upon himself. *Little did I realise when a year ago I left home what a responsibility I was to take on.* He now has a *faint glimmer* at this early age of what he thinks a priest should be.

* * *

St. Columba's College,
Springwood.
May 2nd '28.

Dear Mother,

The month of May has come round to us once again. It is indeed a dear month to my heart, first as it is the month of Mary, my Mother and my Queen and 2ndly because it is the month of my other mother and queen. Glad I am to be able to send this note of love to you wishing you many happy returns on your birthday and asking God in his love, kindness and mercy to bless you and guard you.

I will be short, dear Mother, as time is limited but hope that this coming year will be to you a source of great grace and spiritual progress. As in this month we celebrate the Immaculate purity of Mary – Mary, of whom the Holy Spirit said, "Thou art all fair my beloved and the original stain was never in thee," so, too, do you strive to make that soul of yours yet more pure. Sure I am that Mary will do your part as a recompense for those numberless times in which you have uttered the words, "Hail Mary full of grace." I am sure she will fill your heart with grace and water those flowers of piety and humility that are in your soul.

And as a special means of grace learn to love the Cross. Jesus on Calvary allowed His Sacred Heart to be pierced by the spear, that of His holy Mother by the seven swords of grief and those of all he loved and still loves by many a sharp thorn. As those thorns have only made the heart more and more pure, rejoice, dear Mother, when sorrow comes your way. Turn to the Cross. Take up that Crucifix from your dressing table, hold it in your hands and think of your Saviour. When you rise in the morning, take it up and kiss it, offer the day to Jesus and unite yourself in spirit with His Precious Blood as it is being offered throughout the world. And before you lie down to rest, take it up again, embrace it, press it to your brow and Jesus will indeed pour his divine grace upon your soul and those of the Family.

And above all Mother never give up hope. With that trust which you have shown in the past still go on up the steps of Calvary. I will pray for you and all at home, especially for Father that he may appreciate his holy religion. Implore the eternal Father by the blood of Jesus to bless him and send him grace to become a Catholic worthy of the Faith.

And while I am telling you these things I become conscious of my very own misery, selfishness and want of generosity to the God who loves me so. It hurts me to see him as little loved. Oh! Pray for me that I may be made worthy to the office to which Jesus has called me. Little did I realise when a year ago I left home what a responsibility I was to take on. Only now do I see a faint glimmer of what a priest should be. Ask God to make my heart pure, holy and really humble.

And now I will close, dear Mother, once more asking God and the Immaculate Virgin to shower down on you the choicest graces purchased by the blood of Christ on the Cross. I remain always,

Your loving Son,

Jack

Letter 18 to Mother

I crossed the river by jumping from rock to rock.
On my return I found a lyre bird's feather.
You've got no idea of the roughness
of the country that is covered in thick scrub.

As John writes this four-page letter to his mother (19th August 1928), there is anticipation regarding the upcoming Eucharistic Congress in September. John is annoyed news was not getting through to the students, as he wants to pass on news to his mother, because she is travelling to Sydney for it. During the Congress a gathering of Assumption College ex-students was to be held at Marist College, Sydney – the invitation came from Brother William.

He tells his mother about the *chief events* at the College. They had a retreat, the subject being on *the proper use of time*, and John writes that this is *important in the priest's life.*

The *Catholic Paper discussions* this month focused on three main topics: the need for fostering vocations, parish libraries and the Hibernians. John does not elaborate but he does say that such presentations give ideas to them for when they are in parishes themselves – the idea of parish libraries of course.

From Sydney, *The Arch,* presumably Archbishop Michael Kelly visited for examination of the students, who assembled together with the Professors. Next day he celebrates Mass with them. John tells his mother how he loves the feast of Mary's Assumption, and expounds on the devotional practice of praying the rosary, on this day praying 20 rosaries to honour Mary! He remembers the way Brother William had reflected on the Hail Mary and now shares it with his mother.

The students have another energetic picnic day in the bush. Boarding the train to Blackheath station, they set out. John with three mates is the first to reach the Grose River and the appointed camping grounds in the Grose Valley – twenty-five minutes before anyone else. Being *bushed* for an hour on the return journey, John's imagination gives rise to the possibility and delight of a night around a *campfire* under the stars. He explains that this bushwalk was not like going across the paddocks at Yea! With such energy expended and a complete change to the normal order of day, no wonder he was tired.

* * *

St Columba's College,
Springwood.
Sunday 19.8.28

Dear Mother,

No doubt you have been expecting a letter from me during the last week. Well I did write a short note but did not post it on the hopes of getting Congress news. However I will write tonight without further delay. I am in the best of health as I hope you and all at home are.

I have not much time so I will just give the chief events. The Arch. was up on Monday 6th but went away early. We did not have the Blue Tuesday exam but just the Retreat. The exam was postponed for a week. Fr. Slattery gave the retreat taking as his subject the "Proper use of our time". It is a very good subject and one, which is most important in the priest's life.

I wrote to Marie about a fortnight ago. I got a letter from her next day. She told me that you are sending my letters to her. I thank you very much for this, as it gives me more time.

On Saturday 11th we had "Catholic Papers" as the particular business of the night. The first was on the "Need of Fostering Vocations for Priesthood". The next was on the "Parish Library". The last was on the "Hibernians".⁹ A student read out his paper and then the rest criticised it and added ideas of their own. This is to enable us to get an idea of what practical means we can use as priests.

I wrote to Brother Michael at ACK. I don't think I told you last time that Bro William sent us (Old Marist Boys) an invitation to a gathering at St. Joseph's College [Hunters Hill] on Tuesday the 4th of September – during Congress week. This day is the only free one during the week.

On Monday last, the Archbishop was up for the exam. We had two lectures in the morning. He got here about 4 o'clock. We all gathered in the one room and then he came in with the Professors. I did not get a call. My number was taken out of the box but another student was called. I suppose there was a mistake in the list. The Arch gave a little speech after the exams. The lower classes got the afternoon off but we (2nd [Year] Philosphy) had to go and do Greek in the afternoon. The Archbishop said Mass on Tuesday. Fr. Slattery was up and gave a lecture on the Assumption.

---

9   The Hibernian Australian Catholic Benefit Society was founded in Ballarat in 1868 in order to assist Irish immigrants. It later amalgamated with the Australian Catholic Benefit Society in Melbourne. It also supported St Patrick Day parades.

Wednesday 15th. Assumption Day. This is the day which I love. The Arch said the first Mass and then the Rector sang the High Mass. Then we had Exposition of the Blessed Sacrament. Some students were appointed to go on adoration while the rest made a Pilgrimage to the Grotto. We sang the Litany said the Rosary and many other hymns. It is on this day that each one tries to offer Our Lady 1,000 Hail Mary's – 20 Rosaries – 100 decades. They take some saying – nearly 3½ hours. I thought of ACK. I think this is a beautiful day – when Mary, the one spotless creature of whom the Holy Spirit says, "Thou art all fair very beloved and there is no spot in thee." Our queen and our Mother ascended into Heaven. I often think what a wonderful thing the Immaculate Conception was. The Hail Mary is a Prayer, which is very suitable for meditation. Bro. William used to take it word by word and give a long talk on it. For example, he used to say "Hail Mary", Oh dear Mary, our Mother look on us thy children, weak and faltering on our way through the vale of tears but oh be a Mother, kind and loving and listen to us". Perhaps, Mother, you may be able to do this if you have a spare minute or as you lie in bed. And ask Mary to be a Mother to me who am so weak and careless towards Jesus.

On Thursday last Cricket began. I went to one of the tables in the back to do a bit of writing. In the afternoon I spent my recreation working in front of the College – cleaning it up for the Congress.

Friday was 'Grose day'.[10] *We had a Requiem for Cardinal Moran's soul*[11] *and then came to breakfast. There was an egg, an onion and a few biscuits as well as an apple in a paper bag on each one's place. We took these with us. We left the college at 10 o'clock. It was a wonderful day. I was one of the first to reach the Grose, Jack Tierney, Frank Newman and myself being 25 minutes ahead of the big body of students. We arrived at 25 minutes to 12. I crossed the river by jumping from rock to rock and then went up one bank for about a quarter of a mile. You have no idea of the roughness of the country. It is covered in thick scrub and all kinds of creepers, which are as strong as rope. Jack Tierney and I then crossed back over the stream just above a pretty waterfall. He got some good photos. Even when the water was about 10 feet deep you can see the bottom quite plainly. Some students went in for a swim, but I believe it was very cold. I found a lyre bird's feather on the way back.*

We had not left the half way cave very long on the return journey when we found we were "bushed". We were there for about an hour. At last they got their bearings and found the track and we got home safely. I was looking forward to

---

10   A picnic outing to Grose Valley in the Blue Mountains.
11   Cardinal Patrick Moran, the third Archbishop of Sydney, died at Manly on 16th August 1911. Mass was celebrated on his anniversary. http://adb.anu.edu.au/biography/moran-patrick-francis-7648

a night out under the stars. We would have had some fun around a big campfire. I was very tired on the following day. It is not like walking through the paddock to Yea or somewhere else. But every step of the way is between trees, over rocks and logs. Sometimes we jumped from one rock to another about 4 feet away and with 20 feet of a fall between them.

I went over to the works in the Recreation Hall in the afternoon. They have the 4 walls up and are now preparing to put the roof and floor in.

Sunday: we had High Mass today. The Rector "squashed" about "smoking" and about Particular friends (P.F.)[12] This means associating with only one person and ignoring others in the College. One student went up to the Dean today for smoking. We were expecting to hear Congress News but were disappointed. They called a special meeting to ask the Prefect to ask the Rector but he said he could not tell us anything. I will write as soon as I hear. We may only get two days down there.

I am sending the Oleographs and pictures for you. You will be able to choose. I sent the Immaculate Heart for Chester. Well Mother I will now close in haste with love from

Your loving son,

Jack.

---

12   Particular friendships that were exclusive of others were not acceptable.

Letter 19 to Mother

All through the bush there were flowers of all kinds
– armsful of waratahs.
You have no idea of their beauty.

In this eight-page letter (28th September 1928) to his father, which John intended to be short, the eighteen-year-old has more to say than anticipated. It is written on the eve of the feast of St Michael, the Archangel. He expects his mother, who attended the Eucharistic Congress in Sydney, would tell his father about the Congress, but he has a lot to share too, because it has made a great impact on him. Following the Congress, she had visited John at Springwood. Not only would she and John have talked at length, she would have met some of John's fellow students and professors and would now have an accurate visual understanding of those John writes about in his letters – and where he is training to be a priest.

Like John, Emma loved the bush, and especially the wild flowers. He is disappointed that she would not see the bush in full bloom – she was too early for it. They have just brought home arms full of waratah from the bush. Miss Nance Quinlan from Yea, who appears in this letter, was well known to John's mother and was the Catholic Church organist. She grew up on the property that used belong to Emma's grandparents.

In this letter John tells of the *Congress Night* when the students shared their Congress experiences. John is impressed at the presence of eighty-two bishops and feels the excitement of history in the making for the Australian Church, amazed at the universality of the Church and shocked at the bigotry that exists even among Christian churches, and notes the fine speeches and how superior was the organisation of the event – and more. He orders the relevant local newspapers with reports of the Congress, *The Sydney Morning Herald* and *The Sydney Mail* to be sent to his sister, Marie.

Following the Congress, many visitors had come to the Springwood. One of them, Dr Joseph Dwyer, an Australian born into an Irish family and Bishop of Wagga Wagga, was greatly interested in Australian botany and the native flora. He suggested, in jest, that he change places with the Rector, so he could spend a year collecting native plants, which amuses John.

Study is tough with four main subjects that must be passed, Scripture, English, Latin and the most difficult for John, Philosophy. A little bit of literary wit alleviates his frustration when he says the professor is always telling them to look up *sweated stuff done last year* and to *see sweated stuff to come*. John says to his father, *I tell you it is sweated stuff when one spends four and five hours a day at it!*

John's description of his peers as they presented at the Seminary Oratory competition are colourful. There are varying topics: *Good Drama and Every Day Life; A Plea for Australian Literature; The Catholicity of the Church; Lucient L'Overteur, William Wentworth and The Call of the Bush, Australia,* and *Irish Pioneers*. The adjudicator, Father Dunne, *the nicest of the nice professors,* had been a teacher at Warracknabeal in western Victoria.

There is also Sports news to write about. John gets fourth in the 100 yards, the 220 yards and 880 yards, but *drove them all home in the 440* yards. He does come first in the obstacle race and third in the mile race. Being the feast of St Michael the Archangel tomorrow, there is another picnic day.

* * *

St Columban's College,
Springwood.
[28th September 1928]

Dear Father,

Just a short letter to let you know how things are going on up here, since our little holiday for the Congress. I suppose Mother will tell you all the news about that wonderful event in our Australian history. I am glad she arrived home safe and to know that you are feeling a bit better. I am in the best of health, thank God!

Well the Congress is over and gone but the memory still remains – and the effects too. It was rather hard to get down to the old round again but I think most of us did so after a couple of days. We had the first day after we came back off. It was then that Mother came up.

The following day we had our regular classes. From now till the end of the year we will have some real solid work. There are 4 subjects in which we must pass in order to go to Manly. They are Philosophy, Hermeneutics (Scripture Study), Latin and English. The Philos is the hardest. Besides a lecture in the morning, sometimes two, we have two hours at night. I spend nearly all my time on it alone. The professor is always telling us to look up "sweated stuff done last year", "See sweated stuff to come". I tell you it is sweated stuff when one spends 4 or 5 hours a day at it.

On the Sunday we had a few Bishops up. Dr. Dwyer of Wagga[13] drove three others up in his own car. One was Dr. O'Doherty, Archbishop of Tuam, who spoke during the Congress. Dr. Dwyer is a great naturalist and went off down the "Bush" with a couple of students in search of flowers. He said to the Rector that he would change places for a year so as to be able to get the flowers. Of course the Rector said, "Not on your life". On Thursday we had 12 visiting priests up. They had to get an extra table to fit them all up.

One of the students asked me whether I knew Nance Quinlan or not. He had met her in a Flat in Sydney. She knew some Nurses of the name of Walsh who were staying here. They introduced him to Nance and they had tea together. She wanted to know was Mother over. He said he thought so.

I got a letter from the "Sydney Morning Herald" that they had sent all the Congress numbers to Marie. I had asked them to send them. I also got a Sydney Mail about the Congress. The Mail has some fine pictures.

We had a "Congress Night" on the Saturday following the big event. Different students gave the impressions, which it had made on them. I spoke first on the "Universality of the Church and the Blessed Sacrament". It was truly marvelous. There were Germans, French, English, Irish, Spanish, Polish, Greeks, Indians, Chinese, Japanese and a number of Islanders as well as Maoris. It is only the Catholic Church that can claim children under every flag of the world. There were in all 82 Bishops coming from USA, Europe and Asia. Competent critics say that although the crowd was not as great as that of Chicago, the organisation was far superior. There were some fine speeches given.

I saw where a Methodist minister began to say some hard things about the Papal Legate[14] and Archbishop Kelly, while preaching in the Domain. The

---

13   Dr Joseph Dwyer was appointed the first Bishop of the new Diocese of Wagga Wagga in 1918 and died 1939. His Irish parents initially settled in Albury, then moved to a number of centres in New South Wales, including Newcastle, Goulburn and Bathurst, where the boys were educated at St Stanislaus College. He and his brother, Dr Patrick Vincent Dwyer, were the first Australian-born bishops in the country. The brother, a great pianist, was Bishop of Maitland in New South Wales from 1909-1931.

14   While there was significant concern of disruption, it did not eventuate, even though a number of Protestant bodies had called for the Congress to be prohibited.

crowd of all denominations rushed him and tramped on him. They had to take him away in a car. There are 120 persons receiving instructions at one Church in Sydney while two of the five aviators who formed the Cross with aeroplanes are becoming Catholics. I wrote a long account of the week [of the Congress] to Bro. William. He was unable to get over, and in a recent letter to Alf Schmude said he felt it very much.

Corey Honner took a bad turn at the tea table and had to be taken to bed. He was here in 1926 but owing to his frequent fits he had to stay away for a year. This was the first time he has had one this year but I am afraid he will have to leave for good. He comes from W.A.

A little boy at Valley Heights, a station not far from Springwood was seriously hurt while hanging on to a car when riding his bike. He died a day after. In the following week a similar accident occurred so that the little boy was anointed. However I think he has recovered.

Instead of the usual Spiritual Director we had Fr. Power, a Vincentian up last week. He was a chaplain at the war and told us some very interesting anecdotes. He had us roaring laughing all the time. I would like to have him here for a week or so to tell us more about the things over there.

When Mother was up she was very much taken with the flowers but she missed the best of them. It was only last week that they were at their best. All through the bush for miles, there were flowers of all kinds. You have no idea of their beauty. They brought home armsful of waratahs. I went with a couple of others to an orange grove some miles away to get some oranges.

We had the Oratory competition last week. I intended to go in but could not find time to prepare a speech and learn it off. There were 8 competitors. The prizes were from 25/- to 10/-. The first to speak was Alf Schmude (an old AC boy). He can write a lovely essay but his delivery is not very winning. He is far superior to the majority in Intellectual ability but cannot express himself as a speaker. He should be able to write fine books. His subject was "Good Drama and Every Day Life." He was classed with two others for 3rd place.

Allen Tullins followed with "A Plea for Australian Literature". It was very good but did not seem to be his own. It was too good. He was with Alf for 3rd place.

Next came Vin Callahan with a fine speech on "The Catholicity of the Church". He had a very methodical way of delivery so that when he was finished one could tell all that he had said. This was his chief characteristic and through it he won the Comp. The Church he said is catholic 1st because she teaches all men of all nations; 2nd because she teaches rich and poor, noble and lowly all the same faith; 3rd because of her numbers (320,000,000).

Significantly, a garden party was held at Government House to honour Australia's first appointed papal legate, Cardinal Bonaventura Cerretti. https://dictionaryofsydney.org/entry/international_eucharistic_congress_1928

Jack Garvey told us about an American negro named "Luisant L'Overteur". He was a general first in the British army, then the French and last was himself leader of his people and gained for those of them in the Island of San Domingo, Freedom from all foreign power. It was a good historical account but there was not much oratory. In fact, very few of the speakers showed the signs of Oratory. Last year's performance was far better.

Bob Kennedy, a true son of the soil from the North coast of NSW, spoke on William Wentworth, the originator of Australian freedom in Government. He got 2nd place not so much for his actual speaking as for the effect he left on his hearers. Each one I think just proud of his country and the remarkable freedom he enjoys in it.

Jim Evans gave a speech on the call of the Bush. It was very fine and showed genuine oratorical powers. He spoilt it by pronouncing the "use" of nature too much. His speech was a bit "flash". Nevertheless, when they finished I felt he did not quiet [sic] attain his end and that he did not mean what he said. I am sure he could not endure the "bush" for a day if on his own. Born in the city he is always complaining of the difficulties we have to put up with here. At the word "bush" there was a general titter in the house. We are not supposed to go into the bush without a prefect; but I think there is a pretty big percentage of students who find their way there every day for a little "puff" or else a "feed-up".

Jim Fitzgerald gave a speech on "Australia". It was full of high sounding words but all the same he had good matter. He spoilt it by introducing the names of a number of insignificant boxers and jockeys etc. into the members of Australia's "great men". I thought he was one of the best but was placed lower down by Father Dunn the adjudicator.

Dennis Kenneally was last on the "Irish Pioneers". He spoke well but left us with very indistinct idea of what he was trying to bring home. I do not know now what he wanted to bring out.

Fr. Dunne spoke on each one, criticised them and gave some hints etc. He has only been out from Manly about 10 months. He was a high school teacher at Warracknabeal. He has his M.A. I think he is the nicest of a nice lot of professors.

On Thursday last we had our Sports. We had one class first – Hermenuetics. We had an exam. It was pretty good but too long for the time. I think I did fairly well.

It was a fine day. The first event was the 100 yds. Champ. Lawman (Qld) won it. He is I think the best all rounder sport here and perhaps that has ever been here. He is hand-ball Champion, the best cricketer, good at football (Rugby, Aussie Rules and Soccer), good at tennis, a fair swimmer and good athlete. J. Healy won the 100 yds. handicap. I got fourth in the 100 yds. Junior handicap. Lawman won the Long Jump 19 feet 5". Alf Schumude jumped 5 feet 2 in the high Jump. He did 5'.5½" at Kilmore. I got fourth in the 220 and in the 880. I drove them all home in the 440.

In the obstacle race I got 1st. We had to put our shoes in a bag. We were about 15 yds. away with our backs to the bag. When the pistol went we turned round, ran for our shoes, which had been thrown out of the bag, put them on and tied them up. I was lucky in getting my shoes together and in having good laces for tying. Then we had to turn 3 back summersaults and run to a ladder nearby. After we got through between the rungs (it was standing on its side), we had to run backwards for a while and then run for the tape. I won my heat and then the final.

Today I went in the Novelty Race – chasing the ball but did no good. I then went in the mile. I did not intend to go in as I was so sore and stiff from yesterday's races but I managed to get 3rd. I had a good start (120 yds). We are to have a picnic tomorrow. It is the Feast of St Michael, the Archangel.

Well I am very tired and weary (Have just finished an hour and a half Philosophy) so I will close with fondest love to you and all at home, and asking Jesus and His Holy Mother to bless you in this coming month of the Holy Rosary. I remain,

                Your loving son,
                Jack

Letter 20 to Mother

*It is my last general picnic at St Columba's.
We are down to work now.*

In this two-page letter to his mother (18th November 1928), John tells of the last of the bush picnics before he goes on to the Manly seminary for further studies. He has exams to be passed, especially Hermeneutics, for which he lacks confidence.

This time the picnic is to the Nepean River and they are up early, arriving by 8.30am. The boats came and, with seven in their boat, they row up the river two miles and set up camp. Some others walked along the bank. The picnic food is of great interest, the fruit salad with cream being the highlight.

Holidays are coming up and he reminds his mother he needs money for his fare home and other matters. The money he wins in a raffle he had already promised *in his heart* before winning to give it to charity! The charity is the Dominican School for Deaf Girls at Waratah.

Lastly, he has an antiphon to sing for Vespers, so he must finish off.

* * *

*St. Columba's College,
Springwood.
Sunday 18.11.28*

Dear Mother,
I will not be able to write a long letter. I have only half an hour. I hope that this will find you and all at home in good health as I am, thank God. I am feeling splendid and am looking forward to the holidays.

We had a picnic to Nepean last Thursday. It rained the day before and was very dull in the morning. We were a bit doubtful about the day. However things cleared up about half past seven. We were up at a quarter to five. We got to Nepean about half past eight. It was then a great day, although the sky was overcast. We had to wait for an hour for boats. The Nepean is about 100 yards across. At last the boats came and we rowed up the river, to a spot 2 miles away from the bridge from which we started. There were seven in our boat. The other three walked up the bank. After fixing up our camp we had a swim. Two students went back in the boat for the Rector, whom we invited to our party.

We had a great dinner. It was finished off by a lovely fruit salad. We got some fresh fruit before starting (oranges, apples, etc.) and a bottle of cream. The Cream was the real stuff, not artificial. Then two students went to a house across the river and got a cupful of fresh cream. They cut up the oranges and apples into small pieces and then added the cream and sugar. The Rector said he never ate fruit salad but he did not leave much of all that we gave him.

To wash up we took the plates etc. out into the middle of the river. What with dates, biscuits, lollies and other fruit we were kept busy eating all the day. We went down the river to the big railway bridge and had a second "boil up" there. I had a good row in the boat. Alex Ryder and I went away down the river to have a look at some rapids. Then we were racing in the boats. It is a lovely stretch of water for rowing. The boat races of the University are usually held there. We got home very tired and also very pleased. I hope it is my last General picnic at St. Columba's.

We are down to the work now. There is little more than a week to go. I think I know the Philos alright and also the Latin. I have to start on Hermeneutics now.

As it is now near the end, Mother, would you please send me my fare. I want to send it to Bill McMahon, so that he can get my ticket on the 30th of this month. This is the day of the ordinations. He will get all the Victorian tickets and thus save us a lot of trouble. I think the fare is about £2.0.0. I have not any big debts just a couple of books and a film. However, it would be on the safe side if you could send me £4.0.0 altogether. I can keep what I do not use here. I won 10/- in a raffle but promised before I got it to give to charity. Roley Smyth, another student, added to it and we were going to raffle a leather handbag for Waratah. We hope to get about 3.0.0. It will be something towards the funds.

I got some photos today but I don't know how they will come out. I told Chester I would write but I have so little time to spare. However I might get a few minutes during the week. I got Brian's letter and picture. Did Marie guide his hand? I think it was like her writing. Well dear Mother, it is time for Vespers now, and I have an Antiphon to sing so goodbye with fondest love from,

Jack.

PS   Please pray for me that I may pass. Would you please send the money as soon as possible so that I can get it away.   **Jack**

PEOPLE AT THE HEART OF MINISTRY
St Columba's College, Springwood 1927–1928
Letters 11 – 20

Austin Cooper OMI

Life in a seminary conjures up images of young men far removed from the 'real' world and subjected to a strict routine. In many ways seminary life in those years was both remote and disciplined. At its worst it might have prompted a blind obedience, a mere shallow conformity. John had some experience of such a life at Assumption College Kilmore. He remembered those days with some affection, occasionally mentioning the legendry Brother William. John Wallis displays his depth of character in making the best use of the circumstances.

Throughout these formative years he continued to display his deep affection for home and family exhibiting a touching sensitivity about asking his parents for money. The financial assistance was for books and sharpened his great respect for learning. John made no pretence to be academically inclined. Indeed he had to approach the new and novel world of philosophy with a strong dose of rote learning rather than rational endeavour. Yet he saw the practical value of a priest having a good library, and noted this particularly with the Rector Eris M. O'Brien (later Archbishop of Canberra-Goulburn). While he made no mention of O'Brien's emerging stature as a leading Australian Church historian, he was impressed with his good library. John's love for learning had a real pastoral bent to it.

These young men at Springwood were a very vigorous lot: while cricket did not arouse much enthusiasm, football, tennis, wrestling and *physical jerks* were popular. Indeed a fall from a horizontal bar gave John a nasty accident but he proved remarkably resilient in recovering. These seminarians in a secluded part of the Blue Mountains managed to be surprisingly broad in their interests: their efforts at public speaking covered issues of current interest such as the *death penalty*, very slowly being abolished in various Australian states and territories. They also included a talk on a famous 19th century Catholic social reformer, Bishop William Von Ketteler. A practical lesson in a broad view of Church and world came with the International Eucharistic Congress in Sydney in 1928: bishops and others from around the Catholic world converged on Sydney, helping in no small measure to dispel some of the effects of the tyranny of distance.

Seminarians often had excursions in the nearby bushlands, another carryover from Assumption College Kilmore days perhaps. John revelled in these and once, when temporarily lost, rather lamented that they were not able to spend a night under the stars. This warm familiarity with the natural world, God's first self-revelation, is fascinating and shows an interesting aspect of John's spirituality.

On one occasion when his mother obviously expressed concern about some issue, John was able to give her a warm response with a practical devotional exercise firmly focused on Christ. A similar warm concern comes through in any mention of fellow students who might be ill, 'clipped'[15] or who decided to leave. Despite some initial concerns about whether he should be a diocesan priest or join a religious community, John was sure that the great need was for the Australian priest of *the future [to] have the interest of the people at heart.* With such a clear view in mind this vocation was slowly maturing in these early years.

Austin Cooper OMI

Professor Austin Cooper AM is a Senior Fellow of Catholic Theological College and member of the Department of Church History and the Department of Pastoral and General Studies. He lectures in Church History and Christian Spirituality. He is a priest of the Oblates of Mary Immaculate (OMI).

---

15   'Clipped' meaning a religious ceremony of initiation, where hair is clipped from the head. The ritual marks the next stage of religious commitment in the ordination process.

St Patrick's Seminary, Manly
1929 - 1931
Letters 21 – 30

Introduction

St Patrick's College, Manly, was the first national seminary, built in 1889 and used for this purpose until 1995 when the seminary was re-located to Homebush in Sydney. Like St Columba's at Springwood, St Patrick's was set apart and isolated from the world, understood at the time to be a distraction to the seminarians' spiritual life and their studies. The Sydney Harbour Bridge was not yet built nor, of course, was the Sydney Opera House. The present-day St Mary's Cathedral was built in 1868.

The third chapter consists of ten letters from John, all of which were written from St Patrick's College, Manly. Two letters from 1929 exist, one to his mother and the other to his father. In 1930, six letters are to his mother and one to his father. Only one letter survives in 1931, which is to his ten-year-old brother, Brian.

St Patrick's Seminary, Manly 1933.
Sydney Archdiocesan Archives Photographic Collection.

Letter 21 to Father

> *I am quite settled down here now.*
> *I know a good number of the students.*
> *They are a fine lot of men.*
> *They are more dignified and like real men.*

This three-page letter dated 17th March 1929, St Patrick's Day, is the first one from St Patrick's College, Manly. In this letter it is noticeable that John is maturing, although he is still only eighteen years old. He compares the current situation in Manly to when he was in Springwood: the men here *are very much more dignified*. Some even have *grey hair*! With four subjects, Dogmatic Theology, Scripture Study, Canon Law and Ecclesiastical History, John lives a regular regimented life-style. Every day of the whole year is mapped out and there is greater strictness than at Springwood. Importantly to John, the big library is open every morning.

John must take a number of ritualised steps on the journey toward priesthood. Archbishop Michael Sheehan ordains deacons, who were taking the penultimate step towards being ordained as a priest. He had come to Australia from Ireland in 1922 upon his appointment as Coadjutor Archbishop of Sydney. Prior to this he was Vice-President of Manooth Seminary and a notable Irish language scholar.

Swimming is the *most popular sport*, writes John, giving a full description of the swimming-hole at Manly.

On the Wallis side of the family there were relatives in Gippsland, Victoria. John with his siblings, Don and Marie, had travelled by train to visit them during the January 1929 holidays. Presumably the Sale photos refer to that trip. Films in box cameras had to be finished in order to have them processed. He knows his father would like to see them.

* * *

Dear Father

I meant to get this letter off at an earlier date so that you would get it for your birthday but as circumstances did not permit I thought it is better late than never so I hope you will receive this letter in the same spirit.

I am quite settled down here now. I know a good number of the students and the others I will get to know. They are a fine lot of men. They are very much more dignified and more like real men than were some of the Springwood students. I suppose it is due to the fact that they are older and moreover realise now their duties. There are some of them fairly old – one chap has pure white hair while a few more are grey. All have their own rooms here or at least dogboxes – small partitions made in one big room. At the entrance to each there is a curtain in place of a door. I am in one. We have to study in a classroom, but there is talk of getting permission to study in the dogboxes like the others who study in their rooms.

We have not got into the way of our studies. We do Dogmatic Theology, which treats of the morality of our acts and is of practical use to a priest in Confession. Then we have Scripture Study in detail: Canon Law and ecclesiastical History. These subjects though few in number need a lot of solid graft.

The order of the day is as follows: Rise, 10 to six, Prayers at 6.30, Mass 7 o'clock, Breakfast 8.15. Before breakfast we sweep out our rooms and get our books ready for study. After breakfast we have about twenty minutes for a walk and then the first lecture of the day begins at 9.00. At 10.00 we change over for another Lecture, then recreation. Study from 11.30 to 12.00 and then a third Lecture. Dinner at 1.15. From 2.00 till four we have study and again from 5.40 to 7.40. Coffee at half past five. Tea at 8 o'clock and then recreation till nine. After prayers we go to bed at 9.15p.m.

The most popular recreation at present is swimming. The baths are about 50 yards long. They are very well arranged. There are about 60 partitions for dressing in. On all four sides there is a wide platform to walk on. The springboard is very good. The water at the board is very deep, but up at one end it is rather shallow especially when the tide is out. In the morning the tide is in and then we have some fun doing fancy dives etc. At night the billiard tables (2) are well patronised and also the Ping-pong tables (2).

The big library is open every morning. I think the rules here are stricter than at Springwood. The Dean (Master of Discipline) called all the new arrivals in and gave them a book with all the times marked and the order for each day of the year. He also gave them a card for the rules.

Last Saturday was the ordination day for the deacons. Archbishop Sheehan performed the ceremonies. There were ten subdeacons raised to the order of deacons. We were supposed to march in the St Pat's procession in Sydney but as the previous day had been very wet the procession and also the sports were abandoned. We shall go to Sydney tomorrow for the Mass at St. Mary's Cathedral. It is for St. Pat's day.

I have some photos of the Sale trip. I shall enclose some in this letter and some more in the next. There are too many to send in one lot.

Well dear Father I shall now close with fondest love from

Your loving Son
Jack

*I did not realise how much it means to be a Catholic
Till I began to study the theology on the Church.*

Letter 22 to Mother

This five-page letter to John's mother (September 1929) is written in the month of the feast of Our Lady of Sorrows, as is mentioned. John is concerned for the health of his parents, Abe and Emma. His sister Marie works at the Tearooms with her mother who can communicate with her in sign language more easily than her father.

John seems pleased to have been able to show Don around the seminary and then to sit in the academy hall to chat in Australian-Irish Sign language for an hour and a half. (This was the sign language used in their family home, with a one-handed alphabet.) He notes that Dr Leonard can *talk on 2 hands* to Don, who is still at St Gabriel's mastering the art of tailoring as a trade for future work. The *two-hand alphabet* was based on British Sign Language to later become the Auslan alphabet. John invites Don to come and see him when his school goes to *The Bends* for occasional outings further along the northern beaches of Sydney. Being the bell man this week John was not able to go to for a swim.

John requires money for books and for fees, reminding his mother that he will only get books that will be useful to him. He writes about some Australian professors who have been to the Lateran University in Rome and who have done very well. He assures his mother of the importance of his study of theology – not realising how much it meant to be a Catholic till his studies began.

The horrific martyrdom of the Columban priest, Father Timothy Leonard (brother of Dr Leonard at Manly), makes news in Australia. He had been one of the first missionaries to go to China in the 1920s.

The *kind spiritual Father* Pope Pius XI celebrates the fiftieth anniversary of his priesthood. Having learned about *indulgences* John instructs his mother about them! In the belief of redemptive theology, indulgences were granted when one undertook repetitive pious practices, for example, six visits to a church. This was thought to save souls from purgatory, such theology having had an overhaul since Vatican II.

John writes of the Temperance meeting to take the pledge not to drink alcohol, but that there was no satisfactory outcome in their discussions.

While it had been Archbishop William Barry who accepted John for the Archdiocese of Hobart, he died in 1929. It was thus Archbishop William Hayden, his successor, who took office in 1930 who ordains John in 1932.

* * *

Letter 22

St. Patrick's College,
Manly.
[September 1929]

Dear Mother,

Just at present I have a little time and so will try to tell you all the news which there is for the last few days. I hope this letter finds you and Father in better health than when I wrote last. I am feeling excellent, thank God.

I told Father about the Sports. We finished them on the following Thursday. It was a very warm day and so the competitors found it pretty difficult to keep up for all the events. We had the 880 yds, the long jump, high jump, the 220 yds, the deacons race as well as a "Go as you please." In this the starter fired the gun and all began to walk or run as they pleased. There was a bullet shell hidden in the track and the one who stopped nearest it after three minutes got the prize – an alarm clock. I went in most of the events but did not do very well. I got third in one too and was told today that I got 11/- altogether. They distributed about £17.00 in prizes some getting 30/- and £2.00.

Don was over last Sunday week. He seemed quite pleased to have a look around the College. We went to the Academy hall and talked for about an hour and a half. Then I showed him a few curios etc. in the corridor. I took him into the Library. Dr Leonard was there. He spoke to me and asked about Don. He can use the 2 hands. He told me to take Don up to the tower. This is a very unusual thing even to let priests etc. up. However we went up and had a look around. I had not been up before. It is equivalent to about 8 or 9 floors up and so one can see all Sydney and the harbour. It is a wonderful view. He went away about five o'clock. He may be able to come up some time when they are at the Bends for a picnic. I told him to come when he could but only at four o'clock.

Dr Madden our Dogma Professor is away in Queensland. There is a new Bishopric there now at Toowoomba[1] and he went up to be the Master of Ceremonies. He was originally from Brisbane but after he came back from Rome he came here as a Professor. I hear he is leaving at the end of the year, and Fr Lane will take his place. They are both very clever and were each of them dux of the Lateran University of Rome, one of the greatest Theological schools of the World. However, another Australian won greater honours. His name is Baker. He is only 20 and has the highest pass ever obtained at the Lateran. He was too young to be ordained subdeacon and yet he is a Doctor of divinity. This is exceptional.

---

1 Bishop James Byrne was appointed the first bishop of the Toowoomba Diocese.

We had a "specimina" today – this is just the same as Blue Wednesday[2] only it is no fixed day but usually at the beginning of the month. The rules are longer here and I think they are more disagreeable. They judge on these as well as on the Sermon and everything else for the Orders. It is getting on now towards Order time and some are getting anxious.

Summer is coming round. It is getting warmer now and today they had the first swim of the season. I did not go as I am on the Bell this week. I think it is still a bit cool for the water but a few more days will warm it up. We are to have a Picnic next week to "Wainnora". They proposed Bulli Pass as a Picnic place but the authorities would not permit us to go there.

I think we will have Exposition next Sunday as a memorial of the Eucharistic Congress. It was this day last year that we came down for the opening of [at] St. Mary's Cathedral.

We had a temperance meeting today to try to make the pledge taken here more binding on those who take it, because it seems that priests when on the mission soon forget their pledge and take to drinking with those who never had it. However despite much discussion we did not arrive at any satisfactory conclusion.

I got Cardinal Mercier's Philosophy [book] a few days ago. It cost 25/-. I had the order in for it since early in the year but it has just arrived from Europe. I did not keep the money and at present I have not quite sufficient. Would you please send me some Mother. There is no hurry at all. I have been trying to get only books which will be of real use to me. I am afraid that I would get books which are of no use. And also Mother would you please send me the money for the fees for the half [year] (£15 Pay Fr Foley).

I have heard no more about a [new] Bishop [for Tasmania] but this will not affect me in any way. The Administrator in Hobart will attend to the business when there is a Bishop appointed.

Last time I wrote I told you about Dr Leonard's brother. No doubt you will have seen something of the matter in the Catholic Press. We were told about a week ago. A cable came from China and was sent straight to the College. Fr. Leonard was in a Chinese town and knew that the Bandits were coming on. However he wanted to say Mass and did so about 5 o'clock in the morning. While at Mass the Bandits came and took him and his server and bound them. They asked for his money. He would not give it till they let the servant boy go and then told them where it was. They took him along in their company and while on the way he passed a Church. He knelt down and there prayed for the Bandits. They laughed at him and struck him. Soon after they took him to the town and gashed his neck with an axe and so he died. It is now sure that

---

2   As they had had at St Columba's College, Springwood.

was truly a martyr seeing that he died on account of his sticking firm to his Master's example of praying for those who mocked him and insulted him.

Well Dear Mother I have not much news now. There is just this. This year is the Jubilee of the Pope's ordination to the Priesthood (50 yrs.) and so he had granted an indulgence. The conditions of which are these:

i) To receive Sacraments (Confession and Communion) for the Pope's intentions.

ii) To make six distinct visits to a public church. This would be done by being there each Sunday or it may be done by going to Church, say for Mass and saying a Prayer for the Pope, and then coming out for a minute or so and making another visit. This would do for one day and so on.

iii) To give a small sum (1/-) for Pope's Intentions. I just mentioned this because there is a Plenary Indulgence applicable to the Holy Souls besides many other spiritual Blessings. Thought you and Marie might do it. It is nice to join with the Church in these pious exercises. God has put the Pope over us not so much as a temporal ruler but as a kind Spiritual Father. I did not realise how much it means to be a Catholic till I began to study the theology on the Church. The more truly Catholic we are the more true to the Catholic faith and doctrines in our daily lives so much the more are we like our divine Lord.

I will now close this brief letter dear Mother, asking God and His Holy Mother (especially as the Mother of Sorrows for this is her special month) to bless you and all at home. I remain,

Your Loving Son
Jack.

P.S. I have been wondering about Mr. Cafferey. I have asked the students prayers for him and prayed rather for his soul.

Letter 23 to Mother

*God wants great love, a humble acceptance of God's will
And a confidence that God will keep you aright.*

This four-page letter is written to John's mother (5th March 1930) at the beginning of his second year at Manly. On the rail trip from Seymour to Sydney, described as *fair* even though the students had a fun time, passengers changed trains at Albury, because of the rail gauge being different in New South Wales. They had time to wander, so they head down the street. John is surprised that the town of Albury seemed so modern, *the shops are big and beautifully fitted and would compare with any shop in Melbourne*. He enjoys telling his community and business minded mother. When arriving in Sydney, John immediately enters a bookshop to buy the books he needs.

It is the beginning of Lent and there are 105 students. John has settled in his room with a harbour and city view. With the Jesuit Father Healy as retreat director and valuing the time to reflect, John is stirred by the experience of the retreat as he came to understand *sin and its consequences*.

He tells his mother about two important up-coming aspects of his studies for his life as a priest: in dogmatic theology the topic of the Blessed Sacrament and in moral theology, the topic of Penance. Penance or confession, John reflects, is the one thing *that brings the greatest fruit*. This theme is in its embryonic form here for John, but later became a life mission – being available to people so they could share their life concerns in a safe place of forgiveness, support and discerning steps for the future. St John Vianney, the Cure of Ars, and patron saint of priests became an inspiration for him.

John mentions Pat Carmine, a student a year ahead of him. Pat becomes an influential friend.

John is worried about his mother in this letter. Again we do not know what she has told him in her letters. He wants to encourage her and urges her to know that God does not expect *long prayers and fasting* but for her to accept her situation and to have confidence, to love God and to trust that God will keep her *aright*. Take time out and have a holiday. *Just put things away!* This may not be very practical for her running a shop.

* * *

March 5, 1930

Dear Mother,

I am at last settled down in my new room, with my table and books etc. all arranged in the best order I can get. It is a good room on the west-side and looking out to the harbour and the city beyond.

More than that I have just come out of a retreat, which was I trust most beneficial and certainly much needed. Fr Healy S.J. conducted it. He was very solid and in a way it was a very hard retreat. It was only the one idea of Sin and its consequence, its insult to God and its punishment. Usually there is also something on the life of Our Lord and more practical things. However I think that this method of making more of the terrible havoc of sin gives a better foundation and, meantime, to love and serve God. I often think that if people could seriously enter a retreat there would be not half the sin in the world that there is today and not half the misery and unhappiness.

We had a fair trip over. We had a bit of fun at the expense of Mick Murphy (Springwood) whose pyjamas we tied and knotted. We slept on the floor of the carriage. At Albury some of us went and had a look round the town. We had an hour's wait. I was very much surprised. One would think it was in a city street. All the shops are big and beautifully fitted and would compare well with any Melbourne shop. As it was in the dark we could not see much except the main street.

When I arrived at Sydney I went straight down the street to get books etc. and then came back and had dinner with the other students. There were a great number of new students from Springwood. There will be 105 all together up there, including 2 ex-parsons and a commercial traveller. I heard that Bill Kennedy (Queensland) a class mate and a mate at work had left for the China Mission. I met him afterwards and said Goodbye. He was to enter at Essendon on Monday ...

There is a Benedictine[3] here. He has come to learn to speak English fluently. I have not spoken to him yet but I believe he can talk English fairly well. He is Spanish and was in Rome for three years so that he can talk Latin and Italian with ease.

Some of the West Australian students are still to come. They are detained at Forrest somewhere in the middle of the Nullabor Plain. Pat Carmine also arrived late. This morning after the retreat was finished we had the blessing of the Ashes and the beginning of Lent.

We had a High Mass asking the Holy Ghost to guide us and enlighten us during the year. After this we met the professors who told us what was the scope of our work for this year. In Dogma we will do the Tract on the Blessed Sacrament. This is one of the most beautiful of all and I would like you, dear Mother, to ask God to give me special grace and light in doing the tract. The Blessed Sacrament is the priest's life. When I was home I found far more joy in my Communion or in a visit to the Blessed Sacrament than in any other amusement. People in the world have other objects of love, their family, their partner in life, the business but a priest's love must be for God alone and for other things in so far as they help him to love God.

In Moral [theology] we will treat "Pennance"– the hearing of Confessions and all things relating to them. This too is perhaps the most important tract in Moral because of all the priest's work, the confessional is the one which brings greatest fruit.

We had our first swim today. It was grand. We begin work tomorrow or rather next Monday. There will be a holiday on Friday Feast of St Thomas and Ordination day for the Deaconate. I see in the Calendar for the year that visiting Sundays are limited to three. The first one is on Easter Sunday. I must write to Don and tell him. I will write to Mick Coonan tomorrow. I hope you have posted Leo Hatswell's letter. I was just thinking of it. We will get our books perhaps tomorrow.

Well now, dear Mother, I will close this letter. Do try to get away for a holiday. You want a couple of months. Try at least for a fortnight. Perhaps

---

3   Dom Stephen Mareno (1889-1953) was a Spanish Benedictine musician and, while studying in Rome, was seconded to the monastery in New Norcia, Western Australia in the early 1920s.

too in that time you might be able to go to some Convent for even one day and there have a while with our Lord, away from every thing else. Just put things away. The Nuns may know of some place. You want someone who can help you because I know you want to love God and that you are doing very, very well in the circumstances. God sees this. It is not, after all, long prayers and fasts etc. he wants. It is a great love, a humble acceptance of His will and a confidence that He is and will keep you aright if you love Him.

Good night now, dear Mother, and pray for your loving Son
Jack

Letter 24 to Father

We will go into the city tomorrow for St Patrick's Day. There will be a High Mass and then the Rosary said in Gaelic.

In this three-page short letter to his father (16th March 1930), some of the content is repeated from John's previous letter to his mother. There are a few more details of *the Benedictine*.

The Far East, the Columban magazine, had come into John's home since he was a child and he had read it *religiously*. He is therefore very interested in the young men that he knows who go to Essendon to join the Columban Fathers with the prospect of going to China – and is inspired by them.

St Patrick's Day is of great importance in the local Catholic Irish community with huge St Patrick Day marches and celebrations. A number of priests and religious are Irish. The lecturers are mostly Irish. There are some people who speak Gaelic and pray the Rosary in Gaelic. The Catholic culture is still predominantly Irish in Australia.

Note the reference to the North Head Quarantine station at Manly and the yellow flag which was flown when an infectious disease had developed among those arriving by ship.

In this letter, as in his last letter to his mother, John is quite anxious about his mother not being well. *She will have a serious breakdown* if she does not get away and have a holiday.

* * *

+
AMDG

St Patrick's College,
Manly.
March 16th 1930

Dear Father,

Your birthday has come and gone and I have not yet written to wish you all the best wishes for such a day. I did not think of it until we began to think of the birthday of the great St Patrick, which comes tomorrow. However it is better late than never and now I wish you God's choicest blessings and gifts, and ask Him to spare you for many another such day. I hope you are quite well as I am, thank God.

We have now got down to our work and things are in pretty good swing. We have already got well into the studies for the year. There are two new professors here now. We have a newly ordained priest who did a most brilliant *course in Rome, one of the best in all the big Universities there. Then there is Dr O'Flynn D.D. who had gone to Ireland for a trip and is again in his office as Bursar and Master of Ceremonies. He has travelled in all Europe and has most interesting things to tell of what he has seen adding to the interest by true wit and humour. He has charge of the choir. When on his trip last year he visited all the famous choirs of Rome, Paris, Ireland and England.*

There are three students who did not return. One of them, Bill Kenny[4], a real son of the soil and a "rough diamond" went to the Chinese Mission College at Essendon where Ted Morgan went. He hopes to be off to China in about 4 or 5 years.

We have also here now, a Benedictine[5] from the Monastery of New Norcia, West Australia. He is a Spaniard, has been to school in Genoa and Rome and has come here to learn English while completing his studies. He can talk fairly well and he told me that in the holidays at New Norcia he had read the works of Scott & Dickens as well as parts of Shakespeare and other English authors.

Swimming of course stands alone in the outdoor life. We go down practically every day. There is to be a sports carnival (local) on next week. It provides a good deal of fun as well as some really good examples of swimming. There are a couple here this year who are considered very good. While it takes Queensland and the Southern States all their time to get a good team, New South Wales has one which stands on its own. They are nearly all used to the surf. The Benedictine has a stroke all his own; the "Benedictine Crawl" as we call it. It is a sort of side stroke, but painfully slow. I believe that all those who have been here before had the same stroke. Our baths are just across a small bay from the Quarantine. We often see the people sitting on the rocks etc. They have a pretty tame time there. There has been a yellow flag hoisted since we came back.

The West Australian students have only been back a short time. Some were stuck up at Forrest,[6] others waited till repairs were effected on the line. The last one arrived on Friday.

We were to have gone to the St Patrick's Day sports on Saturday but as it rained we did not. I think they had the sports just the same, despite the rain. We will go into the city tomorrow for St Patrick's Day itself. There will be a High Mass and then the Rosary said in Gaelic. There are about 8 or 9 of the

---

4   Sometimes John has different spellings for the same person. The correct names for example are Bill Kennedy not Kenny, Ted Morganti, not Morgan.
5   The Benedictine monastery in New Norcia was founded by the Spanish in 1846.
6   The small settlement of Forrest is on the Trans-Australian Railway in Western Australia.

Sydney priests who know Gaelic. It sounds funny to hear them talking in a tongue no one else about knows the meaning [of]. We will have a little bit of a concert. I think St. Patrick's day and Corpus Christi day are the only two days of the year on which we miss the night study of 2 hours.

Archbishop Kelly sailed a few days ago. I heard that he was on the same boat as the Australian cricketers. He is going to Rome, to Carthage for the Congress,[7] to Ireland and then back again.

Has Mother had a holiday yet? I am afraid that if she does not get away soon she will have a serious breakdown. I wish she would get help and try to have a few weeks right away. Well, Father, I will close this short letter. There is not a great deal of news but I will try to make up for that in another way. May God bless you and may St Joseph, the patron of a happy family, care for you and all at home, this dear Father is the prayer of

Your loving son
Jack.

---

7   While the 1928 Eucharistic Congress took place in Sydney, Archbishop Michael Kelly needed to travel to Carthage in Tunisia to attend the next Congress in May 1930.

Letter 25 to Mother

The Order list has been announced.
I hope I will fulfil all that is required
and straighten up the inner man.

This was an important but short two-page letter (12th October 1930) that John writes to his mother to say that, after all her prayers, her son is called to full minors, however on condition that he holds his head straighter! John sees the irony of such a condition and quick with his wit switches the meaning: *I hope to be able to straighten up the inner man* to be *up to the mark*. The ordination of full minors refers to Tonsure, Exorcist and Acolyte.

His parents have become familiar with the different students and where they are from and so were interested in them and how they were going. Imagine the tense moment for the men as they learn their fate – accepted or not accepted. John mentions with compassion those who were ill and could not go on to be ordained.

The tradition had been established that the fourth year students before their ordination go to Castle Hill for the day to St Gabriel's School for Deaf Boys, seemingly to have the experience of communicating with Deaf people. They may well meet Deaf people who come to them in the course of their ministry. The students in this period would have met or seen Don and Charlie, John's brothers, and become aware of this different cultural group in society.

John is interested in the book that the Shell Company had put out on Australian Wild Flowers. He suggests his mother get it from Cafferey's, who ran the service station in Seymour.

Dr John Joseph Nevin, President of St Patrick's College, Manly NSW 1929 – 1942.
Sydney Archdiocesan Archives Photographic Collection.

* * *

A.M.D.G.

St Patrick's College,
Manly.
Sunday 12th [October] 1930

Dear Mother,

Just a short and hurried note to tell you that the Order list has been announced yesterday afternoon. Dr Nevin[8] called each individually. I was called to full minors, thank God. However it is conditional on my holding my head straighter. Dr Nevin was very good and said to try hard and then said not to forget to pray for him and the other professors. I hope I will be able to fulfil all that is required and also I hope to be able to straighten up the inner man. It is a step very near to the altar. I know I need not ask your prayers. I do want to be up to the mark.

In 4th year there was one student kept from Orders. Whatever the reasons I do not know. Joe Purcell was called to Diaconate but is too young for priesthood and so he will have to wait for some time. Bill Gilby, Tony Hatswell and Jim Conway are to be ordained in Melb. Gus Lacey and Cyril Cochrane in Bendigo. It will be several weeks from tomorrow till ordinations here. In 3rd year there were two who were not called. They will have to wait till next year for Subdiaconate. In 2nd year: two were not called at all and one was called to half Minors. In 1st year there were 6 who were not called at all and 2 who were called to tonsure only. [Tom] was not called owing to his time away but he will be quite alright. Dr. Nevin said not to worry. He seems to be getting better every day. He preached his sermon today. I had to criticise it. The criticism is a mere formality.

Archbishop Kelly and Dr Leonard... [paper torn] ...a reception in the Cathedral. The... [paper torn] ...stayed at home. Most of the choir was in Sydney one day before also. Monsignor McDermott who was once the President here died. There was a big funeral in his Parish. We are expecting the Archbishop over one of these days. [Justin] who had been in Lewisham for over 12 weeks is going home next week to West Aust. He was in hospital for a long time last year also. He has been having operations and his nerves are gone. I am very sorry. He was a very good student and was also of a very cheerful disposition. Another W.A. student has been in Hospital since August – Cyril Hudson. He had pleurisy.

I will be preaching on Wednesday. I am the only one left now.

Do Caffreys get Shell Petrol? There is a book of Australian Wildflowers got up by that Shell Company showing flowers of the various states. Some of the students have them here. It would be very interesting. You would like it. I

---

8   From County Galway, Ireland, Dr J.J. Nevin was Professor of Canon Law and Moral Theology. He died in 1961.

thought you might get one if they had them. They can be got at the airports.

The 4th year students will be going up to Castle Hill one of these days. Some of them have learnt the signs. Well dear Mother this is a very scrappy letter but I hope the news will make up for the shortness. Did you see the Messenger for October⁹ – the special Intention is for family prayers. It is very good.

Goodbye now dear Mother for the present and may Our dear Lord bless us and preserve us, and help us to do all He asks.

With fondest love from
Your loving Son

Jack

PS. I received Marie's letter. I will write to her soon.

Souvenir of the Tonsure Ceremony

---

9   *The Messenger* was a popular monthly Catholic magazine published by the Sacred Heart Fathers.

Letter 26 to Mother

*I often think we do not realise here
what trials and difficulties people are having outside in the world.*

In John's four-page letter to his mother (26th October 1930), he refers to the societal difficulties of the times. He is relieved his mother is getting on fairly well, *despite the present conditions in Australia* – and globally. Politics were not far from John's mind, Abe and Emma being ever ready to disagree with one another. Abe supported the Liberal Party. Emma was an open supporter of Labour, the Labour Prime Minister Scullin being the first Catholic to take this office. The Catholic fear of Communism was widespread and deepened in the following years.

John likes the fact that an insightful Jesuit in Europe coaxed politicians to do retreats. He praises the Jesuits seeing them as *most deserving*.

Through their spiritual director, Father Hall, John grasps the depths of the simplicity of the spirituality of St Therese of Lisieux, a *great apostle* – a young unknown Carmelite nun, who entirely entrusted her life to God as a good Father, and *went on her way not worrying*. She prayed for priests from her enclosed convent.

John takes to heart Archbishop Michael Kelly's story and how Pope Pius XI said to him: *We serve a good Master!* Throughout John's priesthood he often preached on being sure to be *about the Master's business!* – an embryonic theme for his life as a priest.

Writing about the religious practice of *solemn exposition* on the feast of Christ the King, John shares the insight he has that *the mission of a priest is not for himself alone, but to also spend himself for the greater glory of God and for the extension of the kingdom of God.* Another special feast was All Soul's Day on 2nd November that played an important part in the lives of Catholics who prayed for their deceased loved ones.

* * *

A.M.D.G.
+

*St Patrick's College,
Manly.
26.10.30*

Dear Mother,

I was most pleased to get your letter a few days ago. I am glad to know you are getting along fairly well despite the present conditions in Australia. I often think we do not realise here what trials and difficulties people are having outside. There are a great number of men out of work in Sydney. The Elections were held last Saturday. I believe Labor has got the biggest majority. There were 14 Communist Candidates. The Communists are very strong here. They have special schools every Sunday and have a very strong propaganda work. Dr. Nevin said one day last week he was asked by a prospective candidate to induce the students to vote for him. He replied that he would rather vote for no one: "You are all a bad lot and it's not much good picking and choosing!" It is a pity we can't get some more energetic Catholic men after the style of Mr Scullin.

In Holland some years ago there was a young lawyer, Robert Rouget, in the Parliament. He did not think much of lying to push Catholic interests and ideals. At last a Jesuit got hold of him and pested [pestered] the life out of him till he made him go to a Retreat. This gave him a new outlook on life. He went back and set to work to get all his friends to try the Retreat. He tried especially to get men of Public office to go. At last he had all the Catholic members of the Parliament at a Retreat. They then began in earnest. Though Catholics were a poor minority in a Protestant country they made their influence felt so that today they are the most active Catholics in Europe. They have the great proportion of Priests on the Mission fields and at home they are growing every day. They even have Retreats for Non-Catholics or men who are dissatisfied with Infidelity and are looking for the true Faith. Truly I do not think there is any worth more deserving of our help and our prayers.

Today is the feast of Christ the King. We had Solemn Exposition all day. I thought of you all and offered my poor prayers on behalf of all, for after all distance cannot override love and faith. It was a most acceptable day for helping to prepare for Orders. It helps us to realise that the mission of a priest is not for himself alone; also to spend himself for the greater glory of God; for the extension of the kingdom of God.

St. Therese though she lived in her convent unknown to the world was a great Apostle. She said that she could not go to China but she would send every little act, every little weary footstep, every little trial to her Lord for the conversion of Souls. So too may we do. For after all did not our Lord spend 30 out of 33 years in a hidden life of simple work and poverty? And Our Lady was always hidden except when she came to share the cruel and bitter passion of her Son.

Fr. Hall our spiritual director gave us a most beautiful talk on St Therese. It is wonderful to think that this little girl – for she was only 24 – would come to be so much loved throughout the world. He spoke of her "way of Spiritual childhood". She considered God as her Father and with this thought before her she entrusted herself entirely to Him letting Him dispose of her as He would. She said she was glad when she sometimes committed some fault for then she saw how poor and little she was and how she wanted God. Then asking God's pardon she would go on her way not worrying but able always to say, My good God I put all my trust in You.

This reminds me of what Archbishop Kelly said when he was here last. He told us of his trip and how he went to Ireland and saw all his old pupils, now priests and Bishops etc. Then he went to see the tombs of his Mother and Father. He told us how as a little boy of nine he had tried to be a Sailor and had fallen into the water between the ship and wharf. This he said seemed as yesterday and he would keep it in his mind always. Then he said that as far as he knew he never sought any office of distinction but sought one thing only – the Master and His glory. Then he told us of his last interview with the Pope Pius XI who is now himself an old man, near 80. "Well Your Holiness! I am going away home now. I am an old man now. Will you please give me Your blessing to help me on the way?" The Pope answered, "Don't fear. We serve a good Master." This is a good thought for when we are a little discouraged.

The 4th Year Students went to St. Gabriel's on Wednesday. They were of course agreeably surprised. Some of them learnt the alphabet and had a good talk with the boys. The Brothers showed them how they teach them especially with regard to the idea of a soul, of God and Sin. When asked how many Gods there were one boy said, "There may be one out there or there may be many." Bro. Allen[10] said there are ten children at the State Institute who are Catholics. Bill Gilby got some photos. He gave me the two enclosed with the negatives if you would like to get more copies.

We will soon be on the Month for the Holy souls. The Novena for All Souls Day began today. I thank you very much, Mother, for the cheque enclosed in letter. I do not think there is anything I want just now but I may want something when it comes on for the holidays. I can send you a pamphlet on Ordination of a priest and also a couple of other little pamphlets etc.

Well now, dear Mother, I will close this short letter sending fondest love to all at home with

Love from

Jack

Fr Hayes got to [come to my] Tonsure. I will not send the pamphlet till the 3rd of November. We will be in Sydney on that day for Requiem Mass.

---

10   The Irish Brother Damian Allen cfc was one of three Irish Brothers, who had come in 1922 from St Joseph's School for Deaf Boys in Dublin. Through the initiative of Archbishop Michael Kelly, their purpose was to establish a Catholic school for Deaf boys in Australia.

Letter 27 to Mother

Some students are arranging for big displays for their ordination But I do not like the idea.

In this two-page letter to his mother (6th November, 1930), John writes in haste. He has exams coming up, then a retreat and Orders, the conferring of Tonsure, Exorcist and Acolyte. It will be too early in the morning for Don to attend the ceremony unless he stays the night before nearby with Miss Maloney.

John pleads to pray to the saints for him. They are role models to inspire him. One is St John Berchmans, a pious young Jesuit, born in 1599 and grew up in an atmosphere of political turmoil caused by a religious war between the Catholics and Protestants.[11] Dying at the age of twenty-two, his father had cut him off from financial support, because he had joined the Jesuits. The other saint was the Polish St Stanislaus Kostka, born in 1550,[12] a Jesuit novice who also died young. John, impressed by their youth, saw how much they had done for God in their short lives – and they were both Jesuits.

John observes that at this time of the year the fourth year students were *occupied with the one thought* – their ordination of the priesthood. He knows that his time will come, but John does not want a big display at his ordination, as some of the young men are planning for theirs. He notes that one of the students to be ordained will celebrate Mass at St Gabriel's School for Deaf Boys.

* * *

A.M.D.G
+

St Patrick's College,
Manly.
Wednesday
6th [November] 1930.

Dear Mother,

This is a very hasty note. I seem to be lost in the work to be done. There is the Eucharist tract to be revised. I intend, with God's help, to do the whole tract again before the exams. I have just begun on that. I have begun on my Revision of Moral [theology] too. We have some more to do yet on the Sacrament of Penance in Dogma and some special tracts in Moral. In this latter subject

---

11   https://en.wikipedia.org/wiki/John_Berchmans#cite_note-stevens-1
12   https://en.wikipedia.org/wiki/Stanislaus_Kostka

we are a good way behind so our year had to go over last year's work again for the sake of 1st and 4th years which have no professor at present. However the revision will stand [us] in good stead and we will get through our own work besides.

There is only a fortnight now till the Retreat so that there will not be many more classes. I am looking forward to the retreat and to the Orders. I am afraid the ceremony will be too early for Don [to come from Castle Hill] – half past seven. Perhaps he could stay at Miss Maloney's for the night. That is quite near. I will write to him. There is one more visiting Sunday[13] – last before the Retreat.

I would be very glad if you would make a Novena to St. John Berchmans whose feast is on the 26th of Nov. The ordination will take place on the 28th the 1st two orders and on the 29th the other two. The Novena will begin on 17th of Nov. Any prayer e.g. Hail Marys would be suitable. The feast of St Stanislaus is likewise in this month. Both these were mere youths when they died but they had done much for God in their short lives. I think their lives are in the "Treasury of Cath. [Catholic] Doctrine".

The 4th year students are all occupied with the one thought now. Some are arranging for big displays but I do not like the idea. Charlie Cunningham from W.A. was saying that he is hoping to avoid all the displays etc. He would not have any Ordination Breakfast. He will of course give his blessing in the Church. The Rector is very much for the Ordination Breakfast. Bill Gilby[14] is yet in suspense. Bishop Dwyer said he will ordain him if the professors agree. (He was subject to strokes but has not had one for well over a year). A couple of others are yet in suspense for other reasons. I know you will ask God to help them and let them go on.

We went to Sydney on Monday for Mass for the Holy Souls. We had the opportunity of paying a number of visits to the chapel here on Sunday and Monday. There is a Plenary indulgence granted for every visit to the Blessed Sacrament, provided the person pray for the Pope (6 Our Fathers, HM [Hail Marys], Glorys).[15] The special intention this month is for the Holy Souls.

I went to the Catholic Truth Society[16] depot to get that book on the Ordination of a priest but came away without it. I have one here and will send

---

13   Presumably it is Don who comes on visiting Sunday.
14   Father William Gilby became Inspector of Catholic Schools in the Diocese of Wagga Wagga, NSW.
15   The prayer: Glory be to the Father and to the Son and to the Holy Spirit; as it was in the beginning, is now and ever shall be, world without end. Amen.
16   The Catholic Truth Society printed and published Catholic literature. Originally founded in New York in 1900, it began in Australia in 1904. https://en.wikipedia.org/wiki/Catholic_Truth_Society

it. There is not a great deal in it about each of the orders. I will try to give a little more from some other little books.

I may not get far tonight but I can write again and give an account of the rest. We had a couple of hot days but now it is quite cool again. I am not sorry that it is so. Arthur Bainbridge who will be ordained this year is going to say his third Mass at Castle Hill. He is writing to Brother Allen tonight. Well dear Mother, I will close this letter now sending fondest love to you and all at home from

Your loving Son
Jack

P.S. If I do not get the bit about the orders done tonight I will send it next time I write.

Letter 28 to Mother

I am just going now to sign a document in which I bind myself to obey the Archbishop of Hobart during the whole period of my life and spend myself to the utmost in the service of that diocese.

This short one-page letter (20th November 1930) from John to his mother was written immediately before the retreat that John undertook prior to receiving *full minors*. Following this year of study at St Patrick's College, Manly, Dr John Nevin had reported to Archbishop W. Hayden of Hobart that John was *satisfactory* and indeed *a man of more than usual piety*.[17]

John implores his mother to be thinking about him right at the time of receiving minors on 28th November, *Thursday night at about eight o'clock*. John commits his life to service in the Archdiocese of Hobart. He would enter the clerical state, meaning he was designated to conduct religious duties.

* * *

---

17   Missionary Sisters of Service Archives, Hobart.

+
A.M.D.G

St Patrick's College,
Manly.
Friday [20th November 1930]

Dear Mother,

This is a most hasty letter. I am just getting things fixed up before the Retreat starts. It will begin tonight after tea. Fr Herring a Marist Father is to give it. Dr Nevin said he heard him once and it was the best retreat he had. He must be something very special.

I am writing to send that card I told you of for Leo Hatswell's Ordination. He and Jim Conway are to be ordained at St Patrick's College, [Kilmore]. You may be able to get to it.

I am just going now to sign a document in which I bind myself on oath to obey Dr Hayden and his successors, to reverence him and serve in his diocese during the whole period of my life and spend myself to the utmost in the service of that diocese. It is a serious step and I will be most grateful for all your prayers. I will enter the clerical state please God on Thursday night about eight o'clock. I know my mother will be here in spirit making an offering of all I am to God.

Goodbye now dear Mother, and may God bless you and all at home. With fondest love to all, I hope Archbishop [Michael] Kelly will ordain us.

From **Jack**

P.S. Bill Gilby will be getting our tickets on Monday week. I have enough money to see me home but I thought I had better make sure. So will you please send me some Mother next time you write.

Letter 29 to Mother

*Lastly I have to look to practical kindness.
I may be kind in thought at times but it stays there.*

As John, aged twenty, writes this four-page letter to his mother (1st December 1930), so much has happened in the last two weeks. Pouring out his thoughts, he knows she will listen more attentively than anyone else and will understand his exhilaration coupled with his fears. He now sees himself as *a new man, a man of God called apart* from the multitude *like the apostles* following the ordination of minors – Tonsure, Porter, Lector, Exorcist and Acolyte.

John gives thanks for his family and others, especially Brother William. They have guided and supported him on his path to priesthood. Don is there for the Deaconate ceremony having missed the previous day's ritual when other visitors were present. John and four other students had *a real good talk* with Don, one being his good friend Pat Carmine, who wishes his own mother had lived to see this day on his journey to priesthood.

The young John is profoundly searching the human heart. He is earnest about the upcoming holidays and how to remain faithful to the three resolutions of his recent retreat, making time for prayer and his spiritual exercises. While he admits he has ignored her admonitions, he now asks her to point out when he is out of line. Besides looking at the good practices in his life, he confesses his three perceived failings. Also he needs to be practical in his kindness and not only of thinking kindly.

* * *

A.M.D.G.
St Patrick's College,
Manly.
December 1st 1930.

Dear Mother,
I received your welcome letter today. It was an added joy to a cup already full. Great things have been happening and now dear Mother I write to you as a "man apart", a man "who is segregated", a member of the chosen ones of Jesus Christ. I find it hard dear mother to realise just what it all means but I realise at least this much that from hence forth I have to be a new man, far otherwise to what I have hitherto been. We had a fine retreat, thank God. Father Herring (Marist) was the conductor. He was most practical and insisted on one point all through that we are not to be ordinary men, not the university student, not the ordinary young man of the world but a "man of

God" in all our actions – *homo segregatus* as he said again and again, that is "a man apart", a stranger in the world.

I look back on past years be that at College or as a student and I don't think there has been that habitual atmosphere of God's presence in my life. He insisted repeatedly that we be men of prayer. I recall that many a day of my last holidays especially after the 1st couple of weeks were not what they might have been. This is not the circumstances but it is the want of constancy on my part. If I do not pray in the holidays there is a grave danger that I will not do so as a priest.

My stay with Mick was a happy one but again I wonder how much God had of that holiday. I must learn to make time not by neglecting other work but by putting aside unnecessary waste of time. I am sure dear Mother you want me to be all a priest should be and you want me to be a Saintly priest. This means that I have not to be satisfied with ordinary piety. I must be ready for real sacrifice and self-denial.

Now I am writing to you to ask you to keep in my mind this thought to ask me from time to time

1) Have I made a meditation for at least ¾ of an hour every day?

2) Have I made a particular Examen each day and have I kept an account of it?

3) Have I done my Spiritual Reading?

I made my Retreat Resolutions centre on these three points. It seems that if a priest keeps up these every day, and especially the Meditation he will be a holy priest; if not his lot is a very doubtful one. I will explain re the account of Particular Examen when I go home. Then again, Mother, Fr Herring advised to sit down and review our lives; writing down our good acts as good practices at various times of our life, e.g. [in our] childhood, Boyhood, College, and then side by side the predominant faults of that time. I was wishing I could have you there just to let me see where I failed.

Then he told us to look for the causes of these acts good or bad. I looked and found some. I saw the Rosary and the Act of Contrition, I saw the Blessed Sacrament and Holy Communion, I saw a good Mother, the causes on one side. But on the other I saw a different story. It seems that I have had three failings in a special way

(1) Pride or self conceit

(2) A want of perfect openness of character and truthfulness

(3) A want of resolute fidelity especially when confronted by Human Respect.

Perhaps if you see these faults in me you would let me know, and let me be humbled from time to time. I know you have always been telling me but I *have too often ignored what you said or at least been too indifferent. However I hope to overcome this. Lastly I have to look to practical kindness. I may be kind in thought at times but it stays there.*

The Retreat for us lasted 3 days. They simply flew. The candidates for Major Orders did Six days. The priest was splendid. We went on Retreat on Thursday afternoon. The Tonsure was not given till Friday morning. This was a big day. I was the first to receive Orders. The tonsure was a lovely ceremony. The Archbishop took 5 big pieces of hair off. I felt that Our Lord was very near calling me apart from the multitude as He did the Apostles. I also remembered that this meant putting off the world.

Next came the investing with Surplice. He put it on me and thus I was told to put on the new man – the life of Jesus Christ. I felt happy and knelt holding the candle. I thought of the Apostles of all the Saints through ages – all the priests and clerics – of all this I was now made a brother in a special way. I thought of you offering me to that good Master and I thanked God very, very, much for all you, Father, my brothers and sister all those others and especially Bro William [Molloy] who had led me thus far. Then came Porter, and Lector. Then we went back to our seats.

The Archdeacon (Dr Nevin) called all for the next two orders, Exorcist and Acolyte. I was the last on the list this time. The students wondered if I would come for any more. The Acolyte ceremony, of receiving the candle and cruets was nice. After this came the Subdeaconate. Pat Carmine was among them. He was most recollected. We had breakfast and then the visitors of those raised to Subdeaconate came and had breakfast. The new Subdeacons had a day in town.

I got a few nice cards to commemorate the event from different students. I enclose one which Pat Carmine gave me for you. He gave me one like it for myself. He said he wished his own mother had lived to see it. He hardly remembers her. His father is alive in New Zealand and lives with a brother of Pat's who is a priest.

On Saturday came Deaconate. On the night before tonsure and while we were on retreat I was given a letter from Don to tell me he was coming over on Saturday. He made a mistake and I did not have the chance to tell him in any way. He saw the deaconate. Dr Nevin told me to get him some breakfast etc. and was very kind to him. We had a real good talk as well as a couple of other students Ted O'Bryan, Pat Carmine and 2 others.

The Priesthood was given today. There were 17 in all – 6 from here, 9 from Sacred Heart Monastery and Joe Quinn from the Vincentians (ACK student). I saw Father Jew (I think that is how to spell it) who was ordained at Werribee some time ago and his young son who is to be ordained on the

26th of December. It seemed strange to see Father and son together, Priest and deacon.

I will close this letter now dear Mother and will write again soon. Revision begins tomorrow for 2 days and then exams. I will leave here on Thursday the 11th – Home Friday 12th. God bless you all at home and pray often for your Son from henceforth a son in Jesus Christ.

Jack

PS. I thank you very much for the cheque of £5.00, which I received. Bill got our tickets today. Gus Lacey and Cyril Cochrane ordained Sunday, Bendigo. Maurice Boyara,[18] Adelaide. Ormond Rush at Townsville.[19]

---

18   The spelling of the name may be incorrect.
19   Father Ormond Rush mentioned was the older brother of the Archbishop of Brisbane, Francis Rush and uncle of Professor Ormond Rush, a priest of Townsville diocese and theologian and Terry Rush, a priest of the Archdiocese of Hobart and who knew John Wallis as an elderly priest.

Letter 30 to Brian

A good time can be offered up to God.
We work and play for God.

This is a three-page letter (29th June 1931) that John writes to his ten-year-old brother Brian. One wonders what John's conversations with Brian were while at home, *I told you I would write to you.* Furthermore, we are not privy to their mother's letters to John in relation to Brian, which would have influenced what he writes to Brian.

Brian attends the Sisters of Mercy Convent School in Seymour, and he is now on holidays at home on the farm with his father, who, John says, would have the big fire burning and would cook good meals.

John chooses topics that would relate well to Brian – the graphic description of the deaths of the martyrs, Saints Peter and Paul, the *foreign* game of rugby, the process of blasting sandstone to build the fence around the seminary, the picnics, the Sisters who took the garden soil, and the other siblings, Don, Charlie, Chester and Marie.

While at one level it seems to be a typical conversation between brothers, John, the big brother, especially zealous and training to be a priest, is instructing and coaching a much more junior brother: *See how well you can say the Act of Contrition and the Rosary.*

St Mary's Cathedral, Sydney, 1930s.

Sydney Archdiocesan Archives Photographic Collection.

* * *

A.M.D.G.

St Patrick's College,
Manly.
June 29th '31

Dear Brian,

I told you I would write to you and now at last I am writing. I'll bet you are tired waiting for my letter. Well forgive me please and remember that I don't write to Mother as often as I should. Today is a holiday (holy day) – the feast of St Peter and St Paul. About 1900 years ago they were killed – made martyrs in Rome. St Peter was nailed to a cross like Our Lord but he said he was not good enough to die like Our Lord and asked the men to put his feet in the air and his head at the bottom of the Cross. St Paul had his head cut off with a sword. I suppose the nuns will tell you about them. You see they gave us a holiday today and so I am writing this letter to you. I hope they will bless you and me too.

Marie told me in her letter that you were going to have holidays soon. We are having ours the week after next. The exams begin on Thursday and on Saturday, we will have a week's holiday. How long are yours? I hope you enjoy yourself at the farm. It will be pretty cool there but I suppose you will have a big fire and then Father will be a good cook. Perhaps you will be cook. At any rate see that you have a good time.

I hope to have some fun in the holidays. I will just tell you what we are going to do. On Monday we go to Springwood. Our team will play Springwood Rugby football. Have you seen a game of rugby? It is something like "Keeping it off" only much rougher. Then we will have a picnic. The Springwood students come with us. We get hampers from Sydney. In the hamper (a basket with a lid) there are cups, plates etc. and also meat, fruit, bread, cream, jam etc. They are not as good as the picnics we have at home where we take what we call "loose stuff" – this means just take the raw meat etc. and cook it for ourselves. We used to do this at Springwood.

On Wednesday we have a picnic to Fairfield a place near Liverpool where the military camp is. I hope we have a good day. Then there is an afternoon at the Zoo. I have been there about 5 times now and so I will go to Castle Hill instead to see Don and Charlie. Some of the students have asked to be let go for a "hike" – that is a long walk. I hope to be able to go. So you see we are going to have a good time. This can be all offered up to God too. You see we do our work for God and then we play for God – All work and no play make Jack a dull boy. So too it will make Brian a dull boy. But I wonder if Brian does too much work?

I told Mother in my letter about the gardening here. Ted O'Bryan's the "boss" – foreman. We work according to Union rules. Stop work at 5 o'clock sometimes but sometimes we work till nearly half past five. I nearly got "rung off". This means that we are late – we have to be in time for Coffee at half past five. At present I am carting dirt from a hole in the paddock nearby to put in the beds and also to get ready some holes for palm trees. The Nuns here had a good joke on us. We had 2 loads of soil carted up and heaped up ready to put on the gardens. The Sisters thought we got it for them – and took it away in Buckets. When Ted O'Bryan went for it, it was all gone. We have to go now and cart more. But the Sisters are very good to us and so we are glad they got the dirt. They can't have the fun we can but we can make them happy by little acts of kindness for them. How are the Sisters at the Convent?

Another thing that will interest you is the "blasting". Joe Brennan who was a boy at school at Maitland when Bro William was there used to be a bricklayer before he came here. Pat Shanley who was at Kilmore when I was there used to be a bricklayer too. Dr Nevin the president is getting him to make a Stone fence round the College. They are getting stone by "blasting" in the College grounds. There is a lot of sand stone about here. They make a hole and put in a charge of dynamite and then put a fuse to it and run for their lives. They will be working for a long while on the rocks. Then they will have to cart the stone. The old horse "Ginger" is very slow and will not pull a heavy load.

Well, dear Brian I have told you what little news I have. I have got my sermon to get ready now. It is on the fifth article of the Apostles Creed, "He descended into hell, the third day he rose again". I have not very long to get it ready. On Sunday I will go to St Marys to be "Master of Ceremonies". Every Sunday a deacon, a subdeacon and another student go to Sydney.

That reminds me, how are you going at serving Mass? You know the time is getting close and I want you and Chester to be able to serve. If all goes well, it is only about a year and a half now till I will be a priest. I hope you often pray for me. Each night at the Rosary please think of me and see how well you can say the Act of Contrition and the Rosary.

Well now, I want to write a short note to Marie so I will close this letter. May Our Lord and Our Lady bless you and make you a good holy and cheerful boy.

With love from
Your fond Brother
Jack.

P.S. Show this to Mother and all at home. I will write to Chester soon.

A CLERICAL CITADEL IN A CHANGING TIME
St Patrick's College, Manly 1929–1931
Letters 21 – 30

Edmund Campion

The most startling of John Wallis' letters home from the junior seminary at Springwood is one in August 1928 where he tells his mother that, on the feast of the Assumption among many religious devotions (Masses, litany, hymns, exposition of the Blessed Sacrament and a pilgrimage to the grotto), each student is aiming to say 1,000 *'Hail Marys'*. It is a reminder that Catholicism was once a very arithmetical religion whose believers were busy counting the number of times they performed a religious exercise. *'Novena', 'decade', 'triduum', 'Forty Hours'* – these were familiar words in Catholic speech.

Numbering continued to be a feature of John Wallis's spirituality when he moved to the senior seminary at Manly, in 1929. He urged his mother to make novenas and to seek *'indulgences'* (the temporal remission of punishment for sin attached to some good work, such as a visit to a church). The letters are a rare window into the spiritual life of Catholics in this period.

But it should also be noticed that his letters are remarkable in the way he shared with his family – his mother especially, but the whole family read each letter – his deepest thoughts on religion and his vocation. On retreat, he makes three resolutions: to devote 45 minutes each day to meditation; to examine some aspect of his moral life daily; and to read a spiritual book every day. He tells his mother these resolutions and commissions her to keep a watch on his adherence to them.

At the time, the Manly seminary was a key promoter of clericalism, insisting on the superiority of clergy over laity and marking a clear line between the two. The stone wall erected around the college when John Wallis was there, isolating college from *'the world'*, was symbolic of this ethos. A few years later, the new college chapel, an elongated sanctuary with choir stalls for seminarians but no place for the laity except a dark lobby near the door and a remote gallery, would reinforce such thinking. In his history of the Manly seminary, K J Walsh wrote that the new chapel *'was not a building to foster a sense of the full Church'*.

Readers of the letters will notice that John Wallis gets nervous when the annual call to orders is coming. The reason is simple. If you want to be a lawyer or a doctor you go to university, pass your exams and at the end join your profession. Not so the priesthood. Your passage through the various stages to priesthood depends on your winning approval from the seminary authorities. If they thought you deficient in some way, you would be denied orders – *'clipped'*, in seminary parlance. A junior staff member would write later of the *'sense of fear'* that pervaded the place. Fear of a *'clipping'* was a powerful disciplinary tool. Note in Letter 45 (12 October 1930) when John is told he will be called to minor orders, *'it is conditional on my holding my head straighter'*.

That absurdity came from Dr John Nevin, College president 1929-1942. He was known as a hard man who thought the college rules had the force of canon law. Under him seminarians, fearful of a 'clipping', toed the line.

Manly remained unchanged, a clerical citadel in a changing world. Vatican II came and went and then, one day in 1968, the then president, successor to Dr Nevin, came in to breakfast, unfolded his napkin and was startled to find a revolutionary slogan printed there: WE WANT MATURITY, NOT MAXIMUM SECURITY. It was time to change. By then, however, Father John Wallis had already written many of the chapters of his remarkable life.

Father Edmund Campion is a Sydney priest who taught Church History at the Catholic Institute of Sydney for a quarter of a century. His books include "Rockchoppers: Growing up Catholic in Australia" and "Australian Catholics". For the past thirty years he has contributed biographical sketches to "Madonna" magazine.

Ordination Year *1932*
Letters 31 – 42

Introduction

This is the year of John's final preparation for his ordination, which took place on 18th December at St Patrick's Church, Kilmore, Victoria. Because John was too young to be ordained mid-year, he stayed on at the seminary till the end of the year when he turned twenty-two and a half and was then eligible.

This chapter consists of twelve surviving letters written in 1932. Ten of these are to John's mother one to his father and the other is a short one to his sister, Marie.

Letter 31 to Mother

Just walking with a mate today
talking about our early steps on our varied paths to the one goal.

Emma's birthday is on 5th May, so this two-page letter (2nd May 1932) is particularly to wish his mother a happy birthday.

On the morning of writing, John has *walked with a mate* and they talked about *the early steps* on their *various paths to the one goal* and how grateful he is to his mother through whom he learned the rudiments of the faith. John also says he has *thoughts running through his mind* about what his life as a priest will be like after ordination and can he stay faithful. Only if he keeps *the energy and power* of faith can he be of influence in his work as a priest. He hopes that during his early priesthood he will have a good mentor, a *very holy parish priest*.

Amid his private worries shared with his mother, he recounts that he is continuing his studies on the Eucharist – all in preparation for his life as a priest and in Tasmania.

Fr Pat Carmine, one of John's 'mates', who later worked in Wilcannia-Forbes Diocese.

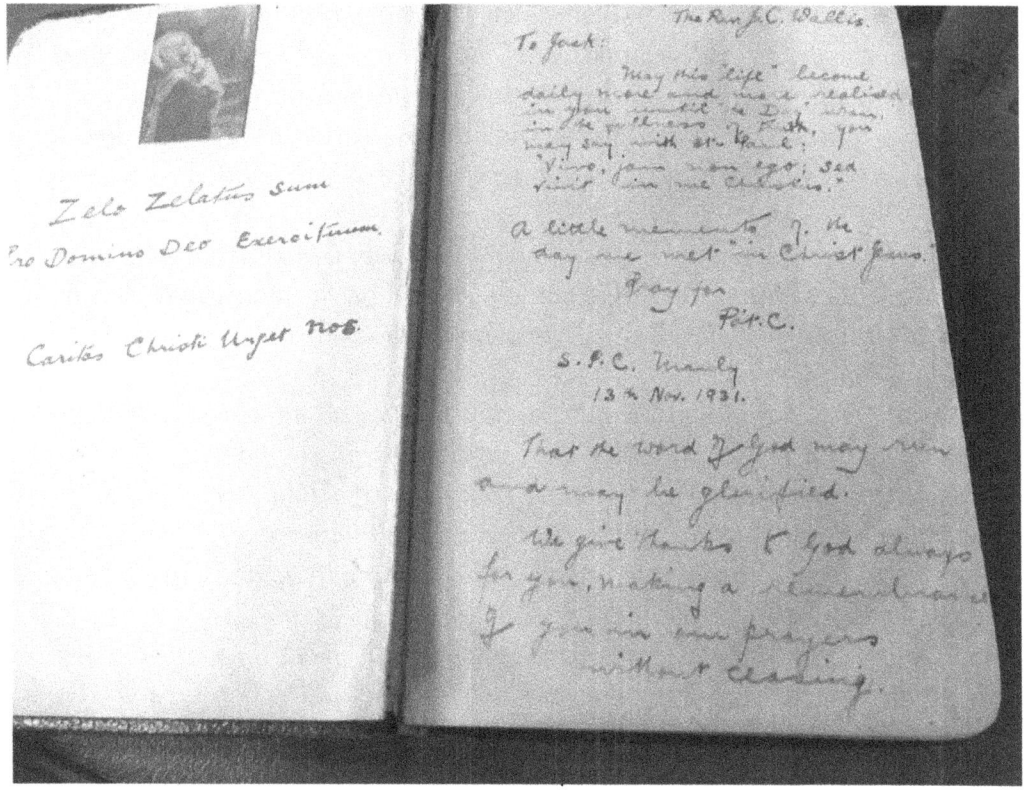

Above: a gift book from Pat to John. The inscription reads:
To Jack: May the "life" become daily more and more realised in you until "the Day" when in the fullness of time you may say with St Paul, "Vivo jam non ego, sed vivit in me Christus".

A little memento of the day we met "in Christ Jesus."
Pray for
Pat. C.
S.P.C. Manly   13 November 1931
That the Word of God may run and be glorified.
We give thanks to God always for you, making a remembrance of you in our prayers without ceasing.

* * *

A.M.D.G.
+

St Patrick's College,
Manly.
May 2nd 1932

Dearest Mother,
I had hoped to write to you a longer letter than I have done so far but again I find myself pressed for time. I have little more than a week till my

Sermon and have not yet finished it. We had a "Specimena" – Blue Monday today. I did not get a call, thank God. I am all out to keep up with the class work. We are at present doing the Eucharist tract in Moral. This is one of the most important, as it has to do with the administration of Holy Communion, the Mass etc. However I know you understand how things are and also that I do not forget you in my prayers.

This letter is especially to wish you a most happy birthday and to promise you that I will not be unmindful of you on Thursday, the feast of the Ascension of Our Lord into Heaven. May He bless you and all at home as He did when ascending from among His apostles.

I was just walking with a mate today talking about our varied paths to the one goal and especially about our early steps on the path. It is now as I look back that I realise dear Mother all that you have done in my regard, more than many others have done. For despite my disinclinations etc. you taught me the rudiments of that Faith, which please God I will go on to teach to some souls waiting for me in Tasmania.

I see now how those simple prayers, especially the daily Act of Contrition before the Rosary have kept me and helped me, and I have resolved that whenever I preach the Rosary which I hope will be often I will remind people of this practice. I ask you now, My mother, to beg God to strengthen and confirm me in that Faith. In a priest's life there is often much to test his Faith, there are special temptations and then there is the danger of faith losing its energy and power. Only when a priest has an intense faith – and intense realisation of God, of the value of a soul, of Eternity, of the meaning of a God Man dying for my soul, and other souls, only when he is filled with this thought can he teach others and waken them to these truths.

However, dear Mother, I know I will find a certain tendency to slacken in the fervour when I am thrown on my own. Every young priest experiences it, he sees others do it. I ask again your maternal prayers, and also Your help to keep up to the ideal. This will be especially so if I do not have the good fortune to get a very holy Parish Priest – the one special grace I now ask of God. These thoughts have been running through my mind. They are not about your birthday but they have been the happenings of days past. Still I know your mother's wish to hear them. Now there goes the bell.

Good night for present and pray for Your loving Son

Jack Wa *['Wa' scratched out]*

P.S.   *I got Marie's letter.*

Letter 32 to Mother

Everything will come alright if I am right in one great thing the spirit of prayer.

This four-page letter to his mother (16th May 1932) is written the day after Pentecost Sunday. John proudly tells her he has done some proof-reading for Dr Leonard for an article to go to *The Press*. He, too, will one day write articles to be proof-read too.

The focus of John's study is the Eucharist and the Incarnation, which he describes as *perhaps the most beautiful of all* studies. Reflectively he shares about what theme he might address in his special study – Sacred Scripture and Dogmatic Theology from a devotional and ascetic perspective. He has committed himself to *a spirit of prayer* – another thread that develops from his seminary life into his priestly ministry, when he becomes the spiritual director for religious communities, and is invited to gives retreats to others in many parts of Australia.

John finds the *lecturettes* by his fellow students very interesting. He enjoys being stimulated. One was about prison life. One of the students gives an account of visiting the Brisbane Gaol with his brother who was a doctor. From another talk John learns about the Irish poet, playwright and novelist Oliver Goldsmith, having already been familiar with parts of the poem, *Deserted Village* written in 1770 – a social commentary on the depopulation of rural areas and the pursuit of excessive wealth.[1] Being interested in literature, perhaps he was thinking that he might use some poems in his preaching. At the end of the letter he asks his mother for the words of a poem by Isaac McLellan that was in his Fifth school reader: *Death of Napoleon* which took place at St Helena in 1821. It begins:

Wild was the night, yet a wilder night
Hung round the soldier's pillow...[2]

John is thinking about his ordination at the end of the year. With Christmas immediately afterwards and being with the family for holidays, he is anxiously preparing his homilies for the public Masses he will subsequently celebrate at Seymour, Tallarook and Yea and especially for the feast days of Christmas, New Year and the Holy Family.

Referring to the political news of 1932, namely, a constitutional crisis, John explains it is *a pretty dose of excitement* when Governor Phillip Game sacked Premier John (Jack) Thomas Lang of New South Wales. At the height of the Great Depression, Lang had defied the Government when it passed the

---
1   https://en.wikipedia.org/wiki/The_Deserted_Village
2   http://www.bartleby.com/297/254.html

Financial Agreement Enforcement Act, by withdrawing all the State's funds from Government bank accounts, so that the Federal Government could not gain access to the money.³

Before he finishes the letter John remembers his grandmother's anniversary and has asked for Masses to be said by his friends Father Pat Carmine and Father Charlie Cunningham who are now ordained.

* * *

+
A.M.D.G.
Manly.
Pentecost Monday, [16.05.1932]

Dear Mother,

I had intended beginning a letter to you yesterday but Dr Leonard asked me to do some work for him so I did not get a chance. He wrote an article on the Holy Ghost for the "Press" and asked me to write a proof sheet for him. I would like the cutting from the "Press" if you or Marie see it.

Yesterday was Pentecost Sunday the 2nd biggest feast day of the year (Easter is first). So we had a holiday and also today. It has been a bit on the cool side and showery on and off. Still there are a few of the boys who go for a swim. We have been in the Academy hall most of the time.

I have written to Frank Toohey. He wrote a few days back. I also wrote to Bishop Hayden. I ought to get a reply soon.

At this holy Season I feel more the need above all of the interior spirit. I gave my sermon last Thursday. The one thing I felt that I wanted was that deep interior fervour and ardour to help me to express from the abundance of the heart what I said with my lips.

As the time goes on I am beginning to get more apprehensive of the work of preaching. I am setting out now to write some sermons for Christmas, New Year, the Holy Family and so on. I must get them done before I go home because there will be a number of unforeseen circumstances which will render my doing them then very hard. I have almost had visions of myself walking up and down learning them off. I will begin one tonight on the Holy Family.

While on this I have been wondering about Mass on Christmas Day, i.e. Sunday after 18th. I will be able to say three Masses. I would like to say Mass at Yea on that day and yet will probably give Fr O'Connor a hand on Christmas Eve. I was thinking of Midnight Mass at Seymour (Convent or Church) – then 10 o'clock at Tallarook and late Mass at Yea. This would be

---

3 https://en.wikipedia.org/wiki/1932_New_South_Wales_constitutional_crisis

a bit of a rush. I would like to know what you think about this. It would give me an idea in preparing a Sermon. If at Yea [we] could make it a little more intimate and personal. The only thing is that we would be away from home. I am not making any other preparations till Mid-Winter. I will thus be able to avoid unnecessary distraction. You would be surprised how easily the thought of these things gets one's mind away from the work.

We are at present on some solid work – the Incarnation. It is a wonderful tract – perhaps the most beautiful of all we have done. In Moral we are doing the Eucharist – i.e. about Communion, Mass etc.

Since I wrote Reg Capely's [Copeley] Father died suddenly. Reg himself is in Lewisham after an operation for Antrinus. He intended going home but has now decided today there are a couple of brothers at home (both Labor Members and contesting seats on 21st). I think his mother is coming down. Brian Doherty (Father Pat's brother) left some weeks back. He has, I heard, applied for the police force. He ought to make a good cop – about 6 feet or more…I have not heard of [Fred] except that he is trying to get work with a dentist. His Mother did not take the news as well as was expected. [Fred] was very worried about her.

The new Wall is finished now and the gates are swung. They make a big difference. We have been preparing for Corpus Christi. It is only a fortnight now. Ted O'Bryan and I will go to the Cathedral on Friday week. All will go on the Thursday – the Feast itself of Corpus Christi and on the Saturday.

We have had a few smatterings of the political news which seem to show a pretty dose of excitement outside. There were more controversies and arguments on Jack Lang who has some ardent admirers here as well as some strong opponents. The last we heard was that he is out of office. There will be an election soon I suppose.

We had a couple of interesting lecturettes last Wednesday Night. One on Goldsmith and his writings. I must confess I have not read any of his works except the parts of the "Deserted Village". The other was on a personal experience of one of the students who visited Brisbane Gaol. His brother is a doctor in attendance there. He happened to be there one day last year – holidays – while Richards a prisoner who escaped from Adelaide gaol was there. He was under the strictest of supervision and yet managed to allude [elude] the warders and scale the 23 feet wall. The Governor of the Gaol had just been saying to his guest that Richards would not get out. Then a warder raced up to tell him.

I must write to Brian some time. I think I will wait till after Corpus Christi as I may have some more "news" for him. Has Chester had his term holidays yet?

Well now, dear Mother, I must close this letter. I have some Office to say yet and also some things to write up with regard to class work. I have been trying to decide what line of study I can take for a special study. I have been thinking of Scripture and Dogmatic Theology considered from a Devotional or Ascetic point of view. I suppose there will be plenty of time for this. These will come alright if I am right in one great thing – the spirit of prayer. I have been trying to give more attention to this point. It is the one thing that shows up in the actual work.

I will also be giving Grandma a special mention this month. I will ask for Mass and am also writing to Father Pat Carmine and Father Charlie Cunningham to ask them to say Mass.

Well now I must close asking once more your loving Prayers and promising you to remember all at home.

Your Loving Son in Jesus Christ
Jack

P.S. Leo Hatswell who got Subdiaconate with us will be ordained next Wednesday. Jack Russell who was in our class also will be ordained in Genoa[4] on Saturday next. I will write to Marie later about the stole and other things like binding for the hands after the anointing with oil, etc. I sent the surplice to wash. It came back in quite good order. I would also like to get that poem in the 5th Reader – the death of Napoleon at St. Helena. It would be alright just copied out. I have been trying to do more reading to improve my speech. Dr Neven said I could speak better than I read. One difficulty is the matter of clear and distinct communication. I am saying the Public Rosary this week.

Goodnight now dearest Mother and God's grace be with you.
Jack

---

4   Genoa is on the Princes Highway in Victoria, the last town before entering New South Wales.

Letter 33

*Study the Breviary, try to understand it
and you will find it a comfort all your life.*

This is part of a letter presumably to John's mother, probably written early June 1932 before *mid-winter* from St Patrick's College, Manly. John begins to think of things he will need as a priest, a pyx,[5] a chalice and remembrance cards to give to people at the time of his ordination. The letter from Archbishop William Hayden would have been about the arrangements for his ordination in Kilmore, which was within Archbishop Mannix's Archdiocese of Melbourne. The former's advice to study the Breviary[6] was taken seriously. Throughout his life John faithfully prayed the Liturgy of the Hours, especially in the morning and evening and Compline before going to bed.

* * *

I was wondering about the boys at Ath. If they are staying back it would seem only decent to give them some memento. Then how about people at gen? The general thing is about 400–500 in all. Then there is the printing also about 8/- per hundred. However I may be able to get some cheaper cards in Sydney. I will write again before the order goes. I got a letter from Bp. All has been finalised by him with Dr Mannix etc. He added a bit of advice: "Study the Breviary, try to understand it and you will find it a comfort all your life." It is not long now dear Mother: I feel that I must redouble efforts – Prayer a life of prayer + all for God. I know you are behind me at home and now the bell is going so Goodbye for the present with fondest love to you + Father Maur + all at home.

Your loving son in Christ,
Jack

---

5   A pyx is a small container to carry consecrated hosts to sick or elderly people who cannot go to the parish for Eucharist.
6   The Breviary was often called the Divine Office or Liturgy of the Hours. It is a book of prayers, hymns, psalms and readings to be prayed at different times of the day.

(Opening pages are missing.)

[Early June 1932]

...charity of her members. At tea time, we have at present "The Genius of Louis Pasteur", the great scientist of fermentation and germs, etc. It is he who gave the world the "Pasteuriser" and also brought in the modern system of packing meats, fruits etc. He was a staunch Catholic.

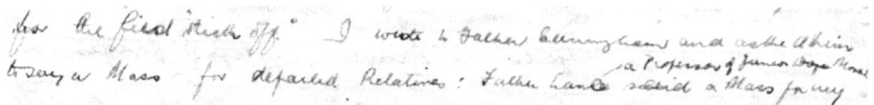

I had intended to write to Brian, but I must wait till I get more time. I am trying to revise some of the work, which will be most practical for the first "kick off". I wrote to Father Cunningham and asked him to say a Mass for departed Relatives. Father Lanke, a Professor of Junior Moral, said a Mass for my Intention and Dr. Roberts said one yesterday for Grandma in particular. I will also write to Father Pat [Carmine] one of these days.

In your last letter you asked about sending on anything I wanted. Well, I think, it would be a good idea to see about the pyx at Mid-winter. I would like to send it home to you to see it before it is blessed. (Only a Chalice is consecrated). I may get Bishop Hayden to bless it. So I think that if you could send on the Jewellery, I could see the Jeweller at the end of this month I heard that he charges about 10/- to 15/- for the making if he has the material. I do not know how much material he will need but certainly no more than in two or three rings. I can then get Marie to make a little Pyx case and burse. I will write about this later.

Now about cards. They are going to be fairly expensive this year, I am afraid. The black and white with gold edge are 15/- per hundred. There are others at 8/- per hundred. I am wondering how many I will want. Of the better ones I will only get a few – at the most 50 for relatives and special friends. The others are quite good and are what most are going to get.

I was wondering about the boys at ACK. If they are staying back it would seem only decent to give them some memento. Then how about people at Yea? The general thing is about 400 – 500 in all. Then there is the printing also about 8/- per hundred. However, I may be able to get some cheaper cards in Sydney. I will write again before the order goes.

I got a letter from Bishop. All has been finalised by him with Dr. Mannix, etc. He added "a bit of advice": "Study the Breviary, try to understand it and you will find it a comfort all your life." It is not long now dear Mother: I feel that I must redouble efforts – Prayer, a life of prayer and all for God. I know you are behind me at home and now the bell is going, so Goodbye for the present with fondest love to you to Father, Marie and All at home,

Your loving Son in Christ,
Jack.

Letter 34 to Mother

I feel very happy to know you see all in the light of Faith.

This is a two-page quickly written letter approximately June 1932 to John's mother. Father Lynch was the parish priest at Sacred Heart Church in Yea where John was baptised. John's thoughts are on the ordination and the initial Mass he will say in Yea and the sermon he will give. Again he talks about the pyx and remembrance cards. Families often gave jewellery to be incorporated into sacred vessels, for example, the gold melted to line a pyx or chalice. Jewels were used to adorn a chalice. It seems his mother has written to John making a suggestion about his first homily – to use the Magnificat as a Marian thanksgiving theme.

* * *

A.M.D.G.
St Patrick's College,
Manly.
Sunday, June 1932.

Dearest Mother,

I am in a great hurry with this note. I have spent longer on the letter to Fr Lynch than I expected. I asked about Dec 20th – about Yea people at the Ordination – and Christmas Day at 10 oclock. As to the last I have been wondering if I could get to Yea from Seymour since the car is sold (though I said Thank God when I heard it as it was a burden on Father and of little use in the town). Perhaps you can tell me. Also would you be able to be present? Would there be someone in the shop for the day itself? I would like this very much – the full joy of the day as I really think there would be many [more] there at the Christmas than at the Mass on the Tuesday.

As to the Pyx I have been thinking it is not necessary immediately after Ordination. I will not need it till at work in Tasmania. And so could wait till after the Ordination. It really hurts me to think of all the expense I am putting you to – there are also the fees for the half [year]. I have here 4 pounds 10/- (having allowed for a shirt etc. which I will get on Wed next). Of this I will want 25/- for cards I am getting here 500. I have ordered about 500 cards from overseas to value of about 30/-. Hence in all cards will be about 30 + 25 + 15 = 3/10/- and printing another 15/-.

To make a Pyx supplying all the gold 5.10.0 (Silver very heavily gilded 2.10.0 and 3.10.00.) The amount of gold I have would not be enough. If you would wish me to get the pyx done now I would like you to take that £2 out of the bank to go towards it. Besides that and the jewellery, it might require about 30/- for the pyx. I would not be surprised if I got Oil stocks[7] at Assumption College Kilmore as they are giving them to Fathers Murtagh, Crowe, Doherty and Marsh. Fr Murtagh was here last Wednesday. His people live here in Sydney. I shall write soon as this is a very wretched note but you understand the way things are. We have a revision in Class tomorrow.

Will you please thank Marie for the Breviary and case. The case is great one and will be especially a protection for the book when travelling.

Goodbye now dearest Mother and may God bless you for your goodness to me. I feel very sad at times when I think of all that [I] have been costing you but then I feel very happy to know you see all in the light of Faith and that I will be able to give you joy on the great day. You too can say a joyous Magnificat – one of my favourite parts of the Office. I too had the idea of making my 1st sermon on these words – and this at Yea. I have nearly finished one Sermon on the Holy Family. I will begin soon on Christmas Sermon.

    Goodnight   Love from

Jack

P.S. Please let me know re the Pyx. But remember I can wait till after – though I want it to be your special priesthood gift.

---

[7] Small containers for the blessed oils to use for the sacraments.

Letter 35 to Mother

*All I want is a little quiet –
perhaps you and I will manage a quiet walk
on the evening of the grand day.*

Twenty-two year old John replies in his two-page letter (16th September 1932) to his mother, regarding arrangements that are being made for the ordination on 18th December at Kilmore. Perhaps his hopes and ideas for a simple ordination have to be adjusted. *I know how you feel, so I will fall in with all you desire,* he writes, and he agrees with his mother and would like the people to feel welcome. Hospitality is important to him and his mother. Working on the details of the ordination requires communication between them. The invitations need to be worked out. One is to be sent to 'Miss Tratford' in Yea, the one in the wheel-chair. The designing of the gold pyx that will be his parents' gift to him has been finalised.

In the meantime John and his peers are required to learn and practice how to celebrate the Mass. They are not seasoned priests overnight. John has a mock-up altar in his room so he can practise in private. His first attempt has taken him three-quarters of an hour and he is only half way through!

John is pleased his friend Father Ted (mentioned also as Ed O'Bryan) called to see his mother at Seymour following his own ordination. Most of all, John wants quiet time with his mother.

* * *

A.M.D.G.
*St. Patrick's College,
Manly.
Friday, 16 Sept 1932*

Dearest Mother,

I was very pleased to get your letter a few days ago. I have been feeling that you are not as well as you might be and, also that you are worried about various matters. I am looking forward to the time when I can see you and I can say in a way these words of Our Lord "I shall see you again and you will rejoice." I am hoping that that time will be a great joy for you and Father. I feel that it will be something for all you have done for me all these years.

I also thank you for the Cheque enclosed (£3/5/-). Since I last wrote I decided to get the solid gold Pyx as the Jeweller said the gilded inside of the other would need to be renewed after some years. I thought that even if there are some advantages from the Silver case I would like to keep this Pyx as it was from the first. This will mean an extra pound. (£4) I think you will be pleased that I have done this. I will send it to you when I get it blessed by the Archbishop [Hayden].

I had my first [practise] attempt at celebrating [a Eucharist] today. I got up to the Creed in 3/4 of hour! And this is the easiest part. I will have to get going a bit more. I have an Altar set up in my room.

I was so glad Father Ted went to see you. He wrote and told me he might go up. We sent his books on to him a few days ago.

About arrangements: I was pleased at the idea of the luncheon for visitors from Yea etc. as it would make them more welcome. I know how you feel and so I will fall in with all you desire here. The only thing I was thinking of is the burden to you. However it will be a joy to you and I know you have been saving for it. I would like to go and see the Yea guests while at the luncheon and say a few words.

As to Invitations: I was thinking it would be as easy for you to get them printed at the Printing office as for me to get them here. I have to write and rewrite and then there is the NSW sales tax, post etc. You could see what you are getting. However if you think better, I will get them at Westmead. Will you post them? (Ed. O'Bryan did so). Cards – better than his way, as they will admit to seats. Try to get as many as possible. Include Maher's at Triangle.[8] I thought of including 2nd Mass on Invitations.

Mr & Mrs Wallis etc.
to Ordination at Kilmore (Guests invited to luncheon etc.)
to 1st Mass at Same Church and to 2nd Mass at Sacred Heart Church Yea.

I have not written to Father Willis or Ellis. Will I do so? Father McHugh may have done so.

I am hoping all will be well with you all and I am looking forward to that day. I can assure you I will do all I can to make guests happy and especially our own. All I want is a little quiet with ourselves and perhaps you and I will manage a quiet walk on the evening of the grand day.

Pray much dear Mother. I will not write so frequently now but I will remember you all just the same. Goodnight and love to all at home from

Your loving Son in Christ

Jack

PS. I would like an invitation sent to Miss Tratford[9] – the one in the [wheel] chair.

---

8   Mrs. Maher lived with her daughter Mrs Dan Ahearn on the corner of Triangle Road and King Parrot Creek Road, Kerrisdale.

9   Cecilia (Sis) Tratford, who had contracted polio, lived with her brother Clyde and sister Win.

Letter 36 to Mother

I am but the instrument in God's hand:
I can water or sow
but God must work by grace in the souls of all.

While he says this is to be a short letter (3rd October 1932) and it is two pages, John pours his heart out to his mother about the things that matter to him. He expresses his gratitude as he looks back and feels he may not have many years of service and *the days are drawing in* on him. His ordination day is approaching and he wants to make the most of his life of service.

Being the feast day of St Therese of Lisieux, John writes again of her spirituality and that she offered her prayer life for priests. John asks his mother and his sister, Marie, to pray for him, as priest. He also writes of St Teresa of Avila, another favourite saint who inspires him. Such lives of prayer are a hidden but powerful work. John also speaks about the call of all to be saints – *to grow daily in the love of God … the Spirit of prayer and patience.*

As is noticeable in this letter, gender inclusive language is not yet in common usage.

* * *

A.M.D.G.
St. Patrick's College,
Manly.
Monday, Oct 3 1932

Dear Mother,
Just a short note in with Father's letter. I intended writing to Marie too this afternoon but the time seemed to fly and I had to source a good deal of Office in this study.
I must get down to the subjects for the exams tomorrow week. I have really so much to revise that I feel almost afraid to get into it; not so much for exams but for the work afterwards. I am feeling more and more that I must make my life a life of hard work. I may not have many years in God's service but I hope

to make the best of them. I will write to Marie when Orders are called.

I want to tell that I got your letter last week and also the money enclosed £16/10/-. I paid Father O'Flynn the last of the fees. Now dear Mother all I can say is that I am deeply grateful to you, as you well know. May God give you good measure pressed down and flowing over for all the good you have done. I often look back now and I feel the days are drawing in.

Today is the feast of St Therese – the marvellous little Saint – so young and yet so wonderfully holy. She is especially dear to priests. I would like you dear Mother to read her own life. It is so simple and yet so sublime in the Sanctity it portrays. As I was reading it today I thought of you and dear Marie. She was saying how she wishes she had a brother a priest. But she had no brothers alive (both died as babes). But God allowed through her superiors that she "adopt" two priests – she was to pray for them – to take a special interest in their work – to be a kind of hidden but powerful worker in their apostolate. She offered her life for their work.

I thought that I have a Mother and sister to whom I may look to be behind the guns – praying for me and offering all their daily sacrifices for me. The more I think on the work ahead the more I realise that after all I am but the instrument in God's hand: I can water or sow but God must work by His grace in the souls of men: He must give the increase. Now how is this increase to come but by Prayer and Sacrifice. Marie will remember how Father Doyle lived the life of prayer and sacrifice in little things in daily life all for the gaining of grace for souls. Who can tell all grace and the conversions won by the hidden austere life of pennance (sic) lived in the Carmelite Convents. God is outraged by men who yield to their every inclination, and it is generous souls who obtain pardon and mercy by their sufferings united with those of Our Divine Lord.

So now dear Mother I am going to rely very, very much on your prayers, and your trials sanctified and daily offered to God for me and all those souls with whom I will have to deal – some sinners – some careless and some who though good can go far higher in the way of the love of God. We are all called to be Saints – to grow daily in the love of God, of Charity, the Spirit of prayer and patience.

I will recommend you to St Therese and to my other patron, St Teresa the Mother of the Carmelite Order, and may they help you to continue to live that life of [the] hidden apostolate which, though unconsciously, perhaps you have been living and may you grow ever deeper in the Love and Knowledge of the hidden life of Our Lady in the little home of Naz. [Nazareth].

This dear Mother is the heartfelt and deep feeling of
Your dear and loving Son,

Jack.

Letter 37 to Father

I do not ever cease to ask God to bless you,
to give you grace and light.

This three-page fragile letter (3rd October 1932) is the only one to his father for the year. In the first paragraph John impresses on his father that the examiners are not staff members. They come from 'outside', presumably, to give authenticity to the examination process. Significantly, there is a confidence in John; he is not worried about his studies.

As is customary before they leave the seminary, the 4th year Manly seminarians go to St Gabriel's School for Deaf Boys for the day. John's brother, Charlie, is eight years old and at school there.

The Irish Jesuit priest, Father William O'Leary, the director of the Jesuit Riverview Observatory, is coming to speak to the seminarians. In 1908, some 24 years earlier, the Jesuit Father Edward Pigot founded the Observatory, which had the first permanent seismograph in Australia and was able to monitor earthquakes as far as Awajas, in the Pacific. Father O'Leary has been at the observatory for some time.

Walls are going up around St Patrick's College, Manly, and a gate is to be installed. As a lawn is to be laid, the rabbits are being trapped. John knows from first hand experience on the farm about rabbit trapping.

Towards the end of the letter John writes of his love and gratitude in appreciation for all his parents have done for him and the family.

* * *

A.M.D.G.

St Patrick's College,
Manly.
October 3rd 1932.

Dear Father,

I was very pleased indeed to get your letter. I did not get time to write during the last few weeks but as we have the afternoon off today I take this opportunity of writing to let you know how things have been going. We had exams today. They were not too bad but were about matters we were not very fresh on. The Order List will most probably be called some time this week. The students of 4th year are not so worried about this as they are sure they will not be stopped now except for some serious reason. There will be another lot of exams on Tuesday week. These [exams] are given by men from outside, but they are not very difficult. On the Wednesday after them, we will go to Castle Hill where we are hoping to have a first rate day's outing.

On the coming Wednesday night, Father O'Leary S.J., the director of the great Riverview observatory, so well known for its fittings in apparatus for detecting earth quakes etc. will give us a lecture. We do not know what the Subject is to be but I suppose it will be about Earthquakes, their causes and so on.

I have given up the garden this half. I could not get all my work in without taking part of Recreation time for it. There are some good men on the work and they are making a big improvement to the grounds. Besides the big new stone wall along the front side of the College, we have new gates erected. The students are now carting soil to make a [new] lawn right back towards the Quadrangle. It is a big [area] but they will get it done in time. It is great exercise and gives a fine relaxation from hard study. One of the gardeners [made] a raid on the rabbits. He got three traps and set them all round about. When he got a catch, one of the tables in the Refectory had the rabbit cooked and served for dinner. A number of students especially the Queenslanders did not know how they set a trap. We had one of them one day going for a walk. We told him about putting green grass on the trap etc. He was quite interested, but was much surprised when we showed him just how they are set.

The weather is beginning to get quite warm here now. The baths are in full swing once more. I am writing this letter in the Academy hall and facing out towards the ocean. It is truly a wonderful sight. There was a very big crowd on the beach today. We can hear the music of the band there quite plainly. There seem to be no end of musicians of every description in Manly. We get snatches of violins, bag-pipes, cornets and all kinds of stringed instruments.

Mother told me you had a talk with Father Lynch again later in the month. I have not had any letter from Kilmore [Assumption College]. I suppose they are very busy with the exams. It seems a long time since I was thinking about the exams there and yet in some ways the time seems to have flown. I have now less than 2 months at St. Pat's [Manly.] I have had a happy time here.

I am looking forward to seeing you all again and to giving you and Mother my first blessing as a newly ordained priest. I cannot say how I feel towards You and her for the way you have helped me, for what you have denied yourselves and borne with for us all. I would wish at times to say what I feel but I don't seem to be able to say it. However I do not ever cease to ask God to bless you, to give you grace and light, and I hope that the day of Ordination will be a source of gladness to you both. I am so glad that all the Yea people will be asked down and I am looking forward to going there to see all again.

For the present I will not write more as it is getting late. It will be no time till I am home again. In the meantime, I will ask you to pray now and then for me, while remaining,

Your loving Son in Christ,
Jack.

Letter 38 to Mother

But by the grace of God I want to be a priest
And a holy priest.

This is a four-page letter (6th November 1932) on A5 size stationery that John writes to his mother. He is still studying and undertaking his last piece of work – on Justice, which he emphasises as both important and extensive. It is two months since he wrote of the first time he practiced saying the Mass in his room. He had been doing it every day since then and he thinks he is *getting on fairly well* now. It is of great importance to him that he prepares for the Masses following his ordination. Arrangements for the ordination continue.

At the end of the letter John shares his worry about temptations he is experiencing and his sense of inadequacy. Fears are looming large about what is ahead for him. He resolves that all will be well if he has *the grace of deep humility* and looks to *the high ideals of the saints* and Jesus himself. Being inspired again by St John Vianney, he desires *to serve God*, as his master.

* * *

A.M.D.G.
+

St Patrick's College,
Manly.
Sunday Nov 6' 32

Dearest Mother,

No doubt you have been expecting some news from me during the last couple of weeks. I received the Ordination cards yesterday. They made me think of how you are looking forward to the great day. Of course there is no need to say how busy I am these days – only a fortnight now till the Ordination Retreat on Nov 22nd.

I am beginning revision of the last tract I will be able to do before I leave here – Justice. This is pretty extensive and also very important for the Confessional. I expected to get a few sermons written but alas I have only one. I will have to write a few short talks.

I wrote to Fathers Willis, Ellis, Egan, Lacey and Lynch. I told Father Lynch the times for the 20th and Christmas Day. I was wondering if they could have a sung Mass on the 20th. I would like to say a Mass of the Holy Ghost but could not do this unless it was a sung Mass. I think I could manage the priest's parts if there was a choir for the rest. I have not written to Father O'Connor yet.

I am wondering about the Mass on Christmas morning. I may be very tired if I say the Midnight Mass at the Convent. I suppose I could go to bed early and then have another rest before the 6 o'clock in the church. If I went to Yea after the 6.00 Mass I would want to be able to rest on the way up and say some office. If I can do this (i.e. not driving myself) I think I will be quite OK for the 10 o'clock Mass at Yea. You might have a talk with Father O'Connor about it. I could say one Mass in the Convent at Midnight, and another right away in the Church or Vice versa. This would be something new for the people. If neither of these, then an early Mass 5.30 in the Convent, and then the 6 o'clock Mass in the Church.

I would be glad too Mother, if you would see the [Mercy] Sisters about Mass in the Convent on the Thursday. I will not be able to write myself. Would you also tell Frank Toohey, when he goes home that he can go to the College and stay there on Saturday night? Bro William [Molloy] wrote to tell me to get as many students as I can. We will give them a whole Dormitory to themselves. I will write to Father McHugh sometime soon.

I am getting on fairly well with the Mass. I will be put through it by Father O'Flynn some day soon. I say it every day in my room. I suppose you will get an account of Archbishop Kelly's Jubilee.

Poor Jim does not know yet whether he is to be ordained or not. He is waiting for the authorities to tell him something definite. I do hope he will go on this year. Please remember him in your prayers.

We are to go to Sydney on Wednesday to get our photos taken and to make any other arrangements necessary. I am expecting my soutane any day now. You asked me about money last time you wrote. At present I am not sure just what I need. I think £5 would be quite sufficient – this includes [my] fare home. There may be some things I have not thought of yet. I have money to pay for [the] soutane and cards.

I will send my books direct to Launceston to Virgil Morgan's place. I can get them when I want them. I will bring home ones that I may need in the meantime. Frank Bowman will take care of my trunk. I will write later about this.

I had a long and very nice letter from Mother Martina a couple of days ago. She said she will put Brian on the spiritual prayer list now as they had me on.

Well now dearest Mother, I must close this letter. I want your prayers very, very much. I am having a hard trial of my own and I want much help from God. I suppose the devil is wanting to frighten me and make me shirk before the priesthood. But by the Grace of God I am here and by the grace of that same good God I want to be a priest and a holy priest. Pray especially dear Mother for the grace of deep humility for me. If I have this all will be well. I want to be in earnest in serving our Divine Master and I hope that the Exercises of St Ignatius will help me to be so. I must look at the high ideals of the Saints and especially of Our Lord. May he indeed make me generous, and something at least of the Cure of Ars.[10]

Would you give me the address of Win Hanlon and Jim Kelly please?

Goodbye now dearest Mother and do not cease to ask the special graces I need for the priesthood. I will, of course, remember Your Special Intentions this month. With fondest love to Father, Marie and all at home. I remain

Your loving Son in Christ
Jack

P.S. I have not written to Chester but may drop him a few lines this week. I got Brian's letter. I was thinking that perhaps the Class want to give me a present. I would like the bound autobiography of St Therese. It would be a thing I would keep all my life and mean much more to me than a stole.[11] I do not like the idea of vestments as a gift. They are always at hand in each church. However I will see Brian when I am home. I often say a prayer for him.

---

10   St John Vianney was known as the Cure of Ars.
11   The stole is a liturgical vestment like a scarf that is placed around the neck and hangs down the front.

Letter 39 to Mother

The retreat will be a long spell in the desert;
I am hoping that it will be of great spiritual value to me.

In this two-page letter (18th November 1932) the anxiety of John is palpable. His mother knows him well. No doubt she feels his nervousness too as he is about to take on, at such a young age, the responsibility of being priest and pastor. John remains worried about the first sermons that he has to give over Christmas and the New Year.

Still at Manly seminary, he is to have a short retreat with the Irish Jesuit who came to speak to the students about the Observatory the previous month. Then some days later John will have a longer one, *a long spell in the desert,* and do the Spiritual Exercises of St Ignatius with Jesuit Father Jack Corcoran before going home to Victoria for his ordination to the priesthood.

Before leaving Manly John had really wanted to go to see the Dominican Sisters at Waratah where both Marie and Don had been to school. The Sisters knew the family well and had shown great support for John, but it seems that Father Nevin did not appreciate the significance of the visit for John. He is disappointed and states *there is quite a deal of unnecessary vetoing* by the powers that be.

He outlines the importance of the valedictory night, which was the opportunity to bid farewell to his friends. Significantly, he misses his friends Ted O'Bryan and Pat Carmine to whom he wished he could have a yarn. They had been ordained mid-year and had gone to serve in their respective dioceses.

* * *

A.M.D.G.
+

St Patrick's College,
Manly.
Friday 18th 1932

Dearest Mother,

We must have been both waiting for a letter. Marie told me you were writing when she wrote and so I thought I would wait till I got your letter. I intended writing tonight if I did not get one from you today. I was so pleased to get yours. Of course I am busy now but not as busy as I was during past weeks. Exams over yesterday – rather a formality. Class today and probably tomorrow. Pack up tomorrow and Monday. Retreat on Monday Evening –

Father O'Leary S.J. the director of Riverview Observatory is giving it. I am hoping it will be good.

I am trying to get through some reading etc. – also do a couple of sermons. I would like to say a few words on Christmas day. I am glad about the arrangement for Christmas day. I will not write a formal sermon for Yea. I do not feel quite up to it. One begins to feel the strain now. I had 2nd try on for Soutane today. I will send it home in trunk with other clothes – Frank Bowman will take care of trunk as far as Seymour. It will be at the Station on Dec 13th. I would like you to get it and take it home – take soutane and then I can get it before I go to Kilmore.

I will write again on Nov 28th or 29th. If you write I would like you to write so as to get letter here on Monday 28th or 29, Preferably 28th. Deaconate is to be given on Monday. Priesthood will not be till Wednesday. I will leave here on Tuesday Nov 29th – going to Loyola for Retreat 16 days. I will come off on Friday Morning. This will be a long spell in the "desert" but I am hoping that it will be of great spiritual value to me. Father Jack Corcoran S.J. said he would welcome me over and put me thro' the Exercises of St Ignatius. I want a lot of graces and much prayer during that time.

I will send a greater part of books direct to Launceston by Boat in care of Virgil Morgan. I have sent Ordination Cards to be printed and will send them home in trunk so that you can pick out any you like and also Marie can pick out a card for each of the [Dominican] Sisters at Waratah.

About going up there – Dr Nevin would not hear of it. One has to look at things from a supernatural point of view. This is especially so in a priest's life. I often feel that there is a great deal of unnecessary vetoing. Of course I should have liked very much to go to Waratah but I could not.

Jim Henry has been called to the priesthood thanks be to God. We had Valedictory Night (Farewell to 4 Years) last Wednesday. It is a night when each of the outgoing students gives a little parting message to his friends. I have had some grand friends here. I have had none like Pat [Carmine] and Ted [O'Bryan.] I often wish I could have a yarn with Pat. He was so sympathetic. We had such a close attachment. I know how you are looking forward to the great day dear Mother. May God give you great joy on that day.

Pray dear Mother [to] our dear Lord that he will keep me in His love, make me holy and lead me to the Sacred Altar.

Jack

Letter 40 to Marie

*Goodbye now, dearest sister,
and pray for your loving brother in Christ.*

John has just received a letter (November 1932) from Marie whose opinions he respects. He writes to his only sister, the eldest in the family, for her birthday on 1st December. She is not only very interested in him and much about his life that is leading to priesthood, she understands the process and has met many of the students and priests, and enjoys learning about the meaning of her faith.

* * *

A.M.D.G.
+

November 1932.

Dear Marie,
You will see the little news I have in the note I wrote to Mother. I was just leaving the College when Father O'Flynn ran out and gave me your letter. I must wish you every blessing of God on your Birthday. I will remember you at Mass and say the Office for you.

Four Manly priests [were] ordained today in Sydney, also one Sacred Heart Father: Slattery, Massey, Ford, Nelson. [In] Brisbane – Henry, Copely, Boland, Concannon. Brown; and Hayes at Rockhampton on 3rd. The College seemed very quiet after the Queenslanders left.

Well, dear Marie, I am just hurrying a few lines to you, as I want to have a sleep. I am feeling very tired after the Retreat, packing up and saying goodbye, etc. I know you will excuse me.

Also tell Mother that I forgot to write to Fr O'Connor and ask her if there is anything to fix up with him. I am sorry I forgot.

Goodbye now, dearest sister, and pray for

Your loving Brother in Christ,
Jack

Letter 41 to Mother

*It is just a fight now
between myself helped with God's grace
and my own pride urged by the evil spirits.*

In this two-page letter (20th November 1932) to his mother, John reveals his continuing spiritual struggle before his ordination. He has sought spiritual guidance from a Vincentian priest, Father Hall. He seems more peaceful, although *feeling just a little run down*. John receives great consolation following a letter from his mother, where she tells him that she has offered up her weary steps for him. He tells her of the spirituality of St Therese of Lisieux yet again.

In this letter he also calls his mother *Monica* as he compares her and himself to St Augustine and his mother, St Monica. John is familiar with *The Confessions of St Augustine* and uses a quote from *The Sixth Book*.

Before leaving St Patrick's, Manly, John will return to see Father Corcoran who will take him through the Spiritual Exercises of St Ignatius Loyola as a final preparation for his life as priest.

* * *

A.M.D.G.
J.C.D.W.
St Patrick's College,
[Manly.]
Sunday, 20th November 1932.

Dear Mother,
You will have noticed the abrupt ending of my last letter. I did not get time to finish just then. As I was going downstairs I remembered I had not mentioned receiving the money in the letter you wrote to me. I am sorry I

failed to let you know. I was so very hurried that I just wrote what came to my mind. I thank you very much for sending the money. I hope I will be able to make a return to you – at least in other coin. I will get my ticket [to Hobart] on Tuesday 27th [December]. I am getting two [photo] groups of the class. I have not yet got a 2nd Manly [photo].

I will send the Pyx on tomorrow. We finished class yesterday. I have my box in my room but will not pack until tomorrow. It will have to be securely nailed down etc. I may get a couple of hours on Tuesday to go to [the Redemptorists at] Pennant Hills to see Father Martin Brannigan and [Brother] Pat Deane.

I have not written to poor old Chester but really I don't get time. I have been taking things somewhat easy lately as I am feeling just a little run down. When you told me of your self, offering up the weary footsteps for me, I felt great consolation and deep gratitude. I thought of St. Therese who did the same for her Missionary "Brothers". Each step, which cost, she offered on their behalf. We are all members of God's household and the works of one can help the others. We are like the hands, eyes, ears, etc. of a body. Each has its part and if it does it for love of God, it contributes much to the welfare of the whole body. I often think of myself as a little cell in the hand. If I am going well, those about me are able to go well too and so the hand goes well and then the body. May Our Divine Lord reward you for all this and may He grant me the graces you ask on my behalf.

As I said in my last letter I want very special help. I went to Eastwood (Vincentians) on the day we went for the photos and saw Father Hall there. He helped me a great deal but it is just a fight now between myself helped with God's grace, and my own pride urged by the evil spirits. I am trying to get on quite evenly and steadily trusting in the good God and praying more.

Now dear mother, I know you will help me. I am looking forward to the Exercises at Loyola to help me. It will be a long time and I can pray quietly there. Father Corcoran is Novice Master there but he said he will help me with the Exercises.

Give my love to dear Marie. I will write to her next week after Diaconate – also to Father, Brian and Don. Mr Healy asks about Don when he comes over.

Now my dear Monica, just a few lines from St Augustine:

"My mother strong in piety followed me by land and sea and in all trials she was secure trusting in thee."[12] *He goes on telling how she was responsible for all that he knew of God and of Our Lord. So, too, dear Mother, I look to your loving prayers – not on your knees but from a sincere and loving heart.*

Pray for me,

Your Loving Son
Jack

---

12   From *The Confessions of St Augustine*

Letter 42 to Mother

I would prefer books to other things.
I would not care to have vestments or a chalice.

John writes this three-page letter to his mother (30th November 1932) while he is on retreat at the Jesuit Loyola College, Greenwich on the lower north shore of Sydney. He is twenty-two and a half and has left Manly after four years following at Springwood for two years before that – and he suddenly knows the aloneness of the next step of his life, *a lone man in the world as I got on the ferry yesterday.*

At the retreat he will rest and he hopes that *it will be a source of joy and a resettling of my mind* in readiness for his Ordination. In the meantime Dr J. Nevin has reported to the Archbishop of Hobart: *Mr Wallis is certainly a very sincere and pious young man and will, I believe, be a very zealous priest. For a while he will probably need prudent direction from an experienced pastor.*[13]

John, the lover of books and libraries, predictably would prefer books as gifts at Ordination time, not vestments or a chalice. Such things are already available in parishes, he explains.

* * *

---

13   MSS Archives, Hobart, Tasmania.

A.M.D.G.
+

"Loyola"
Greenwich.
Wednesday [30 November 1932]

Dearest Mother,

You see by the address that I am now a fledged bird from dear St Pat's [Manly.] I felt quite alone – a lone man in the world as I got on the ferry yesterday. However I know it is for Our Divine Lord's sake and that I will ever have true friends to whom I may turn. I will I hope and trust find my greatest friend in the good Mother God gave me. Yes Mother I was so glad to get your letter the other day when I came off retreat. I got Marie's yesterday as the car was going from the College.

We had a very solid retreat. Deaconate on Monday. I did not go out that day. The Queensland students left in the afternoon. I left on Tuesday about 11.30. I intended to get away earlier if I could but seemed to be continually detained. I went to Castle Hill and then by car to Pennant Hills. Saw Father Brannigan, Brothers Deane and Fiscalini. Charlie was in great form. He told me about his First Holy Communion.

I got here about 8 o'clock at night. Father Corcoran is very kind. Showed me my room – got a glass of hot milk and invited me to go and join in the Community prayers. He also made me do a bit of light reading before I went to bed – to settle [my] mind. I have spent today reading – just saying [the] Office and lying on the bed. I feel fairly knocked out. This is a grand chance for a quiet rest. I am free except for the three meal hours. There is a fairly large garden where I can walk etc. I may begin on Retreat this evening. I will try to take it very easily and have a Siesta each day.

Frank Bowman is taking [the] trunk to Seymour. Cards [are] in it. I would like you to pick the ones you like – also keep me two or three of St Monica and St. Augustine – also of the Sacred Heart. Marie can pick out as many as she wants for [Dominican] Sisters at Waratah. 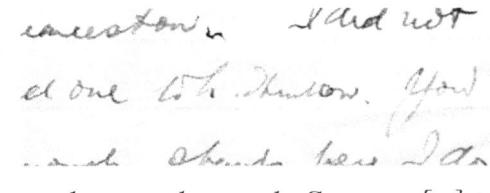 Their names are in a letter somewhere in the trunk. Soutane [is] in [the] trunk. Virgil Morgan will probably travel home with me and come to dinner with me. He is getting books sent to his place (Hotel) in Launceston.

I did not send those Invitations. I will send one to L. Hanlon. You might send one to J. Kelly. I have not enough stamps here. I don't want to bother Father Corcoran. I got ticket yesterday.

Re presents. I do not like to take them in a way because there is that feeling that one is out to get all he can. However I will try to see them as to be used for God's glory. I would prefer books to other things. I would not care to have vestments or a chalice. E.g. Works of J. Henry Newman, Works of St Teresa of Avila, <u>Life of St Vincent de Paul</u> by Bougard. A set of the "Westminster Version of the New Testament". These are just ideas. I could not say just what I might need. Of course I will need their prayers in plenty.

Well dear Mother, I will close this short note and try to get a rest again before tea. I know you will be praying for me and I am hoping that this retreat will be a source of joy to me, and a quiet resettling of my mind. I have been very tightly strained during the year and also as I said troubled with private worries which really played on my nerves. But I can rest here a good deal and so I hope I will be feeling fit when I go home. I will write to Father Pat [Carmine.]

Goodbye now dearest Mother, and may God reward you most abundantly now and hereafter for all you have done for me. Pray still for that great virtue of humility, of a personal love of Our divine Lord and His most holy Mother Mary.

Believe me I am ever your most loving Son in Christ Jesus.

Jack.

P.S. I got Deaconate on Monday.

HINTS OF THE MAN, PRIEST, PASTOR
Ordination 1932
Letters 31 – 42

Corrie van den Bosch

I first met John in 1959, when I joined the Missionary Sisters of Service. During my novitiate, John taught us theology, liturgy and spirituality and directed a number of our retreats. Over the years, he continued his mentoring, teaching and spiritual directing roles, especially during and after Vatican II. I reflect here on a few of the hopes and ideals expressed in these letters. Appearing as small seeds, they matured over the years of his priestly life.

Reflecting on the journey that had brought him to this point in his life, John appreciates the extraordinary role his mother has played. Her faith was the *womb* in which he developed. She laid its foundations, *despite his disinclinations*, as he writes. To her he confides his hopes, fears and doubts, confident of her understanding and her constant support.

Seminary studies opened up for John a way into the depth and richness of the mystery at the heart of the Gospel and the living tradition of the Church. Throughout his long life, John continued to read, study, pray and ponder on the mystery of Christ. During this final year in the seminary, he began to sign his letters *"in Christ"*. Over the years, this became *"In Christo"*, or *"in Xto"*. This was never a formality for him. He came to see everything in Christ, seeking to put on the mind and heart of Christ in his life and ministry.

What John intuitively saw in 1932 became the pattern of his life: *What I wanted was that deep interior fervour and ardour to help me express from the abundance of the heart what I said with my lips.* Years later, he would stress this in the formation of the Missionary Sisters of Service: *From the abundance of the heart the mouth speaks.*

While John appreciated the discipline of seminary life as a necessary support for his growth, he did not buckle down easily under some of its restrictions. In a rare comment (relating to permission refused to visit the Waratah school for the Deaf), he writes, *I often feel that there is a great deal of unnecessary vetoing.* Obedience was important to John, but love must always take priority: *Suprema lex caritas,* as he often said – *the supreme law is charity.* It guided his profound sense of *epikeia,* his freedom in discerning when and how to apply the law.

The *Spiritual Exercises of St Ignatius* provided a significant pattern in the development of John's spirituality. During the year of these letters he started to write *"A.M.D.G"* at the top of his letters, an Ignatian expression meaning, *For the greater glory of God,* an emerging focus in his life. Approaching ordination, he was besieged by anxieties and fears about his capacity to sustain his high ideals. He hoped the retreat based on the *Exercises* would help him in his battle *between myself helped with God's grace, and my own pride urged by the evil spirits.* In subsequent years, he was to give many retreats based on the *Exercises* to priests and religious.

According to the spirituality of the time, John learnt many devotional practices, and urged them onto his mother and sister. St Therese of Lisieux and her devotion to and prayer for priests had a particular appeal for him. Over the years he moved beyond the practice of many devotions to developing depth: *Not many devotions, but much devotion,* became a familiar saying in his spiritual conferences.

Throughout these letters, we see evidence of John's capacity for love and friendship. Here, I highlight particularly John's profound love for his family, his mother first of all, but also for his father, his sister and brothers. He expressed his love unreservedly in his letters.

It is amazing how these letters from his last year at Manly give so many hints of the man, the priest, the pastor, guide and friend John was to become in his priestly life. In the short space of this reflection, I highlight only a few of them. Years have gone by since John died – he continues to be a source of wisdom and inspiration for many.

Corrie van den Bosch *is a Missionary Sister of Service. When her Dutch migrant family settled in Tasmania, the Sisters visited her home in Tullendeena and enrolled the children in the Correspondence Course for religious instruction. Corrie joined the MSS in 1959 when the congregation was fifteen years old. During her novitiate years Father John Wallis was very involved in the formation program. For the rest of his life he remained for her a friend, mentor and guide. Passionate about life, people and creation, over the years the MSS mission took Corrie to five Australian States, serving in various pastoral and formation roles. She lives in Blackburn South, Victoria.*

PHOTOS I

1932 John's Ordination Day at Kilmore, Victoria. Seated- Abraham & Emma Wallis with John. Standing, from left- Charles, Chester, Donald, Marie and Brian Wallis

The Wallis Café at Seymour, run by Emma Wallis to raise money for the education of her family, including, John's seminary fees. Insets- Café promotional items, a match-box holder with 1932 calendar

Bro William Molloy SM. Born at Rosewater, South Australia, principal at Assumption College Kilmore when John was a student there 1924–1926. Photo: Marist Brothers Archives

John's letter to Bro William 30.6.1961 on the occasion of his diamond jubilee, not long before he died

Photo: Assumption College Kilmore, 1925.

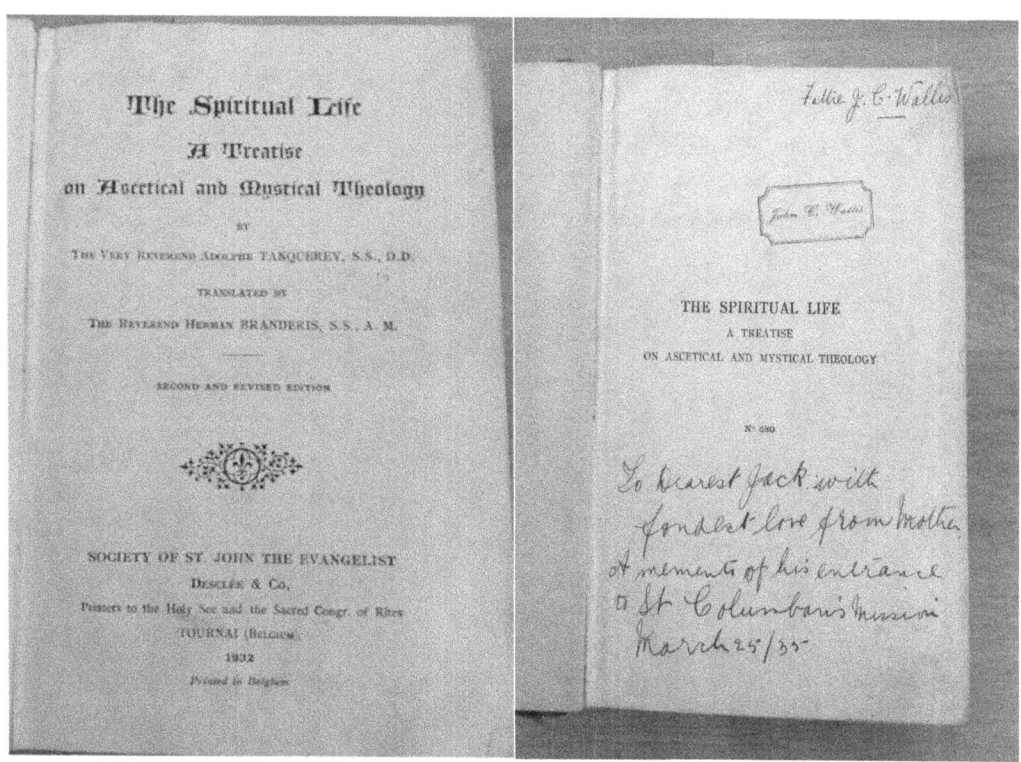

Throughout his life, John appreciated the critical importance of good reading to nourish his mind and spirituality. The gifts he treasured most were good books. The gifts from his mother (above) and his sister Marie (below) are still in his library, now part of the Archives of the Missionary Sisters of Service.

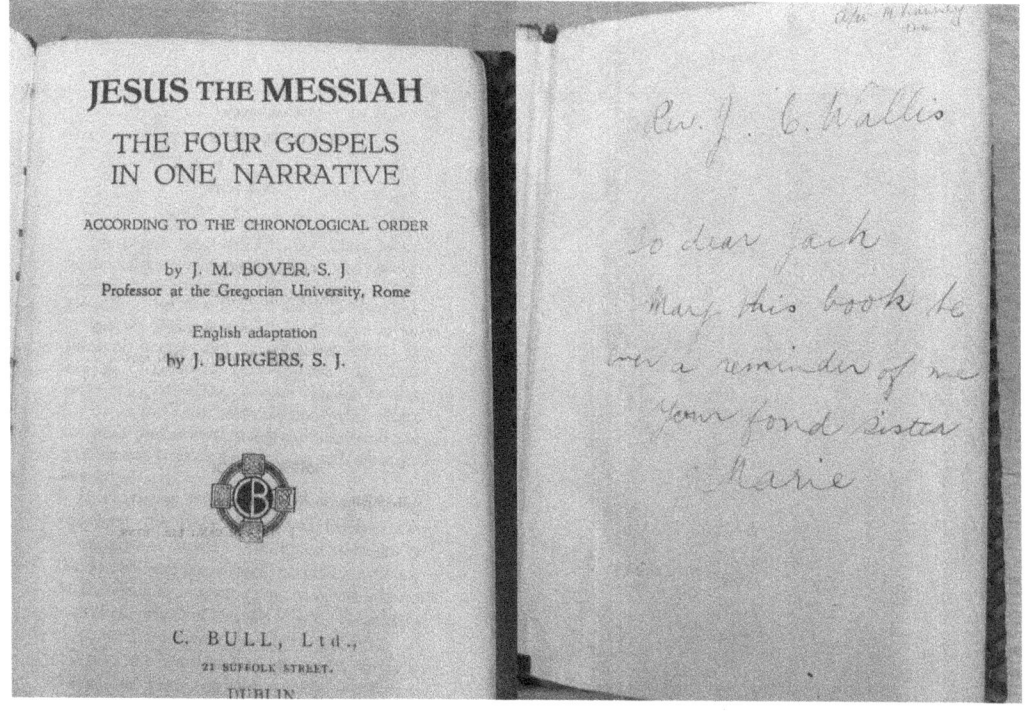

The Wallis Farm at Homewood

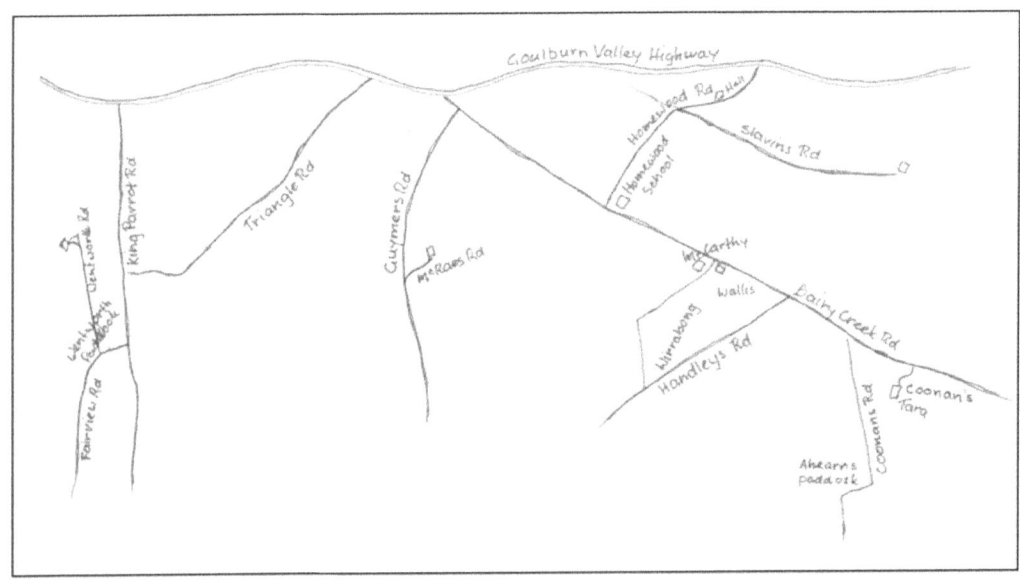

Mudmap of Homewood District

The newly ordained John Wallis, 1932

Fr John Wallis and Archbishop William Hayden 1932

Launceston & Hobart
Tasmania
1933
Letters 43 – 53

Introduction

In John's first year of his priesthood and pastoral work in Tasmania, a grand picture is gleaned of the conditions in Tasmania and John's impressions and experiences as a new priest. His first appointment is to the Deanery of the Church of Apostles, Launceston for ten weeks, before moving to the Bishop's House at St Mary's Cathedral, Hobart.

This chapter consists of eleven surviving letters from John during 1933, nine to his mother and two to his father, four of the letters were written in Launceston, six in Hobart and one letter was written on the boat from Bruny Island after his first visit there mid-year.

Letter 43 to Mother

There is a great deal of poverty here –
Another great trouble is to get the children to the Catholic schools
Or to get them some instruction.

This four-page letter from John at The Deanery in Launceston (14th February 1933), his first from Tasmania, explains to his mother why he has not written for three weeks since arriving there. His pastoral work has begun in Launceston. With a few sick calls at the hospital through the night, and visits to the sick through the day, as well as baptisms, funerals, prospective converts, preparing sermons, Masses, rosaries, Benediction and hearing *confessions*, he has been *kept very busy*. Being busy (and often overstretched) is a thread throughout his letters.

In preparing his sermons for Masses and Benediction, he cannot get his voice to be heard in the big church, the Church of Apostles. People not hearing him, his fellow priests try to assist. Focusing on *converts,* John explains God's mercy and love and helps them to have an understanding of the Catholic faith. He even sends written materials to one person because of commitments he cannot come to him regularly. John also worries about the children not getting the opportunity for instruction in the faith, especially those not in the Catholic school system, either because they live in isolated or rural areas or because they cannot afford to be there.

In Launceston, however, the Catholic education system was well-established with the Christian Brothers and the Presentation Sisters each conducting a college. In Hobart in the Cathedral parish, John also worked along side both congregations.

While Australia was still in the grip of the Great Depression during the 1930s, Prime Minister Joseph Aloysius Lyons, originally from Tasmania, was in office from 1932–1937. Tasmania, in particular, suffered from great poverty, and John could see it in his own street, Margaret Street, where the Church of the Apostles was situated. He also sees what the ongoing effects on a veteran are, fifteen years after the First World War (1914–1918).

On the lighter side, Archbishop Daniel Mannix has been in Tasmania and has given speeches that were written up in the Catholic papers. Additionally, both he and the local Archbishop Hayden had the opportunity of meeting Kurtz and Kalili – the American Olympic champions, Maiola Kalili, a swimmer, and Frank Kurtz, a diver, who competed in the 1932 Games in Los Angeles. They travelled through Tasmania in 1933 and were star attractions, competing in the Swimming Carnival Tasmanian Championships at Sandy Bay.

John hopes to get his car licence. He is led to believe he will go to Latrobe parish, north of Launceston, and be the assistant to Father James O'Connor. This does not happen.

* * *

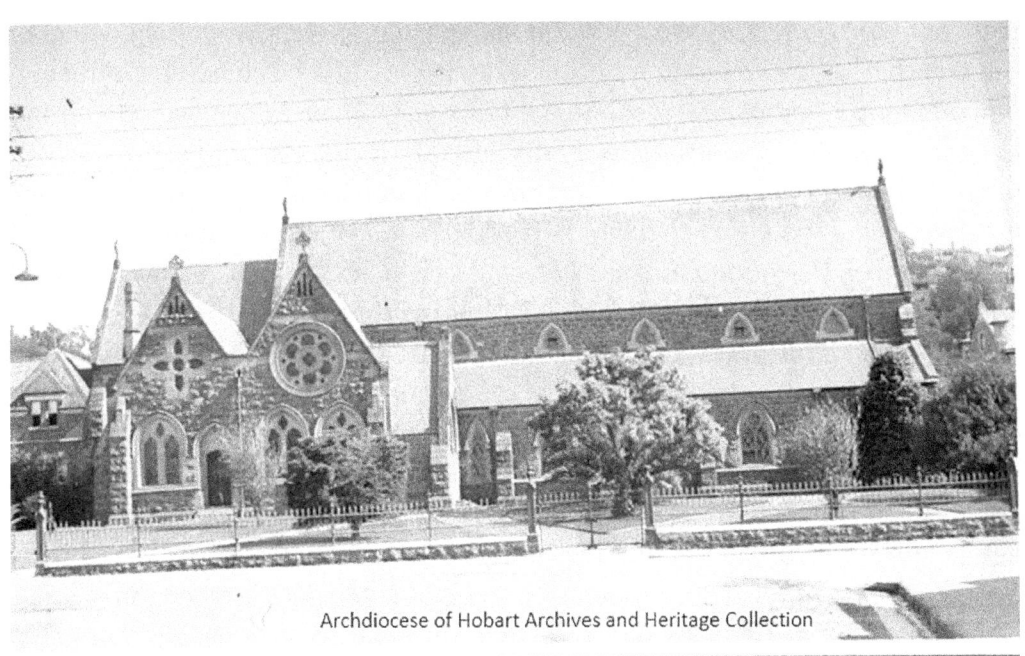

Top: The Church of the Apostles, Launceston 1940s
Left: Interior of the Church
Photos: Archdiocese of Hobart Archives and Heritage Collection

A.M.D.G.
+

The Deanery,
Launceston.
14.2.33

Dearest Mother,

No doubt you have been wondering why I have not written. Well I was the "Priest on duty" for last week and so I have been kept very busy. We take each week about. The man on duty has to attend all sick calls, all Baptisms, funerals, etc. I had one sick call a few days ago. Then I have been doing the hospital with 30 Catholics there. I have also some other sick to see as well as to hunt up people. I think there are a couple of prospective converts here too. I must get away today to see them. We got a call a few nights ago at 4 o'clock.

Yesterday I had two Masses here – 2 sermons and then sermon, Rosary and Benediction. The church here is very big and I find it hard to speak loud enough. Father Bill Ryan got at the back of the Church to listen. He said he did not catch it all. I have to practise a bit. The country churches are easier and I just talk to them.

I began my convert on the Catechism last Friday night. He cannot come regularly so I am going to write out instructions and send them to him. That will be work for this afternoon.

There is a great deal of poverty here, especially in Margaret Street just below the Church. I am getting to know the people there now. Another great trouble here is to get the children to the Catholic schools or get them some instruction. The [Presentation] Sisters here are very nice but I think I like the Mercy Sisters better. They visit the people and also go to the Hospital. The Hospital is fairly hard to do. I am getting good at hunting up patients now. All of them have been very easy to deal with – so far.

I met a man named Reg Smith who said you would know him – Bluey Smith used to drive a truck. He is a sad case of the aftermath of the war. I don't think he will do very well. He is an excellent Catholic. All the men at the Hospital are very good.

There was a very large crowd at Holy Communion for the 7am Mass – We were hearing Confessions on Saturday afternoon and again till nearly ten, and [with] 3 priests. The people here are very easy going – no hurry – half the congregations seem to be on the street when Mass begins.

I could not get over their "floats" for a while, these are carts with very low bodies about 2 feet off the ground. I will have to get a bike soon. The hospital is a nice step from here and one gets tired if there are three trips up in the day – up hill. Then there are the places to be visited etc. I am going to get my licence for a car too. Then I can take Father Ryan's or Father Scarfe's when I am to *go to the country. I would be glad if you would send me my Victorian licence – I have just found it so it will be alright. It may help to make it easier to get.*

Dean Hennessy is expected back tomorrow. He has been away on sick leave – Diabetes. I don't think he will do very well. I am looking forward to meeting him. I will also have a more definite idea of my work, i.e. my district and also whether I will be staying on here or going elsewhere. The weather here has been delightful. Just an ordinary warm day. The natives tell me it is "fearfully hot".

I suppose you saw the account of Dr Mannix's speeches here in the Advocate. Father Scarfe gets The Sun (Melbourne) also Advocate. He is very nice. We are getting on splendidly. I got a letter from Des O'Callaghan also Bernie Massey[14], junior curate at Manly.

I must write to Father next time. I would love you and he to come over here for a trip. Tell Brian that Kurtz showed the Launceston people how they swim in Tasmania. Dr Mannix and Dr Hayden had a few moments with both Kurtz and Kalili.

Well now dearest Mother it is just 12 o'clock and the post closes at one so I must close this note and get off to the Post Office. It is about 15 minutes walk. I have then to get back for dinner at one. I will be looking out for news from home. How is Mr Toohey? I have such a lot of letters to write. I don't know where to begin. I will have to let some of them slip. I have not got my room fixed up yet, nor books unpacked, as I am not quite sure what I am to do.

Goodbye now, dearest Mother, for the present and pray for your ever-loving Son in Christ.

Jack.

P.S. Tell Don Brother O'Shea[15] is in charge of St. Patrick's College here. There are a number of boys here. St Patrick's College, the Church Deanery, Presentation [Sisters'] convent and Sacred Heart College, also the Presentation [Sisters'] Novitiate and the Catholic Parish hall are all on the one block. I say Mass generally at the convent. I may have an aeroplane trip to Flinders Island. It is a way out on the North East Coast. The priests from here go there twice a year and they stay about a week. There are about 400 Catholics there. If I am here, then it will be my turn to go. They go by plane. Tuesday Morning – The boat did not go yesterday afternoon. I am just posting. There is likelihood of the ships coming tomorrow. I may be at Latrobe with Father James O'Connor. I will let you know any news.

---

14 Des O'Callaghan and Bernie Massey were students at Manly with John.
15 In 1923, Brother O'Shea taught Don at St Gabriel's School for Deaf Boys, Castle Hill.

Letter 44 to Father

Seeing my first dead person
brings home to one just what death is
and how when all is said and done
and when all our schemes and plans are made,
life is very short and very uncertain
leaving us with only this great and tremendous certainty
"I must die" and I must at all costs save my Soul.

In this three-page letter to his father (23rd February 1933), John tells more of his pastoral experiences in hilly Launceston. Father Scarfe has lent him his bike but on his way home from visiting he has *to wheel it up the hill.* John visits the gaol and learns about the reality of a death sentence. He has been visiting a woman, a Mrs Wilson with *consumption,* and was with her when she died, his first experience of seeing death. He has another funeral, at which to preside and then religious instructions to give. He has had Benediction and more sermons. There is no time for study. And he still has the problem of his voice not carrying in the Church.

John has also begun to make contacts and friends in Tasmania. The young Father Vincent Green, who attended John's ordination in Kilmore with Archbishop Hayden, became a life-long friend, being appointed as administrator at the Cathedral in Hobart. An *important* appointment, John writes. His classmate from Assumption College, Dr Ned Clarke, *a most painstaking doctor* at the local hospital, came to have a *yarn* with him at night. John is also glad that Father Scarfe gets a Melbourne newspaper, *The Herald Sun*, to read some Victorian news.

John and many Catholics listen to the Sydney-based and most popular Sunday night radio personality, Dr Leslie Audoen Rumble, a Missionary of the Sacred Heart priest and *a convert.* He comes to Tasmania and gives a lecture on the *wireless experience* and on the outside view of Catholics

John is conscious of the pastoral needs of those people who are more isolated and on the perimeter of the parish, but he has not yet had the opportunity to go to the out-lying areas. In the previous letter he mentions Flinders Island, which he says is the responsibility of the Launceston parish – that would be an out-lying place for him to go.

It seems that John will stay on in Launceston because of Dean Hennessy being ill and *sinking fast.* John is *feeling splendid* and eating well, likes the people and the weather, and after three weeks writes that he does not regret committing to this diocese.

The Deanery,
Launceston
Feb 23rd 38

Dearest Father,
I have been trying to get a few spare minutes to write home, but I seem to be all the time on the go. I have been out on sick calls for the last two nights as well as other trips in the morning. I had a trip up to the Gaol yesterday. There was a man brought in with a death sentence on him while I was there. This morning I have just a few minutes before I go off on some rounds. The Dean is back and in charge once more. He has diabetes and cannot [?] be able to stay here, he said himself he is sinking fast. I think I will be staying here now. he seemed to give me that idea a few days ago. I have been on "duty" all last week and also part of this. It is for the priest on duty to answer all sick calls, funerals, Baptisms etc. Father Searle lent me his bike. It is a big help in getting about. The only difficulty is that the hills here are so steep that I have often to wheel the bike up. I have been attending a Mrs Watson who died yesterday morning from consumption. She is the first dead person I have seen. It brings home to me just what death is and how when all is said and done and when all ourselves and plans are made life is very short and very uncertain leaving us with only the great and tremendous certainty "I must die" and I must at all costs, save my Soul.

A.M.D.G.
+

The Deanery,
Launceston.
Feb 23rd, 33

Dearest Father,

I have been trying to get a few spare minutes to write home, but I seem to be all the time on the go. I have been out on [sick] calls for the last two nights as well as other trips in the morning. I had a trip to the Gaol yesterday. There was a man brought in with a death sentence on him when I was there this morning. I have just a few minutes before I go off on some rounds.

The Dean (Hennessy) is back and in charge once more. He has diabetes and so is not likely to stay here. He said himself he is sinking fast. I think I will be staying here now. He seemed to give me that idea a few days ago. I have been "on duty" all last week and also part of this [week]. It is for the priest-on-duty to answer all sick calls, funerals, Baptisms etc.

Father Scarfe lent me his bike. It is a big help in getting about. The only difficulty is that the hills here are so steep that I have often to wheel the bike up.

On Sunday last I had to preach twice as well as give Benediction etc. It is a fairly large church and so it means a continual strain [for my voice] to be able to reach every part. I have been told that I was not heard down the back. I will be going to the country next Sunday doing Beaconsfield and Exeter.[16]

This afternoon there is a funeral then Instructions for a convert, two children to be instructed and then a couple of sermons to prepare with the chance of another Instruction after tea. I thought I would get a bit of study done but to date I have not got any done.

Dr Ned Clarke came down last night for a yarn. He is an old classmate from A.C.K. He has got the name of being a most painstaking doctor in the Hospital. There are about 30 Catholic patients at the General Hospital and a couple in a private Hospital.

Last night Dr Rumble M.S.C. who runs the Question Box on the Wireless station 2SM Sydney gave a lecture on the Wireless Experiences and the Outside Attitude to the Catholic Church. He is a convert himself. His father who was an agnostic (no religion – just indifferent) became a Catholic then his mother and sisters. He used to be a Dogma professor at the Sacred Heat Missionaries Monastery, Randwick, Sydney, but now devotes his whole time to instructions and lectures etc. He is leaving today for Sydney.

---

16   Beaconsfield and Exeter are towns along the western side of the Tamar River north of Launceston.

I have not seen much of the out-lying country yet. Launceston itself is very pretty especially if it is seen from one of the high hills about. The people are all very nice and the climate so far has been delightful.

I am feeling splendid just now, though a bit tired. Father Scarfe says I have a "great stroke" in the way of eating. We get two daily papers here but neither of them has much news – one from Hobart – one a local publication. Father Scarfe gets the "Sun" so I see a bit of Victorian news now and then. I met some people a few days ago who had relations in Kilmore.

Father Ryan is at present preparing for the St Patrick's night concert. He is very good as a conductor of singing etc. I am glad I have nothing to do in this line. I have been looking in The Advocate to see who is at Seymour in Father O'Connor's place. I have not seen any news yet. That young Father [Vincent] Green who was over with the Archbishop has been appointed Administrator at the Cathedral in Hobart. This is one of the most important offices in the Archdiocese.

How is Chester's leg? I have been wondering how he and all at home are getting on. It is three weeks today since I landed here. I am sure I will like it and do not in any way regret having taken on this diocese. I suppose Mother and Marie will see all that I have to say in this little note and I will try to write again when I get a few spare minutes.

I must go now on duty so I shall close this little note wishing you and all at home every choicest blessing and asking your kind prayers now and then for your dear Son in Christ,

Jack

Letter 45 to Mother

I asked, "What I should preach on?"
You answered, "On the mercy of God – tell them about the mercy of God".

This four-page letter to his mother (26th March 1933) was written the day after the feast of the Annunciation. John has had a few more weeks of pastoral experience. He makes new friends. With his visiting at the hospital, he is in touch with vulnerable humanity, people with all kinds of sickness, more *than I have ever seen before*. Expectations are high – he encourages and helps everyone but feels he does not have *the art of getting to their hearts*. A young man of missionary zeal, he tells the people they can be apostles in their daily lives in their homes. Census work, locating the Catholic people in the parish, is another aspect of his day on days when there are no other commitments.

John is pleased to meet an educated but lonely 79-year-old retired teacher, who is familiar with the 19th century poets, the American Henry Wadsworth Longfellow and the Englishman Alfred Lord Tennyson. He is someone of like mind, someone John can connect with at a literary and academic level, whatever about his faith commitment. *We had a great talk,* John writes.

After two months in Launceston and at the age of twenty-two, John gives classes to the young Presentation Sisters to assist with their theological education. He begins forming a closer association with religious in the diocese, later significantly appreciating the work of religious throughout Australia.

At the end of the letter, John writes that people are led by example rather than cold advice. He teaches children through storytelling, *I told them stories,* in his catechetical class at the schools. It is his approach in sermons including storytelling. For example, the story of the venerable Matt Talbot[17] who died in 1925, where Matt, from an Irish working class family in Dublin, was the second of twelve children, suffering from an addiction to alcohol, as did his father and other family members. In his vulnerability he remained faithful to God.

Prayer is important to John. He worries about the hypocrisy of his life, telling the people about prayer and neglecting his own prayer and meditation.

John finally visits the out-lying places – Lilydale and Karoola – travelling by a local train with which he is not impressed. He writes of the great rural people, the land and its beauty, as well as the farm produce, noting especially the apple orchards. Then he takes action. He arranges for the St Vincent de Paul Society to collect the apples that had fallen in a windstorm, and give them to the poor in his street. John also organises to send a box of apples to

---

17   https://aleteia.org/2017/09/14/he-was-a-drunk-and-now-hes-on-the-path-to-sainthood-meet-matt-talbot/

his family in Victoria. John wants members of his family to come to visit and see the places he writes about and to meet the people.

Signing off with *God bless and keep you, Mother Machree*, John could have been inspired by the American-Irish song and lyrics from 1910 stage show, Mother Machree, and the 1928 silent film about a poor Irish immigrant in America with Mother Machree characterised. Machree is the Anglicisation of the Irish *mo chroi*, an exclamation meaning *my heart*.[18]

* * *

---

[18] en.m.wikiedia.org

Letter 45

AMDG

The Deanery,
Launceston.
26.3.33

Dearest Mother,

It is some time since I wrote home. Of course you know how busy I am and that I am ever thinking of you where remembrance is best at the altar of God. I do hope you are all well. I often wonder how you are getting along.

Last week I was on duty here and so busy at the hospital. There were a number of operation cases there last week. You have no idea of all the kinds of sickness one sees in there. I have seen more in the past few weeks than I have ever seen before. I often feel I should do more to help those people to love God but I feel in many ways I have not the art of getting to their hearts. Still prayer can do a lot and I know your prayers are following. I was telling the people tonight during the Holy Hour that they can be apostles in their daily lives – in their homes by their prayer, offering up all they do to God generously for souls, for careless Catholics.

I went today to see an old man (79) who was once a school teacher and a good Catholic, who has not been to the Sacraments, Mass etc. for many years. He did not know who is the head of the Church here. We had a great talk. He said he felt his was a lonely life. He had quite a number of poems of Longfellow, Tennyson and others off by heart. I think he will be quite ready to tow the line now.

Today I recalled to the people at 11 o'clock Mass some words you spoke some years ago. I asked, "What I should preach on?" You answered, "On the mercy of God – tell them about the mercy of God". Then I told them the parable of the Prodigal Son also about St Augustine and Matt Talbot, how they sinned but rose, fought and won through, even to becoming great Saints of God.

During the week I went to the Schools for Catechism instructions. It takes a great deal of time to do about six classes at least each for about ¾ hour and I can say it is very tiring work. I try to tell them stories so as to get them interested. I find that these lessons help me also in preaching, the hardest of all the work. I have six to do. It takes hours to get up a sermon.

I have been going also to the [Presentation Sisters'] Novitiate to give an occasional talk to the Novices on the Catechism etc. trying to give them a clearer idea of the theology. There are two new Irish postulants here.[19] They are very broad. Their accent is delightful. Yesterday morning (Feast of Annunciation)

---

19   A number of young Irish girls came to Tasmania and joined either the Presentation Sisters or the Sisters of St Joseph.

there was a reception of Mary Smart to the white veil. She is now a novice. The Bishop came up. It was a very impressive ceremony.[20] There is a young school teacher here who is entering [the Presentations] at Easter. Another boy Frank Pollington is leaving for the Sacred Heart Monastery in Randwick – to be a lay Brother. There are two or three others here with ideas of the Religious state. Poor Virgil has had no news. I am afraid he will not be able to go on.

I suppose you saw about Dr Nevin being honoured. I wired congratulations to him and got a reply yesterday. He was grateful but was not sure I realised the vanity of a mere title.

Dean Hennessy is in Sydney. He went for treatment for Diabetes. There is a poor Sister here who has the same trouble – affecting her in her eyes so that she is quite blind – Sister Stanislaus. She is in bed most of the day. I go up now and then to have a chat to cheer her up. She is very holy and resigned to the will of God.

On Monday last [I] went to St Patrick's Concert. It was a tremendous success – the hall was packed and many people had to be turned away. There were items by leading artists, by the children of St Pat's College, Sacred Heart College (girls) and St Mary's School. The scene was that of Lourdes with Our Lady standing in the grotto. Then the other children were ranged in tiers on either side. The dresses – the scenery and the lighting effects were beautiful. There is to be a repetition on next Thursday night.

On Sunday last I said Mass at Karoola and Lilydale. I caught the train out on Saturday afternoon. It was my first ride in a Tasmanian train. I was not very impressed after seeing the New South Wales and Victorian trains. It was very slow, just 1 hour and 20 minutes for 17 miles. It pulled up at some ganger's home to drop something and then just crawled along.

---

20   Mary Smart did not continue on to profession with the Sisters.

I had a good walk to the Convent. In the evening I went to one of the McCarthy's places (Neil) (there are about 4 different ones here within a mile of each other). Neil drove me to Lilydale next day where there was a congregation of about 15 or less. At Karoola there were more. After dinner at the convent I went to see some of the people – had tea at McCarthy's and then gave Benediction. It was very cold there but the country is lovely. There is no town though the sisters have a school there and about 37 children. I was thinking of you and wishing you could see it. There were plenty of robins about and the morning was very like a morning in the Blue Mountains.

Karoola is one of the great apple centres. There were from 60 to 100 thousand cases sent off one place. There had been a very heavy wind-storm and they were lying everywhere on the ground. There are hundreds of cases of apples lying there – no good for the market – to be ploughed in as manure. I am going to see about getting some sent to you, and today St Vincent de Paul Society said they would help and get some for the poor about here. There is no doubt about Tasmania for apples. The trees are simply laden with great big fruit.

Did you see that Brother Allen has been transferred to Western Australia? He will be sorely missed at St Gabriel's.

After Easter I hope to be able to meet the account at Assumption College Kilmore.[21] *In this parish (the only one of this sort in Tasmania) we are not given a single penny till after Easter and after Christmas. So far I have had a few stipends but apart from this I have had no money of my own. Of course we get all keep here and that is very good. I may get a new bike after Easter as the one I have (Father Scarfe's) is heavy and also is not very safe.*

I will be off again on the census on Tuesday next. Tomorrow I want to try to have a day of recollection – a day to myself and God alone. This is one of the difficulties of one's work. We must be always ready to go to work and at times one gets careless about prayer about meditation and about being generous with our divine Master. When we read the lives of the Saints we see how mean we are, how cold and coward like. I often feel a hypocrite as I tell people to pray much, to strive hard and especially to "deny themselves for Lent". It is in the confessional that we notice this especially. There are so many good people who are living good lives despite the setbacks they meet. They love God and that is the essence of Sanctity.

I am getting to know a number of people now and have made a few friends. I want to write a few lines to some of the students at Manly, also Father Ted [O'Bryan] to whom I have not written since I was ordained.

---

21   It appears John needs to pay an account, probably for expenses at the time of his Ordination celebrations in Kilmore.

How is poor Auntie Jane and also Auntie May?[22] *I would like to hear about them and I will try to write. Really I seem always to be busy. I would like a letter from Brian. I would like him to come over here to see Tasmania. But that is for you and father first. Marie and Don may manage a trip too sometime.*

For the present I shall close this scattered note. Give my love to all – also to all friends – so many I did not know I had. Prayer can unite us and we will be together with Our Divine Lord and Blessed Lady.

God bless you and keep you, Mother Machree,

John

PS. *(top of page 1)*

I would like my books the sisters have – Life of Pius X, of Matt Talbot and of St Jane Frances de Chantal. I may get a few lines to them but you might kindly ask them some time. I would like them, as they are so useful in sermons etc. People are led more by example than cold advice.

---

22   Auntie May Lovelock

Letter 46 to Mother

*I do like the confessional
and would not mind staying there all day long –
to help to heal the wounds and bring the people nearer
to the Divine Master.*

In this six-page letter to John's mother (Easter Monday 17th April 1933), he writes hoping she has received the wire he sent – a telegram for Easter, because he had been too busy to write. Perhaps he also told her the news that he would soon re-locate to Hobart. Miss Traynor from Launceston is holidaying in Victoria and John arranges for her to meet his mother – on the mainland.

Why does John ask his mother if all was in order with their relationship? Was she hurt by something he had said or done, or was it because he had not written? The mystery remains.

John finds the task of preparing sermons or homilies the most difficult of his chores. After a *poor effort* for his sermon on Holy Thursday night, John realises his sermons have to be *up to standard* otherwise the people will not listen attentively. In one place at Easter he had seventy-two people for the sacrament of penance – *confession* – then more in other places too. In the confessional, he *would not mind staying there all day long*, because it is a *place of healing wounds* and encouraging people to come closer to God.

John was impatient with some people who worried about petty pious practices. He was more concerned that people *pray to be kind and to help the poor.* He is touched by the man who pawned his best boots to buy food for his children. He recognises the practical good that the Children of Mary do and asks his mother if she had clothing she could send across and if Marie would knit clothing, especially socks for the poor.

It is six years since he began his journey at the seminary in Springwood. He is overawed at the trust in him that people have and the deference that they show him at twenty-two, *so much a boy in many ways*. Again he feels a hypocrite, needing to attend to his own relationship with God. He is looking for a confidant, hoping that the young Father Vincent Green would be that person when he goes to Hobart. Understanding the need for supervision, he writes that *we are teaching people, guiding them and so on and yet we so often need guidance ourselves.*

* * *

AMDG

The Deanery,
Launceston.
Easter Monday 1933
[17th April 1933]

Dearest Mother,

I trust you got the wire I sent last week. I did intend to write but really I seemed to be so very busy for the Holy Week that I thought it best to send a wire. Today I have a little spare time so I am trying to get a few letters off. I hope you are all well as I am. I have been feeling splendid ever since I arrived.

It has not been nearly as cold as I had expected – in fact it has been quite warm and pleasant. We have had a few heavy frosts up to date and one or two spells of rain. It is rather inconvenient here when it rains as I have just the bike and so can't take umbrella (which by the way comes in very handy. I have got quite used to it now, as they are very common over here). I had intended getting a new bike after Easter but as I am being shifted to the Cathedral at Hobart this week, I will not need it – at least I don't think so. The Archbishop [Hayden] is coming up on Wednesday and Father Sherry will take me back on Thursday. This will save me the trouble of packing up etc. – I will just put all my books on the back seat.

I have not had much time to study. By the time I get a sermon prepared I seem to be run out of time. It takes a lot of preparation to speak to large congregations like we have here. I am expecting that it will be easier to speak in the Cathedral than here. I find the preaching the hardest part of the work still. People get the fidgets and show their uneasiness unless the sermon is right up to the standard. I had to preach for nearly ¾ hour on Holy Thursday night. I took the Mass as my subject but really though I did prepare for hours on end, I felt that it was a very poor effort especially on so grand a subject.

I do like the Confessional and would not mind staying there all day long. There one gets to know individual souls – to help to heal their wounds and bring them nearer to the Divine Master who loved them and died for them.

Holy Week was very busy. On Palm Sunday I helped the Dean [Hennessy] to give out the Palms, then Holy Communion. I had the nine and eleven o'clock Masses. We had confessions every night from Wednesday on. There was a High Mass on Thursday. The Dean celebrated the Mass. Father Ryan was Dean and I was subdeacon. In our spare time we went around to try to hunt up careless Catholics to get them along for Easter duty. It was wonderful to see the crowds that came. I believe there were tremendous crowds at Holy Communion yesterday.

I went to Karoola for 9.00am Mass – had 72 confessions to hear then 11.00am at Lilydale. I had dinner at Neil McCarthy's out there and then spent the afternoon with the Sisters talking to various ones about their worries etc. There are about 24 [Presentation] Sisters here and 13 Novices. The [Presentation] Novices gave me a nice Holy Card specially designed as a little reminder before I leave [the parish]. There are two sick Sisters here now, Sister Stanislaus who is blind and Sister Ignatius who is a cripple. She is Miss Traynor's sister. I suppose by the time you get this you will have made her acquaintance.

When I go to Hobart I will get *The Catholic Standard*[23] sent on to you each fortnight. You may find some items of interest in it. I will have Father [Vincent] Green as my new superior. He is Administrator of the Cathedral. They say he is fairly exacting but he is a very good and kind man. Father Lynch is the other priest there. Of course the Bishop is there too. I will be at the Bishop's House. Address will be simple, "Bishop's House," Hobart.

Mr Morgan told me he would send a case of apples on to you. I was talking to Virgil. He is still unsettled. There is another man going from here to be a lay brother at the Sacred Heart Fathers. There are also a couple of girls entering the convent. I am going to May Dutton's place for tea this evening. She is joining up here soon.

I had just got to know a lot of people and now I must leave them. Of course it is not for me to say what I like – I came here with that intention of being entirely at the beck and call of my superior and so it does not matter much where I am. There is always work to do and indeed too much. I received my first convert and baptised his three children on Saturday. One man whom I had been instructing had to go away so that I cannot receive him before I leave. I suppose Father Scarfe will do so.

Father Ryan's Mother and sister came in yesterday with Father John Ryan, his brother from Derby.[24] Mrs Ryan keeps house for him out there. I was talking to him for a few minutes last night before Devotions. The new choir gallery has been finished but they have not yet started on the organ. It should be very nice when it is quite finished.

I had a nice letter from Bro. William [Molloy] who said he sees you sometimes – also Marie. He was sick when he wrote. Father Martin Branagan and [Brother] Pat Deane wrote to me, also Father Patrick Kelly CSsR. His letter was most welcome and most beautifully written (the ideas not the handwriting!) They will be having big celebrations over there this week for the Centenary.[25] We get the *Advocate* here and so have a good idea of Melbourne news, also the *Sun*.

23　　The Tasmanian Catholic newspaper
24　　Derby is on the north-east coast of Tasmania
25　　The Redemptorists celebrated the bi-centenary of the Order in Ballarat, Victoria, April 1933.

I was so glad to get a letter from Brian. I was surprised when I looked at the end to see the name of the writer. I must write to him when I go to Hobart. How is Auntie Jane? I will write a note to her today also to Mrs Toohey and Frank. I am sure they will feel it very much but really it was a blessing for poor Mr Toohey and them too. He was a good man. I said Mass for him the day after I heard the news.

Dearest Mother, it was six years last Saturday since I left for the Seminary – six years since I landed. I seem to have gone through a lot in that time and still I seem to be so much a boy in many things. It is a strange feeling that one is looked up to and trusted by all the old and young. They all come to ask advice and guidance and you know how poor a reed they are leaning on. Were it not that I feel there must be special graces with the priesthood, I should be afraid that God uses poor instruments to do His own good work. One thing I do find the need of here is the assistance of another in my own worries. We are teaching people, guiding them and so on and yet we so often need guidance ourselves. I hope to be able to get more help in this way from Father [Vincent] Green.

The last 10 weeks have been one continual rush with scarcely a moment for my own personal sanctification. The only time I can call my own is what may be got by getting up early or going to the Church in the late evening and night. Sometimes it's half past ten before I am finished my business and then there is the office to say after that. Of course there are some "pious" people who are annoying at times with the continual requests for this and that blessing etc. Then there are others – the making of Saints who want really to love God and do His will not worrying so much about petty little devotions but by trying to live in the presence of God – to pray to be kind – to help the poor.

A good deal of good is done here by the Children of Mary[26] in making clothes etc. for poor children. I was just wondering if there were any old articles of clothing at home. Of course it is a long way to send here. Marie may be able to do a little knitting in the winter. I would be so glad of little socks – warm underclothing for children etc. One man I know here was out of work for 2 years and had to pawn his Sunday boots to buy food for his three little children. He was afraid to ask for assistance until I asked him how things were going. He has work this week. I do hope he can keep on going. The St Vincent de Paul men do a great deal of work here in a quiet silent way.

Well now dear Mother I must close this letter as I have a few more to write and just about 20 calls to make before evening. I would be so glad if you could write. I have been looking forward to a letter from you if only a note. I was wondering was there anything other than the fact that you are very busy (as

---

26

I hope you are at this time of the year) which kept you from writing. Is there anything I have done which hurt you or you felt I should not have done? You know there is no letter I look forward to so much as yours. I have many friends here, but as I said there is no deep intimate friend – noone so far to whom I could go like I would go to Father Pat [Carmine]. I miss him very much but it is not God's way. He wants me to stay at my post to work here and try to forego that pleasure in order to do my work where I find myself.

How is the idea of the Retreat going? You can let me know when you want to go and I will take all the costs. It will be some little return for all you have done for me.

Goodbye now dearest Mother. Give my fond love to Father, to Marie and the boys and also to friends in Yea and Seymour. I can't write to them but I do pray for all.

God bless you now and pray for
     Your loving son in Christ
          Jack.

Letter 47 to Mother

There and everywhere I can be praying
by sending up that little dart of love,
My God, I love you, I love you.

This three-page letter to his mother (1st May 1933) in time for her birthday is John's first letter from the Cathedral parish in Hobart, where the presbytery was known as the Archbishop's House. He says he has settled in his new home and situation and he likes the two priests, Father Lynch and Father Vincent Green. Snow has already graced the beautiful Mt Wellington behind the city of Hobart this year.

An *unfortunate occurrence* has taken place – the cathedral has been vandalised, with thieves attempting to take the sacred vessels, which were of considerable worth.

John's pastoral work continues. He prepares to conduct his first marriage. He has been saying Mass at Newtown, taking the tram[27] and walking half an hour home. There are additional responsibilities with the Sacred Heart Sodality, a devotional practice of meeting and prayer, and taking religious classes at the schools. While John still worries about his sermons, his friend Father Pat Carmine in western NSW has sent him some notes on *sermon writing* to help him.

He is also involved with a Deaf couple with children. The mother, Jane Riley, was at school with John's sister, Marie at Waratah and had known the three founding teachers in Catholic Deaf education in Australia, Dominican Sisters Gabrielle Hogan (from Cabra, Ireland) and Columba Dwyer (sister to the two Bishop Dwyers), and the lay Deaf teacher, Miss Marianne Hanney.

John has discovered one of the girls in the Children of Mary association, Mary Giani, is a distant relative, on his mother's maternal side of the family, originally the McAsey's. (It seems he did not ever follow up this family connection.) Thomas and Elizabeth McAsey and their five children from Ballyellen, County Carlow, Ireland settled in Yea, Victoria in 1853. One of the children, Maria, is John's *Grandma*.

John suggests his mother is a *Monica* and himself an *Augustine*, her son. He emphasises the importance of realising God's love and doing loving acts in life so that *our lives are made heavenly, even while on earth*.

* * *

---

27   The tram no longer exists in Hobart.

A.M.D.G.
+

> Archbishop's House,
> Hobart.
> May 1st 1933

Dearest Mother,

It is now late at night but I must get this letter off to get home somewhere about the time of your birthday on Thursday next. I have been writing up the Marriage Book[28] and preparing for my 1st on Wednesday evening – just a quiet private one. I am of course quite settled now in my new home. We had a most pleasant trip down. Father [Vincent] Green is very nice, as is Father Lynch. I am sure I will like being here very much. It is fairly cold but it is a nice kind of cold – nippy but no fogs. There was snow on the Mountain [Mt Wellington] a couple of times. All last week I used to go out to New Town for Mass – about half-hour walk. I used to get [the] tram out and sometimes I walked back.

Then I was out again for Confessions on Saturday – 2 Masses and Benediction on Sunday. I had to come home for the Children of Mary meeting, which has been entrusted to me. There is also the Sacred Heart Sodality – about 200 or more women and then I have the St Mary's College for Christian Doctrine as well as both Primary and Secondary Schools at St Virgil's College. I have to give about a half an hour instruction to the various classes. It takes a great deal of preparation to get ready for these instructions.

We had a most unfortunate occurrence here about a week ago when thieves

---

28   Entering the details into a Marriage Register.

blew open the Tabernacle and desecrated the sacred vessels and outraged the Blessed Sacrament. There is to be a day of Exposition[29] in the Churches here to make Reparation for the sacrilege. Archbishop Sheehan[30] was here for about a day. He is most genial and ready to talk etc. We thoroughly enjoyed his company. He told us about robberies in Sydney where thieves were after the Sacred Vessels. Their object here seemed to be to take the Monstrance, which is worth over £1000 made out of old jewellery, etc. We are all very careful now to put things away in a place of safety.

There are a number of entertainments etc. at which some of us must be present. I have to do my part in introducing people – thanking speakers, etc. I often wish to avoid it so as to get a little study done – and to get down to sermons. These are still my greatest worry. I got a little note from Father Pat [Carmine] on Sermon writing. It was very good and helped me much.

I got a letter from Miss Traynor. I was so glad she went up to see you. There is a lady here who is deaf and dumb married to a deaf and dumb man. Her name is Jane Riley and she went to Waratah [in] 1903. She knew Sister Gabriel Hogan and Mother Columba well. She seemed delighted that I could talk in sign. She has been using the two hands so much that she has almost forgotten the single hand code.[31] She said she would love Marie to come over to see her. Her two boys can speak and hear very well – the older is quite expert on his fingers.

I will write to Marie and Brian etc. when I get a chance. Tell Brian "it is pretty cold in the mornings over here". (He asked me what it was like.)

I met a girl yesterday who said she thought she was a distant relation of mine. Mary Giani. Her mother was a McAssey [McAsey.] She died 2 months ago. She said her mother remarked that I was some relation before she died. They got The Advocate account of [my] ordination. Mr Giani is a policeman here. Mary is one of the Children of Mary office bearers.

Well now dearest Mother it is getting near to eleven and I have more work to get done before I go to bed so I must close this note now. Of course I will offer Mass for you on Thursday – the first time I have been able to do this on your birthday. The feast of St Monica always appeals to me especially as it comes just before your day. I know you are still my Monica and I hope I will try to be your Augustine.

---

29   Exposition of the Blessed Sacrament is an old devotion in the Church. A sacred host from the tabernacle is placed in a monstrance for viewing, while people pray in adoration.
30   The Irish Coadjutor of Sydney, Archbishop Michael Sheehan was an energetic remarkable educator but resigned, returning to Ireland in 1937.
31   Two-hand sign refers to the fingerspelling of the alphabet used for Auslan, which is based on British Sign Language. The one-hand sign refers to the Australian-Irish Sign Language alphabet, which is based on the Irish Sign Language.

Dearest Mother I want many prayers because there is a lot of work to do and I always feel so helpless – so much of a bad workman. It is God's grace alone which saves souls and that is the fruit of prayer – especially your hidden unknown prayers – just like the hidden life of Our Blessed Lady whose month we are now entering upon. It is the love that we put into our lives which makes them worthwhile. "My little children if you want to become Saints love God very much." St Francis de Sales gives us this hint and means all. Little acts of the love of God – ejaculations rising up day-by-day and our lives are made heavenly even on earth. I find that even when I am most busy here, there and everywhere I can be praying by sending up that little dart of love. "My God I love you, I love you".

Be sure I will not forget you and also you have the prayers of the [Presentation] Sisters here. Pray for me now, your poor child trying to do his little bit in the vineyard of the Master.

Best, dearest wishes to you and all at home.

Love from

Your loving Son in Christ
Jack.

St Mary's Cathedral, Hobart 1940s.
Archdiocese Archives Hobart Collection.

Letter 48 to Mother

Unless one has the Love of God burning in his own heart he can do nothing to enkindle it in those of others.

The next pages of letters are in three segments and written to John's mother (possibly early July 1933). They may all be from the one letter. Now twenty-three years of age, John visits Bruny Island for the first time in late June 1933 and it seems that his letter was written while on the ferry on the return journey.

After visiting various people in Hobart, he tells the story of his time on Bruny Island, telling his mother about farming and the land in this part of Australia – very little dairying and just a few sheep for their own mutton. John is interested in everything – the berries, apples and how by planting peas and oats the soil is rejuvenated. He writes that the people *need a tremendous heart to clear the land*. He seems amused that in the slush and wet, *most of the people wear sea-boots* – rubber boots that come right up to their knees. His mother, skilled with horses riding side-saddle, will be interested that John will ride a horse next time to the lighthouse.

Being in such pastoral settings is in complete contrast to the previous years of his life living in the closed realm of the academic seminary, undertaking theological studies. There was no ordinary contact with people outside the seminary itself, no interaction about the every day concerns of people in the home or in the work place. His life has changed overnight.

It was on this visit to Bruny Island that he met Mrs Kit Hawkins with four little children. At Alonnah, in an isolated part of Tasmania, she had asked how her family could be educated in faith and she questioned if the church cared about them in the bush. As we see later, it was this encounter that impressed upon John that something needed to be done.

John, in his enthusiasm and zeal, together with an exaggerated sense of responsibility, thinks he must save everyone: *I try to think of the people I meet as should be redeemed with the Blood of our Divine Saviour. They must be saved.* He is often disillusioned: *Some extremely good souls – hidden saints, then cold godless people.* He obviously feels he could say such things to his mother, but to no-one else. He trusts that she understands him more than anyone, and continues to invite her to come and stay and have some time out for quiet. The Presentation Sisters have a room ready for her for as long as she needs.

*Archbishop's House,
Hobart.
[Possibly Early July 1933]*

... just 1 o'clock when I turned in. The chief industry is fruit growing. An orchard of 10 acres is reckoned a fair holding – would support a family of about 4 or 5. Dillon's have nearly 2 acres of strawberries. They looked beautiful big bushes. It is at present sowing time – they are cutting runners to sell. In normal times they get about 5 pence or 6 pence a lb. for them with somewhere about 3 tons to the acre. They [strawberries] are the best paying fruit at present. Raspberries are also a good proposition. They have a busy time for about 6 workers in December and January picking the berry fruits. It is rather hard work and all hands are out. Then they must keep loosening up the soil – keeping the weeds down. In the apple orchards they are pruning at present. This takes about a month for about 8 acres.

An ordinarily good yield for Apples is 1000 cases to the acre. They plant peas and oats between the trees – then plough it in. The soil is beautiful but it needs a lot of work. It must need a tremendous heart to set to work to clear the land. There are trees – logs – scrub everywhere. As a rule no one of the farmers has more than 20 or 30 acres cleared. There is very little dairying. Just a few sheep for their own mutton.

Most of the people wear sea-boots – long rubber ones coming to the knees. They are grand for the wet slushy ground. I did not go to the lighthouse this time. It is about 13 miles further south. I will go down next time on horseback. There is no track for a trap. I came back to Alonnah on Tuesday – spent the afternoon visiting various people. On Wednesday I got round some more and then rode...

To Mother

*Archbishop's House,
Hobart.
1933.*

... I have a radiator in my room but I do not care for it. I prefer to run round and warm up that way.

At present the boys from St. Virgil's are away – also the girls of St. Mary's. All the [Presentation] Sisters are going to Launceston this week for the election of new superiors. The Sisters are anxious that you would come down and stay with them. They told me there is a room for you and all you want as long as you wish. They are all very anxious to know about all at home. I showed them the photo you sent.

Well dearest Mother we are nearing our port now. I am going to send a case of oranges to the good folk who helped me while I was at Bruny.

One of these days – perhaps tomorrow I am going out to the Sacred Heart Fathers' place at Moonah for a day's retreat. When I am so busy mending the Spiritual needs of other people I sometimes neglect my own. It is very easy to become cold and wanting in fervour. Unless one has the Love of God burning in his own heart he can do nothing to enkindle it in those of others.

Dear Mother wherever I go I feel I have your dear prayers following me helping me. I try to think of the people I meet as should be redeemed with the Blood of our Divine Saviour. They must be saved. I must save them. Pray for me always.

I would like you to make a retreat some time. Just let me know if you can and I will meet all costs. They have a Retreat here in the [Presentation] Convent each year for Lay people – there are about 40 each year. It would be nice if you could be here when it is on. I would wish to write to you more. I seem to be always behind myself with my correspondence. I was so pleased to get Father's letter. He seems to have felt...

To Mother   **1933**

... She asked my advice. I can tell you I need a lot of God's guiding grace to help me in directing people like this. They ask the most difficult questions and always abide by the decision.

Well now dearest Mother I must close this note. God bless you and keep you, helping you day by day to grow more and more in His sweet love. As I saw men slaving on a little block on the Island – clearing out a patch in the bush; burning grubbing ploughing etc. I thought how vain it all was if in the end they had not known God nor loved Him. We meet some strange cases. Some extremely good souls – hidden saints – then cold godless people. It is hard to get through the crusty hearts of some but when you get through there is always a good reward.

Pray for me
Your loving Son in Christ

Jack

P.S. I will write to Marie too soon.

Letter 49 to Mother

There is a great deal of poverty here – people are out of work.

In this two-page letter to his mother (15th August 1933), John says he is remiss for not writing sooner. Miss Traynor, who visited John's mother's café at Seymour at Easter, has set up a shop in Hobart – moving from Launceston. His mother will be interested in how she is going. It is winter with snow on Mt Wellington.

There is a great deal of poverty in the region – the Great Depression still taking its toll at home and in Tasmania. John is still paying off ordination expenses to Brother William at Kilmore, then he will save money for Brian's educational fees to help out his parent's financial difficulties. The Parish Sewing Guild have bought 300 yards of material to make clothing for children.

After preparing a young blind man for first communion, John visits the Blind and Deaf Institute. He also tells of the sad news of the Deaf family in whom he has taken a special interest. Their little boy had died.

His first trip to Port Arthur to the Penal settlement has made an impression on John. He finishes the letter with another invitation to come and see Tasmania.

* * *

A.M.D.G.
+

Archbishop's House,
Hobart.
August 15th 1933

Dearest Mother,
I feel utterly ashamed of myself for not having written to you before. Really I have been extremely busy. At present I have just finished a long delayed batch of Instructions to the poor Children of Bruny Island. I had great difficulty getting them typed – then I have to add a good deal in hand writing. I have one lady to instruct by post – then some more here for Instruction.

We are very shorthanded here. Then there is a visiting priest here from the West Coast who seldom meets a brother priest. I have been playing billiards with him. It is a matter of charity. They wanted me to play cards tonight but I did not as I had to write home. Rene Dando was here today. Father Dando is at Queenstown on the west Coast.

It was a perfect day here. In fact we have had glorious weather all along. Two weeks of really cold weather – snow etc. On Thursday last I took 15 altar boys up the Mountain [Mt Wellington]. There was heavy snow all over the top. They had a great time snow fighting etc. They managed 5 dozen saveloys and 24 chops between them in 2 meals! It is a beautiful walk. I would love you to be able to go up.

During the holidays at St Virgil's, the Brothers went for a day to Port Arthur. Father Green and I went. We had lunch at his Mother's place – then tea on the way home. Port Arthur is a gruesome place. One would think the devil had tried to think out ways of punishing men to see the gaols, etc there. I may be able to describe the day's journey more at length next time I write.

We have a Sewing Guild here for the Poor. I have to see to it in its work. To date they have bought nearly 300 yds of material for boys' shirts, children's flannel jumpers etc. Then there is a depot for old clothes. There is a great deal of poverty here – people out of work.

Tell Marie that Mrs McGrath (Jane Riley that was – she is an old girl of Waratah) lost her little boy. I had to go to the funeral. I go to see her and talk to her. Her husband is also deaf and dumb. Not instructed. I intend to begin instructions for him this week. Last Sunday Chris Simpson – a blind boy aged 19 whom I have been instructing received his first communion. We had a high tea at the place where he boards on Sunday Night. I had a look at the Blind Deaf and Dumb Institute here. They seemed to be glad I came along and asked me to come again.

Miss Traynor has opened up here now. I hope she will do well. I sent £15 to Bro. William £3 yet to pay and then I will begin in advance for Brian – a little at a time.

Well now, dear Mother, it is nearly 11 o'clock. I have Office to say yet and up early tomorrow to go to Newtown. I will write as you asked to Auntie. May God bless you – also Our Blessed Lady on this her dear Feast day. Kind invitations from many here to you to stay with them – also offers of car drives when you come.

Your loving Son in Christ
John

PS. Marie's letter to hand – so pleased. Most interesting.

A.M.D.G.

ARCHBISHOP'S HOUSE
HOBART

August 14, 1933

Dearest Mother,

I feel utterly ashamed of myself for not having written to you before. Really I have been extremely busy. At present I have just finished a long delayed batch of Instructions to the poor Children of Bruny Island. I had great difficulty in getting them typed - then I have to add a good deal in hand writing. I have one lady to instruct the post - then some more here in Instruction. We are very Shorthanded here. Then there is a mission priest here from the West Coast who seldom meets a brother priest. I have been playing Billiards with him. I think matches of charity. They wanted me to play cards & you get that I did not. I had to write home. Father Dando was here today. Father Dando is out of Queenstown on the West Coast. He was a prefect day here. In fact we have had glorious weather all along. Two weeks ago it was cold weather, snow etc. On Thursday last I took 13 boys up the Mt. There was heaps of snow all over the top. They had a great time snow fighting etc. They managed 3 lbs Sandwiches and 24 Chops between them & 2 meals! It is a beautiful walk & I would love you to be able to go up. During the holidays weekends the Brothers went for a day to Port Esperance. Father Green & I went. We had lunch at his Mother's place & then tea on the way home. Port Esperance is a queer

Letter 50 to Mother

I love these poor people –
they are Our Lord's own and I only wish I could do more for them.

This is a three-page letter (30th August 1933) written to John's mother in response to a situation back home: Auntie Kate Neville is very ill. Having been reprimanded for not writing to her, John attempts to explain himself and he reminds his mother of the insistent call on him in his pastoral work, *we are really heavily worked here*. Also because he is in the Cathedral parish, it means work from a diocesan perspective as well. He apologises, *I ask you to bear with my remissness* and will write to Auntie Kate again. He later adds, *I will try for the love of God and the souls of my own near and dear ones, to be more attentive to my correspondence.*

He sees dire poverty. *Dear Mother, people have little idea of the poverty I see, day in day out, in the back streets of the city*. The boys at home, his brothers, have no idea of the poor children he sees. John's tasks are named as attending schools, a school retreat, preparing instructions, hearing Confessions, preaching, visiting and taking sick calls, and managing people who cannot pay their rent and are in need of food and clothing – and he is preparing to go to Bruny Island again.

The weather has been fine, although John was caught in a rain storm and afterwards kindly cared for by the maid, Kathleen. He also writes of the *kind and thoughtful* and a *splendid cook*, Mrs McKenna. (She is actually Miss McKenna, seen in later letters.)

John requests to tell Marie of the Riley family and that he is instructing Jane's husband, Mr McGrath. (John wrote of their little boy dying in his last letter.) Also he notes that Archbishop William Hayden speaks fondly of Waratah from when he was in Newcastle so has a great interest in ex-students from there and Deaf people generally.

* * *

Archbishop's House,
Hobart.
August 30, 1933

My dear Mother,

I was just this minute coming in to write home when I got Marie's letter about Auntie Kate. It seemed from it that she did not get my letter which I was sure would have reached her before the 29th of August (date of Marie's letter). I could not get it off as soon as I wished because we are really very heavily worked here. I often intend to write and then when I come in I find somebody wanting to be seen, or some work to do.

There are three of us here doing the greater part of Hobart between us – schools – confessions – preaching – visits and sick calls etc. Then too as we are at the Cathedral we have a great deal to do, which comes from the rest of the Archdiocese.

However I do not wish to excuse myself for not writing and I ask you to bear with my remissness in the matter. You may be well assured that the thought of you all is very seldom from my mind – I have been thinking of the chances of your coming over here and so on. For the last week or so I have been going to write to Auntie May – but something seems to creep up every time I come into my room. I am not quite sure as to her address. Would you please send it to me when you write? I will write to Auntie Jane today sometime. I have been away all the morning at New Town for the school children's confessions. I shall write again to Auntie Kate and of course remember her and as I have done in a very <u>special</u> way <u>each day</u> your intentions for her and Father.

Sometimes if I am careless in this matter you will remember, dear Mother, that here we see souls perishing on every side. There are a great number of cold and careless Catholics and perhaps at times the actual presence of these urges one to think more of them. As St Paul said "The Charity of God urges us on". But I will try for the love of God and the souls of my own near and dear ones to be more attentive to my correspondence.

It has been fairly fine here lately though I got a good soaking a couple of nights ago. I had gone to see some people whose sister I buried that afternoon. It was not raining when I left and it was pouring when I set out for home. At first I thought it would stop raining but it kept falling all the time. Kathleen (our maid) dried my coat and other clothes. We have a splendid housekeeper – Mrs McKenna. She had been looking after a big family for some time and is very kind and thoughtful as well as being a good cook.

I am at present preparing for another visit to Bruny Island. I hope to have a Euchre and Dance [night] there this time. The writing of Instructions for the children there takes a lot of time.

On Friday week we are to have the Consecration of the Children of Mary and a little social after it. Then there is the Sewing Guild every Tuesday night. They have made up about £14 worth of material (sheeting, flannel etc) to date besides repairing and collecting old clothing etc. Dear Mother, people have little idea of the poverty I see day in day out in the back streets of the city. I met a poor Scotch woman with 3 children without a friend – and in dire need of food and clothing, let alone the money to pay rental etc. I love these poor people – they are Our Lord's own and I only wish I could do more for them. Our boys at home have not any idea of the poor children here and their lot. Another family of six children (baby 15 months old) have been left by their mother.

I am also preparing to give a little retreat to the children of St Columba's School here. This will be my first attempt at anything in this line. It will need preparation and God's blessing too. The children will come for Mass – then Breakfast – 4 talks in the day for 2 days with a preliminary talk and then a final one on the morning of the 3rd day. Miss Traynor is fairly settled now in her new shop. Mrs Traynor has not been at all well.

Well now, dear Mother, I must go to do some business for the Archbishop as well as see some of my sick people. I shall try to write soon to Father, Don, Brian, Marie – all of whom have kindly written to me. Tell Marie I have begun to instruct Mr McGrath – the husband of Kate Riley[32] (that used to be) who is an ex-pupil of Waratah. The Archbishop often speaks of Waratah. He always took a keen interest in the work being done there.

Now dear Mother, I will close sending you my fondest love and begging you remember my poor work here.

I remain, Your loving Son in Christ

Jack

---

32   This is meant to be Jane Riley – not Kate.

Letter 51 to Father

*Every day I am brought into contact with real poverty –
people have no blankets on these cold winter's nights.*

In this letter of three pages (10th September 1933) John writes to his father, Abe, re *Auntie Kate* – she had always been very kind and thoughtful towards him. He also asks how things are after the floods in Victoria. The weather is warmer, he says, but the cold winds come up from the south – Antarctica.

John is concerned about the people on Bruny Island whose *whole outlook on life is one of intense hard work and nothing beyond* that. He has been preparing to send lessons in faith education to the children there. Demanding though it is, he knows it is worth it. People are responding *to a little care and attention*. In detail John outlines for his father his plan for the longer trip to Bruny Island, of approximately ten days, leaving on 14th September – North Bruny, to Barnes Bay, to Adventure Bay, to Allonah, to Lunnawanna, to the Cape Bruny lighthouse and back to Lunnawanna, to Alonnah and to Dennes Point. He will ride a bike, walk or his preferred option is to ride a horse, but he is not sure he will be able to get one. He indicates the remoteness and wildness explaining there is no road to the lighthouse – it is accessed following tracks for nine miles through the bush.

Shedding light on the Tasmanian reality, John tells of *real poverty* in Hobart in 1933. He is responsible for the section of the parish near the old gaol and the wharf. They have no blankets; they eat bread and dripping; their houses are musty and damp. Outside Hobart, the apple season has failed and farmers now hope for a better berry season.

John has been ordained for seven months. He writes, *Study, properly so called, is a thing I seldom or never can indulge in.*

* * *

AMDG

*Archbishops House,
Hobart.
Sunday Sept. 10, 1933*

Dear Father,

Just a hurried note to let you know how I am getting along – very busy. I am just thinking out plans for my next visit to Bruny Island – this time a longer trip. I shall go on Thursday – go to North Bruny and hunt up the Catholics there. I did not touch this part of the Island before. Then on Friday Mass in somebody's home – push on per bike through Barnes Bay – to Adventure Bay, to Alonnah – about 13 to 15 miles. Mass [is] at Alonnah on Saturday [and] again at 8.a.m. on Sunday, then [I go] to Lunnawanna for 10.30 [am Mass].

In the afternoon I will set out for Cape Bruny Lighthouse about 9 miles distance. There is no road so I shall have to ride or walk. I may not be able to get a horse. I shall say Mass at the Lighthouse and then back at Lunnawanna which I leave on Tuesday about noon. Then I may say Mass again at Alonnah and then on the Dennes' Point of North Bruny – Boat home Thursday morning. The country as I told you is quite wild – not as thickly settled as Homewood and like the country at Toolangi[33] – Mother will understand this.

I have been trying to instruct the Children by Correspondence. It entails a good deal of work but it is worth it. These poor children seem to have little or no idea of God who created them, and who with that knowing Him, loving Him and serving Him here below, they see and enjoy Him forever in heaven. Their whole outlook on life is one of intense hard work with nothing beyond. But they are responsive – a real joy and a reward for a little care and attention.

It is rather warm here though now and then we get a cold shower from the south. There is really much need of rain. The poor apple growers have had a bad time this year – in fact they have failed in places to pay expenses. It is hoped that the small fruit Strawberries and Raspberries will be better. I saw that wool has improved – something to be really thankful for! I also saw about the floods and have been anxious to know how you got on.

The St Virgil's boys won the Premiership of the Island on Friday. They beat Grammar School from Launceston. The standard of football here is not very high. I suppose you have seen the name of Billy Barwick[34] in recent athletic roles. Billy is an old St Virgil's boy – and extra good Catholic lad and one of the most unassuming men one could wish to meet. He is really a fine type of man.

We are having a Mission towards the end of the year and I am trying to get round the whole of my district before it comes off, so as to know just whom to draw along – great fun I must say.

Every day I am brought into contact with real poverty – people with no blankets – with one or two, then one to cover them in these cold winter's nights. Other places where they have only bread and dripping with black tea for their food. It is really distressing. There are a great number of old houses [that are] musty, damp and in disrepair especially in the lower part of the city, that is, near the gaol and the Wharf – in my section.

---

33   Toolangi is south of Yea in the Great Dividing Range.
34   E.W. (Billy) Barwick, an ex-student of St Virgil's, was a Tasmanian Olympic runner in the 1930s.

His Grace is away at present doing a tour of Diocese for Confirmation. He is going to West Australia for the Consecration of the new Coadjutor Bishop of Perth.[35]

I must drop a line to Marie also. I seem to be always so busy. This coming Month will be particularly busy. Study, properly so called is a thing I seldom or never can indulge in. I must close this letter now sending you again my priestly blessing, begging God to make [it] a rich and full one. Do you please remember me from time to time by a little prayer.

With fondest love from Your Loving son
John

P.S. How is Auntie Kate? Mother told me she is very sick. I often think of them. She was always kind and thoughtful towards me.

---

[35] John Archbishop Hayden attended the ceremonies for the new Coadjutor Archbishop of Perth, who was an Irishman, Dr Redmond Prendiville, and who succeeded the then Archbishop there in 1935.

Letter 52 to Mother

As I arrive home I feel the need of a few hours for quiet prayer to bring myself back into the presence of God.

This is a most informative 10-page letter (22nd September 1933) from the twenty-three year old John to his Mother on his return trip from Bruny Island on the *S.S. Mangana*, a Port Huon fruit boat. The weather is *fearfully cold* with south winds and snow on nearby ranges. It was his second trip and he now refers to Bruny Island as his *little Island mission*. He longs for his mother to meet the country people, to share in his experience and to see the wild bush that reminded him of home.

Describing the plethora of birdlife, the flora and the landscape on Bruny Island, John outlines his week's journey. Through rough terrain, wet moorlands, on beaches and in thick scrubby bush, he walked, rode a horse which nearly bogged, and rode a bike, which he wheeled for four miles through virgin bush. Altogether he worked out he had done 160 miles on an island that is 40 miles from top to bottom. He visited many people and families, a number of people entrusting their precious personal stories to him:

- Thursday to Dennes Point, the northern end of Bruny Island
- Friday Mass and visiting
- Saturday to South Bruny Island to Adventure Bay, then Alonnah
- Sunday after Mass to Lunnawanna
- Monday visiting
- Tuesday Cape Bruny Island lighthouse
- Wednesday returned to Allonah
- Thursday visiting
- Friday home to Hobart

Furthermore, John writes of the views from various points and explains in detail the Cape Bruny Island lighthouse itself, the families there and how they lived. A priest had never previously visited the lighthouse. Other lighthouses in southern Tasmania are remote too, he explains.

The return trip was long because the boat calls in at every jetty on the Channel for goods, fruit and carbide, the latter presumably used for lamps. He finishes the letter when he returns to Hobart. While he has correspondence lessons waiting for him to attend to and an article to write about the Deaf schools at Waratah and Castle Hill, he says he needs quiet reflection to be more present to God and to people. He has in fact been so very present to the beauty of his extraordinary experience on Bruny Island, both to the land and the people. Perhaps he needed to process the impact of the experience on him.

Letter 52

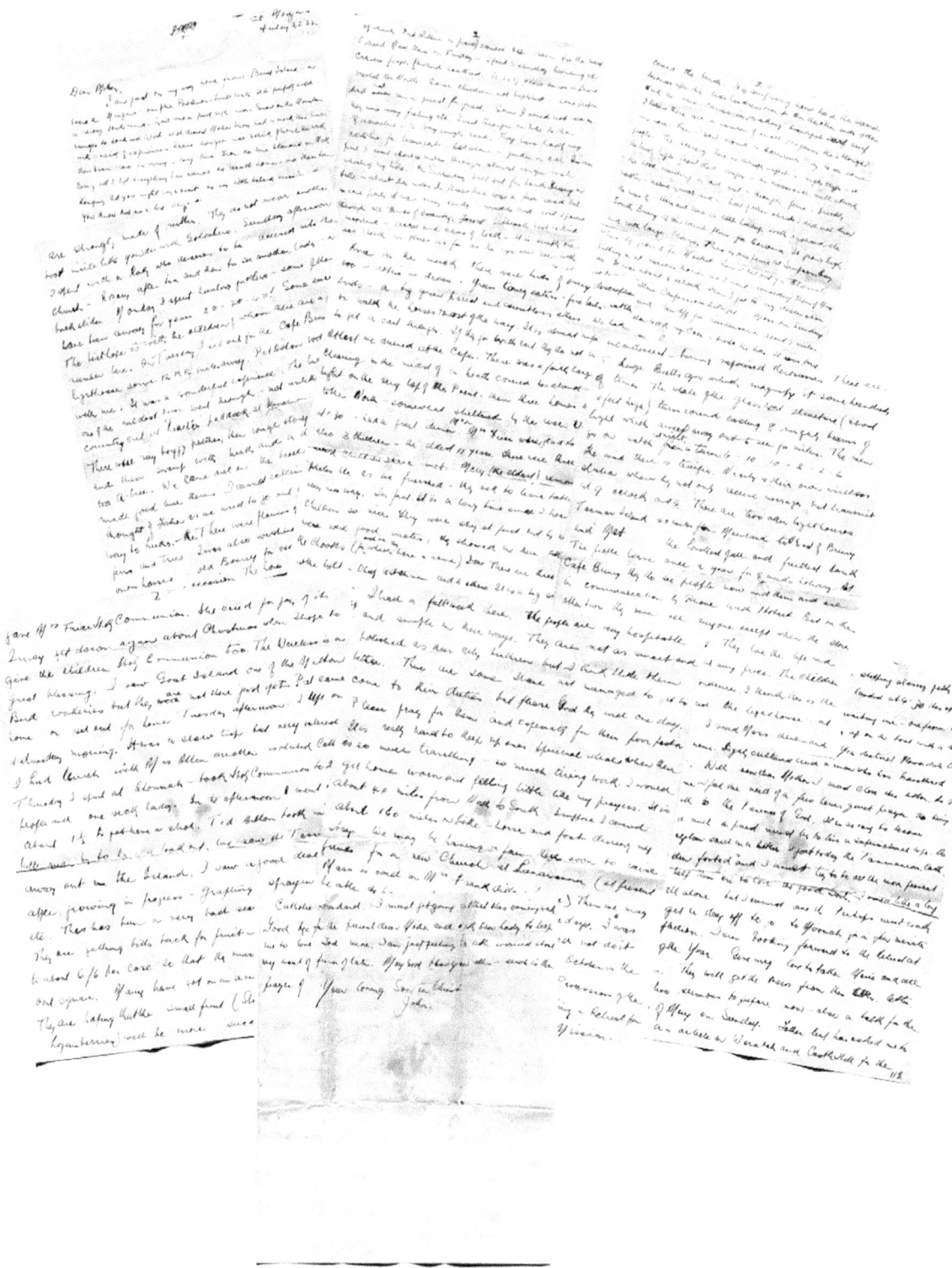

Letter of John Wallis written to his Mother on Friday, 22 September 1933

A.M.D.G.

+

SS Mangana.
Friday 22, 33
[22nd September 1933]

Dear Mother,

I am just on my way home from Bruny Island – on board the Mangana – one of the Port Huon fruit boats. It is fearfully cold – a strong south wind – hail and a fairly high sea. Snow on the Mountain ranges to south and west.

Well dearest Mother I have had a week this time with a variety of experience. I have thought more I think of home this week than I have done for many a long time. From the time I landed on North Bruny till I left everything has seemed to recall home – and I have been longing that you might pay a visit to my little Island mission. For you know that as a lad I had thought of the Foreign Missions. Well my work here is something in the nature of a little Mission. I shall try to give you some account of the trip.

I set out on Thursday – case full of books, prayer books, Messengers etc., Rosaries, Mass Kit etc. I took a little over an hour to reach Dennes Point – the northernmost part of the Island. My case was taken about 4 miles along – I followed on a bike. I stayed with a Mrs. Bottomley. The house was away back in the bush – on a hill overlooking the sea – Storm Bay, Barnes Bay and Bull Bay. It was a glorious sight to see the sun rising out of the sea. Tasman Peninsula (of which Port Arthur is part) could be seen to the east.

I said Mass there on Friday – spent Saturday hunting up Catholic people few and scattered. It is 9 years since a priest visited the North. Some children not baptised – some people had not seen a priest for years. Some I could not see as they were away fishing etc. I went through on bike to the Quarantine – a very rough road. They have hardly any carts here for transport, let alone a jinker or car. In one part I went about 4 miles through almost virgin bush wheeling my bike. On Saturday I set out for South Bruny on bike – about 24 miles. In places there was a fair road but in some parts it was very sandy – muddy and wet. I passed through all kinds of country. Forest – sheok bush – a kind of moorland – acres and acres of heath – it is simply one mass of heath in places as far as the eye can see – with water underfoot and a kind of moorgrass everywhere. I had to walk through the sandy places.

At last the road led onto the Neck – a strip of land about 100 to 200 yds. wide 4 miles long connecting North and South Bruny. There is a good beach and I rode along that just on the very verge of the water, at times running through the water. The tide was rising but I got along just a bit before it covered the beach. It is surprising how hard the sand becomes after the tide has been over it. On the other side of the Neck the ocean comes in, making beautiful surf. I believe there are a number of small penguins there though I saw none.

I went around to Adventure Bay to see some people. The scenery there is simply superb – high cliffs – at the back high forest clad ranges – an occasional mill at work – the road winding in and out – through ferns – prickly wattle – native Laurel and a host of other shrubs I did not know the name of. Here and there a little holding with orchard etc. South Bruny is an ideal place for Boronia. It grows high and with large blooms. There is one place at Simpsons Bay where they grow it for Market.

Then I set out for Alonnah pulling in at various homes as I went reminding them of Mass etc. It was about 6 o'clock when I got to my destination at Mrs Ted Dillon's. Confessions that night – Mass on Sunday at Alonnah and then off for Lunnawanna about 7 miles. Terence Dillon took my case – I rode the bike. It was fairly wet on the way. As I said once before, they have plenty of rain – not heavy but continual. Quite a lot wear sea-boots or gum boots – they come right up to the knee are strongly made of rubber. They do not wear another boot inside like you do with Goloshes.

Sunday afternoon I spent with a lady who desires to be received into the Church – Rosary after tea and then to see another lady. Monday I spent hunting for others! Some success. The best hope is with the children of whom there are a good number here.

On Tuesday I set out for Cape Bruny lighthouse some 12 or 14 miles away. Pat Dillon rode there with me. It was a wonderful experience. The track was one of the wildest I ever went through – not unlike the country out of Leach's paddock at Junction[36] – only rougher. There were very boggy patches, then rough stony strips – forest and then swamp with heath and a kind of swamp ti-tree.

We came out on the beach three times and made good time there. I cannot explain all I saw. I thought of Father as we used to go out over that swamp on the way to Leach's. There were flowers of all descriptions ferns and trees. I was also wishing I had one of our own horses – old Bonny for example. I nearly got bogged one occasion. The horse got down below her knees in the muck. There were birds of every description too – robins in droves – green honey-eaters – fire tails, wattle birds, a big green parrot and countless others. We had to walk the horses most of the way. It is almost impossible to get a cart through. If they go with cart they do not ride in it.

At last we arrived at the Cape. There was a fairly large clearing in the midst of a heath covered headland – the Light on the very top of the Point – then three homes down to the North – somewhat sheltered by the rise. We

---

36 Near Yea in Victoria

arrived at 1.30 – had a great dinner. Mr & Mrs Friar were glad to see us, also 3 children – the eldest 11 years. These were three of the nicest children I have ever met. Mary (the eldest) removed the plates etc. as we finished – they asked to leave later in a very nice way. In fact it is a long time since I heard children so nice. They were shy at first but by next day were good mates, they showed me their little garden [and] the chooks (for which each one they have a name).

There are three Families at the Light – Chief Watchman and two others. It is a big stone construction – [the] walls 6 feet through – no rooms inside but a big spiral staircase going up. I saw the Light itself incandescent – burning vaporised kerosene. There are eight huge Bull's eyes, which magnify it some hundreds of times. The whole of the glass structure (about 10 feet high) turns round casting eight mighty beams of light, which sweep away out to sea for miles. The men go on watch at night in turn 6 – 10; 10 – 2; 2 – 6.

The wind there is terrific. Nearby is their own wireless station where they not only receive messages but transmit at 9 o'clock and 4 o'clock. There are two other Lighthouses – Tasman Island, 40 miles from the Mainland to North East of Bruny and Maatsuyker, the loneliest of all and furthest South. The people leave once a year for five weeks holiday. At Cape Bruny they do see people now and then and are in communication by phone with Hobart. But on the other two, they never see anyone except when the store boat comes in with provisions.

They love the life and would not be in the city for any price. The children receive schooling by correspondence. I think this is the first time a priest has visited the lighthouse – at least in his official capacity. I said Mass there and gave Mrs Friar Holy Communion. She cried for joy of it. I may get down again about Christmas when I hope to give the children Holy Communion too. The Wireless is a great blessing.

I saw Goat Island, one of the Mutton Bird rookeries, but they are not there just yet. Pat [Dillon] came home or set out for home Tuesday afternoon. I left on Wednesday morning. It was a slow trip but very interesting. I had lunch with Mrs Allen another educated Catholic. Thursday I spent at Alonnah – two Holy communions to two old people and one sick lady. In the afternoon I went out for about 1½ (hours) to have a shot. Ted Dillon took me up to the hill nearby to have a look out. We saw the Tasman Light away out in the Island.

I saw a good deal of the apple growing in progress – grafting, spraying – ploughing etc. This has been a very bad season for the growers. They are getting bills back for fruit. The expenses amounted to about 6/6 per case so that they must get that to come out square. Many have got on an average about 4/-. They are hoping that the small fruit (Strawberries, Raspberries, Loganberries) will be more successful.

I had a full week there. The people are very hospitable. I like them. Please pray for them and especially for their poor pastor. It is really hard to keep up one's Spiritual ideals when there is so much travelling – so much tiring work. I would get home worn out feeling little like my prayers. It is about 40 miles from north to South. I suppose I covered about 160 miles on bike, horse and foot during my stay.

We may be having a fair there soon to raise funds for a new church at Lunawanna (at present Mass is said in Mrs Frank Dillon's house).[37] *Then we may be able to have a Mission there for 3 or 4 days.*

I was due back in Hobart on Wednesday but I could not do it conveniently. We have a busy time ahead. October is the Month of the Rosary, then the 40 hours' [adoration], the Procession of the Blessed Sacrament on the Feast of Christ the King, a Retreat for the children and the preparations for the Mission.

<u>At home.</u> It was a very slow trip – stopping at every jetty on the Channel for goods – fruit, Carbide etc. We landed at 4.30 this afternoon. I had a little package of letters awaiting me – one from Bro. William which was most welcome. I came up on the boat with a man who has a house at Toolangi. [He] knows Yea district, Flowerdale etc. McKay by name. Highly cultured and a man who has travelled extensively.

Well now, dear Mother, I must close this letter. As I arrive home I feel the need of a few hours quiet prayer to bring myself back to the Presence of God. It is so easy to become dissipated and a priest must try to live a supernatural life... I must try to be more present to the Tasmanian people so as to help them on to love the good God. I would like a long Retreat, all alone but I cannot have it. Perhaps next week I shall get a day off to go to Moonah [Missionaries of the Sacred Heart] for a few minutes quiet reflection. I am looking forward to the Retreat at the end of the year.

Give my love to Father, Marie and all at home. They will get the news from this letter. I have two sermons to prepare now – also a talk for the Children of Mary on Sunday. Father Kent has asked me to write an article on Waratah and Castle Hill for The Catholic Standard. I must get going at that this coming week.

Goodbye for the present dear Mother and ask Our Lady to help me love God more. I am just feeling a little worried about my want of fervour of late.

May God bless you all – such is the prayer of
Your loving Son in Christ,

John

---

37   Mrs Amy Dillon.

Letter 53 to Mother

*I feel so weak and so much a boy still.
It surprises me at times that people trust me.*

This seven-page letter to John's mother (11th November 1933) is written on the back and front of stationery as are many of the letters. It is almost twelve months since John's ordination. While he writes that he has learnt much and that he is supremely happy, he pours out anguish, *Oh dear Mother ... people trust me with so much reverence and they seek my advice as if I were an old and experienced man.* The responsibility is great.

In the meantime he writes of his tiredness and weariness, the seeming chaos in his room, instructions to give, the all-absorbing mission, visiting all in the district and *finding backsliders*.[38] He also has concerts to attend – the most trying of all the priest duties. In all this *his mind lacks taste for deep thinking.* Also missing his hours of study and reading and still longing for space and time, for solitude, peace and quiet, he writes, *of course my special attention must be to the sick and poor,* and *despite a hundred and one things that grate on human nature.* At the seminary, *one had no anxieties, no bustling here and there.* He admits to being *irritable* and speaking *sharply to good people whom I should treat kindly and tenderly* and says he is *needy and poor in his spiritual life* and begs her prayers.

Finally, he invites his mother and father to come and see where he lives and works; then he adds a goodnight with all his heart *a priestly blessing* and he adds, *as evening is closing in, I am going for a quiet walk in the garden to think of you all and to pray for you all.*

* * *

[*11th November 1933*]

Dearest Mother,

At long last I sit down to pen the letter I have been promising. I am tired and weary after a strenuous fortnight for the Mission. Somehow I seem to be at a loose end today. There are so many things I must do and yet I cannot decide just where to begin. Letters to answer, bills galore – instructions to prepare – concerts to attend (one of the most trying of a priest's duties) – people to instruct. My room is at present like a Chinese shop – books, papers etc. everywhere. I am going to have a big clean up before Christmas – get it in order and then I want to get going on some steady study. I miss my hours of study and reading very much. One is so busy visiting people etc. that his mind lacks taste for deep thinking. I hope to be able to get in a couple of hours each day. We have had plenty to do in the last couple of months.

---

38   Backsliders – slang for people who were not attending Church.

After the big procession for the feast of Christ the King, we had the November devotions. I spent some time also with a few girls who were preparing for the Merit exam. I hope to give them a few hours each week next year in History and Geography. It will be a good exercise for me too. I have forgotten all my history. I suppose Marie got the letters from the girls. When you allow for the proneness of girls like them to exaggerate, I trust you will not take all they may have said (what they said I do not know) very seriously. I do love the children and find my happiest hours with them.

Of course my special attention must be to the sick and poor. There I need more of God's grace to help me to be true and gentle to them despite a hundred and one things that grate on human nature. They are having their concert tonight. I must go. It is a time quite inconvenient to be going to these entertainments but one must appear. Then there is another affair tomorrow afternoon – another on Wednesday and one on Wednesday evening. I managed to get out of a couple but I must go to the others.

The Mission has been the all absorbing interest for some two months past. We had to visit our entire districts – to find out the backsliders and to bring them along. Many people seem to have no religion at all – some are so lost in the cause of getting a meagre livelihood that they will not listen to anything about their souls or God. Many even wondered if they had a soul or not. It is a sad thing to see big boys and girls many of them 20 or 25 years old who were baptised as Catholics and yet had no further instruction. I have quite a number on my books at present. I hope God will be very merciful and I pray Him to spare those parents who are responsible. Now I realise more than ever before, that it is the Home and the Home above all else – school sisters, brothers or priests – which is responsible for good or bad Catholics.

I hope to make an intensive effort to introduce the practice of consecrating the Homes in my own district. I have also a scheme on hand to secure the desired ideal of a Catholic paper in every Catholic Home.

Fathers O'Loughlin and Forrest conducted the Mission. They are Sacred Heart Fathers. Father O'Loughlin is the P.P. at Moonah, an outlying district or suburb of Hobart. He is a great preacher – a tremendous voice and sweet and musical. Father Forrest was for some time Editor of the Annals – a teacher and then he went to America and Ireland giving Missions. He is an excellent speaker – more of the cool logician who appeals to the intellect. He has a particular interest in converts. He will give our retreat, which begins on Jan 8th. We do it at St Virgil's College while the Brothers go away for a month's holiday. We had three Masses in the morning 6 o'clock 7.00 and 9.00. A short instruction was given after the 6 o'clock Mass – an instruction of ½ hour after the 9 o'clock for the children.

There were grand congregations for the evening exercises. Quite a number of Non-Catholics came. Some have asked for Instruction. I have about seven people at present to instruct. Last night the Cathedral was packed. Every available space was occupied. After the Sermon we had the renewal of Baptismal vows. All brought candles and lit them. The Cathedral lights were put out and this left the whole building to be lit up by their candles. It was most impressive. We had solemn Benediction and then this morning there were three Black Masses for the departed souls of the Relatives and friends of all who had made the Mission. A good deal of good was done – many long timers came along.

It was a great joy to bring some poor soul back to God after years of carelessness. We had about 1,000 confessions and over 5,000 Communions in the time. Of course there are many whom we could not bring to receive the Sacraments. This only reminds one that he may never rest till he has done his best to help them.

I trust that your prayers, dear Mother – your daily work and trials and sorrows will all be offered to God that He will do what man cannot – that He will give to these poor people a special impulse of His holy Grace. We hope to be able to keep struggling for the rest. Retreat on Thursday.

We shall have a busy time for Christmas. On New Year's Eve from 11 o'clock to Midnight we will have the "Holy Hour," that is, the Blessed Sacrament exposed and special prayers said by the whole Congregation.

I hope to go to Bruny after the New Year and then back for our Retreat. After that we shall have the Men's Retreat and in the following week the Ladies' Retreat given by Father Forrest. We hope to have good attendance at both of those. They are the most telling of all the affairs we have through the year. Most of the St. Vincent de Paul Society will make the Retreat.

Yesterday there was a Conference of all the Tasmanian St V. de P. at Oatlands about midway between Launceston and Hobart. I went up with Father [Vincent] Green. We had to leave early so as to be back for the closing of the Mission. It was a beautiful drive. The country is quite fresh, green grass everywhere. I was wondering if it was so in Victoria.

It is warm here – hot for Tasmania. I had a letter from Mrs. Sier. I must set to work and write some Christmas letters. It means a lot of time but it may be some help to them – [the] only end I wish to have in all I do or say [is] that God be praised, loved and served by all. I often wish I could do more but I do hope I am trying to do something. God must do the rest.

It is nearly 12 months now since I stepped forward to receive the great dignity of the priesthood. Those twelve months have sped by and I have learnt much in the time. I am supremely happy and only wish I could thank God for the blessing He gave to me. I think of my anticipation of the day – the generous desires and grand resolves many of which have not been fulfilled. Oh dear Mother, I feel so weak and so much a boy still. It surprises me at times that people trust me with so much reverence and that they seek my advice as if I were an old and experienced man. St. Paul said truly God has chosen the weak ones of this world – and the foolish – the contemptible things, the base things and those that are not 'that no flesh might glory in His sight.'

I have a long letter from Father Pat [Carmine.] I must write to him also. I should like to be away in a quiet lonely place like a Monastery there to rest awhile with God. I miss the Seminary in many ways. One had no anxieties, no bustling here and there as one does on the Mission. However I know I am doing God's work and all I beg of Him is that He will protect and keep me "lest perhaps when I have preached to others I myself become a cast away."

If I go back to Victoria some times, I hope to spend some days in one of the Religious houses or at the Redemptorist monastery where I can enjoy a few quiet hours away from all the distracting cares. At times I become irritable and speak sharply to good people whom I should treat kindly and tenderly. So now Mother, you see I am needy and poor in my spiritual life and how grateful I shall be for the alms of your prayers.

I have been wondering if you and Father could come over. I shall pay your boat fare over. As Father O'Loughlin said, when I asked him about this, I have a duty to do something like that to repay all your care and trouble in my regard. I must write to Father and Marie. Tell them how things are going here.

Goodnight now, dearest Mother. Evening is closing in – I look out over the city – I am going for a quiet walk in the garden to think of you all, to pray for you all and beg of God that as He has been good and merciful to us so far, He will be so to the end of that time when we set out for that Eternal city which is above, the home where we will be united in never ending happiness as the Act of Consecration of the Family says: to sing the _glories_ and the _mercies_ of God.

Allow me in closing, dearest Mother, to send with all my heart to you all, my priestly blessing, which I first imparted to you 12 months ago. Believe me, dearest Mother

Your loving son in Christ.
John C. Wallis

Gloria in excelsis Deo.

To Wish you

A Happy and a Holy Christmas

A Bright and Prosperous New Year

St. Mary's Cathedral
Hobart

Jack

10(a)

Letters 43 – 53

WITH ENTHUSIASM AND ENERGY
Launceston and Hobart, Tasmania 1933
Letters 43–53

Graeme Howard

As a Tasmanian originally from Zeehan on the West coast and as a fellow diocesan priest, I found the letters in this chapter a wonderful insight into John Wallis' first year as a priest on the Island in 1933. I knew John from my youth as a senior student when I was at St Virgil's College in Hobart. It was to John I went to discuss the idea of the priesthood – and how surprised I was to hear him encouraging me to think about a missionary vocation.

John came to Tasmania as a very, very young priest, 22 years of age, faced with a new Archbishop and priests and people whom he did not know. What a challenge for one so young, yet John responded to the challenge, the call of the Lord to serve the people with enthusiasm and energy in this most southern part of Australia where he had never been.

John threw himself into parish life with all its variety of works, taking on the responsibilities that were given to him immediately upon his arrival – firstly for ten weeks in Launceston, then settling in the Archbishop's House, Hobart. However, in the letters, it also becomes clear that gradually the pressure of the work was taking its toll. John felt lonely and the need for support from someone on the local scene to whom he could turn and confide. Also, the pressure of constant activity meant he felt his spiritual life was not getting the attention it required. John was conscious of the need to have time apart, time for prayer and study.

There is no doubt John received great support from his family, especially from his mother. His mother's common sense and perceptive guidance were so important to this young priest, he confided in her as he struggled with his youthfulness and lack of experience. … *I seem to be so much a boy in many things. It is a strange feeling that one is looked up to and trusted by all the old and young. They all come to ask advice and guidance and you know how poor a reed they are leaning on … We are teaching people, guiding them and so on and yet we so often need guidance ourselves.*

Yet John pushed on and engaged in his pastoral work of visiting, sermon preparation and care of the poor. The letters portray very clearly his concern for the poor and how aware he was of the need to do whatever he could to help them. He went out of his way to organise food and clothing for people in need, as we see in the early letters in Launceston, when he organised for the St Vincent de Paul Society to take a truck to the orchards and gather the apples on the ground after a windstorm. He saw that the fruit was delivered to the poor in his own street.

The first year of his priesthood saw John make his initial visit to Bruny Island. The Island and its people had a profound affect upon the young priest. The children and the families and the need to know more about God's love for them moved John. This, of course, lead in years later to the founding of the Missionary Sisters of Service. John loved the Island getting around it on horseback, by bicycle and boat. He took a great interest in all activities of the Island, including the farm practices, as well as the bushland and its flowers and trees.

These letters give us an amazing insight into the lived experience of this young pastoral priest; they portray his faithfulness, his vulnerability, his love of his family and his tremendous commitment to follow his call to be priest, to serve and love God and his people.

Graeme Howard

Father Graeme Howard, a Tasmanian diocesan priest, was born in 1936 and grew up in Zeehan on the West coast of Tasmania. He was educated at the Convent school in Zeehan run by the Josephite Sisters, then St Virgil's College, Hobart, by the Christian Brothers. His studies at Corpus Christi Seminary in Victoria followed, and he was ordained in 1962 for the Archdiocese of Hobart. Greatly involved in parish life with a pastoral focus through the years, Graeme found his long time friendship with John to be an immense source of support and enjoyment and certainly filled with treasured memories.

Tasmania
1934
Letters 54 – 64

Introduction

In the early part of this second busy year as a priest in Tasmania, John's parents, Abe and Emma Wallis, visit him in Hobart. His brother Brian travels with them and begins a year of schooling at St Vigil's College, Hobart. He was fourteen and ten years younger than John and had potential for further studies. John's desire to join the mission in China increases and he finally makes the decision to apply to the Columban Fathers in Essendon, Melbourne, to begin the following year.

This sixth chapter consists of eleven letters of John's to his mother in 1934. They are written from the Archbishop's House, 99 Barrack Street, Hobart.

* * *

Letter 54 to Mother

My desire is to start to arouse some apostolic zeal in their hearts.

John's two-page letter (April 1934) to his mother is the first surviving one of the year. John is enjoying the cold weather with snow on Mt Wellington. While in Hobart his mother, Emma, establishes a relationship with the Presentation Sisters and especially with Mother Paul. She meets many of John's friends and contacts, including Miss Traynor, the Bratt family and others as revealed through the letters. In this letter there is a suggestion that John realises some works of the priest do not show apparent results.

* * *

Hobart
Monday
April 23rd [1934]

My Dearest Mother,
Your letter to hand today – also cheque for £7 which you enclosed. I thank you for it and I want now to pay it on to Brother Garvey for Brian. I know how hard you are finding it to keep going under the circumstances. I can manage that quite alright. I have been fairly busy – and yet I seem not to be busy. There are some kinds of work, which do not seem to show results.
I am going to have a Children of Mary Retreat on the 1st Sunday of

May. They will begin about 2.30p.m. and go on till after Benediction in the evening. My desire is to start to arouse some Apostolic zeal in their hearts. To make them feel that they are needed in the work of saving souls and making Australia Catholic.

It is very cold now – there has been a good deal of sleet and snow on the Mountain [Mt Wellington]. I like this kind of weather.

I shall see Mother Paul and tell her your wish. I write [to] you today to tell you that next Saturday is her feast day – 28th of April. It would be a joy to her to get a telegram from you if not a letter. I see Brian fairly often. He seems to be getting along quite well. Had a go in the Boxing Competition. I must write to Father sometime soon also to Chester.

We shall have a Requiem Mass on Wednesday next for Anzac day. Fr O'Donnell[1] will preach. They generally fall back on him for such occasions.

This letter has been written rather in haste and I hope to write to you more at length in a short while. I have to see to the Altar boys now. We are trying to establish the Crusaders of the Blessed Sacrament[2] amongst the boys and girls. I shall now close this brief note and promise a longer one shortly.

Please remember me in your prayers, especially in the Month of May. I am always mindful of you. Goodbye for the present, dearest Mother. Give my love to all at home.

From Your loving Son in Christ,

Jack.

---

1   Father T.J. O'Donnell had served as a chaplain in the 11th Battalion.
2   Australian Manual of the Crusaders of the Blessed Sacrament: edited by Eustace Boylan 1927-1940 https://catalogue.nla.gov.au/Record/1863661.

Letter 55 to Mother

One of the chief dangers of a priest
is that he fixes all his attention on the work,
forgetting the motive for whom he works.

In this four-page, full and interesting letter to his mother (May 1934), John reminisces Rosary in the *'boys room'* at home and Mother has sent ideas about his work. Brian is doing well, except for his handwriting which is not satisfactory – perhaps a family trait. It is polling day for the Legislative Council and John notes he is not up with the politics of the day, especially in Tasmania. An invitation to the priests' dinner at Franklin, south of Hobart comes his way, but he is not into *these special formal dinners*.

Involved with young people, John is giving a retreat to the girls and planning to take the boys up the mountain, the weather being cold but fine. He identifies his need to do a retreat for himself again longing for *solitude* to *pray and think*. His *fighting spirit* is waning. What he is doing and how he is thinking and living, is somehow not sustaining him.

Fr Mullaney of the Columban Fathers in Essendon has written and invites John to stay any time he was on the mainland, so it seems he has raised with them his interest in joining them.

As with the times and in his early priestly ministry, John focuses on bringing *converts into the Catholic Church* and gives them an informed understanding of the Catholic Church. He expresses in this letter how he wants *to warm up people's hearts* in his *crusading*. In a judgmental practice he worries about people who do not show up for religious *duties*. He refers to a *hard case*, people who were *careless* in the practice of their faith, *a renegade* regarding his life and faith, a *Mason, non-Catholics and mixed marriages* and more. This attitude changes in John's life with maturity and with social change and the development of ecclesial theology and spirituality. Witnessing the harshness of the bigotry between Christian denominations, and as well how it affected the Irish Catholics, John must come to realise that this does not match his desire for the mind and heart of Christ.

To be noted in this letter is that Miss Traynor after hard times with her new business has won Tatts[3] much to everyone's surprise and delight.

---

3   George Adams, a rich publican was the cornerstone of Tattersalls sweeps, known as Tatts. In 1881 he ran the first public Tattersalls sweep on the Sydney Cup. Because of regulations by governments in New South Wales and Queensland, he moved his business to Hobart in Tasmania in 1895 and eventually set up in Collins Street, where many people were employed. Tickets were sold across Australia and New Zealand by post.

A.M.D.G.

+

Archbishop's House,
Hobart.
May 1934

Dearest Mother,

It is now getting well into the night but I must at least begin this letter to you now hoping to finish it as soon as may be. I generally have two or three attempts at a letter. There are so many things which call one away.

I was sorry I could not write more than the scrappy note I sent you for your birthday but then I understood that you would also understand. Of course I remembered you where remembrance is best at the Holy Altar. It is truly a great joy for me to be able to do that. As I pronounced the words of Consecration I went back to the "boys room" where we said the Rosary. May our dear Mother obtain of our Lord a big reward for you, dear Mother, for the way you taught us there. I am only hoping that Brian with his opportunity will also be a priest.

We had the miniature Retreat on Sunday. The girls met on retreat 2.45 and came off after Benediction. They brought sandwiches, scones, cakes, etc. and so had luncheon and tea in one of the school rooms. There was a large fire there – also booklets, etc. if they wished to read. I gave them the first talk on Our Lady as the ideal of Personal Holiness for a Child of Mary – specially noting two characteristics in Mary – her unworldly spirit – unworldliness and her pure Intention – doing all for one only motive – to please God.

Then we had the Blessed Sacrament exposed and they said the Office of Our Lady in choir. Another talk at 5 o'clock – this on Our Lady as a Model of Zeal – not only holy herself but anxious to make others good too. I do hope that God in His goodness will inspire them with a spirit of apostolic zeal. They could do so much good if they only tried – distributing Catholic literature, visiting the sick, caring for neglected children, etc. I hope to urge them to get new members also for the Sodality.

Next week I hope to be able to get away for a quiet retreat myself. I feel like what Our Lord and the Apostles were, "There were many coming and going", whereupon our Master said to them, "Come apart and rest awhile." And He took them into a desert place apart. A quiet time of prayer and meditation helps one very much. One of the chief dangers of a priest is that he fixes all his attention on the work – this duty and that – to the forgetting of the motive for whom he works. It seems strange but God's work can often draw us away from God, and so one needs to frequently redirect his aim – a fine intention.

There will be a big procession for the Feast of Our Lady Help of Christians.[4] *Then too we hope to send representatives to Melbourne for the Congress. Yesterday I got word to say all has been arranged for Violet Dillon*[5] *to go to the Good Shepherd Nuns. I saw the Rev. Mother at Mt St Canice*[6] *yesterday. She wishes to be remembered to you and Father. I wrote to Violet last night. She will be going to Melbourne fairly soon to begin her novitiate. She may get up to Seymour before she enters.*

I want to go to Bruny soon to give them an opportunity for their Easter Duty. Brian enjoyed his stay there. He is much interested in Football now. He got a Season ticket (5/-) for the games played on Saturday afternoons. Brother Garvey told me he is doing well. He passed a particular remark about his writing and said that if it does not improve under persuasion, he will have to adopt other methods, e.g. to put in an afternoon rewriting his letter or transcribing.

We also have Confirmation here on May 20. His Grace is still in Sydney – expected back next Monday.

Here is news! Miss Traynor and Mrs John Traynor won £500 in Tatts. There was great rejoicing. Miss Traynor was just beginning to become very despondent about a big draught owing to Burns Oates and Washbourne.[7] *This will set her on her feet. God looks after His own and I am very glad. She has been extraordinarily charitable to the French ladies who have had a very hard struggle to keep body and soul together.*

We shall have the Sodality at St Virgil's soon. It should do much good amongst the boys. The Crusaders of the Blessed Sacrament will also do much good. I am most anxious to see this movement flourish.

A few days ago I was at the Public Hospital. Sister Kilmartin told me of a "hard" case. He had been careless. At last he agreed to do to [fulfil his religious] duty. I heard confession on Friday. Took Communion on Saturday – also anointed him – almost as an afterthought. A couple of days later he was taken to Newtown Infirmary and then a day or so after he died. I am sure God had a special providence over that man. Thanks be to Him for His Mercy. At present I am [looking] after a renegade Catholic who is very sick – also a Mason. Remember them in your prayers.

The Cathedral appeal is going on slowly. The new drain [at the cathedral] is finished now. More tomorrow – I must go to bed now as it is nearly midnight.

Wednesday Morning. I had a short note from Mother Alphonsus at the [Presentation] Novitiate Launceston. She asked how you were and wished

---

4 Our Lady Help of Christians is known as a patroness of Australia – her feast on the 24th May has been celebrated since 1844.
5 Violet Dillon (Sister Justine RGS) from Bruny Island, the Dillon family offering the priests hospitality whenever they were on the Island.
6 Mt St Canice, Sandy Bay, Tasmania, was originally built to serve as a reformatory for women and was run by the Sisters of the Good Shepherd.
7 A publishing company.

to be remembered. Mother Teresa feels better and the blood pressure is going up instead of down. May Dutton, the young girl at Karoola, has entered the Novitiate and seems to be settling down. I hope she will persevere. They are short of sisters at present. We had to get a teacher in for St Columba's school. Unfortunately she is not a Catholic. One of the Sisters does the instructions.

Today is Polling day for the Legislative Council. I must go down to vote. I am not very conversant with politics anywhere, and least of all in Tasmania. We have been having beautiful weather – cold but fine. I hope to take the Altar Boys up the Mountain [Mt Wellington] some time soon. They dearly love a day's outing like that.

Father Fitzpatrick invited us all to his place for dinner on May 24th. He is the priest at Franklin. I am not sure yet if I shall be going. I do not like these special formal dinners.

I suppose there are great preparations going ahead for the Congress. I do not know yet what arrangements are being made here for representation. I got a letter from St Columbans, Essendon, inviting me to stay there any time I chose – "a towel and a piece of soap always ready" – so wrote Father Mullaney.

Well now, dearest Mother, I must close this letter as I am on duty this week and so have many little affairs to attend to. I want to get an Instruction for the Brunyites finished. Give my love to all at home. I am always intending to write to Father and Marie but I seem to let it slip.

Father Lynch's Father died recently in Ireland. Both his parents are dead now. His sister is alive. He will perhaps go home next year or in 1936.

I was glad for the few ideas you expressed in your letter about my work. I only want to do more and to try harder to be a Saint. Of course I am not my own. I am God's and he may use me where He will. It may be that I am a coward shirking from work to be done here and yet I feel that the other is the more complete and generous sacrifice.[8] I am longing to go away into a place of retreat or solitude for a month or so and there to pray and think. I do hope to be able next year to do this at the Redemptorist Monastery. For the present I place myself in the hands of Providence and I want to try to do all I can. I only wish that I had more of the fighting spirit in me – it needs not only simple preaching it here, but vigorous crusading to warm up the hearts of the people.

May the Holy Spirit come down on us and fill our hearts with the fire of divine love. We began the novena to the Holy Spirit on Friday. I often remember the 3rd Glorious.[9]

Goodbye now dearest Mother and believe me as always

Your loving Son in Christ
Jack

---

8   This is a reference to joining the Columbans and going to the missions.
9   The third Glorious Mystery of the Rosary is the story of Pentecost, where the Holy Spirit comes down upon the disciples gathered in the upper room.

Letter 56 to Mother

Always try to do the right and the generous thing.

In this four-page letter to his mother (Monday 11th or 23rd June), John begins ... *I seem to have been doing but little lately. I do not know just what it is. I hope to stir myself.* His visiting of the parish people has suffered and, while he has lost some of his enthusiasm, he is still very involved, including doing a Latin course to refresh all he learned at the seminary. It is cooler now and the evenings are cold. So far this winter little snow has fallen on Mt Wellington, and rain is needed.

There is a problem at home, an unexpected trouble, seemingly about a business or financial matter that disturbs his mother greatly. How it is impacting on her life is unknown except that *God sees, God knows* the truth as to what happened, he reassures her. He thinks of her in the evenings when he is alone in his room or when he walks up and down the grove at the back of the Bishop's house. His loneliness, perhaps homesickness, is evident. Local people from home come to mind as well – Mrs H. McRae and the Misses Conroy.

He may also need to improve on his writing, as his mother will notice that maybe his writing, as in this letter, is on a par with Brian's!

* * *

A.M.D.G.
+

Archbishop' House,
Hobart.
June 1934

My dearest Mother,

Your welcome letter to hand a few days back. I am sure you are waiting for one from me. I seem somehow to have been very busy and yet I seem to have been doing but little lately. I do not know just what it is. I hope to stir myself up again and to get to work this week. I had to help prepare some children for their First Holy communion as well as attend to other affairs in the school. I think I shall have a little more time to give more directly to the Parochial Visitation which has suffered so much of late weeks.

Today was King's Birthday – very quiet. Fr Green went home for [the] day I have not been out at all. I had some study to do. I must begin now for the retreat to the St. Mary's girls. It will entail a lot of hard application. Father Lynch and I went to the [Christian] Brothers for dinner today. This gives our girls a rest. His Grace is away in the North.

It is getting quite cool now – not yet like it was last year. In fact there is a great want of rain yet. At Queenstown the situation is still serious. There has been snow only a few times on the Mountain [Mt Wellington] this year.

I shall be able quite easily to meet the fee[10] for next term. I have been trying to save some, as times goes on and then the Bishop gives us some extra allowances at times. Apart from calls, etc. – I have not so much expense. There is no car to run and then I do not smoke so I want to try to help you all I can.

This is especially so, seeing the trouble you are [having] at present having. I have remembered your intentions in Holy Mass. You have indeed had many reverses – many times too from most unexpected quarters, but then, dearest Mother, I am sure that deep down in your heart you have one great consolation. You have always tried to do the right and the generous thing. God is your witness – you can say, despite what men may say, "God sees, God knows." I have not told Brian yet but I shall do so on one day when he is over. I intend to write to Chester sometime soon. I do be often thinking of you especially on the cold evenings when I am alone in my room or when I go for a little walk up and down the grove of trees behind the [Archbishop's] Palace.

I got a letter from Mrs H. McRae[11] thanking me for a letter I wrote. I also sent a crucifix. I was glad to be able to do something for the woman. That reminds me too of the Misses Conroy. Please remember me to them and tell them that I will remember them at Holy Mass. If I can, I will write to them.

Mother Paul wishes to be remembered to you – also other friends especially the Bratt's. Poor Thelma is gradually getting worse.[12]

I am still going on with the Latin course. It is a kind of revision for me recalling much that I had forgotten.

We had a big procession here on Trinity Sunday – the day before the Feast of Our Lady Help of Christians. All the Children of Mary from the Cathedral, from Newtown, Moonah and Glenorchy took part in it as well as the boys and girls of the schools. We had a special frame made to carry a statue of Our Lady. They sang a very beautiful hymn, "This is the Image of Our Queen," during the procession. Then we had Solemn Benediction given by his Grace. There was a High Mass on the Feast day itself.

On Thursday last we had exposition all day. Quite a large number of people attended the evening devotions and also they were very fervent in their visits during the day. The Communions on that day and also on the First Friday were quite pleasing.

We are hoping for a repetition of this on Friday next, the Feast of the Sacred Heart. I hope that Our Divine Lord will enkindle some of the fire of

---

10   The fee is for Brian's schooling at St Virgil's.
11   Mrs McRae on McRae's Road, Homewood.
12   Thelma Bratt's daughter, Mabel, helped establish a Catholic library with John and worked in the Catholic Centre Bookshop as an employee until she retired.

divine love in my own heart and help me to labour more steadily for the souls He loves so tenderly. I am sending a little leaflet with the "Promises" on it. Pray that the 10th will be realised in my regard.

Violet Dillon[13] left on Sunday last for Launceston. She was to sail today. She seems quite glad. Mrs Dillon is also quite pleased though she is naturally feeling parting with the second of the only two girls she had. I shall be going to Bruny this month, probably for the 17th. I must send some Catholic papers on to them.

Brian will have his Mid-winter holidays at the end of this month. He has not decided just what he will do as yet. He came over to me to ask me what I think is best.

You asked me to send The Standard. Sometimes I see it, sometimes I do not, so that I could not guarantee to send it myself. So I shall go to the office and ask them to forward it to you direct each week. I suppose you will be able to follow many of the items of local interest after your visit.

I went and stayed one evening with Father Kent in his den at Sandy Bay. I said Mass for him next day and he came and celebrated the High Mass here.

Well now, dear Mother, it is getting late and I must close this letter. I am thinking you will consider my writing on a par with Brian's but I have been writing in haste. Remember me to all at home. I suppose all will have a read of this note. To all I send my deepest love.

Goodnight now dearest Mother and remember in your prayers as always,
Your loving Son in Christ,
Jack.

Tuesday

Had a visit from Bro Gregory, Marist Brother from St Joseph's – [an] old friend of Bro William, who was his first Superior after he began teaching. [He is] going to Turin Italy for a 2nd Novitiate. [He is] going to see Bro William on the way. I went to [see the] boat "Ballarat" – 1st time on an Ocean liner – certainly very interesting. Saw about [getting a] photo for Bro William. Will get it tomorrow and send [it] on when taken. Will close now
Love from
Jack.

---

13   Violet Dillon joined the Sisters of the Good Shepherd in Melbourne.

Letter 57 to Mother

I need God's guiding light, a great spirit of prayer and above all the grace of being humble.

This is a three-page letter to John's mother (15th July 1934) packed with thoughts not all in order or in sentences. Martin O'Loughlin's ordination has taken place in the cathedral and the occasion brings to his mind his own ordination and he exclaims it is so long ago – nineteen months! John is the second master of ceremonies, so must attend to many details. Brian, his brother, is at the ordination and in a *splendid* seat where he could see all.

One of John's further responsibilities on the day of the ordination was to conduct the Holy Hour at Newtown, and he then returns for solemn Benediction. He is not sorry to miss some ordination proceedings, as they are such *formal things*, he says.

John is trying to systemise his work and as well he has ideas about some new schemes, one being a library for young people. At the end of the letter, he confesses his pride and, while acknowledging God's generosity, he pleads for prayer that he may be as a child trusting God.

Since her holiday, Emma has written to a number of people including Mother Paul of the Presentation Sisters. John's family are now associated with his part of the world in Tasmania. He reports that Brian enjoyed his holiday with the Dwyers, and notes he is savvy with money. Local people look forward to his sister, Marie, coming later in the year.

* * *

A.M.D.G.
+
Hobart
July 15th 1934

Dear Mother,

Ten thirty finds me very tired and weary after a long day. It took me back to Dec 18th at Kilmore – the Ordination of a New priest. Father Martin O'Loughlin was ordained today in St Mary's Cathedral. We had been preparing – yesterday was a time of all kinds of affairs to attend to. Boys to instruct – directions for the requests for Ceremony etc. I said the early Mass this morning and then we had to bustle to arrange everything for the Eleven o'clock Mass. A huge crowd there – many friends of the Ordinand. His Mother, Father, two Brothers, two Sisters and one in the Convent, Sister Dolores. Fr Green was 1st MC. I was 2nd. We managed between us.

Brian had a splendid seat – saw all, got blessing almost immediately after the family got it. He was very keenly interested in it all and would not have missed [it] for anything. Father O'Loughlin gave Blessing to most of people – then we told them to wait till tonight. Dinner at Palace – a very informal thing. Benediction at Mt St Canice at 4.30. Brian went. I did not. I went later to a tea at 5.30. His Grace, priests and family of newly ordained were entertained by [Good Shepherd] Sisters. I heard Mrs Dillon was up. [I] did not see her but is doing well.

I had to hurry away (for which I was not sorry) to give Holy Hour at Newtown then back for Solemn Benediction at Cathedral. Big crowd and good Sermon by Fr Dalton M.S.C., who has been with us for the retreat to Brothers. A very interesting man. I had a good talk. [He was an] old pupil of Brother Michael.

Father Martin is staying with us. 1st Holy Mass tomorrow at 8 o'clock. He goes back to Werribee [seminary] for 25th July. He will then be over here at end of year. I may be sent elsewhere then. I thought of my own day. It is near 19 months – a long time.

I am trying to make a more constant effort to systematise my work. This means more done with less expenditure of energy. I have a couple of schemes in mind over which I need God's guiding light. One is about a Library for young people here, also a select group of Catholic youths ready to join in work of instructing careless Catholics – hunting them out – distributing Catholic papers etc. I had four children for instruction today. They have not clothes to go to Mass in, so I go to (their) home. Pray for this work.

I read Brian's letter and saw 10/- in it. He is very savvy with money. I have been surprised more than once to see how little he spent while going about. He has not taken after his brother in this direction.

Mother Paul got (your) letter – very pleased indeed. This is a very hurried letter. I am tired but I thought I could not let the day go without a short note at least. It brought back memories.

I am thinking of getting a portable typewriter. It will cost £7.00 but I think it will help me in [my] work. I can save up for it in little ways. I wonder if you knew anyone in that line who could get it for me at reduced price.

Well now, dearest Mother, I must close. I am always in [a] hurry but you will understand. Please remember me to all at home. I shall be glad to see Marie in Oct. The sisters are anxious for her to come too.

Goodnight now, my dear Mother, and beg God to give to me those priestly graces I so much need – above all a great spirit of prayer and above all the grace of being humble. Oh this is my terrible trouble I am so proud, so fond of the lime light in all that goes – ceremonies, at table in conversation, etc. The

Saints loved a hidden retired life – to be united at one with God – a life too of great self-denial but I feel so proud. Please beg the Divine master to teach me to be as a child. I am asking you to pray for many things but after all I need them and God is so generous. I have had no reply from Fr Hall[14] to date.

Goodbye once more dearest Mother and good night. Love from

Your Loving Son in Christ

(John, crossed out) Jack.

P.S. Brian enjoyed holidays. I shall send case of oranges to Dwyer's later. They are very good to him. Holiday in all cost about £1.00. He is very pleasing in every way. Old Brother Flood – a saintly old man from Launceston was very much taken with him and asked him to visit him when he is on way home.

---

14   Fr Hall is the Columban Father in Essendon that John is corresponding with in regard to joining them.

Letter 58 to Mother

And God is saying, Who will go?
Whom shall we send?
Shall we stand by and answer No!
Shall we say, "I am not ready".

In this important four-page letter to his mother (11th August 1934), John finally shares of his discernment to join the Columban Fathers and go to the *Far East*, to China as a missionary. He reminds his mother that when he was a child she explained the words on the cover of *The Far East*, "The harvest indeed is great but the labourers are few." He asks but *Who will go, who shall be sent, is it I? Should I go I want it to be quietly*, he writes, and he worries how his mother will manage and what others think. Imagining he may one day be celebrating Mass in a *remote Chinese village*, he thinks surely not a martyr, as Father Pat Leonard SSC suffered.

The young John still lives as though he is fully responsible for *saving souls*, and especially *pagan souls*, the language and terminology of the day. His discernment has also raised his perceived responsibility to his family, including his Deaf siblings. He suggests that he offer funds through his insurance policy if he leaves the diocese.

Of particular note is the biography he is reading – the life of Jesuit priest, Charles Plater, born in England in 1875. Plater studied industrial economics and the importance of education for social justice. He organised retreats and delivered lectures for working people throughout Britain to enrich their spiritual lives and encourage social reform.[15] Even while John is working out his future, he sees possibilities for the local scene that if he organised more retreats he could be *warming the hearts* of Tasmanians with *a spark of love of the Sacred Heart*. But alas, when it comes to fund-raising, especially through parish fairs, John is not an enthusiast!

---

15   https://www.jesuit.org.uk/profile/charles-plater-sj

A.M.D.G.
+

Archbishop's House,
99 Barrack Street,
Hobart.
August 11th 1934

Dearest Mother,

You must be waiting patiently for a letter. Although Brian can write to tell you I am well etc., I know you look forward to my hurried notes. I am busy as usual. Alas, at a Fair. Going here and there about house parties, bridge parties, this and that affair. It is a very distracting business and I fear that I am not an expert at asking [for funds.] People are good with all helping as they can. I have seen quite a number.

There was meeting on Wednesday evening. Three stalls – Children of Mary, Children's Stall and one other – I don't know if it has been christened yet – I am in a sense the patron of the Children of Mary stall. Miss Traynor gave a nice statue of the Sacred Heart to be raffled. We are having a picture benefit, parties at a house, a concert, dances, tuck shop, Paddy's Market. So far no rows! It will last for about 8 to 10 weeks.

Also [we] have a proposed Novena[16] in hand for preparation for the Assumption.[17] Then for the St Mary's College girls [there is a] retreat from the evening of 14th to the 18th August, i.e. three days [before the feast of the] Assumption and two [days] following the Assumption. Please pray for me that I may make it what I want it to be – an occasion of "warming" their hearts with a spark of the love of the Sacred Heart. It is the hearts of Tasmanians that must be touched. May our Blessed Lady watch over it to make it a success.

Later there will be our Retreat to St Columbanites [students] – this is an easier task. Boys have not had retreat yet. Fr O'Donnell [is] to give it. Brian is looking forward to it. I see him from time to time, I hope he gets to hard work this half (of the year). There is keen interest in cricket here – Fr Green [is] particularly enthusiastic. I am afraid I am rather behind times – old fashioned. However [I] have plenty to do – though I seem to get but little of it done.

Am reading life of Fr Plater SJ, the great worker for having retreats in England. Would like to make more of them here. I want to get some of the boys interested and to get it here and to push the movement. The Money Question is the biggest difficulty. No funds. This can be met by means of a weekly subscription of 6d. to some responsible person. The St Vincent de Paul Society will discuss it next Sunday. I hope to be at the meeting.

---

16   A novena is a long-standing traditional practice of prayer over nine days or weeks, usually leading up to a feast or for a special intention, from the Latin *novem* meaning *nine*. A tridium is a similar practice but of three days of prayer.
17   The Feast of the Assumption of Mary into heaven was celebrated on 15th August.

The Bratt family [is] expecting Marie over in October. Others too have asked if she is coming. I often have enquiries about yourself and Father.

Had a lovely note from Fr Jim Henley at Rockhampton. He seems to be doing well. I would like to have a chat to him. Maybe I shall see him some time. No letter from Fr. Pat [Carmine.] One from Bob Kennedy telling me a good deal of Manly news. I often think of Manly. I will be writing to Bro William for the Assumption.

And now, dearest Mother, I come to some news which has been in my mind for some time but more so over the last few days. You will remember what I said to you about China. I know this will cause you a feeling of suspense but I am glad I told it to you before. Well, dearest Mother, the thought is ever there. The Missions[18] are it seems to me the dearest work of the Sacred Heart.

I often think of the church as a great growing power ever drawing in assimilating peoples of other tongues and classes. It is the Kingdom growing (and) growing. Such is God's will – such is our desire at least so we pray. No all this is to give glory to God. This is the first thought that appeals that God is glorified known and loved. That these poor pagans be taught to love the true God not idols. Yes dear Mother how glorious to labour that God be praised. And He is saying "Who will go? Whom shall we send? Shall we stand by and answer No! Shall we say, I am not ready".

Dearest Mother I feel that Our Lord is asking me to give myself. Send me. Behold Lord here am I. I may be a weak poor thing but then He is so merciful as to choose the weak for His own wise purpose. Then there are the souls. I often think of Our Lord on Calvary! What does it all mean? It means Souls Souls Souls! I think of the happiness they know nothing of: Then there is heaven their true home and they walk in darkness.

I go back many years to when you my own dear Mother explained to me the meaning of the words on the cover of The Far East, "The harvest indeed is great but the labourers are few". Send labourers! That is to be our prayer. So I have been thinking much. At times I wonder if I am shirking present work for an uncertain future.

However I wrote to Father Hall my spiritual director at St Patrick's Manly. None I think knew me as well as he, so I made up my mind that his word would be to me as an indication of God's will. He said to pray and to make a retreat in Victoria at end of year. I put objections to him against my going e.g. My duty to [the] Bishop – but there will be enough priests with three coming

---

18   '*The missions*' was understood, firstly, as a foreign place to establish Christianity. The term has been understood differently from the time of Vatican Council II, such that now *the mission* is active wherever we are and in whatever we are doing. The theology of mission is enriched with an understanding that God's perspective is ever generous and loving in relation to humanity.

at end of year. As to finance I would gladly come to [an] arrangement with the Far East people to let my Insurance policy go to the Diocese. I shall write later to Essendon.[19]

Of course one consideration I put to Father Hall was that I would be leaving my near and dear ones – My Mother and Father, Brothers and dear Sister Marie. Now that his letter has come I feel this more: I felt that the break would be hard for me. It seems to be the one thing that really unsettles me but I know what I would feel in the light of a Retreat. I know what I would wish to have done when I am awaiting my summons on my death bed.

I do not know what I shall have to do. I shall take time to think and pray: I ask your prayers and then if I feel I must go I shall approach his Grace. I may have difficulty in getting off. I suppose I would have a year at Essendon probably two years and then embark for Ireland or for the Far East. May God guide me and His Holy Mother help me.

At present I am continuing work as usual making no change. I shall await your letter. Please do not tell this news to any at present. Should I go I want it to be quietly without any publicity. I am wondering what Marie will say. You might kindly tell her I look to her prayers to help me to know God's will and [have the] generosity to do it. There is one question that set me thinking. I feel that in a sense I am to be responsible for the rest of the family especially for Marie, Don and Charlie. I am wondering if I would be doing wrong in leaving them. What do you think? In a way I suppose I am not able to do much but still the thought worries me.

Well dearest Mother, I know that this news will come hard to you and I might have feared I may hurt you and might have feared it would cut deep, were it not that I know the depth of your understanding heart and your deep generous Faith.

Oh what it is to have the gift of faith, to see that this life is but the antechamber to Eternal life – that to live for God, even to lose all for God is the grandest noblest thing of all. To you under God I owe that faith. By Our Crucified Saviour to help us both to give all for His Eternal Love. One joy I will ever have – to have had you all at my ordination and at my First Holy Mass. God knows that perhaps I shall be celebrating it far away in the North East – some remote Chinese village. I even think at times (though I desire it not) that I may have the prize of a martyr's crown.

Goodnight now my most loving Mother and please write me soon.
Your ever loving and loved son in Christ Jesus,
Jack.

---

19   The Columban Fathers had their Australian Administration Centre in Essendon, Victoria, and the General Administration in Ireland.

ARCHBISHOP'S HOUSE
99 BARRACK STREET
HOBART   Aug 11th 19

Dearest Mother,

You must be waiting patiently for a letter. Although I know I can write to tell you I am well & I know you look forward to my hurried notes. I am busy as usual — alas at a Fair. Going here there about house parties, bridge parties, this and that affair. It is a very distracting business and I fear I am not an expert at asking. People are good and all helping as they can — have sent quite a number. There was mostly a Stall we,. 5 stalls Child of Mary, Children's Stall & one other I can't know if it has been Christened yet. I am in a sense the patron of the Child of Mary tho' Mass & may not join a nice statue of the Sacred Heart is to applied. home lay a lecture benefit — parties at home concert. Clowns truck shop Paddy's Market. So far no news! It will last for about 8 to so days. Also have a proposed Novena in hand in prep for Assumption. then Retreat from busy Sick to the 16th is three days Assumption & a follow to St Mary's girls. Please pray for me that it may make & what I want it to be we reason for "warming" their hearts with a spark of love of the Sacred Heart. Her the hands of [?] hot maythe hundred. May our Blessed Lady watch over to make it a success. Later there will be the Retreat to St Columba the this an easier task. Boys have not had retreat yet Fr O'Donnell to give it him is looking forward to it. I see him from time to time he is fitting more

Letter 59 to Mother

A dry prayer said in the spirit of Faith is far more precious than prayers coming from pious emotional feelings.

In this two-page letter (15th October 1934) in response to his mother's letters to Brian and himself, John writes *I felt a tremendous feeling of joy and gratitude.* She has surrendered to John's plans although she no doubt feels great sorrow – her son, in whom she confides and trusts, may go even further away in pursuing his desire to go to China. She writes of her *dry prayer* and, in the role of a young spiritual director, John responds that prayer said *in a spirit of faith is far more precious than prayers coming from pious emotional feelings.* His mother's lifetime wish was that her priestly son would be at her death-bed – John attempts to console her, writing that if it is God's plan it would be such a privilege and it could still be so. But it may be a sacrifice that is asked of them.

From Hanyang in North China and China's first Columban bishop, the Irish Bishop Edward Galvin, as a young priest, had inspired John during a visit to the Yea parish to speak about *The Far East*. So since John's childhood the Columban magazine had come to their family home. The Bishop is in Melbourne at the Eucharistic Congress but John, due to commitments, cannot go to meet him. Two of the Brothers at Assumption College think John as *too weak* for the mission, but change their minds later and encourage him. The application papers to join the Columbans have been sent to Ireland.

In this time of waiting, John still wants to live as though his Hobart ministries *were my fixed field of action until arrangements are settled.* He visits the newly ordained Father Martin O'Loughlin and still sees needy people around him. John uses the word *pagans* in such a way that he would never have done later.

In looking forward to a holiday home and being with her before he goes to the Columbans, he speaks of two special places, *May we yet say the rosary together and may I yet celebrate Mass in the little chapel at Yea and at Assumption College Kilmore – the two dear spots of my heart.* John is not demonstrative, but his written words are.

* * *

A.M.D.G.

Archbishop's House,
Hobart.
October 15th 1934

My Dearest Mother,
It is now 11.30pm but I want to drop you a line tonight if I can. I have been out all evening to Moonah to see Fr O'Loughlin; to Newtown to see

Mr Ross Long who is planning the platform and canopy for the Eucharistic Procession of Christ the King and then to a dance at Newtown – and home in rain with Fr Lynch. His Grace is in the North. Fr Green in Hospital so there is a small household. I have a good deal to do – most of Fr Green's work, as I will be on my own.

I was so pleased to get your letter today. And then Brian's.[20] Well Mother – when I read them I felt a tremendous feeling of joy – of gratitude to God and the spontaneous expression "Oh woman great is thy faith". How proud I am of my dear good "little" Mother[21] for the generosity of her heart. I feel so much my want of response to that love but this I can say, if I do seem to be wanting in demonstrativeness it is only because I must be at my work day and night and I am offering that as my return. God I hope will accept it. I feel every day that I do so little – so much left undone – so many people I might have helped and encouraged. So little effort to "give myself to the people."

You know dearest Mother that I do want to be a Saint but have little faith when I put myself beside the Saints. To make the Sacrifice for China – and it is a sacrifice to leave all I love at home and here – I feel leaving my work in Tasmania, especially the dear children – all this I hope will be a little more to realising my ideal.

I had a letter from Dr Mullaney today. He has sent my papers to Ireland. It is a question of waiting now till news comes back – about 3 months. He suggested that I enter at Essendon on March 1st 1935. Stay here till mid-January accordingly as the Bishop desires. Then a holiday, which I am sure I will be able to benefit by.

With Fr Green off the list it means a lot of extra work. The Fair, Feast of Christ the King, Mission 40 hours and then the Congress and Christmas. Following them the Retreats. I have made up my mind to work here as though this were my fixed field of action until arrangements are settled. The part of China to which the St Columban's Missioners go is in the North of China.

I know it is hard but that is just one reason to urge me to go. If God wants me, if He has smoothed the way I am sure He will give me the grace. It is not so much the hard life I fear as (my own) cowardice and the want of deep humility and perfect obedience. That has been always difficult; it will be more so seeing that for 2 years I will have had a very great deal of independence.[22] Bishop Galvin is coming for Congress. I would like to see him but I suppose I shall not.

---

20   John's mother wrote to Brian as well, so he reads both letters that she wrote.
21   This is in reference to the little Irish Mother in John O'Brien's poems, *Around the Boree Log*.
22   For a priest who belongs to an order, community is central to his life of mission with a particular charism or focus. The diocesan priest belongs to a diocese and commits his life to serving under the Bishop of the particular diocese.

I do not know that the Christian Brothers have Missions – they did have but not now. Of course the Marists have. I am not surprised at Bro Michael and Bro Gonzales thinking me too weak but as I said we must not look merely at the human aspect. Even if it were God's will – which I hope it is not – that I were never to actually reach the Mission but to stay in some College at home – in Australia or Ireland – I should still be quite happy.

I must have a good long talk with Brian. I thought that if Marie came over in November she could go over with Brian. He will be leaving about Nov 30th. I shall book his passage.

There is one thought that concerns me – that when we are praying especially when at Mass we are and will be together, the same God to whom you speak is present here. The same Blessed Sacrament is here as is present at the Mass or in the Tabernacle when you visit the church. As to your prayers there is just this thought. That you could write as you have is more and ample proof that your prayers are indeed pleasing to God. A dry prayer said even against the grain but in a spirit of Faith is far more precious than prayers coming more or less from pious emotional feelings.

May we yet say the rosary together and may I yet celebrate Mass in the little chapel at Yea and at Assumption College Kilmore – the two dear spots of my heart.

I would love to help pour out something of God's grace on the souls of the people. They always seem to me like a big dry dusty paddock with dried up withered crops – parched. I hope to offer my life to Our Lord not only for the Mission but also for Tasmania. It may seem that I am leaving pagans for pagans but there is a truth we must never forget – Grace can convert souls – and grace is won by prayer and Sacrifice.

Now dearest Mother it is late and [I] must be up early tomorrow so I shall close these notes with all the fondest love of my heart – I just thought of what you said about assisting you at your death. To do that would be joy unspeakable but still I feel that your death will be yet more happy for sacrificing even that. Fr Mullaney told me his parents felt it but they both had remarkably happy deaths. And who can say but that in God's good plan I shall indeed have that privilege.

Goodnight dearest Mother. Love to all and to you from
Your loving Son in Christ Jesus
Jack.

Letter 60 to Mother

God's grace works in extraordinary ways.

In this three-page letter to his mother (5th November 1934), John writes that he awaits news from the Columbans in Ireland, and reminds her the news is not in the public arena yet. He is pleased to hear from Brothers Michael and William. A fellow priest from Tasmania, George Stonor, who was also thinking about entering the Columbans, ultimately joins the Franciscan Order and serves in Papua New Guinea.

    John recounts what is happening in his life at the present time. With the Administrator Father Vincent Green on sick leave at his mother's place in Sorell, John is seeing to parish accounts. He needs to see him and goes with, it seems, Brother Joyce from St Virgil's. As well John is organising the Redemptorist mission, preparing for different retreats as well as seeking out *some careless people*, most likely those who do not attend Mass for various reasons.

    John does not enjoy the priests' formal dinners and, alas, the fair was not a great success. He admits he is not meant to be an organiser.

* * *

A.M.D.G.

+

Hobart.
Nov 5th 1934

Dear Mother,

    It is now late but I must write a few lines before I go to bed. I have just come back from Sorell. Bro Joyce and I took a run down after tea. I had to see Fr Green about accounts etc. He is still on sick leave and has left his Administration work to me. It means a very busy time.

    And then there is a Mission coming. So far I have done barely anything [nothing] to prepare for it. I hope to get going tomorrow on A… Street to hunt up some careless people. Please remember it in your prayers. The Redemptorists are giving it. One is a Father Wallace. I have not heard yet what they are like. At present they are giving "two weeks" mission at St. Joseph's in the city of Hobart. Fr Cullen has invited us to dinner there tomorrow. I suppose I shall go though I do not like these formal dinners.

    We had the Fair a while back. It was not a great success. All along there was [a] great lack of interest. Of course I know we might have done more in organising but am afraid I was not meant to be an organiser. I am not an expert at making money. The whole Fair proceedings will conclude with a crowning on the 26th of this month. I shall be glad when it is over.

There are a few going to the Congress. His Grace leaves here on or about Nov 20th and will ordain Frank Bowman on Oct 30th. He asked me about going but I prefer to wait till it is all over.

There will also be the Retreats to prepare for. Fr Power S.J. of Werribee is giving the priests' Retreat, Fr Hehir S.J. the Men's and Ladies' (retreat) and then a series of lectures in St Mary's Cathedral. St Mary's will be on the Air next Sunday – 7ZL Hobart for 11 o'clock Mass. You will see [an] account of [the] Eucharistic Procession in The Standard. It was a glorious day – the Procession was fine. Fr Kent has a great knack of organising. The only drawback was that the dance had been on the night before and I fear made our number of Communions less than we might have expected. After all it is the earnest desire to be more fervent in our Holy Church that we need.

I see Brian from time to time but lately have been so busy that I do not get the chance to talk much.

I am still awaiting news from Ireland. As far as Essendon authorities go there is now nothing to prevent my going ahead. I suppose word will come in December. Bro Michael wrote a nice letter – also Bro William: "Dear Father John (Chinaman)." Father Hall wrote also saying that he approved of the decision. I must try to write to Father this week. I know it will all seem so strange and even unnecessary, but then God's grace works in extraordinary ways.

I should be glad to read that pamphlet again on the Mission – also to give a talk on it to [the] Boys so I would be glad dear Mother if you could let me have it some time. As yet it is not public that I have decided on leaving. I asked Father Mullaney to send you a "Far East" Calendar. I should like very much to meet Bishop Galvin who is coming to [the] Congress. He may call in here on his way back to Ireland.

I had a very nice letter from Charlie. The writing is very good. I gave it to His Grace to read. He was quite surprised at it. I want to write to him also this week. How is Anne going along? I wrote to her and I fear I may have spoken too harshly. You may have heard from her of it. I do hope all will be well.

I am getting Miss McKenna to see what is the quality of the material in a suit for Brian. I shall see about his passage home probably about 29th or 30th of November. I want to try to get a suit too and have a little money to fix up some small affairs in Melbourne. I have opened an account at the Savings Bank with the Resolution: not to take money out once in. I wonder how long this will last.

George Stoner is also thinking of the Missions. We are still at the ... He is doing very well.

Well now dearest Mother, I must get off to bed. It is now nearly 12 o'clock and I have to rise early. Many friends ask after you and send you best wishes. Give my love to all at home. I think the Flu is nearly all gone now and fine weather has been the order of the day. I would like to know more about Marie – whether she is coming soon or not. If not before December it were better after December and then we could go home in mid January unless His Grace wants me to stay till end of January or the beginning of February.

Goodnight now my dearest Mother and believe me to be

Your loving Son in Christ

Jack.

PS I shall say Mass on Nov 12[23] for Deceased Relatives, etc.

---

23   John's father died on 12th November 1945, eleven years later.

Letter 61 to Mother

*There have been missionaries who were not saints
but I hope by God's grace to be
both missionary and at least something of a saint.*

A short two-page letter (November 1934) from John to his mother again mentions the *special intention* of going to the missions in China. He is still hesitant as he thinks of the aloneness of such a vocation, and he awaits his mother's next letter to see what she might say to enlighten his discernment. Mission and language as expressed in John's letter, such as helping *millions of pagan souls* and noting *superstitious worship,* was reconsidered and changed with Vatican II, and particularly with its new theology of missiology.

As he invites the young men in Hobart *to come along* to Church activities, John seems to have a great influence on them in his teaching; he will give input that will enrich their lives in faith. Expecting about forty men to come to a forthcoming event, he is respectful of them, recognising their generosity of heart when they respond.

John refers to his Irish heritage and the strong Faith that has been handed on, especially through his mother and his maternal grandmother, Maria, who was still alive when he was a child. He also reflects on the Irish faithful in earlier times gathered in secret on a hill in Ireland for Mass while priests were *hunted and persecuted* by the British regime. It is November, the month of the Holy Souls, and his mother has asked him to remember deceased relatives at Mass.

St Therese of Lisieux, of whom John has written in earlier letters, comes to the fore again. Her mission was to pray for priests, so John asks his mother to pray for him as a priest and not only as a priest, but a son. He signs off referring to his mother as *Mother Machree,* the little Irish mother in John O'Brien's poem from *Around the Boree Log*.[24]

* * *

[Hobart]
Wed Night

My dear Mother,

As I write I am surrounded with all kinds of papers, notes pamphlets & books – the mines so to speak from which I am trying to extract ideas for

---

24   Around the Boree Log; A Seletion from Around the Boree Log and Parish of St. Mel's, John O'Brien, Angus & Robertson, London, 1980.

the young men. I hope to have about 40 lads ranging from 16 to 26 years of age. Some were not quite taken with the idea but after a little persuasion they consented. It has meant hunting them up in offices, shops – in [the] street, etc. I met one lad making sausages – and he agreed to come along. I trust that God will reward their generosity. One thing that has become more and more evident to me is the grand generosity of lads if they are only put to something worthwhile.

As you asked me in your letter, I have been giving deceased relatives a special memento at Holy Mass during the past week or so. Please keep my intention in your prayers. I have been praying still for the grace to do God's will. I did feel almost ready to hesitate as I thought of myself alone on the way to a strange land but I still feel that God calls and I may not resist nor refuse. The only thing I want now of God is that He will help me to give myself to Him in all things not only in the big things but also in the little things in bearing little annoyances, limitations etc. There have been missionaries who were not saints but I hope by God's grace to be both Missionary and at least something of a Saint.

I am quite anxiously waiting your next letter. I must also write to Father. He will find it hard to understand but oh! how I think of the millions of pagan souls and of the superstitious worship given to the devil and his rebel angels.

You also mentioned the gift of Faith in your letter. Yes indeed, dear Mother. I owe it to you and to your forebears. As I was preaching last Sunday on the love we should have for our Faith, the thought of the Irish priest hunted and persecuted surrounded by his faithful flock out on the hill side came to my mind. Oh how I feel grateful to God for the gift of Faith. It is the desire to sow the seeds of the Faith in Pagan lands that has prompted my resolution – to share in the work of encircling the world with the Church of God.

Dear Mother I would like you to read if you have it The Life of St Therese – especially the Chapter on her Apostolate of Prayer and her missionary "Brothers". After all they were only adopted – you will, please God, have not a Brother a missionary but what is more i.e. son.

Dear Mother, it is late now and I must close. God bless you and keep you Mother Machree – so prays

Your loving Son in Christ
Jack.

Letter 62 to Mother

I pray to be a saintly priest –
otherwise all we do is of little value.

In this four-page letter to his mother (late November 1934), disturbingly John writes he is *not getting going* and is *very forgetful of late* and has *many things to think of*. He has *fervent resolutions and good intentions* and fails again, feeling *so lazy and so slow at times*. He prays for *a burning zeal to drive my lazy self to work*. He feels *hopeless*, longing for space and time to rest and think awhile. It is a dark time for him, critical of himself. Imagine the concern of his mother! While he has many involvements coming up, he writes he will have to be *like the lamplighter*, working at night. He may have heard stories of his great-grandfather who was the first lamplighter in the town of Yea in the latter part of the 19th century.

No news regarding the Columban Fathers has come yet from Ireland. Acceptance would impact on his future plans and his spirits. Thinking of China, he would have to endure the hard conditions, poverty, strange food and isolation and a difficult language to learn.

John's older twenty-five year old sister, Marie, arrives in Tasmania mid-November at the same time that the Duke of Gloucester, Prince Henry, visits Hobart. She communicates effectively with pen and paper, besides Sign language. Besides seeing her brother Brian at St Virgil's, she is drawn into the Catholic community and welcomed with warm hospitality. She visits the Presentation Sisters, and school classrooms, sees the boarders at St Mary's, and is invited to dinner by John's friends and the housekeeper at the Archbishop's *Palace*.

Again John concludes with reference to the Irish mother, Mother Machree, and her son, Soggarth Aroon, a dear priest, counsellor, comforter and friend.

* * *

A.M.D.G.
+

Archbishop's House,
Hobart.
[late November 1934]

Dear Mother,

I should have written to you before this to tell you of Marie's arrival and especially to thank you for the cheque you sent for £15/15. I gave it to Brother next day.[25]

---

25   The cheque for the Brothers was for Brian's educational fees.

I got quite a surprise when the wire came about Marie. At present we are working up a Mission to begin on Sunday next. It means a lot of house to house visiting. However I am glad she came now as there is a good deal of interest in the affairs of the city, the Duke etc. I missed her at the train – late one – and found her already at the Palace.[26] Miss McKenna had already given her a cup of tea etc. I took her to Miss Mitchell's. There are a number of boarders at St. Mary's as well as some lay teachers so that I thought it better not to stay there. We had breakfast together at [the] Convent on Sunday. I have been doing my work, giving Marie what time I can. She understands that till the Mission is over I cannot spare much time. The week after the Mission I can give her more time. In fact it will be a holiday for me too.

After that I will be hard at it again – Retreat to St Columba's children – a miniature Retreat to St. V.C. boys[27] – this will be harder and probably a Recollection day to Young men. Then Christmas and Retreats after. I also want to get to Bruny.

Marie went to [the] National Park, also down the [Huon Valley] with Miss Jones of Seymour whom she met on the boat over. She has been at [the] Convent a few times – [she] also saw [a] number of children in class. The Boarders at St Mary's are most anxious for her to come to see them. Of course Mother Paul is teaching her tatting. Tonight she went to Bratt's for tea. Brian will be able to go off with her on Saturday or Sunday. I simply will have to go like the lamplighter [the] next few days.

Fr. Green is not at home yet – probably he will be home on Saturday. Even then he will have to take things quietly. We shall have big confessions for the Mission. Marie comes up to the Palace for meals rather than I go to Miss Mitchell's. She finds it more homely. She and Miss McKenna and Eileen get along very well. She is very interested in the Electric cooker, etc.

Re Brian: He has exams on Saturday 1st of December – end about Dec. 12th. He will miss the Congress but, as you say, the exams are the test of his year's work. Then I suppose he will go home about 16th or a day or so later for Christmas. I shall not be home till later in January.

So far no news has come from Ireland. It may come about middle of December. Some of priests are going to the Congress in Melbourne. Bishop Galvin is coming. I should like very much to see him. Do you remember him coming to Yea when he was still just a priest? I can remember quite well how you told me about a priest from Northcote going [to China.] I think it was Father Hayes though I am not sure.

I have not had a talk with Brian lately. Somehow I have a lot to do and do not "get going" at it. I am also very forgetful of late. It may be there are so many things to think of. Mission begins on Morning of Sunday next. Only a

---

26   Referring to the Archbishop's House, where John lives.
27   St Virgil's College.

week this time – then week at Newtown and then the Forty Hours on Dec. 2nd, 3rd and 4th. We will then be joining in with Melbourne [Congress.] I am sorry we are not having a fortnight Mission.

I think it would be better for Brian to get a suit in Melbourne. You could pick stuff better than I could. He had his teeth attended to. It cost about £3.0.0 but I thought it wise to have them done. I must have my plate reformed – and a couple of teeth drawn.

I had a letter from Bro. Michael, also Bro. William [Molloy] – both rather surprised.[28] Dear Mother, I am still needing your prayers. I am always beginning again. Fervent resolutions good intentions etc. etc. and then I am falling again. Please beg of God for me the gift of zeal – a burning zeal to drive my lazy self to work. I feel so lazy and so slow at times. Also beg of God the Spirit of Sacrifice.

If I go to China it will mean hard conditions, poverty – strange food and isolation. Then there is the language one of the hardest of all to learn. So I am trying to make effort now but almost feel myself to be "hopeless", except that I know God's grace can make me what I should be. I am longing for the Spiritual Year at Essendon where I will be able to rest awhile from the Mission work to think over things – to benefit by my two years experience and so set out my life again according to higher grander ideals. The Chinese Mission has a reputation for grand ideals. Archbishop Hayden is very keen on them. "They will do anything," he said meaning that they have a certain spirit of bold daring ready to suffer even to die for the cause of the Faith. I still want you to pray that I may be a Saintly priest – that is all that counts. We must be holy otherwise all we do is of little value.

Now dearest Mother, it is late and I must be closing this letter. I am thinking always of you and looking forward to seeing all – especially Father. I would like you to have a holiday while I am home. I want to give you a few weeks off. It may be our last time at home like that because I would become in a way a member of a community and so not at freedom to go at pleasure. I have not heard from Anne. I may be able to see her when home and talk matters over.

Give my love to all. I have remembered Auntie Kate at Mass. Black Mass[29] last Monday for deceased relatives.

God bless you now Mother Machree and pray for
    Your loving Son (Soggarth Aroon)

              Jack.

---

28 It seems the Brothers have changed their tone since the previous letter.
29 A Black Mass meant using black vestments for the deceased. This practice changed after Vatican II.

Letter 63 to Mother

I poured my heartfelt thanks to God for the gift of faith.

This four-page letter on a *scribbling pad* from John to his mother (11th December 1934) is written while he supervises a student doing an exam. It differs from the majority of others in 1934 letters, which are on the Archbishop's House stationery.

In early December, Abe's sister, Auntie Kate Neville, who the family seem to see regularly, has died in Seymour. At this time, the Victorian floods were especially severe in Melbourne where seven inches of rain fell and thirty people died. While John worries, it seems that Emma and Abe were not seriously affected, although their café is not far from the Goulburn River.

With the Congress on in Melbourne, much Catholic activity is taking place. John supposes that his Archbishop, who is there, will speak with Bishop Galvin regarding the Columban mission. The outcome of his application is still on John's mind. He does not know when he will be able to go home but he must see his friend Fr Pat Carmine before *his departure*.

Alas, it is the end of year with school picnics and speech nights – *I loathe them!*

***

A.M.D.G.
+

[Hobart]
Dec 11th 1934

Dearest Mother,

I am at present sitting as supervisor for a Leaving Examination. Peter Green, a St Virgil's College boy, took ill and is doing his exam in bed. I was asked to act as supervisor. Another University Undergraduate is assisting. It is tiresome from the very fact that one seems to be so idle. I have said my Office, read a little, thought a bit over sermons and now I am writing this note on a scribbling pad for want of better.

I was so sorry to hear about Auntie Kate. I have been thinking over the telegram I sent. I should have sent it to Father I suppose. But at the time I got it I was tired after long confessions – we ended at 9.45. Fr Green is back but not doing parochial work as yet.

I said Mass for Auntie on Sunday – also asked prayers of [the] Sisters and [the] congregation. Hers was a good life but I am glad in one way that God has taken her – I always felt sorry for her. I also told Brian. I shall write to Nora[30] later. I suppose you will have seen Marie by the time this letter reaches you. She will tell you Tasmanian news. I have been anxious to hear how you got on in the floods. We have had fine weather here though there was some heavy rain on Friday and Saturday last.

We had 40 Hours devotion[31] – began on Sunday 2nd – ended on the Tuesday. Listened in to Congress on Thursday night – also Friday morning. I also heard a good deal of the Procession being broadcast and was there for the Benediction.

I was thrilled through and through and poured my heartfelt thanks to God for the gift of faith – and for the Mother who under God gave me that Faith. Yes dear Mother I see every day the sad results of a careless mother and I see too the fruits of good Catholic homes. I often wonder how parents can be so terribly indifferent to the spiritual wellbeing of their children. Sunday's display was for me a glorious tribute to the pioneer Catholics of Australia – and not a little to the Little Irish Mothers who have laboured and toiled to keep alive the Faith amid all manner of setbacks.

Brian has finished his exams and is anxious to be on his way home. He wishes to stay at Launceston for a few days. I thought he might as well as he may not have another chance. The Brothers know he will not be back. I am hoping he will be able to get on at Assumption College Kilmore. I shall book his passage tomorrow. He will have tea with me tonight as I am all alone at present – Fr Green in Launceston, Fr Lynch on Fishing trip to Great Lakes, His Grace[32] in Melbourne. I suppose Charlie is home now. There will be great home coming this year.

I do not know yet just when I am coming. I suppose his Grace had a talk to the St Columban's people and to Bishop Galvin. I would like to see Bishop Galvin.

At present there is little school work being done – a few yet for exams. Picnic of St Columba's School tomorrow, St Mary's next day – two speech nights and the St Columba's Concert. These are the functions I loathe especially speech nights.

Had a wire from Father Pat[33] who wished to meet me in Melbourne. I had to say, "I can't". He may be able to come over I do hope so. He is the only priest of my college days whom I would really wish in a special way to meet and talk to. I must see him before my final departure.

Now dear Mother, I must close this note as time is drawing to a close. I

---

30   Abraham's sister, Auntie Kate (Catherine Neville) had six children, Honora being the fifth child and John's first cousin.
31   A time of prayer and adoration lasting 40 hours.
32   Archbishop William Hayden
33   Fr Pat Carmine was the good friend from seminary days, who worked in

shall write again before Christmas. Give my fondest love to all especially to Father.

Your loving Son in Christ Jesus
Jack.

P.S. I have given Brian £6.10 (cheque £3 and £2.5.0.) I have also fixed up about his teeth. I shall bring home some of his things as I have a trunk and a case. I should be very glad if you would kindly keep the newspapers with account of Congress in them.

Remember me please on Dec 18th my ordination day. Two years a priest now. I hope that God will accept what efforts I have made in that time.

Wilcannia-Forbes diocese.

Letter 64 to Mother

> *I would like to go over my theology again –*
> *so much that I have forgotten*
> *and also so much that I would now view*
> *in the new light of experience.*

It is Christmas Day as John writes his four-page letter to his mother (25th December 1934). On this day, he also takes the newly arrived, homesick Irish priest Peter Murphy for a walk. John too possibly needed companionship on such a day as families came together for Christmas. He misses his brother Brian who has returned to Victoria.

In January, the Irish Jesuit priest, Father Albert Power, a respected theologian, Scripture scholar and church historian is to give the retreat to the Tasmanian priests. In 1919, Archbishop Daniel Mannix of Melbourne had insisted that Power be appointed as Rector of Newman College, then in 1923 he was the first Rector of the newly established Corpus Christi Seminary at Werribee in Melbourne.[34] The retreat would provide the priests with solid input.

During the retreat, John's *intention of leaving* to join the Columban Fathers would be made public and he fears being in the *lime-light*. He does not want *fuss* but to *go quietly*. Impatient for news, John thinks about the missions every day and he wonders about *the pagan millions who know nothing of Christmas*, not yet understanding the depth of culture and history of the people. However, he looks forward to an opportunity for further study and to review his theology after two years of being in the *hurly burly* of pastoral life; as he says *there is so much that I have forgotten* and also so much he would see differently now. The harsh attitudes towards *mixed marriages* and other aspects of Catholic life change in the light of a changing Church and society.

Presently, his life is full as he attends to his commitments and being involved with the schools, particularly enjoying the simple concert at St Columba's, where the children give him a photo of the pupils at the end of the year. Through the children's donations, he sees the poor helping the poor. On Christmas Eve, he listens for hours to confessions, responds to a call to the hospital, and prepares sermons for the three Masses on Christmas Day. He does a blessing of a home and sends Christmas cards to people. He plans to visit Alf, a sick parishioner, who is to be confirmed by the Archbishop. Now he is falling asleep at the end of a long day with the first Mass at 6.00am next morning.

---

34   https://en.wikipedia.org/wiki/Albert_Power_(priest)#

Archbishop's House,
Hobart.
Dec 25th 1934

Dearest Mother,

At last I am getting to write to you. Somehow or other I have wasted a great deal of time. We had heavy confessions last night 4 – 6, 7.15 – 10.45, 10.45 – 12.30. There was a great congregation at the Midnight Mass. His Grace said it. Fr Green and I helped give Holy Communion. I am sure great graces came on the Parish with this holy day though one feels sad indeed to see so many who fail. They made a mockery of Christmas.

I had a call to hospital about eleven last night. To bed about 1.30am then to the 6 o'clock Mass, 6.30 and 7.30. The 10 o'clock Mass was a Sung one.

We have Fr Peter Murphy here now. He has been in Australia five weeks and felt very home sick today. It was not like Ireland. I took him for a walk in the afternoon. I feel sorry for him; he seems to be so sad. We are expecting Father Frank Bowman over soon. I hope for great things from Frank. Fr Hehir SJ is here at present to give [a] Retreat to [the Presentation] Sisters and then to give lectures in [the] Cathedral. He is a very nice man.

Our Retreat comes on January 7th – Fr Power (Albert) SJ is to give it. I will want your prayers then especially. My intention of leaving will then be made public. I do not [want] a fuss but would like to get away quietly. One of my continual worries is my pride and love of lime-light. I seem to seek for applause from others. May the humble Christ child of Bethlehem help me to conquer here. The thought is always in my mind. I am still waiting and I fear am impatient to hear news from Ireland.

I hope to go to Bruny Island early in the New Year. The [Christian] Brothers want me to have a few days with them when they go to Orford for holidays. I may. Fr [Vincent] Green has gone home for Christmas but will be back soon I expect. I received various presents, handkerchiefs to a special degree – also a beautiful razor and shaving brush. It has been warm here – but there is nearly always a sea breeze.

I was so glad you got to the Congress. We listened in. It was certainly a glorious display of Faith and more than that; it made one thrill with gratitude for that Faith. Today I have been thinking of the pagan millions who know nothing of Christmas, of Bethlehem and the Christ Jesus. I thought especially of pagan children who are strangers to our dear Saviour and it makes me long the more to go to give all, even my poor life, if God so wills for them.

The St Columba children gave me a photo of their pupils. They had a very simple but enjoyable concert. They also gave little donations in kind to St Vincent de Paul appeal for Christmas presents for poor. It was indeed the poor helping the poor.

I had a nice letter from Mrs Toohey. I shall write to her and try to see her when in Melbourne. I have been going to write to [Auntie] Kit[35] for some time. It was a joy to me to know that the old breach of friendship had been healed.

I hope that Brian will not opt out. I am all the time thinking of him and pray for him. I miss him here very much. I shall bring his bed linen up with me. I have quite a lot of books to pack up and bring also. I shall write to Father also.

I am at present trying to prepare a sermon for Sunday before New Year. Of late I have not been as careful in preparation of Sermons as I might be. This means speaking at random, saying a lot of words but not saying much that matters. I would very much like to put in a couple of years studying. I would like to go all over my Theology again. There is so much that I have forgotten – and also so much that I would now view in the new light of experience.

I may be able to do some at Essendon though the principal part of the year there will be spent entirely on Spiritual formation. There is a 30-day retreat shortly after the seminary opens. In a way it is like a novitiate and there is a good deal done to try one's vocation. I shall be very glad of this after two years in the hurly burly of parish work. Can see what helps and what does not and also I am learning that the spiritual element is of supreme importance. It is possible that I should go to Ireland or to one of the Societies' seminaries in China till I have learnt the language. This is one of the difficulties I am apprehensive of.

I was grateful for remarks in your letter. I, of course, did not advert to others reading my letter to Anne [Douglas.] She sent me a Christmas card. I do feel it a tragedy but dear Mother it only goes to emphasise the old, old story of mixed marriage. One of the sorrows of my life as a priest is the havoc wrought by mixed marriages. Today two persons came to arrange a marriage. One had not been to Confession for five years and the other about three years! I have had only three or four really good respectable Catholic marriages. That is truly appalling. I am hoping that Chinese Catholics will at least be strong in faith and have a great desire to keep it unsullied and unimpaired.

Fr Hehir has been telling me about the Legion of Mary in which Marie is interested. I want to know more about it. It seems to me to be the means of great good in the Church. They seek out careless Catholics, see that children go to Catholic Schools etc. Our schools cost us dear but they are worth it all.

Bro William invited me to call to see him when home. It was nice for Don and Chester to join in procession. I meant to go to see Alf today but did not. I must do so tomorrow. I also want to take His Grace to confirm Alf. He is asking me often when he can be made a soldier of Christ. I sent Christmas

---

35   Auntie Kit Ahearn

Card to Mr & Mrs McCarthy at Karoola to thank them for kindness shown to us.

The [Presentation] Sisters got Marie's letter. They were very pleased. I am going to bless Mrs Bratt's home and consecrate it to the Sacred Heart. She has been so very good to me. They gave me handkerchiefs for Christmas.

Now dearest Mother I am feeling sleepy and have 6.15 Mass in morning so I must now close this note. I send my fondest love to all at home wishing them all the graces of God for the New Year. I offered up my 2nd Holy Mass for you all this morning.

Goodnight now my dear Mother and please continue prayers for me.

Your loving Son in Christ Jesus
Jack.

P.S. I am enclosing £3 for you and Father to use as you please for Christmas. It is not much but I feel that you would not wish me to make a return in monetary ways. I suppose that once I am in the Society of St Columban I shall not be able to get any money at all for my own uses apart from keep etc. **J.C.W.**

Pagans, The Careless And Mixed Marriages!
Tasmania 1934
Letters 54–64

Bobby Court

This privileged glimpse into the heart and mind of a young, newly ordained, restless and quite isolated John Wallis, reminds us of a time when our world, its politics and religious perspectives were insular and defensive of the many barriers and exclusions we had built with great righteousness and conviction, and informed by fear. John's conversation with himself, pouring out with no inhibition into the letters to his mother, reflect a moment in time, one that he would, in his mature years, have looked upon with either amusement or embarrassment or both, but certainly with wise humility. The language of the era and for decades beyond, spoke of the battle of lines drawn, rushed, subjective judgments of people and the Church's great and continued crusade to convert and save pagans in their millions.[36]

John's missionary zeal to be on the frontline and his innate sense of responsibility have their genesis in his brave aspiration to join the Columban Fathers in Essendon and head to China to take up the fight. His letters reflect the extremes of his priestly experience. He is unsettled and wanting to take on the 'mission' challenge which he himself describes as the dearest work of the Sacred Heart;[37] yet his own day-to-day existence is confined by the regimen of his clerical duties, managing a demanding workload, the distance from his family, poverty and a naïve, frustrated understanding of human existence and the complexity of our faith journey.

His effusive description of his own formation, nurtured so completely by his mother, establishes a point of comparison which he applies to those whom he suggests are 'careless'[38] about their faith and the responsibilities that come with it and those who make the choice of 'mixed marriage'.[39] His view of Church, the world and the well accepted language he used to describe it, bear little resemblance to the John Wallis of later years; and he was not alone in this priestly transformation.

---

36   Letter 61
37   Letter 58
38   Letters 55 & 57
39   Letter 55

His focus on pursuing every opportunity to find holiness and solace in the scriptures, meditation, further study, the silence and prayer of retreat and his want to leave behind the security of and his frustrations with his local ministry to adventure to far away lands, speak of his struggle with connecting confidently at every level with those immediately around him. One wonders if his letters, written usually late at night, are his only safe avenue for demonstrating the reality of his hopes and fears.

He longed for a burning zeal to drive himself to work.[40] He did not enjoy the social company of fellow clerics, saw himself as lacking organisational skills,[41] and struggled with official duties attached to the Cathedral, naming school speech nights as something he loathed.[42] Others probably shared his dislike of the latter and possibly still do! He happily avoided formal things.[43] After long demanding days, John usually hurriedly wrote his mother[44] just before retiring, often asking for the strength to labour more steadily,[45] anticipating an early start to another day of doing God's work.[46]

His and his mother's determination to pay for his younger brother Brian's school fees at St Virgil's and his reference to St Mary's and the alternate school for poorer students, St Columba's, portray the reality of access to Catholic education at the time and for decades afterwards. In later years, as parish priest in some of our poorer and more isolated areas, he was unrelenting in his want to establish and support Catholic schools with fees reasonably afforded by families so children could be further nourished in their faith. Success with his own teaching, initially to groups of young men, began in these early days and continued, with a fresh Vatican 11 perspective into his later years.

The Father John Wallis whom I first knew as a child and later as a servant of Catholic education, had moved well beyond the persona communicated by his letters of 1934. The quiet, strong determination was still there, but his embrace and encouragement of the laity to become fully involved in the life of the Church reflected a firmer confidence and contentment alongside a worldlier wisdom, compassionate acceptance of the frailty of human existence and the need to walk strongly yet gently alongside his people as pastor and advocate.

40	Letter 62
41	Letter 60
42	Letter 63
43	Letter 57
44	Letter 57
45	Letter 56
46	Letter 55

Bobby (Barbara) Court BA, Dip Ed, M Ed Leadership, FACE, MAICD was educated by the Dominican Sisters at St John's Primary School and Holy Name School in Glenorchy. John Wallis, her parish priest, was a significant person in her life and that of her family. She was the first from her school to graduate from the University of Tasmania and went on to devote the next four decades to the service of Catholic Education in Tasmania and independent schools nationally. John followed her career, offering wise counsel and encouragement whenever the opportunity arose. She now serves on a number of Boards including Edmund Rice Education Australia and Southern Cross Care and mentors new principals around Australia.

Priesthood and Columbans
1935
Letters 65 – 79

Introduction

In this chapter, a picture emerges of John's leaving Tasmania, joining the Columban Fathers, then returning to pastoral work in Tasmania, including visiting Bruny Island. Towards the end of the year, John is in hospital and is unwell for the rest of the year.

Fifteen surviving letters are incorporated into this chapter, thirteen to John's mother and two to his father, the majority written in the latter part of the year 1935.

Letter 65 to Mother

Give my kind and loving wishes to all at home.
I am longing to see them all.

This four-page letter to his mother (17th January 1935) is dated 1934; John has forgotten it is a new year 1935. He is again on his way to Bruny Island, his favourite place – and he wants to go there before he leaves Tasmania. This time he is on the S.S. Dover, which ferried people and goods down the River Derwent and its surrounds.

He knows his mother will be disappointed when he breaks the news that he will not be home in January; it is a setback and a trial. His holiday has been *postponed indefinitely* and there is no definite answer as to when he will go to the Columbans. At their diocesan retreat, the Archbishop, as usual, informed the priests who would be moving to another position or parish and this time there are priests going back to Ireland. Some priests are sick too, so John is required to fill in the gaps. Archbishop Hayden had already written to the Columban superior, Father Mullaney, to inform him that he would not release John yet. The reply came back with the deadline date for this year's intake into the Columban novitiate as 28th April.

John would do a 30-day retreat immediately upon entering the Columbans, then a year's probation before he would join them officially. He thinks about what it will mean for him to give up all his privately collected, precious books and donate them to the Columban community to which he would belong. Everyone is posing the question to him: Why does he really want to go to the Columban mission?

With all of this on his mind, John still has his feet on the ground and attends to his ministry. He uses his contacts to find a job for a friend. He is on the way to visit families on Bruny Island, which means riding a bike, walking or riding a horse over very rough terrain; he is interested in the 1935 situation in the U.S.A. with regard to schools, the wireless, the *black* question and secret societies. He has taken down names of *careless* people to visit on the mainland at the request of their relatives. For him it would be a friendly visit to give news of their families in Tasmania, and who knows where that will lead.

John's immediate family and Aunties May, Clare and Jane are waiting to see him. Subsequently and surprisingly, the Archbishop releases John by mid-February and John has his long holiday at home.

* * *

A.M.D.G.   +
S.S. Dover.
Thurs. Jan. 17th 1934

Dearest Mother,

Once again I am on the Dover on my way to Bruny. I meant to get away earlier in the week but have been detained for one reason or another. I have lots of things I would like to write in this letter but the boat is bumping a great deal and I am writing under difficulties. Your own welcome letter is to hand. Mrs. Dillon just came to me on [the] boat. I shall be at their place on Sunday next.

Well dear Mother our retreat is over and now I must tell you that my home-coming has been postponed indefinitely. Usually at retreat time, shifts come out. Three priests are going home to Ireland and the Dean of Launceston is too sick to continue work. All was well till news came that Frank Bowman was seriously sick – really serious breakdown. He may not be able to work for some months.

His Grace[1] has written to Fr. Mullaney to ask if I may remain on. Today I got [a] letter saying that the Superior General has given consent and asking me over. However he said that though he would like me to be there on March 1st he will let me wait till April 28th when the long retreat of 30 days begins. I am going to ask His Grace to let me go before March 1st. I told him I want a holiday for a while at home. "Of course," he said. He will be back from Launceston next week and then I shall try to get final news. I am sorry but it is the only setback I have had and I am sure it has been sent as a trial. One

---

1   Archbishop William Hayden

year probation at Essendon and then please God I shall be admitted to the [Columban] Society.

Fr. A. Power S.J. of Werribee gave our retreat. He was pleased to see me ordained and was exceedingly kind. He thinks very highly of the St. Columban priests – "Very holy men these" he said, "and all of them potential martyrs." I am only praying now that I shall be worthy of such company. I know it will be a hard life – with few of the pleasures of our civilised world.

The retreat was very good. We made it at St. Virgil's College. We have two other Jesuits over, Fr. Noel Hehir who is giving a series of lectures. You will see a mention of them in The Standard. He is a particularly nice man and also a saintly little man. Fr. Perrott from Xavier is here for the Lay Retreats. 28 men made a retreat last weekend – there are 47 names in for the Ladies' retreat. I hope it will be a success – I would like to be there for it. Fr. Hackett is over also. He is at St. Joseph's[2] for a holiday. Fr. Green and the four S.J. [Jesuit] men went to Port Arthur. They enjoyed the trip. We also had two American priests here – both highly educated and extremely interesting in their news about U.S.A. – about the schools – wireless – black question, secret societies etc.

Today just a short time before I left, Bro Esmonde[3] arrived for a little spell with Brothers at Orford.[4] We had a chat for a while. He will be here for a day or so after I come back. He looks well indeed.

V.M. was down a few days back looking for work. I introduced him to a man who does travelling. He gave him a couple of agencies for small liners.[5] They are something for the present and with effort that should mean about £20 to £30 in the year. It is a start at something and if he gets right liners, specialties, he could do really well. I feel sorry for him and hope he gets on well.

At present the [Presentation] Sisters are away at Blackman's Bay. I have never been there. I suppose I shall not get away now till after school begins. I thought I might be away before that. I will have to pack up all books. If we wish we can keep personal property or if we wish we can give all over to the Society. That is what I want to do. It will mean a greater detaching of self from the things of this world. People here ask me why I want to go there. Of course it is now generally known.

I am looking forward to going home. I want to go to Yea to see old friends

---

2   St Joseph's Church, the first Catholic Church in Hobart, and presbytery are situated in downtown Hobart.
3   Brother Edmonde was one of the first Irish Christian Brothers to teach at St Gabriel's School for Deaf Boys at Castle Hill.
4   On the East coast of Tasmania.
5   Liners – travelling ships.

there, also to A.C.K. Apart from these I do not want to go about, I feel tired and am hoping to have a rest. I will need to be in form for the [Columban] Novitiate. One thing about that year is that I will have a regular life and not the constant changing of the parish work. I have also been asked to look up careless people for different relations here.[6]

I would like very much to see May and Clare but I do not want to go all the way up.[7] Perhaps I could do it by a car trip on a couple of days. I shall call at Auntie Jane's on way home. Well now dear Mother I shall close this note, as I want to post it at Alonnah. Please pray for my intention and in particular that if it be God's Will I may enter the College in March. I shall write again next week when I get some definite answer.

Give my kind and loving wishes to all at home. I am longing to see them all. Goodbye dear Mother now and may God bless you with all that is choice and holy.

With fondest love from **Jack**.

---

6   Presumably this means visiting people on the mainland who have relatives in Tasmania.
7   Aunties May Lovelock and Clare Keating live in Gippsland.

Letter 66 to Mother

Whichever way things go I can still say I am in God's hands, prepared to do his holy will in all things.

This is a two-page letter from John to his mother (1st April 1935); he has arrived at St Columban's College, Essendon. His mother had already been to visit him and to see the College. Settled and rested, he is *very, very happy*. However, John senses that the doctor who conducted his medical examination has some doubts as to his health, maybe an undiagnosed heart issue from childhood. This could be very disappointing.

The regularity of the order of his day satisfies him. He studies ascetic theology, the practice of the spiritual life in the Christian tradition with its sacred scripture. In self-examination, he notices his shortcomings and failings, resolving to be more *mortified* and to be more like Jesus, the crucified Master, who *chose poverty, suffering and humiliation*. John will be required to deny himself on the mission field so he decides he must practise denying himself now, becoming *more like a disciple*. The gospel passage is his inspiration: *Unless you renounce yourself and all that you possess you cannot be my disciple.* Luke:14:33. The thirty-day retreat will soon begin.

* * *

Monday April 1st 1935

Dearest Mother,

I have just been studying some Ascetic theology – a rather new and unexplored world for me as well in practice I fear as in theory. I am now quite settled and needless to say happy very, very, happy indeed. I was so glad you came out and saw the College and I am only longing now to be able to show Father and Marie round the grounds also.

I have a very full program – every few minutes ear-marked. I am to do my probation work and quite a lot of study privately. In all things also I am with the priests of the house. They are all so wonderfully kind and good – all of them having a certain "spirit" that seems the special possession of St. Columbanites. May God give me that spirit too and help me to be at least a little less unworthy of their company.

There are seven probationers. I meet them when out for manual labour – digging in the garden etc. It is hard. After Mass Breakfast etc. there is a walk in the grounds – then I go to my room for study – a revision of my Theology, Scripture and Liturgy. It first seemed strange to be back to student life but now

I am getting into it. Dinner at 1.00pm. Then from 2.00 – 3.00 some form of vigorous recreation. I have been doing the garden. Cricket on Wednesday and Sunday – other games or walk, if desired. Study after tea – Benediction and prayers at nine. To bed about 10.15. We will begin the Long Retreat a month from yesterday.

I seem to be always going and yet do not feel the strain. It is really quite restful after Hobart. I have written a few letters to a few people and shall write more next Sunday when I have time to write. One of my duties is to give a lecture each Monday night to the house staff.

The Bill from Pellegrini[8] arrived. I am so glad we got that book for Marie. It is now time to go down. I must learn to obey bells etc. Will finish this tomorrow.

Tuesday. I have just finished an hour's fairly solid study and so will finish this as a break. I had to go to the Doctor to be thoroughly examined. It was a long process – worse I do believe than Dr Doyle. So far I am not sure of the verdict. Of course my continuance here depends on it. I know the doctor was not over enthusiastic. He said he would get in touch with Doctor Costigan. However I think all will be well and certainly pray for it. Whichever way things go I can still say I am in God's hands and that I am fully prepared to do His holy will in all things.

I wrote to Auntie May and Charlie[9] – not yet to Auntie Clare.

We will soon be having the holy week ceremonies. I believe they are done with considerable elaborateness here and I am looking forward to them. I am to start Chinese probably tonight. Fr. Mullaney is to teach it.

The principal work is of course to enable us to build up our Spiritual life. Two years away from the College discipline with much work and many distractions and external occupations have not been without their effect on my interior life. It is only now that I am beginning to feel and see how far I have fallen below those ideals I had as a student and newly ordained priest. There is not the same spirit of prayer and of self denial that I once tried to cultivate. I have set out now today to become a much more mortified man trying to be a little more like my Master – a crucified Master who chose poverty and suffering and humiliation as His lot in life.

Moreover one of the special virtues required of us is that of being able to deny ourselves as we must do that in the Mission fields. Please pray for me that I may be very generous with our Lord and especially that learning to renounce myself more and more now I may become more and more His disciple. "Unless a man renounce all that he possess he cannot be my disciple." These are the

---

8 Pelligrini's was a store in Melbourne that provided religious books and religious goods.
9 Charlie, his brother, is still away at St Gabriel's School at Castle Hill.

very words of Our Lord and when I measure myself by them I feel how far – very far I am from what I ought to be.

Now dearest Mother, I must begin my next set of work and so close this letter. Give my kindest love to all at home especially to Father and to Marie. I have been remembering the special intentions we spoke of.

Goodbye for a while dearest Mother and may God bless you and all my dear ones at home. With fondest love to all from

Your loving Son in Christ

Jack.

PS. Did Elsie get the books? I meant to write: may do so when I get a chance.

Letter 67 to Mother

I must try to see that the Bruny children are helped to learn their faith.

It is the feast of Pentecost (4th June 1935) when John writes this poignant two-page letter to his mother. He finished the thirty-day retreat on Sunday 28th May; then within the week he had left the Columbans. On the morning of 29th May, the day after the retreat, John wrote to Archbishop Hayden: *I am glad in one way to be going back to Tasmania since it appears to be the evident will of God.* His dreams of going to China had collapsed – on health grounds and no more is known. The long retreat helped him – giving details to his parents when he visited them before returning to Hobart.

Sadly, something has happened with his father – a break in their relationship. It takes its toll – *I feel a load in my own soul.* He wants the chance *to draw nearer together.*

Everything has changed in Hobart since he left. His previous responsibilities have been taken over by others. He does visit Alf, the sick elderly man whom he visits – Alf has been pleased to see him, as are friends and parishioners. Mr and Mrs Noel McCarthy spotted him going through Launceston – and followed him. Father Vincent Green is anxious he stays in Hobart. John is glad Father Bob Kennedy, who was a pal at the seminary, is there – they have much in common. He recognises that he has support even though he feels lonelier than when he first arrived in Tasmania.

The faith of the children of Bruny Island is still of concern to John. It is two years since he first met Mrs Kit Hawkins, who asked about the care of families like hers in the bush. John sees that catechism lessons are now available in the Tasmanian Catholic paper, *The Standard*, due to the work of Father Cullen, and ensures that the Bruny Island families receive this paper. Then they are in touch with something of the life of the church in Tasmania.

As a source of inspiration for his own life, John comes across the life of St John Vianney (1786 – 1859), whose feast, previously on 9th August is now 4th August. A French parish priest, venerated for his extraordinary work as a confessor, St John Vianney had been declared the patron saint of parish priests, relating closely to John. John died sixty-six years later on 3rd August, the eve of the feast of St John Vianney.

A.M.D.G
+

> Archbishop's House,
> Hobart.
> [4th June 1935]

My Dearest Mother,

I am once more back at my old post at least for a while.

I intended writing on Friday but was kept busy after my arrival about dinner time, so that I had only a few minutes off. Today I have been fairly free. I had two Masses at New Town. It was a change to be duplicating again.

I feel just a little strange yet but everybody has been very good and kind to me. Have met quite a lot of friends, some came along to the Palace. I have not yet seen the Brothers[10] but am going over this evening. They have invited me over to supper in honour of the Holy Ghost. I felt leaving home this time and some how I feel more lonely than perhaps last time I came. In a way I think I will be a missionary here – there is I feel a great deal to do and there are opportunities for the sacrifices of the Missionary life.

I have been wondering how Father is now and have been remembering him in my Mass. All the people, nuns and priests have been asking how you and he are, also about Marie and Brian. I met Mr and Mrs Neil McCarthy in Launceston. They saw me in the street and followed me in the car. They were particularly anxious to know how you were and also disappointed that Marie did not go to see them. They asked me not to let you or her miss them next time when over.

It is at present very cold here. There was heavy snow last night on the Mountain. This time my room is on the balcony side so that I do not get the afternoon sun. I do not know what I am to do yet. Father Green is going for a holiday to Sydney for a month so I shall take over his work during that time. It is quite strange to be at the old work again. Please excuse the writing but my fingers have been made stiff by the cold. After a while I suppose I shall become quite used to it again. Fr Bob Kennedy is here also. He has been working hard

---

10   The Christian Brothers at St Virgil's College, which was literally down the hill from where John lived.

and has met quite a number of people about Hobart. He is thought by them to be very shy but I think he will overcome that soon. I am glad he is here. We were pals at Manly and we have much in common.

Fr Green is much brighter and more sociable since I went away. I have made up my mind to try to foster as far as in me lies that spirit of fraternal charity and mutual help amongst ourselves that I noticed at St Columban's. When Fr Green comes back I may still be kept on here. He is anxious that I stay. Fr Lynch will be going home to Ireland next year so that if I stay I shall have his work to do.

Fr Fitzgerald left about a fortnight ago to join the Redemptorists. I do not know how he will get on. I hope he finds his vocation there. It is possible that I will be sent to his parish at Richmond. This is a big district, perhaps the most extensive parish in Tasmania. It entails a great deal of travelling and there are a great number of country districts where the children and the people too have had but little opportunity for instruction.

I intend to do as much study as I can while I am here. For the present I shall not have much to do in the way of Parish visitation. There are many I would like to visit but I do not like encroaching on another man's patch – as Fr Kennedy has now taken over my district. I went to see Alf. He was glad I came back. Fr Kennedy has now been very kind to him.

I do not know yet what is to be done about Bruny. So far there has been no priest there. Fr Cullen is at present preparing a series of Catechism lessons to be given in the "Standard". I must try to see that all the Bruny people get the paper and that the children are helped to learn their faith in this way.

I find that the Retreat helped me a great deal and am again offering myself and my work to our Lord for Tasmania. I intend to get the Life of St John Vianney and read it so that I may have his example and his ideals before me.

I spoke to Miss Traynor for a few minutes today also her Mother and the two French ladies.

Please give my love to all at home and especially to Father. I have been praying that the Holy Spirit will in His own good time pour out more fully on him the light of faith and keep him in all things. I feel that I have still a load in my own soul in this respect. Please God we will get a chance to draw nearer together.

Well now dear Mother I shall close this note and shall write again soon.

Your loving Son
Jack

Letter 68 to Father

I feel sorry for so many of the people who have been finding it hard to get a little wood for the fire.

It is a very cold winter's day in Hobart and snow is thick on Mt Wellington. Aged twenty-five, John writes a three-page letter to his father (23rd June 1935) telling him that he worries about so many of the Hobart people who have no wood for their fires. This winter is worse than last year and the level of poverty has increased in the city.

John is concerned about his mother still working such long hours in the café at Seymour. While he is *fairly well settled again* but without his books, John's workload is not at full capacity yet because other priests are available. He is even taking some French lessons and is meeting with old friends too. He has arranged for a second-hand bike to be done up. He is very glad there is no fair this year. A new system of raising funds has been put in place.

Because Miss McKenna is to be married soon, she is leaving her job as the presbytery housekeeper, as was then customary that once married, a woman was required to leave her paid work! Now they must find another woman with the special capacity to do the job, John writes. No doubt it has been a challenge for Miss McKenna. Father Green is even looking out for someone from the mainland.

The letter recounts a controversy from the Hobart community involving Father Thomas Joseph O'Donnell, who was born in 1876 in Buninyong, Victoria, and was a colourful figure of Irish descent. Having studied for the priesthood at All Hallows College in Ireland, he was ordained in 1907 and ends up in Tasmania. In World War 1, he joined the Australian Imperial Force as a chaplain with the rank of captain and served in France with the 11th Battalion. With his strong views expressed in public statements, he was arrested in Ireland and ended up in the Tower of London for a short period. In Tasmania, he has been on a number of hospital boards, including the Royal Hobart Hospital, (the chair from 1934 to 1936). As a central figure in the 1935 royal commission into the management of the Royal Hobart Hospital, he was described as a passionate man who became known as one who stood up for the under-dog.[11]

The Archbishop, Father Kennedy and Charlie Walters had been in a slight accident, but in the last paragraph it is to be noted that John himself was also in an accident during his holiday home in Victoria. While it was minor, rumours abounded about his wellbeing, and in fact that he had died. There is a further rumour that John is to go as parish priest to Zeehan on the isolated west coast of Tasmania.

---

11 http://adb.anu.edu.au/biography/odonnell-thomas-joseph-7880

Archbishop's House,
Hobart.
Sunday 23.6.35

Dear Father,

I think the thermometer is somewhere very close to freezing point here now – if it is not below it. It certainly has been extremely cold here all day while the snow is very thick on the Mountain. It began to rain on Friday night and then cleared up yesterday but there was a heavy frost this morning and it seems to have chilled the air. I feel sorry for so many of the people about who have been finding it hard to get a little wood for the fire. I think that in some ways things are worse here than they were this time last year. For one thing there has been an unusually long spell of cold days.

Well I am fairly settled again in my old home – in a different room this time and as yet without my books, they are to come soon I hope. I have been often thinking of all at home especially of Mother at all hours in the shop. So far I have not been doing a great deal of work myself but I suppose as time goes on it will accumulate.

Fr Green went away over a week ago to Sydney. He took his car with him on the Zealandia – £7.00 return for the car. He is, I think, to be absent for about a month. I have been doing his work in his absence. This time there is not the worry there was before, as there is no fair and also because he was able before he left to set all affairs in order.

Then too Fr Bob Kennedy is here to assist as well as Fr Lynch. Fr Kennedy is a College mate of mine so that we have many a good yarn about Manly days. He is very cheerful and jolly and also a hard worker.

The Archbishop is not in the best of health. He has failed a great deal since I saw him last although during the last week or so he has been remarkably bright and cheerful. He and Fr Kennedy together with a lad named Charlie Walters who was driving them in a car nearly came to grief. They had a trailer on behind and were going to the Huon for apples. On the road over the Mountain they came on a frosty bit of road, the trailer skidded and nearly turned them over the bank.

There are new additions going on here just now. A couple of new rooms are being added so as to make more accommodation for visitors and there is also a new bathroom. The big room you were in is being cut into two, one part to be an office and the other a room for the priests to read in, etc.

I have been across to Bratt's once and was talking to Mabel a couple of times. As time goes on I am meeting my old friends.

Fr Kennedy has taken over my district and I shall probably take Fr Green's section of the Parish for Census work. This year we are not having a fair for which I am mighty thankful. Instead they have introduced the Block Collection System by which all are reached and money usually spent in getting up functions etc. is saved.

I have not a bike yet but have arranged for a second-hand one to be done up. Mr Keenan is a very reliable man so that I am quite sure that the job when done will be a good one. I miss the bike very much in getting from place to place. It means that a lot of my time is spent in travelling instead of in other work. Fr Kennedy has a bike also so that there will be three of them soon in the Sacristy of the Cathedral.

Quite recently there has been a change of priests here. Fr Kent has been made Parish Priest of a new parish or rather a part of the old Parish of Richmond. It is to include Richmond, Sorell and Bellerive. The others parts of the original Richmond parish, Kempton and Brighton are to be a new Parish. At present the Sacred Heart Fathers are going to take this over. I just heard that the rumour has it that I am to go to Zeehan. It is the first I have heard of it but it is quite possible. I would get plenty of rain and cold there. We will not know definitely what is being done till Fr Green comes back from his holiday.

The Brothers asked after Brian, also the boys. The numbers at St Virgil's have increased considerably this year. It is a remarkable thing that hardly any of the boys are from fruit growing areas. Most of them are from the North West coast, Launceston and up New Norfolk way.

Miss McKenna, our housekeeper, is leaving sometime soon to get married. It will be hard to get another like her. Fr Green is looking out for one on the mainland. Priests' housekeepers have to be of a special brand almost, and many who would suit other people are not what are needed in a presbytery.

Monday:

I began this letter yesterday but had to drop it for a while owing to other things coming up for attention. I said it was cold – now I add to that with a vengeance. There was a very heavy frost this morning and there has been a keen frosty nip in the air all the day.

I have sent a telegram to Bro William [Molloy]. It is his feast day tomorrow. Tonight I had about an hour's class in French. I go of a Monday evening to

Madamoiselle ? (I can't manage her other name) for some lessons. I want to pick up what I have lost in regard to this language, which is so important to anyone who wishes to study.

I saw in today's paper that you are having a cold spell in Victoria also. I hope it will not interfere with the business of the shop. Fr Green said he might call in[12] if he comes through to Melbourne in his car and [I] think he will probably do so.

At present there is a good deal of excitement here over the Hobart Public Hospital. Father T.J. O'Donnell is one of the Board of Control – in fact he is Chairman. They have dismissed the Matron and so have raised a hornet's nest about themselves. Of course we all keep very much away from it all looking on as interested spectators only.

I suppose you are still getting The Standard at home. I shall see about having the subscription renewed.

Well now dearest Father, I shall not write more for the present. I have a couple of other letters waiting and it is actually getting late. Give my kind love to all at home, especially to Mother. I am always remembering you all at my Mass and also often through the day. I hope you will be able to come over sometime but I advise you to wait till it warms up. I am feeling the cold more this time than I did before. It may be I had got used to warmer weather in Victoria.

I heard today that I had only a few months to live – from one quarter I heard that I was dead already. It is quite amusing to the extent to which the accident was exaggerated. Everybody heard of it – but I hear it grew beyond all proportion by the time it reached here.

Love from

Your fond son in Christ,
Jack.

---

12   At Seymour

Letter 69 to Mother

Visiting friends –
old sheep who are just inclined to nibble again
in places they should not.

In this four-page letter (12th July 1935) written from the Presentation Sisters' holiday house at Blackmans Bay, John is excited to tell his mother he has been appointed as priest-in-charge at the mining town of Zeehan on the west coast of Tasmania. On the positive side, the Sisters of St Joseph run the school there. However, John points out a number of hardships that he will experience. There are no roads to outlying places, not even to Queenstown fifty miles away. The only travel is by rail. He plans to get a horse, although others say it would be of no use. Zeehan is isolated, the presbytery has no housekeeper – John does not cook – and it rains every day.

John keeps his interest in the Columbans and their mission; he hears someone is to go to the newly established mission in Korea. A friend, George Stoner from Tasmania, like John, has not been accepted for the China mission. Both of them have discerned God's plan that did not coincide with their own.

As an after-thought to this letter, John has more to tell his mother. He had been reading about the lives of two faith-filled women who perhaps reminded him of her deep faith. In the village of Riese in the Province of Treviso in Italy, Margarita Sarto, experienced much hardship after her husband's death, supporting a family of nine children by selling farm produce and sewing. She was the mother of Joseph who became Pope Pius X. The other woman, also Italian, Margarita Bosco, was the mother of St John Bosco, who was the founder of the Salesian Fathers and Brothers. Her husband also died young leaving her to raise three sons. She was an example of faith, facing difficulties with wisdom and courage. At the age of 58 and illiterate herself, she moved to the city of Turin and assisted her son in his work serving as a surrogate mother for the hundreds of boys being cared for and educated by the first Salesians.

In recognising his faith-filled mother, who faced many difficulties, John declares his love for her and expresses his gratitude to her, *a Mother whom I love as only God can tell and perhaps I have not shown.* He can never repay her except through prayer and remembrance at the Eucharist.

***

A.M.D.G.
+

[Presentation Sisters,
Blackman's Bay.]
Thursday 12.7.1935

My Dear Mother,

I am writing this note from Blackmans Bay where the [Presentation] Sisters have their country house for holiday time. It is down past Kingston – past the Shot Tower you and Father saw when you were over. I came down to say Mass for them and am taking three home in a car. It is a most delightful spot – quiet – peaceful. I heard the magpies singing at their top while I was saying Mass. It is an ideal place for the Sisters to spend their few days off from school work. Tomorrow they are to begin their retreat.

I have been going to write for some time but so far had to be called away with various duties. Fr Green is still away – in NSW somewhere. He will be back about Monday week.

I can break the news now that I am to be sent to Zeehan on the West Coast. His Grace told me some time back. Fr Joe Cullen who was there for 14 years has had a serious illness and has to have a long rest. He will take over the chaplaincy of Mt St Canice where Fr Kent was. Fr Kent is parish priest of the new Richmond-Bellerive parish.

I am leaving Hobart on Tuesday week and hope to be in Zeehan on the following Thursday. I do not know a great deal about it. It is a rather small town – mostly mining. It was once very flourishing but is not now. There is a Convent school – three sisters [Sisters of St Joseph[13]] there. I do not think there is a housekeeper. The priest has his meals at the hotel or else "batches". I have not yet decided how to manage. They say it is a great place for rain – rain practically every day.

There are no roads to the outlying places so that one has to go by rail. I am told that it is even out of the question to get to them by horse. If I can I will get a horse. Queenstown is about 50 miles away but there is no road through [to] there either. As far as I know I shall be there for some time. I am glad to be going because I will be able to do work with country districts and also have my own district. I hope also to be able to do a good deal of study in the spare time.

I will be expecting you and Father over – via Burnie to stay at my presbytery – a four-roomed house so I am told. They say there is a nice Church there – a hall and school. Next time I write I can tell you more about it all. It will be very isolated – the most isolated parish on the Island. His Grace was very nice to me and said he wanted a priest there who was ready for a hard mission. I am told also that the people there are mostly poor so that is another reason to be

---
13   The Sisters of St Joseph left Zeehan in 1976.

grateful. I am getting a few little odds and ends that may help me there and also trying to see friends – old sheep who are just inclined to nibble again in places they should not.

I had a very nice letter from the Carmelites[14] telling me to let my life in Tasmania be one of self-immolation and self-sacrifice for souls. I hope too in Zeehan to prepare a series of instructions to send to country children.

Mrs Bratt and family send best wishes to you, Father and Marie. Marie will be glad to know the Legion is going well here in Hobart. I have been at the meetings in Fr Green's absence. There is only the one branch as yet. I have seen Alf only once but I must go to see him again. Poor Brian will be wondering when I am going to write to him. So far he has been on the waiting list but no more. I wrote to Charlie. Miss Traynor took her mother for a trip to Sydney. She will be back in about a fortnight. Fr Kennedy is now in charge of Bruny.

Fr Devlin of St Columban's is to sail for Korea[15] in August next. I am so glad he is going. He was a priest in N.S.W. for some years before he joined the Mission.

The Brothers have been on holiday for a few days. Also old Brother Hood asked about Brian. He has great faith in him, "There is something good in that boy!"

I am going to see George Stoner's people on Monday. He is still plodding along, still with the one idea in his mind. He told me he is now quite prepared for any work that God might send him even if it be not in China. He too has come to see that we are to do "God's will" not to be too much wedded to a particular fancy of our own.

Well now my dear Mother I am going to leave here now with the Sisters who are ready, so goodbye for the present with fondest love to all at home from

Your loving Son in Christ Jesus

Jack.

P.S.   I shall write to Marie when I arrive in Zeehan and also to Father. I do hope he is keeping well as you told me in your last letter. I am now going a step further in God's work – I am to have the responsibility of a parish (Priest in Charge) and you will, I know, beg God to help me to be zealous. I hope not just to do the bare essential duties but labour to make the Catholic people better and holier, to bring others into the bosom of the one true Church. Dearest Mother, I am now your "poor parish priest" and I am relying on your prayers to help me.

---

14   These were the Carmelite Sisters in Melbourne who were founded from Sydney in 1922.

15   The Columban Fathers first went to Korea in 1933.

I have been reading the lives of the Mother of Pius X Margaret Sarto – a poor peasant woman and the village dressmaker, and Margaritta Bosco,[16] another peasant woman who through years of toil helped her son on the way to God's altar and then later threw in her lot to help him keep a home for the waifs and strays of Turin. One day she nearly gave in. The toil, the trials, the hours of unremitting hardship nearly crushed her noble heart. Then her son simply pointed to the Crucifix and said nothing. "Oh John", she said, "I am sorry. I had forgotten." Once more she took up her work and today all the world honours her as the Mother of a great and holy priest St John Bosco.

Dearest Mother, we will not seek to be honoured by the world – please God both of us will leave this world with little of its praise but may we be together in Heaven – a Mother whom I love as only God can tell and perhaps I have not shown – and a Priest son for whom you have shown love that he can never repay – or should I say could never repay were it not for the Holy Mass wherein thine is ever the first name that rises to his lips.

Love from
Jack.

---

16   https://en.wikipedia.org/wiki/Margherita_Occhiena

Letter 70 to Mother

Beg Our Lord for me for a greater zeal, a greater spirit of prayer and a greater spirit of self-sacrifice.

In this one-page letter to his Mother Machree (10th August 1935), John, after the anticipation of being appointed to Zeehan in his last letter, is dispirited and downhearted. He is not going to Zeehan. It is the middle of winter in Hobart and, besides being miserable with a cold, he is unsettled and feeling depressed not knowing where he is to go or what he will be doing. He sees so many poor people and there is so much to do. His peer Father Bob Kennedy has gone to another parish and there is no-one with whom he can talk. With his self-esteem knocked around this year, and that despite everything, all is well. She will understand. The Archbishop's house has had renovations done, but John is uncomfortable with what appears to him as luxury – *I would like a poor little cottage with not so much convenience.* He prays for detachment from comfort.

* * *

A.M.D.G.

Archbishop's House,
Hobart.
Aug 10th [1935]

Dear Mother,

I am so sorry to have let you go for so long without news but I have been very busy and also a little off colour. I had a very sore throat, but it is better now, also a cold in [the] head. It is now improving. I had Marie's letter sometime before I posted it.

There is a lot to do now that Fr Kennedy has gone. I don't seem to be getting down to the work as I wish. There is such a lot to do – so many careless people, poor people etc. I am of course somewhat unsettled as yet waiting to know where to next. I am sending this note to let you know all is well and will write later on in month.

The carpenters are out of [the] house now – two new rooms and a bathroom etc. It is all very nice but somehow I would like a poor little cottage where there was not so much convenience etc. I always feel that it is not being like my Master.

Pray for me dearest Mother at times I seem to do so little and to get so slack and negligent that I feel depressed. I know you can understand. I miss very much the benefit of some priest to whom I can talk – like Fr Hall or Fr McGlynn.[17] *However that is part of one's life and so I simply want to go ahead.*

Beg Our Lord for me a greater zeal, a greater spirit of prayer and a greater spirit of self-sacrifice and detachment from the comforts, etc. of life. St John Vianney whose feast it was yesterday makes me blush with utter shame and confusion.

God bless you and keep you, Mother Machree.
J.C.W

---

17 Fathers Hall and McGlynn are Columban priests from Essendon in Melbourne.

Letter 71 to Mother

*Country people seem to be able to appreciate
the presence of God more keenly.*

In the midst of this five-page letter to his mother (22nd September 1935), John, longing for a better world, hopes that the missioner will *stir the possum in this land*. In contrast to his previous letter, this one does have a tone of positivity. It is springtime and *it is such a lovely day*. His spirits are uplifted as he hears the cuckoo, sees the young magpie, the new foliage and the flowers in bud. He is reminded of home when he used look for *cowslips, the harbinger of spring and the purple orchids*.

However, John still struggles with his sermons, finding it hard to get ideas and express them simply and in a convincing way. While he says he is not keeping in touch with people, he writes of many situations where he is relating with people, including his friends the Bratt family and Miss Traynor.

Recounting the people with whom he is engaged in the parish – the *old lady in the tin shanty*, the *poor man in an awful tangle* of relationships who calls himself the black sheep, and another man in a wheelchair, John sees the incongruity of things – the beauty of nature, then the degradation of poverty and how, beneath the most repulsive exterior, *one can find amazing beauty*.

Other things are happening in the parish and need to be done: the month of the Rosary, October, is coming up, the census in preparation for the mission, and teachers have to be paid, but *making money is no easy job*.

John mulls over the Columbans – their generosity to him and that Father Devlin would be on his way to Korea. *At last* he has written to his friend, Father Pat Carmine, in western New South Wales. Years later, John pondered on his seminary formation and on the vivid memories he had of very long walks with Pat and the value of the lengthy discussions on their theology lectures and the theological reading they were doing, solidifying their long-term friendship.

John tells his mother of meeting Jim Noonan who knew her family in Yea. With Christmas coming up, he would dearly like to see any family member, wondering about the concession that would be available if his brothers belonged to the Tennis Club. Is there any chance of coming over? *I suppose it is nil*.

* * *

[Archbishop's House,]
Hobart.
Sept 22nd [1935]

My dear Mother,

I know you will be looking out for a letter. My letters of late have been having a bad time. I seem to be [writing too] late at night – what with sermons, instructions etc. to prepare I am always kept busy.

Somehow I have been finding great difficulty with these sermons etc. At times I find it hard to get any ideas or any way of expressing simply and in a convincing manner what is in my mind. And then I seem to be letting so much parish work drift – not keeping in touch with people as I would wish. With God's grace I want to begin more rigorously this week.

I shall be glad to hear from home. I often think of you all. Of late especially I have been thinking a great deal of the old home when Spring was coming. I think of when as a lad I went for cowslips, the harbinger of Spring, and how we looked for the purple orchids. We used to be very close to God then. There is a certain note about country people that they seem to be able to appreciate the presence of God more keenly than the city people.

I heard a Cuckoo a couple of days ago and it brought me back to the trees outside the house – and then a young magpie – the first I think I have heard over here. We have had a most glorious day here today. I do not think I ever remember such a lovely day especially, as we were walking in the patch of ground behind the Palace where the trees are just in their new foliage and the flowers coming. I used to love to look for new birds and the flowers but now there are other things to seek – often amid sordid and revolting settings.

The other day I went to a tin shanty to find an old lady living there who seems to spend most of her time lying on the floor with all kinds of rubbish about her. The room was shockingly dirty and the atmosphere was sickening. I got quite sick and had to take quite a good dose of fresh air before I felt myself again. She is a Catholic. I must go to see her this week. Result I hope will be a working bee – two boys and myself cleaning out her house. Sometimes one finds amazing beauty under the most repulsive exterior.

Before I forget: Do you remember Jim Noonan whose father was station master (at least I think it was that) at Yea when you were young. He knew Fanny and Charles[18] *and Emma Corcoran. He said they got milk from Grandma. He is living here now.*

I ask that you would pray that all may come right for a poor man, he has got himself into an awful tangle – the old story of more than one woman. Still he is true at heart and is anxious – very anxious to do the right thing. He tells me he is the black sheep and so does not want his whereabouts known to his people. I will be so glad of your prayers for him and indeed for many more like him. Oh that men and women would only think and pray and step warily before they get married. I have about twelve cases of wrecked lives – or wrecked families – all of them in my own immediate district.

Another man has been twice to St Mary's [cathedral.] A young lad Cyril Patterson brings him – wheels him to the Cathedral. Cyril is now most fervent. His sister Lola is going to join the Marist Sisters in Sydney soon. I am trying to help her get what things she needs, as she is very poor. But for what she lacks of this world's goods so she has ample abundance of the spiritual qualities needed for a good sister.

I have written at long last to Fr Pat Carmine. I often wish I could see him and have a long yarn. I get letters now and then from St. Columban's. They have been very good to me and have positively forbidden me from trying to make good any expenses I have caused them. Of course I can help them by sending a little now and then as I save it. Fr Devlin will be on his way by this [time] for Korea. I am glad he is going.

You will see by The Standard that there is to be a big Tennis Tournament here at Christmas. I suppose there will be no chance of any of you coming over. The fares are reduced for members of the Clubs. I was thinking Don or Chester might get over. They could join up with the Victorian Association and then would have benefit of all travelling concessions etc. I was wondering what chance you or Father or Marie would have. I suppose it is nil.

Making money is no easy job, but we have to raise £300 somehow or other for the Presentation Convent to pay for teachers. So far there is £180

---

18   His mother's siblings, Fanny (Frances) and Charles Corcoran, both died in their 20s before John was born.

in hand. I have Art Union tickets here but I have not liked to send them over to Marie to sell because I know you all have your calls. However if you think some could be sold I will send them.

No news from Assumption College Kilmore. The Retreat will be on I suppose in a short time. I hope the missioner will "stir the possum" in our land. October is a busy Month – Rosary Month – the Eucharistic procession and some other feast days. Then the Mission is to begin on Sept 17th.[19] *So I must get busy with census now.*

My letters are few and far between but then you can understand. One place there is where there is no forgetting and that is at the Holy Mass. What news [is there] of Anne? [Have you] Any letter from Auntie Clare? I must write this week to poor Auntie May. I would dearly love her to get over for a while in Tasmania. I shall send her some photos of Hobart. The Bratt's send best wishes also Miss Traynor. I think Fr Lynch is off to Ireland at the end of Dec.

Goodnight now dearest Mother and may God's blessing be rich upon you. With fondest love from

Your loving son in Christ

Jack.

PS. *Love to all and to Father.*

This prayer of Offering was with John's letters.

---

19   Does John mean 17th October? It is already 22nd September.

Letter 72 to Mother

*Every day the choicest flowers are picked
and put on Our Lady's altar.*

In this note to his mother (1935), accompanying a letter to his father, John tells of the two Dillon girls, Lily and Violet from Bruny Island, who have joined different religious congregations. Violet has received the Good Shepherd Sisters' habit and her mother had been to Melbourne for the occasion. Emma now knew the Dillon family and had corresponded with Mrs Dillon.

John's particular interest is that he had prepared religious instruction lessons for the Dillon girls, encouraging them in their chosen life pathways.

* * *

[1935]

Dear Mother,

You will find Bruny News in Father's letter. I am enclosing a photo of Violet Dillon in her Good Shepherd habit. Mrs Dillon went over. She does be constantly thinking of her two flowers – her Lily and her Violet whom she gave to the Master. Every day she picks her choicest flowers and puts them on Our Lady's altar for the girls! Mrs Stan Dillon wishes to be remembered to you and would love you to come to see her. She has six children now – all well though four of them did get the flu and pneumonia.

Love to Marie Don & Chester. Give regards to Kit. I must try to write during [the]weekend.

Your loving Son in Christ
Jack.

Letter 73 to Father

*I was called to an old man who was fairly sick –
I had to go with the mail man as my bike did not come.*

This letter (16th October 1935) that John writes to his father has three pages that have survived – and at least one page is missing. His father is not well. Hearing about the farm at home, John admits he is homesick.

He gives an account of a wet Bruny Island, describing the farms on the Island – the apple blossom is out, men are hoeing the early potatoes and peas are being picked, the strawberries will be picked in December. The locals are very busy this season and it is hard to visit them. Usually *all hands are on deck from dawn to dusk.* But with heavy spring rain and consequent flooding he saw newly planted potatoes floating and strawberry patches washed away. Roads were damaged too. John was caught in the rain-storm and arrives at the Dillon's late at night for shelter – a fire is lit, his clothes are dried and a bed is made up for him. Being so wet, the menfolk cannot work, so they are at home and he can see them. With Mr Smith and Mrs Dillon travelling to attend a Council meeting next day, John accepts the transport opportunity. John recounts having had a pleasant time overall, despite having left his bike on the wharf and travelling with the mailman and everything else. In particular, he notes the warmth of the homes with their huge fires.

Fundraising is a constant in parish life. Besides the two fairs to be held on Bruny Island, there is the drive for the Convent Appeal in Hobart. John refers to money as *filthy lucre!* A nuisance for him really.

On the last page, John refers to the possible development of tourism on Mt Wellington and in the whole of Tasmania.

***

A.M.D.G.
+

Hobart.
Oct 16th 1935

Dearest Father,

Your letter was a welcome surprise awaiting me as I arrived back from Bruny. I did intend to write to you on [the] boat but as there was no table on the SS Mangana, it is fairly difficult to do any writing.

I was glad indeed to know that you are getting over the effects of your falls. I thought they were more serious though I know they were quite serious enough. What you told me about the farm made me feel very homesick.

The Spring here is really very pleasant – the apple trees are all in blossom now. They make a wonderful sight. Spraying operations are in full swing though the recent heavy rain held them up for some time. There are quite a lot of early potatoes on Bruny – also peas. On all sides now can be seen men working in the potato paddocks hoeing them etc. They go to great pains with all their crops here. They are also at the strawberries now. Strawberry season begins about the 3rd week of Dec. When it comes all hands are out from dawn to dusk. It is no use visiting people then. They must pick the fruit just as they ripen – that is within a few days, before they get over ripe.

I had a very pleasant even if wet time at Bruny. Arrived on Wednesday and mustered the children. Then on Thursday did the rounds – visiting most of the people at Alonnah. I left my bike behind at the wharf – rang for it, waited for it and got it on the boat when I was coming home.

Rain began on Thursday. That night I was called to Lunawanna to an old man who was fairly sick. I had to go with the mail man as my bike did not come. The rain simply poured – We had 2 ½ miles up hill Friday morning. After attending to the old man I had to walk from near the Lunawanna jetty out to Dillon's – to find them all in bed. They got up – lit a fire and dried my clothes and fixed up a bed. Next day Friday the rain continued but as my time was limited I had to go out to visit all I could. They had huge fires everywhere – all the men folk at home as it was too wet to work. I had to ride through flood waters in places. Whole patches of strawberries were washed away; newly sown potatoes were floating around in the water the roads were badly damaged. It was too wet and rough for me to go back to Alonnah on Friday night so I stayed the night at Dillon's.

Next day it was a bit finer – though the rain continued on and off all day. I went up with Mr Smith and Mrs Dillon as they were to attend a council meeting. On Sunday after Mass at Alonnah I came back to Lunawanna this time by motor bike. There were quite a lot at Mass at the second station. It was decided that they have a Fair (bazaar) to raise funds for a little Church. I have inspected some blocks and shall make arrangements today. It will cost about £15 (including transfer – surveying fees etc). They are also having a Fair at Alonnah with a view to improving the Church, painting it – fencing round, clearing ferns and putting in new piping etc. There is to be a mission there early in December. Fr O'Loughlin MSC will probably go – I shall

(A page is missing here.)

can raise a few shillings. It is hard to do so now. There is not I think the poverty about that was noticeable a couple of years back. Now that summer is coming people have not to buy wood so much and this makes things a bit better. Still there are a lot out of work – many of them really genuine cases.

Attempts are being made to open up the tourist trade more. I think that Tasmania would become most popular with tourists if it were advertised and the travelling facilities improved. There is a road now almost to the top of Mt Wellington. It is to go to the Pinnacle. So far I have not been along there.

Well now dear Father I have not a great deal more news and I have to get off to the Bank with some more filthy lucre! for the Convent Appeal. I wrote to Mother last week and then she will read this note so I shall not write more just now. I must also write to Don.

Give my kind regards to friends – in Yea and Seymour. I was very pleased to get your letter and I pray that God will bless you in all good things.

With all love and affection, I remain

Your fond Son in Christ

Jack.

P.S. You mentioned the superphosphate. It is used very extensively in the apple orchards and fairly constantly in the paddocks. The rains this time washed away quite a lot as they have just been manuring in the last few weeks.

Letter 74 to Mother

Sometimes we begin to think we can't be done without, then God steps in to show that He does not need our work.

In this four-page, back and front, letter to his mother (4th November 1935), John explains his health issues and that he is to have surgery tonight for the removal of his appendix and to have a hernia attended to while under chloroform. This means he will avoid the fair! A wire will be sent to his mother when he comes out of the operation to reassure her that all was well.

John reflects that *sometimes we can begin to think we can't be done without*. It is a reality check for him. God's mission continues. All he needs to do is respond with love and obey God's will, keeping things in right relationship.

* * *

Hobart
Nov 4th [1935]

Dear Mother,
You will be wondering about me by [the] time you get this letter and I will please God be once more out of the chloroform etc.

I have been not at all well for past month or two. Had nine X-ray photos – Heart, Lungs, Kidneys – Gall bladder etc. – all in order. Diagnosed as appendix – not immediate danger but best to have done now in early stages. Likely to develop at any time. I will also have the hernia attended to. I am going to Stowell Hospital – send letters to Archbishop's House. Dr Rogers is doing operation. I expect to be a week in Hospital – two weeks off after that possibly at St Mary's on the East coast.

I am not worrying at all – in fact [I] will be glad to have it fixed up as it has been more or less troublesome for months past. Dr Rogers said that was the cause of stomach trouble – retching etc. I am sorry I could not wait till after the Fair but doctor thought it best not to. The Fair is on Friday and Saturday.

I have a lot of things to fix up before I go into the Hospital tonight. I do hope you will not worry too much. The Appendix operation is not so terrible now and I hope to be well again soon. I am glad in one sense – because it takes me from the Fair.

Sometimes we begin to think we can't be done without. But God has stepped in to show that He does not need my work. He does in His mercy deign to need my love and obedience to His holy Will. That I may ever do His will is my prayer and I know it is yours too.

I had intended writing a long letter but circumstances took a sudden turn and I am now in a hurry over everything. I shall get them to wire you when operation [is] over. I said a Mass for all deceased relatives on Sunday – also of course on All Souls.[20]

Love to all and especially to Father. Goodbye for the present dearest Mother,

Love from your loving Son in Christ,

Jack.

---

20   The feast of All Souls is celebrated on 2nd November.

Letter 75 to Mother

Being in hospital is one way of realising how God is able to dispense with our service in an active way though we can still work by prayer and sacrifice.

With some text missing from this four-page letter to his mother (18th November 1935) John writes from hospital, and, after two weeks as a patient that he is feeling fit again, although he is still on his back. He expects to have a week at Mt St Canice, where the Good Shepherd Sisters will care for him. Then he thinks he will go to St Marys on the east coast with Father Tim Murphy for further recuperation. Father Sherry brings him communion each day.

He also wonders if his mother will come over – he has received a lecture from her about the will to live, which he notes. With all the gifts he has been given from food – fruit, lollies, biscuits – to flowers and books, he quips that he could set up a *little joint,* a shop, as his mother has. While he enjoys the care and kindness *propped with soft pillows and with kind nurses and kind friends always attending to my every want,* he feels a false guilt, thinking about the asceticism of the saints and Jesus on Calvary *how they suffered in poverty and hardship and even in death.* John is learning that he can serve God without feverish activity, but he writes *I will be stronger in health – a new lease of life to do more for my Master.*

* * *

Stowell Hospital,
Hobart.
Nov 18th [1935]

Dearest Mother,

I intended to write to you before but have just been waiting a while. I have had a good number of visitors and I feel played out when they are gone. Now however I am feeling fit again, though still on my back. Possibly I will be let up for a while on Thursday or Friday and can leave early next week. Doctor told me I am to go away for a rest – right away from work etc. I will stay at Mt St Canice for a week or so and then may go to St Marys on the East Coast with Fr Tim Murphy.

I have been wondering if you will be coming over. If so I can make my arrangements to suit us both. I shall be glad to hear from you soon. I shall be able to go back to work about middle of December or near Christmas time. Even then I shall have to be fairly quiet. It is hard to be inactive so long but I try to see God's will in it all. I keep thinking that it is one way of realising how God is able to dispense with our service in an active way though we can still work by prayer and sacrifice.

I have been most kindly treated by all the nurses and by the many kind visitors. I am thinking of starting a "little joint" here – fruit (all descriptions), biscuits, lollies, cake, flowers and books. There seems to be a new stock in every day. The nurses enjoy the lollies, strawberries and cream (from Mt St Canice[21] nearly every day). I read a good deal although that tires the eyes. Fr Sherry brings me Holy Communion every day so that I ought to be most grateful.

The Mission is on at present. There again I am out of it – again too, a check on tendency to stake too much to feverish external activity. I am trying to say a few Rosaries for its success. Fathers Dalton and Conlan, Sacred Heart Fathers, are giving it. I hope it will do much good. One thing I am glad of is that I will be quite fit by the time of our Retreat in January next.

I must write to poor Auntie May. I have been going to each day but I find it hard yet to write. When I can sit up it will be better. The wound is not very big and is now fairly well healed. There is a little pain when I move and I expect it will be more so when I try to walk. It is very low down in the groin.

I am enclosing a little poem I found in The Advocate some months ago. I have been keeping it but thought you might like it.

There is one Catholic nurse here Sister McRae. She is particularly nice and often speaks to me of her Mother whom she hopes soon to go and see in N.S.W. She worries about not being able easily to get to Mass here. The hours on duty are awkward so that it is only once a month that she can get to Mass.

I have not written to Father yet. But I know he will be able to know from this that I am doing well. I will certainly write to him this week.

Mrs Bratt was in today to see how I was. Everyone has been wonderfully kind. I feel that I am being spoilt and I sometimes think that I am too fond of the esteem and attentiveness of people. I have often told

(A page is missing here.)

... humility and am very proud in my head though it may not always appear. I am sorry for it and beg your loving prayers that I may overcome it. I also still feel that craving for the "hard life" and to be more generous to the Master. As I lie (propped with soft pillows and with kind nurses and kind friends always attending to my every want) I think of Him on Calvary and I think of His Saints how they suffered in poverty and hardship and even in death.

---

21 The Sisters of the Good Shepherd were at Mount St Canice Convent, which was not far from Stowell Hospital.

Still I hope that after this stay in Hospital I will be stronger in health – a new lease of life to do more for my Master. Indeed I did appreciate the hint in your lecture about the will to live. Yes if it pleases Him I want to do a lot yet. I did not have the least fear of the operation and would not hesitate about another. After it the pain is all killed and then I think of God's Mercy. I hope and trust I am in His Grace so why should we fear.

Love – my fondest love to all – to Father and Marie, Don & Chester. I must write to Brian and Charlie too. Love dearest Mother mine

From Your priest son in Christ
Jack.

Letter 76 to Mother

Hasten slowly and let the plans of God work themselves out.

This two-page letter to his mother (November 1935) reveals that twenty-five-year old John is still in hospital after another two weeks. Father Vincent Green has taken his breviary away. No need to be so disciplined with his spiritual practice while he is sick! He attempts to pray the rosary, but John hates *wasting time*. Various people are visiting him, including Mrs Bratt and one of his converts, Mr Roberts, the Christian Brothers and two girls from St Mary's College. He remembers the advice *Hasten slowly!* Let the plans of God work themselves out. After all, maybe his dream of going to the East will be realised later in the journey of his life.

* * *

> Stowell Hospital,
> Hobart.
> [November 1935]

Dearest Mother,

I am still abed and so my writing may be a bit scewwiff (sic) but I want just to let you know how I am faring. I feel much better than when last letter was written – able to sit up in bed and move a little. Doctor said he may remove the stitches today or tomorrow but I do not expect to get up till Thursday or Friday.

I have had a few visitors – Fr Green comes in every day – also Fr Sherry who brought me Holy Communion this morning. I am not doing much in the prayer line now. I can say the Rosary and a few other short prayers. I am not saying Breviary. Fr Green saw it on [the] table and took it away while I was under the anisthetic (sic). I can hear you saying "I am glad."

The Mt St Canice Sisters[22] sent me some flowers and later some Strawberries and Cream. The S.C.S. [St Columbas School] children sent letters and fruit. A Mr Roberts and his wife were in also. He was formerly a Grand Master of Masons. Became Catholic. I had privilege of instructing him and also of receiving him and his wife into Church. The Brothers have been in, also Sheila Lyons[23] and

---

22   Good Shepherd Sisters.
23   This name may not be accurate.

Helen Leahy of St Mary's. I think their fair was a success. I have not been anxious to have visitors up till yesterday. They made me very tired but I am feeling better now though I still get weary easily.

I am able to read now so this helps to counteract the monotony. It is hard to get a book just such as I want – not heavy and yet of some use to me from a knowledge gaining point of view. I don't like the idea of wasting time or rather of not using time in best way I can under the circumstances. I have first got to let a lot of work go but I can be gathering material for sermons etc.

I saw in today's paper about a fire in which poor Harry Tye was burned.[24] May God be good to him.

I was told by Matron about your wire. She told me she would send one back right away. I was glad to know what you thought of the future.

Fr Hall of whom I have told you before told me to "Hasten Slowly" – and to let the plans of God work themselves out. He says that to his mind I should still keep the East in Mind – but not for some years. One of the priest Missioners in China today, Fr McGoldrick, did not join up till he had been many years a priest.

I hope this operation will mean an improvement in health – will close now as I am feeling the strain of effort to write. I shall write to Father during the week also to Don. I often think of him indeed. Give my love to all at home and tell them that I won't be long till I am able to get about again.

Believe me dearest Mother as always,

Your most loving Child in Christ
Jack

---

[24] In Seymour, the Chinese market gardener, Harry Tye and his blind father Charles Tye died as a result of burns in a tragic fire in their home. Before Harry died he rescued his brother, Albert, who was an invalid. *Examiner (Launceston, Tasmania) Monday 11 November 1935.*

Letter 77 to Mother

The holiday is nearly over. Must get down to earnest work again.

John writes a short one-page note to his mother (December 1935) from Orford on the south-east coast of Tasmania on Christian Brothers' stationery. He sounds well again as he takes a holiday as part of his recuperation.

The east coast of Tasmania has magnificent scenery. A day's trip to St Marys, where Father Murphy is, requires that they go up the Elephant Pass, known as treacherous and especially in wet weather. John is the driver, changing gears being a tricky challenge. The day has been pleasant, especially after the previous six weeks or so.

* * *

Orford.
Tuesday, 9.o'clock.

Dear Mother,
I did not get your letter posted yet. The mail goes out at irregular hours from here. We have just come home from St Marys on [the] East Coast, 95 miles from here. In all we did 194 miles today. The car behaved splendidly. There is one long pull – about 5 or 6 miles of very winding road. They call it Elephant Pass. I had to change gear at one very sharp point – Fr Sherry took us to a hotel for Dinner. We went to Falmouth great surfing resort. Arrived home about 8.30. Very hungry and tired. A most pleasant trip. To bed right away this evening.

I feel my holiday is nearly over. Must get down to earnest work again.
Love to all

Letter 78 to Father

One of the greatest joys of my life was to give you my blessing on my ordination day and so see my own dear Father so pleased that that day had come.

This is a four-page letter to John's father (11th December 1935) two weeks before Christmas and a week before his third ordination anniversary. Because of an abscess on his wound, John has moved into St Canice's Presbytery next door to the Good Shepherd Convent at Sandy Bay for further rest while he is still *getting mended*.

At the Good Shepherd convent, there are twenty-six nuns and 180 girls at the Girl's Institution. They have cows, fowls, chicks, and pigs. The elderly Belgian Sister Antoinette with her scientific farming skills and expertise interests John and would his father too. The Sisters treat John with attentive and *kindly* care during his recuperation, sending strawberries and cream and other goodies while in hospital. Now the nurses from the hospital visit him and he introduces them to the Sisters, *the nuns*.

Home from holidays, Father Bob Kennedy brings a souvenir for John – a little booklet about his *best friend and pal*, Pat Carmine whose church was now *the open air with the car as a background,* in the Wilcannia-Forbes Diocese[25] in western New South Wales. Father Pat travels in his most impressive 1935 Southern Cross on the thousands of kilometres of dirt roads. This image stays with John. In 1941, John visited his friend in Broken Hill. Later in 1957, the Missionary Sisters of Service made their first mainland foundation in Parkes to work within that diocese.

John still expects to be moved to a country parish, while, at this point officially Zeehan, he thinks it might be Derby, a mining town in north-east Tasmania.

With the tourist industry developing in Tasmania, John recognises that, especially during the upcoming Christmas holiday season, the hospitality businesses will be hit hard, because of the 1935 national shipping strike that extended longer than anticipated, and in which the Tasmanian Prime Minister Joseph Lyons was a key figure.[26]

In the last paragraph, John breaks open the heart-rending silent chasm between himself and his *dearest and loving* Father who has not been well. John has *a longing to be more* to him. He admits he has not adequately shown his love for his father and they are not as close as he would like. He

---

25   Archbishop William Hayden of Hobart was previously Bishop of Wilcannia-Forbes diocese from 1918–1930.
26   nla.gov.au/nla.news-article11861211

writes *"Still I know that you want to have deep faith"*, and his father may have been *getting it*, his faith and communication in stark contrast to his mother's expression of her faith easily shared. Charlie is home on school holidays. Don has been out of work and now has a tailoring job in Melbourne.

* * *

A.M.D.G.
*Mt St Canice Presbytery,
Sandy Bay.
Dec 11th '35*

My dear Father,

I have been promising myself, and others, too that I would write to you. I intended to do so when I came down here but am sorry I have been so long about it. I received Mother's letter yesterday in which she told me that you are far from well. I am so sorry and I have been wondering about going over if only for a short time. At present there seems to be a shortage of priests all around. Fr Kennedy is at the Cathedral all on his own. Fr Green has gone to bring His Grace back from Sydney.[27] *However I will go over if you are not feeling better after Christmas.*

At present I am still "getting mended" – taking things fairly easily. The [Good Shepherd] Sisters here are exceedingly kind. They try to have every kind of comfort and delicacy at table etc. for me. I feel that it is not good for me. I will be collar proud when I get away and won't want to settle down to work again. I can walk about quite freely now, though the wound has not quite healed yet. There is a stitch abscess, which has been discharging. Doctor said it may take 10 days or more to heal up.

I expect now to be here till after Christmas. Fr Kennedy will most likely stay at St Mary's Cathedral at least till the changes come in January. Some of us I expect will be sent to the country. I should very much like it. Derby is a possibility. As far as can be seen the Zeehan appointment will be let pass. Officially I am still to be at Zeehan.

I do a great deal of reading here and am trying to write some sermons. It is seldom that I have time when on duty so I want to get a few put aside for a rainy day.

It is by the way quite a rainy day here though we have had some fairly hot days. I saw where it was very hot in Melbourne.

Some of the Nurses from the Hospital where I was came down last week

---

27   Father Vincent Green travelled to Sydney to bring home Archbishop William Hayden, who was very sick.

to see the Convent etc. A couple I think had not seen a nun before – all were rather shy at first but after a while quite at home with the [Good Shepherd] Sisters. They were quite taken with the Laundry and were anxious to know all about it.[28] *They also had a look in a Nun's cell for which they were very pleased. It was quite ordinary – to their surprise. Yesterday two more [nurses] came down. They were very fascinated by all they saw. They had a look at the farm also. There is a very big block of farm buildings, sheds etc. at the back of the main building. They have about 20 cows milking just now. There are about 600 fowls and about 400 chicks. They also have 30 pigs.*

The old Sister who has charge of all this part of the Institution (Sister Antoinette) is a Belgian. She was the eldest girl of 10 and when her father died she was about 14 and had to set to work to manage the farm. She was given a special scientific training by a friend next to their place and so carried on their own [place] for years. She studied all about the various diseases of stock and fowls and so was quite an acquisition to the Sisters. She did not join up with them till some years later – having left her home after the war.

There are about 180 girls here at present with 26 Sisters. They have occasional concerts, two last week. I did not go to the first but went to bed instead. On Sunday last I went to a short musical concert given by some artists brought by a Mr Harris, a businessman of the city. None of the party were Catholics, some had not been in a convent before. They were very pleased with their evening and they certainly gave us a pleasant hour and a half. The Violinist was exceedingly good. They said he used to ride a bike twenty miles to learn to play.

Fr Kennedy had a lot of news to tell of Sydney and of old associations there. He told me that Castle Hill got a lot of tailoring from St Pat's.[29] *He brought home some souvenirs.*

In one there was a little mention of Father Pat Carmine in Broken Hill Diocese. Mother and Marie would know of him. He was my very best friend and pal at Manly and I think the only one to whom I felt a really special and intimate attachment. He was the ideal student and yet very kindly with it all. His parish stretches from the Murray to the Queensland border. He goes out in his car – The Southern Cross – taking all kinds of things from petrol and shovels ropes etc. in case he gets bogged, to books, lollies etc. It said in this little booklet that his name is a household word through the West, in station homestead and hut. There were some pictures of him baptising a black child

---

28   The Good Shepherd Sisters conducted a laundry business in which girls in the institution worked. This enabled finance in order to run the institution.

29   The older students at St Gabriel's School for Deaf Boys trained in tailoring are engaged for the task of customising soutanes and suits for students at St Patrick's College, Manly, as well as for Springwood seminary.

and teaching Catechism to [a] motely crowd of black and white children. His Church was the open air with the car as a background. If there is one of my old mates I would really like to see it is Father Pat. He always asks after You and Mother and Charlie in his letters.

I suppose Charlie is glad to be home again. He must be grown a big lad now. It is nearly three years since I saw him. It will be three years on Wednesday next since I was ordained. It does not seem that. I seem to have lost a lot of time this last year. It will be New Year before I begin to do anything yet.

The shipping strike is causing a good deal of worry here in Tasmania. They had been looking forward to a particularly good Tourist Season. I believe Tasmania is being advertised everywhere on the mainland. The hotels and boarding houses will be hard hit here.

It was great news to hear that Don has got something to do. I had often wondered about him and been looking out for something over here but there was never anything offering. I hope he will be able to keep it. I must write to him also. Bill Drysdale's letter must be still on the way but I have written to him. Please give my kind regards to your friends especially Siers, Coonans and to Staffords. Is Michael [Coonan] wedded yet? And Nell McCarthy?[30]

Well now dear Father, I shall close this letter and go down to the letter box before it is too late. I have been remembering you in my prayers and at Mass especially. I do be often thinking of you and wish too that I could see you. I think that somehow you and I must come more together. I feel that I have been wanting in filial love in many ways – at least in showing it but really in myself I feel a longing to be able to be more to you and you to me. I pray for one grace for you that God will give you the gift of faith. I often think that has been between us. We view things perhaps in different ways. Still I know that you want to have deep faith, and I felt too while I was home that you were getting it. In fact one of the greatest joys of my life was to give you my blessing on my ordination day and so see that you my own dear Father seemed so pleased that that day had come.

Goodbye now dearest and loving Father with all love from
Your loving Son in Christ
Jack.

---

30   The Drysdales, Siers, Coonans, Staffords and McCarthys were people from the district of Homewood. Michael Coonan born in 1911, who lived at 'Tara' next door to Wirrabong where John Wallis, grew up, married Annie Mary McCarthy in 1938 and had five children. They lived at Worrough, Trawool. Nell McCarthy was four years older than John and married Jack Fallon in 1937. They lived at the Post Office in Yarra Glen and had four children. The two Miss Staffords, Et and Dora ran the drapery in High Street, Yea.

Letter 79 to Mother

*Goodbye, now dear Mother, for the present,
and please give me a special remembrance
on my ordination anniversary.*

John's short two-page back and front letter to his mother (December 1935) accompanies the important letter to his father. John and his mother have spoken of the difficulty in the father-son relationship and she has possibly encouraged him to write to his father – *you will be pleased ..."* John indicates he thought they may have come when he was ill, and reality dawned on him – namely, the struggle to get away from home with father not well, plus financial issues. Also they are still educating the younger boys.

* * *

A.M.D.G.
+

[December 1935]

Dearest Mother,

Again a short note with another letter that I know you will be pleased that it is so. Really I have felt sad about poor dear Father. And I pray for him always – especially for the gift of Faith.

I would not have been a bit surprised had I seen you and he walk into the Hospital. I remember saying so to one of the Nurses. Then I thought of your struggle to get away.

I have not written to Miss Conroy yet but shall do so tonight or tomorrow. Also to Auntie Kate. Tell her I do not forget her. I wrote to Auntie May. I would be glad if she and Auntie Clare could get a little place to settle down. Auntie Jane will be expecting a letter as I sent Auntie May's letter c/- her, as I was not sure of her address.

Mother Joseph was grateful for your kind letter. She was broken up and has become a sad woman. She was very attached to Mother Paul.

I shall read your letter again and answer later. At present I am in hurry to catch [the] post with Father's letter. Goodbye, now dear Mother, for the present and please give me a special remembrance on 18th. Give love to all, especially Charlie.

Love from

Your loving Son in Christ
Jack.

P.S. Pat Carmine makes me feel very mean indeed. I would like you sometime to meet. We may both meet at Seymour. I don't know Rosie Tehan's address and so am sending papers for the Legion [of Mary] c/o Marie.

MISSIONARY COOPERATION[31]
Priesthood & Columbans 1935
Letters 65 – 79

Gabrielle McMullen

Seeming to lack robust health, 16-year-old John Wallis was not accepted as a seminarian for the Archdiocese of Melbourne. He pursued other options and was welcomed as a student for the priesthood by the Archdiocese of Hobart. He was a seminarian in Sydney in the years 1927–1932.

The letters from that period reveal that John explored whether he was perhaps called to be a religious order priest rather than a diocesan priest. He made contact with the Redemptorist Fathers about joining them. The advice that he received was to persist in his current life as a diocesan seminarian and in *"preparing to be a 'good' priest"*.[32] John remained steadfast in his commitment to his priestly vocation and generally relished his years in the seminary, although he found the studies demanding. In the letters, he occasionally mentioned other religious congregations – the Vincentians, the Jesuits, the Columbans – and obliquely elements of their charisms which he found attractive.

Just before Christmas 1932, John was ordained for the Archdiocese of Hobart. The first years of his priestly ministry in Tasmania are demanding and, as during his years in the seminary, John sometimes questioned his worthiness for priestly ministry.

The letters recount numerous examples of John's faithful service and commitment to his parish duties. However, his heavy workload due to the shortage of priests, the social impacts of the Great Depression and the demands of many Church agencies on his time tested John's physical, spiritual and mental wellbeing. Further discernment about his priestly mission surfaced again in the mid-1930s and he felt called to join St Columban's Mission Society in Essendon in preparation for going to China as a missionary. The Columbans had been in Australia for just over a decade but John knew others, including a fellow old boy from Assumption College, Kilmore who had joined

---

31   In his 1990 encyclical letter, *Redemptoris Missio:* On the Permanent Validity of the Church's Missionary Mandate, Pope John Paul II wrote: "Since they are members of the Church by virtue of their Baptism, all Christians share responsibility for missionary activity. 'Missionary cooperation' is the expression used to describe the sharing by communities and individual Christians in this right and duty"; accessed at w2.vatican.va/.
32   Letter 11, September 1927.

them. For a short period, John did go to Essendon but the Mission Society proved not to be his calling. However, the thirty-day retreat at Essendon was a turning point in his missionary spirituality.[33]

John returned to a lifetime of priestly work in Tasmania, his *'island mission'*,[34] having deepened his understanding of mission – the *"missionary ideal"*[35] is realised not only through the Redemptorist who is invited to give a parish mission or the Columban who goes to the 'foreign' missions but also through ministry in your own parish or neighbourhood. As a seminarian John had written to his mother: "The mission of a priest is not for himself alone" but "also ... *for the greater glory of God; for the extension of the kingdom of God"*.[36]

Mission is the way that we as individual Christians are sent out into the world to proclaim the Gospel. John Wallis realised that he was called to mission as a priest in Tasmania – to the precious ministering of the sacraments to the Catholic community, including in isolated corners of the island, to visitations and being with people in the joys and sorrows of their ordinary lives. His place of mission led him to a new missionary endeavour – a vision of religious sisters who could go onto the *"highways and byways"* on mission to those outside the centres of population and with little or no access to the ministries of the Church. The vision became the reality of the Missionary Sisters of Service.

In his message for World Mission Day 2017, Pope Francis invited us *"to reflect anew on the mission at the heart of the Christian faith"*. He spoke of *"missionary responsibility that needs ... rich imagination and creativity"* and working *"to develop a missionary heart"*.[37] He might have been speaking of Fr John Wallis and his developing sense of mission as reflected in the treasure of his surviving letters.

---

[33] In 1965 the Vatican Council released the Decree *Ad Gentes*: On the Missionary Activity of the Church, which developed John's thinking further: "The pilgrim Church is missionary by her very nature" (Art. 2); accessed at www.vatican.va/.
[34] Letter 52, 22nd September 1933.
[35] Letter 71, 22nd September 1935.
[36] Letter 26, 26 October 1930.
[37] Pope Francis (2017), Message for the World Mission Day 2017, accessed at w2.vatican.va/.

Professor Gabrielle McMullen AM FRACI BSc(Hons) PhD (Monash)

Following postdoctoral research in Germany, Professor Gabrielle McMullen AM joined the Faculty of Medicine at Monash University and was also appointed Dean of its Catholic residence, Mannix College, in 1981. She was then Rector of Australian Catholic University's (ACU) Ballarat campus from 1995-2000 and its Pro- and Deputy Vice-Chancellor (Academic) until February 2011. From July 2011 until December 2017, Professor McMullen was a Trustee of Mary Aikenhead Ministries and since November 2015 has been one of four lay appointees to the Stewardship Council of the Missionary Sisters of Service. She is a member of the Council of the University of Divinity and also of the Council of the Divine Word University in Madang, Papua New Guinea. Her other community contributions have encompassed membership of education, health, theological, community services and pastoral research boards.

Tasmania

1936-1937
Letters 80 – 88

Introduction

This eighth chapter covers a period of intense pastoral encounters and John's further involvement in Church administrative matters.

It consists of nine letters from John, seven to his mother and two to his father. Seven of the letters are written in 1936, two in 1937.

Letter 80 to Mother

I am leg weary and could wish for a nice car
to pick me up and run me up the hill.
But that is some way
of preaching the poverty of Christ.

In this four-page letter to his mother (14th January 1936), John encourages her, but she is clearly unwell, another reason why she did not come to see him in hospital. In January the priests' retreat had taken place in the north of the State. John had stayed overnight with Father Vincent Allen at Invermay, a suburb of Launceston. He also stays at the Deanery in Launceston where he first worked after his ordination three years earlier. Visiting the Morgan family, he notes that Mary Morgan is to join the Sisters of St. Joseph, but in fact she joins the Presentation Sisters, as Sister Mary Gertrude, and she later becomes their congregational leader.

In returning to the Archbishop's House John is *squaring things up*, getting things in place, his *timetable* and such things for the year ahead. He collects his things from St Canice presbytery at Sandy Bay where he had recuperated, visits the Good Shepherd Sisters and *picks up the strings* again wanting to *make up for lost time* – time lost during his sickness and absence on retreat.

There are the men's and women's retreats to organise, instructions for those wanting to know more about the Catholic faith, people to see like the Bratt family, the old man Alf, and Mother Joseph who is in hospital. He wants to visit other sick people and take communion to them. Besides this, there is a Deaf family with whom he has come into contact and he wants time with them.

John notes the Columban who is going to Ireland for further training. He also adds an opinion on his friend, George Stoner from Hobart.

With no bike, he is now getting plenty of exercise walking to the hospitals and around the parish in the course of his work. He believes, as does Father Hehir, that it is easier for people to approach them while walking or riding a bike rather than driving a car, from which it can appear that *the priest is above them*.

* * *

A.M.D.G
✝

Archbishops House,
[Hobart.]
Jan 14th [1936]

Dear Mother,

You will be wondering when I am going to write. We came off retreat on Friday last and since then I have been trying to square things up – to get my room in order, timetable for work, letters on business answered etc. So that it is only now that I am getting a little time to spare. I had quite a pleasant trip over arriving about 4.10. Went into Launceston and stayed at St Finn Barr's Presbytery Invermay with Fr Allen.

Next day I was at Deanery, also to Morgan's. Mary is going to join the Brown Josephites in Vic. I saw the few sisters at the convent – most of them are at Low Head for holidays. On Sunday I said 9am Mass and preached at devotions. We got away early on Monday.

Father Hanohoe[1] came down to take up duties at St. Joseph's [parish in Hobart]. He has Fr Pat Hanlon[2] for companion. Fr Bob Kennedy is my fellow curate. Fr Lynch will be going away soon. There were many speculations as to new order after Retreat but we are all where we were before.

Fr Hehir gave the Retreat. He is splendid. Also the Men's Retreat. 30 men [are booked] in. We are now working to get as many ladies as possible for Retreat. He is to give it – begins on Saturday next 3.30 p.m. ends on Monday morning. I hope it will be a grand success. There should be about 40 ladies [booked] in for it.

It is hard to make up for lost time and I am now trying to pick up the strings again. There are a few for instructions to be attended to and I hope to be allowed to have an Instruction Class this year. This would make that work lighter. I have not been to see Bratt's yet nor indeed any of the people. Will see Alf today.

George Stoner has arranged to seek admission to Loyola – Jesuit Novitiate. I am very glad as I feel that that will be the ideal place for him. More so than the Chinese Mission. He is of an intellectual turn of mind and wants guidance such as [he] would get with [the] S.J. [Society of Jesus.]

The [Christian] Brothers [from St Virgil's school] are on holidays.

Came across a family today with three children and [the] mother [is] deaf and dumb. [The] mother is Catholic. Married about 30 years. Children baptised in another Church.

---

1   Joe Hanahoe, an Irishman who sang Irish songs, was later parish priest of Latrobe in Tasmania for many years, but not being very strong in health returned to Ireland.

2   Pat Hanlon, who was well-respected as a parish priest loved poetry.

I had a letter from Rosie. I am so glad. We will see how God works in His own quiet way and is able to easily dispense with assistance of any of us. I went to Mt St Canice [presbytery] for my things and saw [the Good Shepherd] sisters. They asked after you all.

Jack O'Meara a student from Essendon is here just now. Comes from Launceston. He is very lonely in a way – feels that he has not the old companions, etc. They[3] *are really scared of students and keep their distance generally. I also had letter from Hubert Hayward who left this year for Dalgan [Park south of Navan, County Meath in Ireland].*

Mother Joseph is very sick in "Stowell" hospital. She will be unable to do work for some six months or so. I went to the hospital to see her – saw some of nurses also and got my account.

I shall not write longer now dear Mother, as I have to visit the sick people in my district to arrange about Communion. It is a good long job now with no bike. I have plenty of exercise now. Father Hehir is against driving the car. He said that the people like to see their priest in a way they can approach him. He thinks the car makes people feel that the priest is above them. I feel that way myself except when I am leg weary and could wish for a nice car to pick me up and run me up the hill. But that is some way of preaching the poverty of Christ.

Goodbye now dear Mother till I find a little more spare time. Give my fond love to all. I do hope that you will go back to the doctor and take the treatment ordered. I will be writing to Father in a few days. Now I will close this time so may God bless you dearest Mother and pray for me please.

Your loving Son in Christ
Jack

---

3   The professors did not usually mix with the students.

Letter 81

*People in the city do not see
a great deal of good in going to Bruny Island,
there are only a few people
but I feel that they are some of Tasmania's best.*

John writes five pages of his news (25th February 1936), especially about Bruny Island and its families, in response to his mother's letter read while on the boat travelling to Bruny Island. It is a relief she has sold the shop and she will return at Homewood, Yea – where his father can sit in the big chair with his feet up in front of a big fire. John looks forward to the next holiday back on the farm.

John adds his thanks for his mother's spiritual care, noting comparability to Mrs Dillon, *a Catholic mother in name and deed, one of the grandest women* he has met. Twelve months earlier, John had taken his mother and father, Emma and Abe, to Bruny Island to visit the friends he has made there, including the Dillons. Emma corresponds with Mrs Dillon who *cherishes your kindly thoughts and encouragement.*

On this trip, John accompanies the *good* Missionary of the Sacred Heart preacher Father O'Loughlin with whom he gives the first mission on the island – a *simple and humble* mission giving spiritual nourishment to the people, who have been exceptional in their efforts to attend *despite the difficulties.* Children are gathered together for *instructions* and some make their First Communion. Being apple season, John enjoys eating as many as he can, but it is not a good year for apples.

He lets his mother know of letters he has received and the ones he must write, and that the *nice man*, Mr Jack Traynor, has had to sell his business.

* * *

A.M.D.G.
Hobart
Feb 25th 1936

My dearest Mother,

Before Lent and before I get back to routine work I must drop you a line to thank you for your letter and to say how pleased I was at news in it. I was on way to Bruny when it came and as we went along in the boat I read it.

Fr O'Loughlin MSC and I led a Mission there. We went on Saturday 15th and stayed till yesterday. Of course it was a simple and a humble one but on the whole I was very well pleased. Fr O'Loughlin is a good preacher and has also a "way" with him.

At Lunawanna there are 7 boys in one family. One family is almost entirely devoid of religious knowledge or religious sense. I feel very sorry for them. I have often thanked God for your care etc. even when I did not want to learn the "Catty" or say even a "dec".[4]

Of course there was some wonderful fervour shown. I will not soon forget the Dillon's and the way they made the Mission. We said Mass in the hall and they brought lunch etc. and had breakfast sitting on steps – then off to hard work. Mrs Stan [Dillon] was there despite all the difficulties – 6 children and the distance. She is one of the grandest women I have yet met. She cherishes your kindly thoughts and encouragement as (one) of the only women who has spoken to her in that way. Yesterday she rode a horse and Stan a bicycle to Mass at 5.30. They asked me to say it early otherwise they would miss it as Stan had to get off to work at 7.00am. Little Patricia made her first Holy Communion also two other little girls. In all, I had about 25 children for instruction. I think it is the first time a priest has gathered the Lunawanna children together for special instruction.

They are anxious to get on with their Church. Fr O'Loughlin was very much impressed by the generous spirit of sacrifice Mrs Dillon showed. One lad says he is going to be a priest. I do hope so. A Mrs Albert Conley convert with her three children also came to the Mission. She is very firm. Doreen the only girl is 15 and has an idea of being a Nun.

I am sure you will keep poor little Bruny in your prayers. People in the city here – priests amongst them – do not see a great deal of good in going there. They think that there are only a few people but I feel that they are some of Tasmania's best. There were a few non-Catholics present also and I expect two of them to carry their enquiries further. Mrs Dillon sends her regards to you and was wondering if you could come over again to see them all.

Well Mother, I am so glad to know that you are rid of the shop and back at [the] farm. I could have cried as I read your letter and felt myself back at [the] farm [as] a child and all that it meant to us all. I may as well say that I am looking forward to holidays now as never before. Somehow I could not feel "at home" at [the] shop but I can see myself next time I am home enjoying every moment. Please God I shall be able to say Mass there at least a few times and then to be with you and Father more.

I expect you are planning little alternations etc. to the garden! I was wondering about fruit trees or berries from over here. I asked Walkers to send a catalogue but it will not be posted till berry season (transplanting) begins.

---

4   'Catty' refers to the catechism; 'dec' refers to a decade of the rosary.

The apple season is on here. I ate apples till I could eat no more while at Bruny. Poor people they are not likely to make much this year. I always feel sorry for them. They have a harder time than any other primary producer. I shall get Mrs Dillon to send a case over. Terry [Dillon] gave me a piece of figured hard wood which I shall try to have made up and sent to you and Father as a memento of Bruny Mission.

Glad – so glad to hear that Brian is back at Assumption College Kilmore! I have not written to him yet. I shall say nothing of what you said.

I must write to Misses Conroy and to Mrs Pearce. Had letter from Sr de Sales [Presentation Sister.] Also Mother Margaret Mary who was Superior at Mt St Canice [Convent] when you were here and so kind to me and now [she is] Superior at Good Shepherd Convent, Albert Park [Melbourne]. She would be delighted to see you. She was anxious to know how you and Father are keeping. I owe much to them for care of me after [my] operation.

Now dear Mother it is late and I have been up since about 4.30 this morning. It has been a long and full day so that I think I shall get off to bed – (about 11 oclock). Poor Jack Traynor had to sell up his business. I am sorry for him – he is such a nice man ... Pat is at school still – a much-changed girl in the last year or so. I have hopes of Pat entering the convent. I can't say how [Sister] M. Joseph is. I have not heard since I came back.

Now dear Mother please pray for me and remember the decades said by the little altar. My trip to Bruny and my meeting the good simple folk there has refreshed all the pleasant memories of [the] past. May God bless you Mother dear and reward you with the graces of a Mother's life consecrated to God's service. As I saw the mother here on Bruny – the Catholic Mother in name and deed – Mrs Dillon, I thought of you and said a fervent "Deo Gratias". Thanks be to God for you too. I always pray for holy and saintly Catholic Mothers in the world.

Will send photo of Stan Dillon's family when numbering 5. (New addition since the photo taken). Give fondest love to all and tell Father I hope next time I am home to see him in [the] big chair with feet up at [the] fireplace and a good big fire as when we were little. However I cannot say when I will be home. We must be generous to the Master and make sacrifices for Him.

Goodnight now once again to yourself dear Mother and Father, Marie and all at home. With fondest love from

Your loving Son in Christ
Jack

Letter 82 to Mother

I feel as though I want the interior spirit renewed and refreshed so as to give life and richness to the externals of the spiritual life.

In this six-page letter (15th April 1936), John reminds his mother that it is nine years to the day since he first arrived at the seminary in Springwood.

It is Easter time. On special occasions, he feels a depth of loneliness and isolation being in Tasmania and away from family. However, the *cable*, namely the telephone, connects him with his family. This *filled his Easter with a lightness* that he has not known at Easter in a while. He captures the scene of running up the hill from the Cathedral to the Archbishop's House to be there for the telephone call and, when it comes, he imagines his mother and father on the other end of the line, as they talk.

Archbishop Hayden is very unwell and John spends more time in his company now, finding him a delightful person. In this letter, he also writes of two good friends whom he would love to see, one being his school friend, Redemptorist, Father Pat Deane, who later works with the poor in the Philippines. The second is Pat Carmine, who sent a telegram, *a wire* using the terminology of the time to say he was beginning *a mission to blacks*, having endeared himself to the Indigenous people. He understood Australia's colonial history of Aboriginal people of the land being so dismal and unjust.

Painting the amusing scene of himself and two of his peers getting the *giggles* at the Solemn High Mass gives an insight of normal impish young men, who also carry the onerous responsibilities of pastoral priests in the tough 1930s. John is still oscillating as to whether he will buy a car or not – will it be a single-seater Morris? The doctor has banned riding a bike for health reasons, so it is a matter of walking up and down the hills of Hobart. He also wishes to buy books for his instructional work with adults interested in the Catholic faith. He cannot do both financially. As well, he wants to buy a bookcase to set up a library for the Children of Mary society.

Interested in the economy of Tasmania, he tells of the apple season being in full swing, with the ship the *Balranald* taking 50,000 cases of the apples to the mainland. The dryness of the season has affected the growth of the crop this year so the apples are not being exported overseas. If not sold in Australia, the alternative was to discard them. In Hobart, Premier Albert George Ogilvie, has announced that much money will be outlaid on a new hospital, the new paper pulp industry, which will provide many with employment, and a seven-storey insurance building. This is good for the Tasmania economy.

There are a number of mentions of different people in this letter, one being George Stoner, who has been looking at various religious orders that he might join. He wants John to talk with his parents about what the life of the Jesuits would entail. George meets him at Cornelian Bay cemetery after a funeral, and rows him over the Derwent River to Lindisfarne on the eastern shore.

John sends his love to the family and regards to all his friends. He wants *a little quiet reflection* and *to be renewed and refreshed,* seeing the importance of a rich life that flows from his spirituality. While he always asks her to pray for the grace to be a better priest, he includes all his brother priests.

* * *

AMDG
Hobart
April 15th [1936].

Dearest Mother,
At last I put pen to paper to write you my Easter greetings, which I have already given you over the cable. Is it not a wonderful thing for us to hear each other and to talk as we did? Really Mother it was a great joy for me – filled my Easter with a lightness I have not known at this season for sometime except of course last Easter when I was home. Usually Easter here is very depressing. This time it was most happy. Thank you ever so much for ringing. I was only afraid I would miss the call as I had a lot of confessions, which took me on till 6.25 so that I had only 5 min. to run up the hill. I was at tea when the call came. I was so glad to speak to Father too. I could see you both there and felt that you would be glad to have had even so short a chat as we did have. We have rung Sydney a couple of times since the phone was set in action. Our wireless reception of the Mainland stations is also much better now – no static.

It is 9 years today since I left for St Columba's Springwood. How the time goes. I have been 3 years in Hobart now. I expect you were busy for Easter. We see a good deal about the traffic etc. on holidays. We had a busy time here for Easter week. I was Master of Ceremonies for all functions so that it meant a lot of work. Besides that, I had a few [sessions for preparation of] marriages – more or less complicated ones too, and then a sick call at 4 o'clock Good Friday Morning.

On Sunday we had a Solemn High Mass. It went off well except that I got a fit of the giggles together with the Deacon and Celebrant. It was one of the most trying ordeals I have had. Fr [Vincent] Green was preaching. He began thus: "Your grace, Rev. Fathers, Ladies and..." This tickled us (Fr Kennedy,

Fr W. Ryan and myself) and we could not overcome ourselves. I am sure the congregation must have seen it and perhaps been scandalised. The Altar Boys certainly made capital of it.

Fr Sherry went by plane to Melbourne for the Holy Oils as His Grace was not in form to consecrate them.[5] They were here in Hobart about 6 hours after the Mass [in Melbourne] at which they were blessed had finished.

There have been a great number of visitors in Tasmania this last few weeks 1000 off one boat. The Apple Season is still in full swing – as many as 50,000 cases went off in the Balranald. There have been a few visiting priests with us when boats come in.

The children are on holidays just now so that we have a rest for a while from our school-work. The Instruction Class is going on in a satisfactory way. About 20 to 30 each night. I shall be receiving a few into the Church towards the end of May or in June. I am also trying to get a Library going for the Children of Mary. We have some books but a bookcase such as I want would cost about £3.00 or £4.00. This is a bit too much for our funds. I am going to inspect one today or tomorrow. It is priced at £2.00 – cedar.

On Monday I went over to see the Stonors. George met me at Cornelian Bay after a funeral and rowed me over the Derwent in a boat. They were very anxious to learn all about the life of a Jesuit. Of course they find it hard to understand in some ways – the idea of not being able to come home etc. is very difficult for a Non Catholic to grasp. Still they are pleased that George has his mind settled at last. He may be going to Melbourne early in January of next year.

I have had a letter from Fr Mullaney – also from Jack O'Meara a Launceston lad at Essendon.[6] He may be going to Ireland next year.

I paid £5 down on the Lunawanna[7] block with 6 months to pay the balance of £10. At present there is a credit of 17/6 so you can see there is a good deal to make up between now and September next. I must try to get some raffles or an Art Union going to help raise the funds.

I did not get a car as I had been thinking of doing. I priced various ones. The one, which I would have liked, was a Morris – a Single Seater but it was a little too high for me to think of £120 payable over 12 months. Somehow as I think over it, it may be better if I could use that money in getting Catholic Books and literature etc. for the Convert Instruction class. This is for Non Catholic inquirers as well. Still I have opened an account at the Commonwealth Savings

---

5   It was the duty of the bishop to bless the Holy Oils – the oil of catechumens, holy chrism, and oil of the sick – which were used by the priests throughout the year.
6   With the Columban order.
7   Lunawanna is a small town on the western side of Bruny Island, which faces the D'Entrecasteaux Channel.

Bank to save a little up. I may then consider a car at the end of the year. I asked the Doctor about a bike but he was very definite against it. I spoke to Fr Green and he said he would rather me not to get a car as he thought it would be a burden to me and said he would cut out some of my duties. This would make things easier. At any rate I have now definitely decided not to think more about the matter till next year.

So far I have not written to Auntie May or to Auntie Jane. As a matter of fact I have written to no one except a couple of urgent business letters. There are quite a number of letters here awaiting replies. No news update from Assumption College Kilmore – either from Brother William or from Brian. I wrote to Os. [Oswald] Dunn some time ago. No reply to date. Tell Marie the lost surplice has come to life. It was found where we suspected it to have been at St Francis Xavier Church. Fr Pat Hanlon brought it back a few days ago.

His Grace [Archbishop Hayden] is not in best of health – he still manages to say Mass but does not do other work. He gets lonely and likes to have us about him. I have been more in his company of late. He is a delightful man to know.

Had a wire from Pat Carmine to say he was beginning Mission to Blacks. A wire a few days ago to report progress. I am longing to see Pat sometime. I have been thinking that next time I get over to the Mainland I will try to go up by Mildura to Broken Hill to see him or else get him down to home. A holiday would not be undeserved by him. I have not written to him for some time. Rosie Tehan wrote to me telling me news about herself. I expect you have heard it by this.

I saw in [The] Advocate that Pat Deane has been Ordained – also Charlie Fiscalini. Both are Redemptorists. I should be glad to meet Pat again. He is one of my really near friends of school days. Fr Fitzgerald has been with us for some time. He has an ulcer in the stomach. I expect the food and life of CSsR was too solid for him. He tells us quite a lot about the life in the Monastery. I often wondered how he would stand it, as he is a man with all kinds of fads etc. It is hard to see how a man like this could knuckle down to Redemptorist discipline. It is not likely that he will be able to do active duty for some time. I hope Frank Toohey and Mick Long go through right enough.

We have had no rain to date. It is very hard for the apple growers. Their apples are too small for overseas shipment and so are simply thrown out or sent to sales in Sydney. There is a good deal of money to be spent in Tasmania this year – new hospital will be £62,000; then about £100,000 on paper pulp industry besides two new Insurance buildings, one of them a 7-storey building.

Well now dearest Mother, it is getting late and I have a lad coming to receive instructions at 5 o'clock so I shall not write more just now. I must write to Marie too as soon as I can. I did get the book she sent. I could not make out where it came from. It is very helpful for the children. They quite enjoy looking through the pictures. Give my love to all at home and kind regards to friends.

I hope to have a day off this week or next week for a little quiet reflection. With all the hustle and bustle of Easter and then the schools, etc. one grows careless and gets out of touch with things spiritual. I feel as though I want the interior Spirit renewed and refreshed so as to give life and richness to the externals of the Spiritual life. Please pray for me always, and beg the grace of a more and more priestly life for myself and my brother priests. You may be reading the Pope's letter on the Priesthood.[8] It is available in booklet form from the Australian Catholic Truth Society.[9]

Goodbye dearest Mother, with fondest love from
Your loving Son in Christ
Jack.

---

8 On 20th December 1935 Pope Pius XI announced his encyclical *Ad Catholici Sacerdotii*, On the Catholic Priesthood.
9 The Australian Catholic Truth Society was begun in 1904.

Letter 83 to Mother

Would you let me help you somewhat,
I would like to send money to you for any needs you have.

In this five-page letter (5th May 1936) written on his mother's birthday, John writes that he had thought of calling her on the *new phone*. Almost twenty-six years old, he tells of many activities and responsibilities in his life; as well he gives a glimpse into how he feels. He still does not have the *pep* he had three years previously, although people are saying how well he looks. He remembers that twelve months earlier he was on his 30-day retreat and insistently asks for prayers.

The Sisters of the Good Shepherd still offer their care, especially since he was in hospital. He appreciates their goodness – doing his washing and, this time, have replaced his worn shirt with a good quality *Crimean shirt*, which he recognises as very generous.

As in many previous letters, John is concerned about his mother's health. It seems she has not moved out of the shop, Wallis' Café. Because of her hard work for the family he encourages her, ensuring she will be rewarded in terms that cannot be calculated in this life. He also remembers Grandma's anniversary coming up on 12th May – it is ten years since she died.

Through the letters, it is easy to observe the vulnerability of ministry in Tasmania that relies on few priests, with a number of local priests, including the Archbishop, sick and not able to work. John is concerned for them and the situation. In describing the Archbishop as *wonderfully loveable,* John points out the former's anxiousness to attend the concert where the local Tasmanian pianist Eileen Joyce is playing. Six months later, the Archbishop dies.

To note in this letter is John's vision for the development of the Church in Tasmania – and its financial affairs. He has the Bruny Island parishioners fundraising for their church development and he is very aware of all that has to happen at St Mary's Cathedral in Hobart – repair of the steps, the windows and the altar rails, as well bitumen on the road outside, tiling the porch and improving the ventilation. Following the renovations, there will be the parish hall to be built.

Enthusing people when *visiting, coaxing and cajoling*, John has various groups fundraising for the many different needs. He recognises leaders and supporters in the parish. Another charity is the Lenten *Mite Boxes* that children take home to save their pennies for the missions. This is an initiative of the Columban Fathers for their work overseas. The Columbans will send to those who raised at least four shillings, *The Far East*, which John considers as good literature in the home.

In Australia in 1936, abandoned children were placed in orphanages. Today's society demands that safe-guarding protocols be in place for children and vulnerable people. John tells his mother of the case of a two-year-old boy abused by his foster mother and how he organises for the child to be taken into institutional care with the Sisters of Nazareth in Victoria, where he believes the child will be better cared for. He also arranges financial support through the Sisters of the Good Shepherd. Aware and involved in the local community and with many Catholic connections, John has his finger on the pulse. He seizes on what he understands to be opportunities for good.

* * *

A.M.D.G.
Hobart.
May 5th '36

My Dearest Mother,
I have been setting out to write each night this past week but I seem to be all behind myself and to have work on all sides so that I thought I could wait

till tonight as I am a little freer on Tuesday nights. On Monday I am kept till late with the Instruction Class and the little details connected with it.

I did not forget your birthday and celebrated Holy Mass for you and your intentions begging God to pour out His choicest and best graces on to you. I was going to ring you on the new phone but I was not sure when it would be best to ring and I was out for a good part of time when it might have been best to ring.

We are beginning an appeal for the Cathedral. I am in a way the organiser of the functions, Dances, Bridge Evenings, Car Drive and sundry other ways of raising money. It means a lot of visiting, coaxing and often a little cajoling to get people going. Once they begin to move, things are easier. I spent most of today calling on likely helpers. We hope to have our 1st Old Time Dance on May 21st, Bridge evening May 18th. The Car Drive possibly will come about May 31st.

The particular objective this year is to repair the steps of the Cathedral; to concrete it and cover with bitumen the approaches to cathedral; tile the porch and rear portion, to repair the windows, improve ventilation and to have [the] altar rails repaired. Then there is question of a new Parish Hall. This will mean a big task – about £2,000 or £3,000. Still I think it can be done well enough.

I had a letter from Bruny today with cheque for £3/12/00 so that our credit balance now stands at £4/9/00. This is really very good. They are to have another function on Saturday next. They hope to have the whole £10 raised by the next time I visit them. This is really fine for them.

While down last time I brought up a piece of Tasmanian Oak – Hardwood – which Terry Dillon cut out for me. It was just a little block. I sent it to a friend – a Mr Hepworth in Launceston and he made it up for me. I told him to make what he liked. I wanted it for you. I am enclosing his letter and am sending the article on. He is an old man between 70 and 80. I thought you would like this memento of Bruny – also from the Mission there in January.

During Lent I gave out a lot of Mite boxes to children. Quite a lot returned them more or less filled so that I shall have about £9 or £12 to send way. Those who had 4/- in their boxes will have [The] Far East sent them for 12 months. It is one way of getting Catholic literature into homes. I think The Far East is still as good and even better than the other Catholic periodicals.

I am also at present trying to write a sketch of the life of St Gabriel the Passionist – to put in next Standard. The articles there are all a little on the "high brow" side. You may see in The Standard about the Educational Conference we are to have here at Christmas. It is intended to help the teachers to exchange ideas and to get new ideas from the best authorities on Education,

Religious and Secular. I should like Brother William to be coming but there is no question of his doing so.

Instruction class is going well. I hope to receive two ladies into the Church on May 23rd previous to the Feast of Our Lady Help of Christians. On that day we are to have [a] Retreat (1/2 day) for [the] Children of Mary. I shall give it myself in default of some one better. It would mean expense to get another priest to come in and at present the Children of Mary are trying to use any spare money on hand to buy a few books for a little library we have been preparing.

... A little lad went off to the Boys home at Sebastopol (Nazareth Sisters in Ballarat). He has been badly treated by a foster mother so I thought it best to let the Sisters care for him. The Good Shepherd Sisters have undertaken to pay all expenses of the keep. Of course there is no fare for him to Ballarat. I asked a young Melbourne visitor to care for him on the way. She kindly took charge of him. There are many good people about us if only we could draw the goodness out of them.

The Good Shepherd Sisters have been most kind to me in many ways. Just one instance: They got a shirt of mine in [the] wash – found it worn and sent a new one – beautiful Cremean [sic] flannel in its place. The next week they commandeered another and replaced it also. I told them I must get even but it is hard. I cannot go down there so often now as it takes time waiting for trams etc. Still I do want to do all I can to help them. I gave the Holy Hours there last Friday.

Fr Fitzgerald is back with us – he is a sick man – ulcer in the stomach. I doubt if he will ever be much good. He is now at Invermay. Dean Hennessy I heard has resigned from Launceston. He is very sick in Melbourne. His Grace is having indifferent health – sometimes bright other times very languid. He seems not to be able to grasp things in conversation, etc. He is a wonderfully lovable man. He is most anxious to hear Eileen Joyce the pianist. She is to play tomorrow night. He is hoping to be well enough to go. Tasmania is quite excited about her as she is a "local", born at Zeehan. I think she will be giving a private recital at Mt St Canice for the Good Shepherd Sisters there.

I had a letter from Fr McGlynn asking for prayers for lads on a Long Retreat. They come off about May 19th. This time last year I was on Retreat myself. I am most grateful for the opportunity that was presented to me.

Well now dear Mother I have told you a good deal about ourselves and I have asked but little about all at home. But I do often wonder about each of you all. Many of the people here also ask after you. A few weeks ago a young man came to Confession and when he had finished he asked me if I minded him asking a question. I had no objections. He wanted to know how Brian was *getting on. He had been at St Virgil's with him ... I must try to write to him sometime ...*

Really I have done next to nothing to repay you and Father for all you have done for us all. Now I have been wondering if you [would] let me help you somewhat. As I said in [my] last letter I have let the car idea drop indefinitely and I have some money to spare in [the] Bank. I have about £15 and then there is about £24 due to me from the House Account, as I have not received any salary for February March and April. I have not asked for it. I can get along without it and it would be safe where it is. Now dear Mother I would like to send it to you to help with any needs you have.

I have paid off my hospital account and have to refund Fr Mullaney too for a cheque he sent me when in Hospital. I am doing that at present. However I have little worry on that score as I have helped in various ways to make up for all they have done for me. I am feeling very fit – everyone tells me I look very well. I sometimes feel that this is a backhanded compliment in that it can mean want of effort on my part with work.

Are you still in the shop? I hope not. I suppose it is like hard work getting away from this and that thing to be attended to. I am also wondering about the Retreat. I am sure you must be tired of hearing my insistence on this, but I am also sure you are really anxious to try it. I would love to be able to have a few days off myself for quiet prayer and Recollection. Perhaps in the coming week I shall be able to get one day to myself.

I must write to Marie too. Her letter has been lying on my table for weeks and I make resolutions – only to find them still not kept at end of the day. Still you all know at home that I don't forget you at the Holy Mass and in my other poor prayers. I trust that Our Blessed Lady will bring her May blessings to you all and help you to come to know Our Divine Lord yet more and more. I shall be offering Holy Mass for Grandma's soul this month. The 12th of May will be the 1st available date when I can say it. That will be this day week.

Now dearest Mother it is getting on towards midnight and I have to be up early tomorrow to take Holy Communion to sick people so I shall not write more. Give my love to all at home and please keep praying for me. I often feel that I have not the "pep" and go that I had two or 3 years back.

May God bless you and may His Blessed Mother keep you dearest Mother and may she give you much grace and joy and peace in the next year of your life and may she help you to lay up yet more treasure where the worm and moth do not consume nor thieves break through and steal. It is good that we are not working for this world but for [the] next. It helps us to go [to] that world with a greater joy and detachment.

Dear Mother I know you will think yourself to be working for the world but I feel that such is not the case. Your life has been lived for your children

and if that be so it has been for God and God will reward you most abundantly. Goodnight now dear and bless your son in Christ,
Jack
PS. Give Father my love and affection. Also Marie, Chester and Don. Poor Charlie will be thinking I have forgotten him too.

Interior St Mary's Cathedral, Hobart 1936
Archdiocese of Hobart Archives and Heritage Collection

Letter 84 to Mother

Every day a prayer of gratitude
for the Mother that taught me to love the Holy Faith.

In this short note to his mother (3rd September 1936), John wants her to know how much her letters mean to him. They serve *as spiritual reading* and are a support in his pastoral work, he writes. She understands him and he tells her of fighting unsettled movements within. In the *coming and going* in life, John identifies with this term from Mark's gospel chapter 6, 31-33 when Jesus invites his apostles to come away to a quiet place, because people were *coming and going* and they did not even have time to eat. Resonating with John, he expresses his desire for time out for quiet prayer yet again.

* * *

A.M.D.G.
Hobart
Sept 3rd [1936]

Dear Mother,

A short note with Father's letter.

As you see there is much work – "much going and coming" as we are told about Our Lord in the Gospel. So that at times it cuts into the time one would wish to have for letters and also for quiet prayer. I seem to want more and more a life of prayer. Beg of God for me the grace of perfect resignation and abandon to His Holy Will in all things. I have at times to fight down any ['feelings' crossed out] movings of an unsettled feeling. I want only to serve my Master where and as long as He wills.

I am looking forward to your letter which when it comes serves me as spiritual reading. It helps me very much in my work. If I do not write as often as you and I could both wish for, remember that your (sic) ever in my heart – every day a prayer of gratitude for the Mother that taught me to love the Holy Faith goes up with the adoration of the very Son of God Himself as He rests in your son's hands at the Holy Sacrifice of the Mass.

Goodnight dearest Mother and God be with you always,

Jack

A.M.D.G.

Hobart
Sept 3rd.

Dear Mother,

A short note with Father's letter. As you see there is much work — "much going & coming" as we are tired of at our Our Lord in the Gospel. So that at times it cuts into the time one would wish to have for letters and also for quiet prayer. I seem to want more and more a life of prayer. Beg of God for me the grace of perfect resignation and abandon to His Holy Will in all things. I have at times to fight down any moving or unsettled feeling. I want only to serve my Master where and as long as He wills. I am looking forward to your letter which when it comes serves me as Spiritual reading. It helps me very much in my work. If I do not write as often as you and I would both wish for remember that you are in my heart — every day a prayer of gratitude for the Mother that taught me to love my Holy Faith, joining with the adoration of the very Son of God Himself as He rests in your son's hands at the Holy Sacrifice of the Mass.

Goodnight dearest Mother & God bless you always
Jack.

Letter 85 to Father

I had five funerals in one week.
Pleurisy, Bronchitis, Influenza, Pneumonia and Diptheria
have been very prevalent.

This four-page letter to his father (3rd September 1936) tells the old story that John is *busy – very busy* – with all his responsibilities. The Archbishop is ill and Father Vincent Green is unwell. *At times I wonder just where to begin,* he writes.

Having a variety of involvements, some seem to be less important, others more serious, but all must be attended to. As secretary for the fund-raising appeal for the Presentation Sisters and their convent, one of his duties is to attend the Bridge night to declare the prize-winners! There are concerts to attend too. He is training twenty altar servers. Then with a considerable outbreak of illnesses this past winter, he presumably has been called to visit many families and, particularly with so many deaths, he has had *five funerals in one week*.

New Church buildings are being built with the Bellerive Catholic School just completed. Renovations are finished at the Bishop's House with significant improvements. The new *smoke room* for the priests would be one that John, as a non-smoker, did not frequent. With great speculations as to who the new Bishop could be, one thing John wants is a younger and vigorous Bishop, *someone to stir things up*.

John plays his part in the conspiracy to buy land for a Catholic hospital – Calvary Hospital. *We have to be very innocent looking.*

Lastly he is riding a bike again and is looking for a new one – trading in the heavier one although the replacement will cost more. It will be worth it.

As he concludes this letter sending fond love to everyone at home, he sends an accolade of how he and his siblings received the guidance they needed and that they were never ashamed of anything their parents did.

* * *

A.M.D.G.

Hobart.
3rd September 1936

Dear Father,

No doubt you are all wondering what has happened to me that I have not written. Well it is just the old story – busy – very busy. It is now 11.30 on Sunday night. Fr [Bob] Kennedy has gone to Launceston and Fr [Vincent] Green is not in the best of health so that there is more for me to do. At times I wonder just where to begin.

There is also an appeal for the [Presentation] Convent, I am secretary to that also. It entails a good deal of rather finicky care and worry. We have about £143 to date. There are two more months to go. On Monday night I have to go to the "Nook" for a Bridge Evening. I just look in – see that all is going well and then later in the night call in and declare the prize winners etc.

How are all at home? I had a letter from Brian some while back. It told me about the football etc. Brother William also wrote telling me some A.C.K. news. I do not expect to be going to Zeehan now though officially I am still due there. I think Fr Cullen will be hard to shift from there.

The Archbishop is still in St Vincent's Hospital Sydney. He is not at all well – it appears he had a slight stroke and is suffering from a general paralysis. We do not expect him to do much good. I would not be at all surprised if he went off quickly – or resigned his Archbishopric. At any rate it is certain we will have a Coadjutor Bishop.[10] *There are great speculations as to who it will be. I hope that whoever he is he will be a young and vigorous man. We want someone to stir things up here.*

One of our greatest needs is a Catholic Hospital. It will cost a lot but it must come. At present we are quietly looking around for a block – about 5 to

---

10   The main role of the Coadjutor Bishop is to assist the Archbishop in the administration of the diocese and he is the Archbishop's designated successor.

6 acres. Of course we have to be very innocent looking – the last people who would dream of buying some place.

Tuesday Night. Since I began this letter a few days have slipped by. I have been kept busy in one way or another. It is now late in the night and I am just writing a little more.

Last night there was a Bridge Evening at the "Nook" Tea Rooms. There were only 10 tables but we cleared about £11. This was due in part to a picture which was raffled to defray expenses and which really brought in a considerable sum over and above the expenses. There are to be some private Bridge evenings etc. An American Tea is on the cards – also a dance.

The St Mary's College Concert is on Wednesday week, Sept 11th and St Virgil's Concert follows the next week. There are great preparations in both camps – and a good deal of rivalry. The boys do quite a lot of gymnastics etc.

I have about 20 boys in training for the Altar. This time I am being much more hard on them insisting on the correct thing in every way.

My bike is not like the old one – much heavier. I find it rather exhausting so have put an order [in] for a new one made to order like the one I had before. It will cost only £7.10.00 over and above the value of the one I have (about £6). Even if it does cost a bit it will be worth it in the long run.

Since I have been back there have been many improvements in the building. A new bathroom, two more spare rooms and a partition in the big sitting room. One half is to be Fr Green's office, the other half to be a smoke room for the priests.

Fr Kent, the Editor of The Standard, has taken up his residence in Bellerive now. He will have his new Church School built by Christmas and ready for school next year. The Presentation Sisters are to take it over. It should make good progress.

I saw in the paper about an accident at Seymour. It must have been a very serious affair. Brian told me of the death of Mr Chas. Hamilton.[11] I wrote to his wife a few days back. I got quite a surprise to know it.

There has been quite a lot of sickness about of late. Pleurisy, Bronchitis, Influenza, Pneumonia and Diptheria have been very prevalent. I had five funerals in one week. There has also been quite a lot of trouble over the Hobart Public Hospital. There is a Royal Commission at present enquiring into the conduct of the Hospital for the past 4 years or so. Fr O'Donnell is the Chairman of the present Hospital Board.

Well now dearest Father it is late and I am very tired and sleepy. It was half past 12 when I got to bed last night. So I must close this letter with all

---

11 Charlie Hamilton was a local of Homewood. His family originally settled in Hamilton, Victoria, when they came from Scotland prior to settling in the district of Yea.

fond love to everyone at home. I am often asked about yourself and Mother, especially by the [Presentation] Sisters who met you both. I always thank God for having given me a good Father and Mother. When I see the parents of others and the lack of even the elementary guidance in good clean living, I look back to think of my parents who gave us all good example and never did anything for which we might ever be ashamed.

Dear Father let me say goodnight now and may God bless you and my dear Mother, Brothers and Sister.

John

Letter 86 to Father

I don't want much in the way of this world's goods.

This three-page letter of John's (22nd December 1936) is the last to his father in the collection that has survived. John responds in detail as to why he did not speak long on the telephone when his father called on the anniversary of his ordination. Further, it is Christmas and he is homesick and misses home.

Times have moved on and John now has a car. The main concerns are his car expenses and going home for holidays whenever he is given leave to go. Belatedly, the most important message is *a hearty wish* for a happy Christmas!

* * *

Hobart.
22.12.36

Dear Father,

I said I would write for Christmas. I meant to get my letter off before this, but I have not been at all well myself lately. I have felt very off colour – tired and unable to think much. Last night I was sent to bed and given a stiff lemon and whisky. I felt better this morning. I was not allowed up early. Tonight I feel fairly fit but am going off to bed a little earlier. I hope I will be able to carry on quite alright for Christmas. I think it is a touch of flu. Of course there is nothing serious. I have also been taking some tonic for the last few days. This had a good effect.

I was feeling very rundown when you rang on Friday night. I had gone to lie down and had gone to sleep. I could not hear very clearly. There are two phones here. One is very good and the other one is not at all good. I could not get into the office for the good phone. Anne [Douglas] and Auntie Jane rang on Saturday but I had a wheezy voice and found it hard to talk.

I hope to be able to get going in good style for Christmas. I shall miss being home. Christmas here is generally a lonely day – homesick. I have been hoping to get off for a few days after New Year – if it is only two or three days. I don't know when I can get home.

I am trying to put aside a few shillings here and there for the trip. The car is a big expense to me. I just paid off £25 yesterday. I have to cut out all extras – of course I don't mind this. I don't want much in the way of this world's goods. I made enquiries about [the] cost of taking car over to Victoria. They told me it would be about £11 or £12 return. I am going to see what the Royal

Automobile Club can do. I think they can get a very considerable deduction. At any rate I shall have to let that rest till I can get off. At present I see no prospect till Easter or even till the middle of the year.

Well now, dear Father, I will not write more but will get off to bed. I don't want to be taking chances just at present. If I am sick for Christmas they will not be able to get any other priest to supply.

I will write again soon. Give my love to all at home and believe me

Your loving Son
Jack

PS. I didn't mention Christmas greetings after all! I send them now with a hearty wish that it will be a happy Christmas indeed.

JCW

Letter 87 to Mother

Be sure I will have you all in my Mass on Christmas day.
May the Christ Child bless you all with His rarest and choicest graces.

In this Christmas note to his mother (22nd December 1936), John apologises that he was not in *good form* on the telephone the previous week. Phone calls are still a rarity and expensive. Praying the Christ Child bless all with the rarest and choicest of blessings, he offers the 7.30am Mass on Christmas morning for all the family. A woman has died, he tells his mother – the one he had told her about.

* * *

[22nd December 1936]

Dear Mother,

Just a note with Father's letter. I was sorry I could not quite catch your voice on [the] phone. I was not in good form: had been feeling rather sick in the day and was asleep when [the] ring came. I knew it was coming but went to my room early and hoped to remain awake. I am feeling better now but have still a heavy cold. It has been very strange and oppressive weather here.

I will say Mass at 7.30, 9.00 and 10 o'clock on Christmas Day. I shall say 7.30 Mass for all at home. I have not sent presents but I am trying to save a few pounds so as to get over when I can get off.

Goodnight now, dear Mother, and may the Christ Child bless you all with His rarest and choicest graces. Be sure I will have you all in my Mass on Christmas day. By the way that woman I spoke of died the day or so after I saw her.

Love to all from

Your loving son in Christ
Jack

Letter 88 to Mother

Converts are good Catholics. They appreciate what they receive.

In this four-page letter to his mother (6th March 1937), John reports, among other things, that he will be home on St Patrick's Day for holidays. He is not taking his car as he had earlier hoped. His mother is still in the café at Seymour, but John wants to go to the farm at Homewood to have the opportunity to celebrate Mass there. The farm is more of a home to him.

Again John is not well – the anaesthetic for a tooth extraction in Hobart has upset him. Later in July 1937, a report in *The Mercury* of an inquest into the death of a woman undergoing dental procedures took place, with a witness indicating that there was *no known method of estimating the amount of anaesthetic* given for any individual.[12] Discoveries are still being made in the field of anaesthetics. Maybe it is no wonder John was feeling unwell!

He is pleased that Father Vincent Green met with his mother in Melbourne. But the big news is that Dr Justin Simonds has been appointed as Archbishop of Hobart. *He will be a very good zealous and capable man*, writes John authoritatively. He knows him from seminary days. A visit from the Columban Father Luke Mullany is most welcome – a confidante with whom he can talk.

John notes that adult *converts* are more responsive and appreciative of the Catholic faith – they have an understanding of what they received. Signing off on this letter and as always running late, he notes that he still has his office and the rosary to pray.

* * *

A.M.D.G.
Hobart.
6.3.37

My dearest Mother,

I had intended writing to tell you I would be able to get off for a few days at home before Easter but Father [Vincent] Green forestalled me. He told me he met you in Melbourne. He arrived home last night full of news about the Cricket. We were kept busy during his absence and I have had a bad cold. In one way and another I have not been feeling the best lately, though tonight I feel much better. I had two teeth out – the eye tooth on top and the anaesthetic upset me a good deal.

---

12   *The Mercury*, 23rd July 1937, https://trove.nla.gov.au/newspaper/article/25415127

I did not make final arrangements for my absence till Father Green returned. I can get a priest supply for me on one Sunday so that I will be leaving here on Wed 17th. I cannot possibly get away before that. It is so difficult to get supplies. I have booked a seat on the plane. Will say the first Mass for St Patrick's Day and then get off. Should be in Melbourne about 12.00. I have to do a good deal of business in Melbourne. I will ring you when I arrive [in Melbourne.]

I expect you to have all the news about the new Archbishop Dr Simonds. I am very pleased indeed. I am sure he will be a very good zealous and capable man. We do not expect him to come till about [the] end of April.

Fr Luke Mullaney is coming down from Launceston on Sunday. I shall be glad to see him. Fr McPoland was down for a couple of days. There was also a Missionary priest from Samoa with us for a couple of days. He was a most interesting character.

There are great preparations going on for the St Patrick's College concert immediately after Easter. We have to begin on a Fair for the [Presentation] Sisters. Indications are that I will have to bear the burden of the organisation. I dread the thought of it as I hoped to be able to get down to a systematic revisitation of my district.

I had the pleasure of receiving one of the converts into [the] Church on Tuesday last. He is an excellent young man, son of a Commissioner of Railways. There are a number of persons interested. I think there are in all about 12 actually being prepared for reception and about 20 to 30 Non Catholics who are coming. It means a lot of work but it has great consolations. Converts are good Catholics. They appreciate what they receive.

I shall write to Father for his birthday. I am sorry that I cannot be home for it but there is no chance. I was wondering if we could go to Kilmore on the Sunday I am home or would I call on the way up.

I have not written to Brian just recently. I shall not write more now, dear Mother, as I have to say my Office and Rosary yet, and it is now quite late in the night. I seem to be always running late.

With fondest love to all and hoping soon to see you all. I am
Your loving Son
Jack

PS. I would love to have a day up at the farm and to say Mass at Yea. We may be able to manage it. **Jack**

Further Insights Into A Remarkable Man
Tasmania 1936–1937
Letters 80-88

Adrian L. Doyle

It was something of a coincidence that I have been asked to offer some reflections on the letters written by John Wallis to his mother during the years 1936 and 1937. 1936 was an important year in my life, the year of my birth. I have always been interested in the particular events of that year, the middle year of the 1930s.

It was the decade in which the Nazi regime came to power in Germany and, by 1936, the belligerent intentions of the new regime were certainly becoming obvious, with far worse to come at the end of the decade. It was in 1936 that the then British Empire was rocked by the decision of the King to abdicate. More locally, our own Joseph Lyons was trying to lead a rebuild in Australia after the damage of the Great Depression.

My first impression from the letters was the depth of the relationship between John and his "dearest mother". He was most open in relating to her all the challenges of his ministry, including some serious health problems, which he apparently faced around Christmas in 1935. One can only imagine the concerns, which would have arisen in the heart of his mother when she became aware of some of the difficulties her son faced. There are times when he felt a deep homesickness, which was understandable, particularly in those days of such isolation from his family.

I note a very deep sense of urgency in the description of his ministry, with a focus on instruction classes, numerous funerals, and a deep concern for those who lived in remote places. Clearly Bruny Island features strongly in his concerns. But there were many late nights, when his only time to write these letters was around midnight, when very likely he would have been expected to rise early for the commitments of the next day.

At the commencement of these letters, John was operating without any form of transport. He had been advised not to continue to ride his bike, which would always have been a challenge in Hobart, and the purchase of his first car was still months away. He must had been relying on public transport and walking much of the time.

I was reading recently that it was in 1936 that an undersea cable across Bass Strait was completed, enabling telephone communication with Melbourne for the first time. A three-minute conversation cost four shillings and sixpence, no small amount in those days. We all know how important the telephone became for John in later years, long before mobile phones became available.

It was during these two years in the 1930s that there was a change in Archbishop. John describes the final years of Archbishop Hayden, as he was resident in the Archbishop's house. Clearly the Archbishop was a very sick man and following his death, mention is made of the appointment in March 1937 of Archbishop Justin Simonds as his successor. He was the first Australian-born Archbishop.

On a personal note, I was very interested in the reference to the purchase of the land where Calvary Hospital would eventually be built. I know, from what I have been told, that the whole process was very difficult. My father, Leo Doyle, acted as the lawyer for the Sisters of the Little Company of Mary in those negotiations and there were some big challenges to overcome, particularly with the opposition of the local residents.

I have very much appreciated the opportunity to gain some further insight into the life of this remarkable man, deeply committed to his vocation as a priest.

Emeritus Archbishop Adrian Doyle OAM

Adrian Doyle was born in Hobart in 1936 and educated in Hobart at St Mary's College, Sacred Heart College, and St Virgil's College. He began his studies for the priesthood in 1955 at Corpus Christi College, Werribee, in Victoria, before transferring to Collegio Propaganda Fide, Rome, in 1956. He completed a Doctorate in Canon Law from the Gregorian University, Rome. Returning to Tasmania in 1965, Father Doyle's appointments over the ensuing years included responsibility for the Marriage Tribunal, Judge on the Appeal Tribunal and President of the Canon Law Society of Australia and New Zealand, while serving in various parishes in Hobart.

From 1999 to 2013, he was Archbishop of Hobart and undertook several key roles for the Australian Catholic Bishops Conference. When John Wallis died in Hobart in 2001, Archbishop Doyle was the main celebrant at his funeral Mass at St Mary's Cathedral, Hobart.

PHOTOS II

Archbishop William Barry
1919 – 1929 accepted John for Tasmania

Archbishop William Hayden
1930 – 1936 ordained John

Archbishop Ernest Tweedy
1943 – 1955

Archbishop Justin Simonds
1937 – 1942

John Wallis was accepted for Tasmania by Archbishop Barry, Ordained by Archbishop Hayden and served under five more bishops during his long life.

Photos: Archdiocese of Hobart Archives and Historical Collection.

Archbishop Eric D'Arcy
1988 – 1989

Archbishop Guilford Young
1955 – 1988

Archbishop Adrian Doyle
1999 – 2013

Above: Dean Vincent Green, Archdiocese of Hobart Archives and Photographic Collection

Right: St Mary's College Hobart, Courtesy St Mary's College

Below: St Virgil's College Hobart, Courtesy St Virgil's

Cathedral presbytery, Hobart, 1930s, John's home for many of his early years of priesthood.

John Wallis regularly visited Bruny Island in the early years of his priestly ministry. He travelled with his bicycle on the SS Dover, shown here moored at Denne's Point, the northern port of Bruny. It was on one of his first visits to Bruny Island that Mrs Kit Hawkins challenged him with the question, "Why can't we ...", the challenge that eventually led to John founding the Home Missionary Sisters of Our Lady, now known as Missionary Sisters of Service.

Photos II

Father John and Kit Hawkins in 1969, the time of the silver jubilee of the Missionary Sisters of Service.

The founding group of Home Missionary Sisters of Our Lady with the Presentation Sisters (in habits); from left: Sister Augustine Healy, Kath Moore, Gwen Morse, Monica Carroll, Sister Ita Heery, and Joyce O'Brien, 1944.

Above: 1 Frederick St. Launceston, the first home of the Home Missionary Sisters of Our Lady

432 Elizabeth Street. The first residence in Hobart of The Home Missionary Sisters of Our Lady 1946 – 1967. It served as the Novitiate for a period of time.

Photos II

Right: The Home Missionary Sisters of Our Lady Alice Fox (Sr Gabriel) and Margaret Kenny (Sr Maria Goretti) working in the correspondence school for religious education in the 1950s.

Below: The Dillon family, an early correspondence family on Bruny Island. Back: Monica (Lal) holding Violet, and Stan; centre: Patricia (Sr Mechtilde rsj), Michael, and Agnes; front: David, Lilian and Bernard.

Emma Wallis with sons John and Brian in 1947

Photos II

John's cousin, Anne Douglas with Emma visiting John in Tasmania 1948.

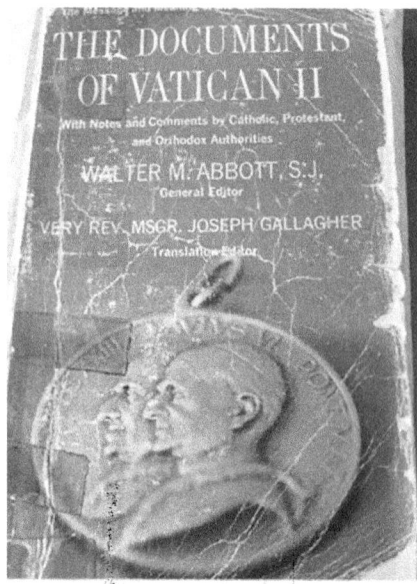

One of the biggest events of John's life was the Second Vatican Council (1962-1965); he relished the changes that brought the Church alive for people in a new way. He lived and breathed its documents, as his well-used copy shows.

Father John Wallis 1960s

Father John Wallis 1990s

Photos II

Father John Wallis with Archbishop Adrian Doyle AM in 1990s
Archdiocese of Hobart Archives Collection

Far right: Father John Wallis with Archbishop Adrian Doyle AM, fellow priests and acolyte. Archdiocese of Hobart Archives Collection.

Part of John Wallis' extensive library held at The Wallis Centre MSS Archives, Hobart.

Right: Father John Wallis 1950s

Below: Bernadette Wallis mss at the Bruny Island memorial depicting John on his bike and panels that tell the story of the Missionary Sisters of Service and the John Wallis Foundation installed in November 2018.

Tasmania
1946-1949
Letters 89 – 95

Introduction

This chapter comes after a nine-year gap since the previous surviving letters of John to his parents. The next and final chapter is dedicated to the letters he wrote to his brother Brian, while he was in the seminary at Werribee, Victoria. Two of those letters pre-date some of the letters in this chapter, where there are seven letters from 1946 to 1949, the last of the collection. All the letters here are to John's mother – one from 1946, four from 1947, one in 1948 and one in 1949. Two letters are written from the Deanery in Launceston, two from the Home Missionary Sisters of Our Lady's[1] house in Frederick Street, Launceston, one from the presbytery in Derby in north-east Tasmania, one from St Finn Barr's Presbytery, Invermay and one from the Presbytery in Burnie.

In the intervening period, World War II took place, John has been celebrant for the weddings of his brother, Don, and his sister, Marie, and now he has three nieces. He has also witnessed his father's death in 1945.

Industrious and continuing his pastoral and administrative work, John has been appointed Diocesan director of the Propagation of Faith, director of Catholic Action, established the lending library and is doing relief work in various parishes. He has been writing his ideas for ministry to those in the bush, as well as inviting review and criticism of his work as he has further developed his vision and strategies.

In November 1941, he wrote a paper, *Perigrinating Sisters,* stating his ideas about a mobile community of women. He had seen an article in *The*

---

1 *The Home Missionary Sisters* is the terminology John uses in this letter. Other names used are: *The Home Missionary Sisters of Our Lady*, *Rosary House Sisters*, *Rosary House Missionary Sisters*. In 1972, the Sisters changed their title to *Missionary Sisters of Service*. Each house where the Sisters lived was called *Rosary House*.

Melbourne Advocate about the Sisters of Service in Canada who lived and worked in the wider community, especially with the migrant population. John asked for further information, explaining he wanted Sisters *who will live in remote country areas, who will be able to go about alone, to do any work they are called on to do – Sisters whose rule of life and mode of dress are adapted to the exigencies of their work …* He continued: *We are trying to meet the problem by means of Correspondence courses, Vocational Holiday Schools… But I have always felt that there is nothing like the personal contact with these people in their own milieu – their own homes.* The Home Missionary Sisters of Our Lady was founded in July 1944 and set up their community in Launceston. John also moved to Launceston and lived in the Deanery, at the Church of Apostles in Margaret Street. Emma is very interested in the whole venture recognising how access to this ministry would have helped her.

One of the interpretive panels telling the story of Fr John and the Missionary Sisters of Service.

Letter 89 to Mother

Learn about 'travelling light'.

In this three-page letter (5th February 1946) written to John's mother from Launceston in early February 1946, temperatures are high in Victoria. Bushfires are raging in the State. John wonders if his home is safe.

Two months have passed since his father, Abraham, died on 12th November 1945 at the age of eighty. John was present at his father's deathbed and celebrant for the funeral at Sacred Heart Church, Yea, and the burial in the pioneer cemetery. There is no reference to or description of the event itself in the letters. John writes focusing on his mother's situation. *I have been worrying about you.* Emma had cared for Abe at home. She is exhausted. He often asks that she come across Bass Strait and he would find a place for her to have a break. He will be more regular with his letters to her now. Sensitively, he writes that he prayed for *Father's soul* on the 22nd January, their wedding anniversary.

John's childhood home was to be sold – a wrench for John. He asks about the *little crucifix* that had been in the kitchen. Could he have it or would his mother put it in her new home? At the time, it was difficult to buy property and housing was at a premium. However, the Treasury granted the purchase contract to buy a new property at Sunday Creek, Broadford, jointly with her son Chester. In this letter there is the mention of Charlie and his job, Brian returning to Corpus Christi College and Auntie Kit who has been so good despite the *sermonettes* given to the boys!

A solid section of the letter is devoted to the new Sisters living in Launceston, where John is responsible for their foundation and formation. Archbishop Tweedy[2] has been to see the Sisters. There are presently eight women – Gwen Morse, Kathleen Moore, Monica Carroll, Joyce O'Brien, Valerie Casey, Winifred Ryan,[3] Anne Murphy and Monica Franklin. John uses their surnames with the title Sister at this stage. How this changes in the years to come! Experiencing a summer school for children from the bush, they realise how much they did not know, so now have a higher motivation for learning how to teach children. Significantly, John understands the importance of study for their work. He wants five years of study, similar to seminarians preparing for the priesthood. He has an appreciation of the kind of spirituality

---

2   Archbishop E.V. Tweedy was ordained Archbishop of Hobart in March 1943 after Archbishop Justin Simonds was appointed to Melbourne as Coadjutor Archbishop to Archbishop Daniel Mannix.
3   Later Winifred Ryan uses her second name Agnes. Her religious name for some years was Sr Magdalen.

these women require for their work among the people. He identifies Father McGlynn, a Missionary of the Sacred Heart priest, as the ideal retreat director. He himself gives the retreat to the novices. One thing the Sisters will need to learn, he says, is to *travel light*!

* * *

> Deanery,
> Launceston. 5/2/46

My dear Mother,

I thought I would have a letter to you before this but the days have slipped by very quickly. The last few weeks have been busy ones indeed and it is only today that I have had a chance to settle down to clear up all my letters. And even then I had interruptions from visitors, etc.

Just at present I will have a break from the work at Rosary House as the Sisters have gone away for two or three weeks at Low Head – a seaside place at the mouth of the Tamar River. They left yesterday – all of them packed into a big bus together with all their luggage – pots, pans, etc. etc. I am always telling them they will need to learn a great deal yet about 'travelling light'. When they go out on their Mission work they will not be able to carry everything with them, but will need to have just a minimum.

A couple of weeks ago they went to Cygnet to take part in the Children's Summer School. It was a great experience. Sisters Morse, O'Brien, Moore and Casey were the first to go. Sisters Moore and Casey came home after some days and then I went down taking Sisters Carroll and Ryan. They had a very strenuous time being on duty almost all the time from five o'clock till 10 or 11 o'clock at night. They learned quite a deal – the chief thing being how little they did know. I can see them much keener now about their study and about finding ways and means of teaching the children.

They are as yet unsettled about their uniform as it is so hard to get materials.[4] *I am hoping that they will have some finality before the middle of the year. After returning from Cygnet I had an eight days' Retreat for the Novices, who were to be professed. It meant a good deal of work, but was a useful experience. I shall have another 8 days retreat for Sisters Murphy and Franklin. This will begin on March 17th and conclude on March 25th. I will be grateful for prayers for that occasion. Though it is for the two Juniors the other Sisters will be present and I want to take the chance of re-stating again the ideals I put to them in their first Retreat. We are having a Mission at the end of the month so that the next few weeks will be fully taken up in preparation for it.*

All this has been about myself! I was so pleased to receive your letter, as I have been worrying about you. I was glad to learn from Brian's letter, which I received today that you were going to see a Doctor. I am sure the thing you need most of all is rest, and if I could help you to have it, I would be happy indeed.

Brian told me that the Treasury has passed the purchase contract for the property at Sunday Creek. I am pleased that you have something definite and I hope you can get into the house soon. It must be difficult for you in your present situation. The housing problem here is acute. People are constantly coming, asking for assistance to secure accommodation. In fact, recently we had a case of a man and his wife sleeping out in the park for nights; after that they slept in a shelter shed behind a school and later managed to be allowed to sleep on a sofa. It is really very sad. There seems also to be a danger of a good deal of unemployment.

I am glad Charl is getting out of where he is at work. He was not happy there and he will be happy in the work that has always appealed to him. Brother O'Neill of St. Gabriel's who is a Launceston man, has been over to see his people and has, at the same time, been busy looking for Deaf children. He has managed to find a few, who will be going to St. Gabriel's or to Waratah. He is very keen and a devoted friend of the Deaf.

The Archbishop has been up for a few days – came up for the profession of the Sisters of the Presentation Order. He visited Rosary House and expressed his pleasure at the progress they are making in their preparation. I only hope he will let them have plenty of time to finish their training. I would like another five years with them until I feel they are what I would like them to be. I am delighted to be having Fr. McGlynn in July to give them their Annual Retreat. He has the spirit I want them to have. I asked his Grace especially for permission to write him to give it.

I should write to Auntie Kit. She has been so good in all your trouble despite the "sermonettes" to the boys. Indeed, I could put in days writing to

---

4 Post-War restrictions included the rationing of cloth and clothing in Australia, because of less imports, service demands and less labour for local production of textiles.

the people I should write to, but it just can't be done. I often have to let urgent business letters wait for days.

I expect Brian will be going back to CCC [Corpus Christi College][5] soon. The time slips by very quickly. I am always praying that he will reach the goal – and that he will be indeed a really good and holy priest. Please God next holidays will see him a subdeacon! I think Geo Stoner is to be ordained this year – in July. I hope his Mother will be able to be present. There seems to be just a chance that he could be ordained in Hobart. We will have an ordination here in Launceston next July. Bernie Reed will be the ordinand.

Were you in danger from bush fires? We have had some mildly warm days lately, but nothing like they seem to have had in Melbourne. In fact, this has been a lovely summer – ideal for holiday people.

Now, Mother dear, I must close this letter and get it off to catch the late mail. I meant to send you a letter for Jan 22nd to let you know I was saying Mass for the repose of Father's Soul. I was then at Cygnet. I would like a couple of the cards for my Breviary. And I also was wondering about that little crucifix which used to hang in the Kitchen at home! Of course, I would not like to take it if you would like to keep it. In any case, I think it would be nice to put it up in the kitchen of the new place – that the blessing of God be upon all who dwell therein. You ought sometime to ask the local priest to bless the house.

Goodnight now, dear Mother. I hope to write again and to be more regular with my mail. Love to all. Your loving Son in Christ,

Jack

Back: Monica Franklin, Gwen Morse (Sr Teresa), Kath Moore (Sr Vianney)
Front: Verna Coad (Sr Paul), Imelda McMahon, Edith Moore and Peg Fitzgerald

---

5   Corpus Christi College was the seminary for Victoria and Tasmania.

Letter 90 to Mother

All things work out for the best;
Simply leave things to the Providence of God.

In this two-page letter to his mother (23rd January 1947), John writes from the Deanery in Launceston towards the end of the holiday period. Tasmania is having a wonderful growth season and the threat of fires is real in the *scorching* weather of Victoria.

At the request of Archbishop Tweedy, two of the Home Missionary Sisters, Kathleen Moore and Winifred Ryan, have moved into *Rosary House*, 432 Elizabeth Street, North Hobart, the first base in the south. John continues his work with them all supervising their classes at this stage of their training.

Brian is on holidays before returning to Corpus Christi College, Werribee for the last year before his ordination for the Archdiocese of Melbourne. However, arrangements are being made for Brian to serve instead as a priest in Tasmania (1948–1952).

Chester plans to do an organised tour of Tasmania and John hopes to meet up with him. His sister Marie's second child is named John now eight-weeks old, John's first nephew. He reports that he has written to Auntie Jane and received a card from cousin Anne Douglas.

John passes on the sad news of Mrs Sullivan's family. Presumably Emma met Mrs Sullivan (and her husband, a renowned journalist), in Launceston when she was visiting two years earlier. Their daughter was Sister Attracta, a Presentation Sister.

In completing the letter, John reports on going out to visit people in the parish, a task he has set for himself for this day.

* * *

The Deanery,
Launceston.
23/1/47

My dear Mother,
Just a line while I have a few minutes before I go out to do some visitation. People are coming back from holidays and so one can see them a bit now. I expect you have been scorching the last few days. It has been warm here but not at all as it appears to have been on the mainland. I read about the weather – also the fires etc. in Victoria. We have had a wonderful season here – lovely green grass everywhere about. In some places they have had 2 crops of grass

hay off the one place! They have tried here and there to burn off. But had no success. There is just a great deal of green grass. Stock look well and selling well.

I was in Hobart last week – went down in the morning, back at night. It is a long run driving all the time. The Dean (Upton) had to go down so I took him. Had a short visit to Hobart Rosary House – saw the two Sisters there and saw the work done by the men who came to clear the grounds.

The Archbishop still has no voice – cannot speak at all. Has been like that for months. All he can do is whisper. Otherwise he appears to be quite well. We are expecting him up here at the weekend.

I do not know just when the Sisters will be going down South – and as a consequence I am at a loss to know just what work to do with them in the way of classes. It may be that they will be there for some time before I can go down. I do not care for this, as I want to supervise their classes and work for some time, until I feel they are really competent to go along on their own. However all things work out for the best and I am simply leaving things to the Providence of God.

I did not hear more from Brian. Expect he has gone on his big trek. I don't get much chance for letters at present. I will be glad to hear news of Chester's plans – also other news from home. How is John? Give my love to all. I feel that I don't get letters to them as I could.

I said Mass for you on Wednesday last Jan. 22nd – and for the repose of Father's Soul. I meant to let you know before hand but I had a touch of flu as well as being busy and I just let it slip. How is Auntie Jane? I sent a letter for Christmas – I had a card from Anne [Douglas]. Now Mother I will not write more as I want to see a number of people this morning. I just wanted to let you know about the Mass.

Mrs. Sullivan's Mother died recently. I think I told you; also her brother – and her husband almost died too. He is very sick. Poor woman. She has had a great lot of trouble but is bearing up well under all.

Love to you and all.

Jack

Letter 91 to Mother

At Flinders Island
I used every means of transport available
except motor bike, and riding twenty miles with three different horses.

In the one envelope, John posts two letters to his mother (beginning 29th November 1947) and written a day or two apart, six pages in total, one from the presbytery at Derby in the northeast, where he is for the weekend Masses, and the other from Launceston when he arrives home. He has plenty to report as he reflects on how a priest could live contentedly in an isolated village. He is still not sure where he will be placed.

John has also been to Flinders Island off the north-east coast, a place that has been pastorally neglected, measured by the fact of *eleven months since the residents had had Mass*. As with his experience on Bruny Island, he took different modes of transport and in particular riding three different horses.

After a dearth of priests being available for ministry in Tasmania, where will the four new priests be placed? The young Irishman, Father Bernard Rogers, comes from Northern Ireland after studying at Maynooth near Dublin. Both Father Rex Donohue, who became the meticulous liturgist and rubricist for the Archdiocese, and Father Joe McMahon, who subsequently worked in various parishes, were Tasmanians, having studied at Corpus Christi College, Werribee together with John's brother Brian. Brian has temporarily offered himself for the Archdiocese of Hobart – John being very pleased to have a brother on the island, even though he suspects they will be in different parts of the State. Chester has finally made concrete plans for his first trip to Tasmania.

John's letters always have news of the Home Missionary Sisters who have become part of his life. He has been teaching nearly every afternoon. The Sisters have gathered together their jewellery with gold content to be made into a monstrance for Benediction in their chapel. The precious metal was sent to Gaunt's Jewellers in Bourke Street, Melbourne. Hopefully the monstrance will be ready for Christmas. Gwen Morse and Monica Carroll are in Burnie for a holiday – with Gwen's family. To be noted is the restriction on the Sisters that it is Archbishop Tweedy who gives permission for Monica to attend her nephew's ordination in Sydney!

It appears the Sisters will move from *Rosary House* in Frederick Street, but it seems to depend on the Archbishop and the availability of housing in Hobart in this post-War period. In 1949, some Sisters move into the *Mission House* at Longford, 24 kilometres south of Launceston. John hopes to do a recruiting tour on the mainland for women to join the Sisters. He has also written an article about them in the magazine, *Catholic Missions*.

It is two years since his father died, and he is concerned that his mother has not yet settled in a home of her own where she can be rest and be comfortable.

* * *

Presbytery,
Derby.
29.11.1947

My dear Mother,
You will wonder at the address given at the head of this letter. I am not stationed here, but have come to relieve Father Flynn who has gone to Cygnet for the Ordination of Rex Donohue. I came this afternoon and will go back to Launceston tomorrow night. Expect [to] get home about 10.30. Three Masses – Derby, Ringarooma and Branxholm, and Benediction at Scottsdale in the evening.

Derby is a small derelict mining town with very few Catholics. Strange enough I missed it as a place of permanent appointment. I can understand a man who was not interested in reading or [doing] odd jobs about the place finding it very lonely. The nearest priest is 60 miles away. The little presbytery is reasonably comfortable – and it can be made more so. Maybe some day Brian will land here – one never knows.

I have not landed anywhere new – as yet. There are all kinds of rumours, especially in view of the fact that we have four new men to be placed. Fr. Bernard Rogers just arrived from Ireland. Then there are Frs. McMahon, and Brian and Rex Donohue.

As yet no news of the move of Rosary House to Hobart. The two Sisters there are both very busy. Sisters Carroll and Morse are still away. I hope they have enjoyed their holiday – 2 weeks next Monday. I am going to Burnie for them on Tuesday.

The junior sisters had an end of the year test on work done – all did quite well. The four novices are due to give their lecturettes some time soon. I don't know if I told you about the other lecturettes. Each Sister must give a talk – an address to the other Sisters – and then be ready to answer questions etc. It is good training for public speaking. I am the only outsider – apart from the rest of the Sisters. After it is all over I give a few criticisms, and suggestions – not that I am at all competent but they put up with me all the same!

I was glad to get your letter. Indeed I did set out to write to you the day yours came but I did not get under way. The last few weeks have been busy. It is quite a rest for me to be here in this presbytery without a soul to disturb or distract me. I have been very busy with marriages and instructions.

I was at Flinders Island a couple of weeks ago. Enjoyed the trip though it was a very hectic one in some ways. Used every means of transport available except motorbike – and I nearly had to resort to that also. Had three different horses: on one day I road about 20 miles. Was a bit on the stiff side next day. I feel very sorry for the Flinders people. They do not get much attention. It was eleven months since they had had Mass!

Sent all the gold etc. collected by the Sisters to Gaunt's. Miss Gillie[6] told me the Monstrance is well on its way. I would like you to see it before it is sent over. There is just a chance that it might be done in time for Brian to bring it with him. I have not yet an estimate of the value of the Jewellery collected – it might be as much as £100. The Sisters are looking forward to having it for Benediction on Christmas Day.

I hope you got to Corpus Christi College before Brian left. It has had many happy associations for him – and for me too. The Jesuits have always been very kind and thoughtful to me on any occasion I went down. Am looking forward to Brian's coming though very likely we will be a good way apart. It often happens that brothers are separated though not always.

Interested in Chester's plans. The Pioneer tours are popular; they do see a good deal of Tas – especially the 12 days one. The 10 days tour misses the West Coast, which is rather worth seeing. Then too there is no trouble about accommodation. Of course while he is in Launceston he will not go on all the trips on the bus but could come with me. I will be delighted if he can come and I will try to help him enjoy the trip. Of course in some ways I will be tied up but he will understand that. We had a priest staying with us a couple of nights. He came over on an Ansett-Pioneer Tour and enjoyed it very much. Let me know if he has made further plans.

Sr. Carroll's nephew got subdiaconate a few days ago. She is very pleased. The Archbishop has told me he will allow her to go over for his ordination to

---

6 Miss Gillie is a staff member at Gaunt's Jewellery.

the priesthood. It may take place in Sydney. I know she would like very much to go.

I would not be surprised if I get over to the mainland some time next year. I have in mind to make something of a recruiting tour – would go to Melbourne, possibly Adelaide and Sydney. There will be an article on Rosary House in the Catholic Missions for Jan-Feb. Also some photos. I will send you a copy.

Now Mother I am really very tired and am thinking that bed is the best place for me. I have had a lot of late nights and am feeling weary. If I go off now I will get a good long sleep. Will try – I mean it – to write again fairly soon. Am very interested to know of any moves re a little home for yourself where you can have an easier life and some of the little comforts that you so richly deserve. Also somewhere near a church where you can get to Mass now and then. Let me know your plans and please let me know if there is anything you think I can do. If needs be I could go over by plane for a couple of days – between Sundays – provided I have enough notice.

Goodnight and God bless you.

Jack.

The Deanery,
Launceston.   Tasmania

Monday evening.

I did not post the letter I wrote, and am just adding a few lines before I go down to post it now. It is very close and hot just now. Hope it will rain.

I had a big day yesterday. Mass at Derby 8.00, at Ringarooma 9.30 and Branxholm 11.00. Called to see a family where the mother died – an old lady of 83. Scottsdale Benediction at 7.00. Called to see Manion's there and had tea with them at the Hotel. Came on home then. Got home about 10.15. I have just come in now from visiting St Vincent's Hospital. I think I will call it a day and go off to bed.

Just told Rosary House that we will end classes at the end of the week. I think they are feeing a little rundown and tired. I won't be sorry as I have a lot of other things to pick up on – and I will be glad to have a break from the teaching nearly every afternoon.

I will send a wire to Marie tomorrow. [7] Meant to write to her but have not had a chance. Will be saying Mass for her. Now Mother dear I am really tired, so you will pardon the brevity of this note.

Goodnight and God bless you. Will be so glad to hear from you again when you can find a few minutes.

Jack.

---

7   Marie's birthday is 1st December.

Letter 92 to Mother

*Cars are hard to come by – as is petrol.
I have been collecting a little here and a little there
and putting it in drums –
so as not to run short over the Christmas weeks.*

This is a four-page letter from John to his mother (18th December 1947) on the date of his ordination anniversary. He has used the Rosary House, Home Missionary Sisters of Our Lady stationery, their address being 1 Frederick Street, Launceston. The three major themes in the letter are the arrival of his brother Brian, who has been appointed to Cygnet parish, the Home Missionary Sisters of Our Lady or Rosary House Sisters as he has referred to them, and matters related to his family and especially his Deaf siblings.

His mother has farewelled another son to Tasmania. John books a telephone call to his mother for 9.30pm the day Brian arrives, but it is late when they connect. John apologises. He is still living and working in Launceston, and Brian spends his first few days with him before travelling to Hobart and on to Cygnet parish.

However, Brian is immediately connected to *Rosary House.* To mark John's ordination anniversary and Brian's arrival on the island, the Sisters have staged a concert. A little light entertainment! Brian has brought the new monstrance from Melbourne for the Sisters and celebrates Mass and Benediction with them. All the gemstones collected, the diamonds and rubies, were not used in the monstrance, but John reassures the Sisters that the jewellery could be used in other sacred vessels. The Sisters will have a holiday at the Presentation Sisters' convent at Karoola near Launceston, and John also arranges for a three-day retreat for Kath Moore and Winifred Ryan, who had been in Hobart and who return to Launceston for Christmas.

Appointed as a parish assistant to the kind and pastoral Father Kent, Brian has plenty to do, including visiting Bruny Island, which is part of Cygnet parish. John tells his mother that the phone number for Brian is 67. Father Kent has the welfare of young people in the rural areas at heart and has established an agricultural school conducted by the Christian Brothers, who share the big presbytery. Of concern is Brian's transport around the parish with the difficulty of acquiring a car and obtaining petrol. John has been collecting petrol and putting it in a drum so he would have enough during the Christmas period.

The Silver Jubilee book on St Gabriel's School for Deaf Boys has arrived. John writes of an ex-student from St Gabriel's, the young Deaf man Darcey Counsel, a schoolmate of his brother, Charlie, who needed an interpreter and bit of support. Darcey later moves to Melbourne and becomes lifelong friends of both John's Deaf brothers. John also comments that the Dominican Sisters will establish a Deaf residential school in Victoria at Delgany, Portsea, firmly backed by Archbishop Daniel Mannix.

Lastly we note John's current concern for Premier Robert Cosgrove at the time of the Royal Commission into bribery and corruption. While the Premier stood down on 18th December, he was acquitted in January and resumed his office to become the longest serving Premier in Tasmania.

* * *

HOME MISSIONARY SISTERS OF OUR LADY

'Phone L'ton 552

ROSARY HOUSE,
1 FREDERICK STREET,
LAUNCESTON.

18/12/47

My dear Mother,

18/12/1947

My dear Mother,

It is Thursday morning and I am waiting for a lad to turn up for instructions. It looks as if he will not be here but I am waiting a while for him. For days I have made a note on my desk-pad to write to you but have not had a chance as yet. At any rate, here is a beginning with hopes for the best that it will get off to you in the next day or two.

I am looking forward to Brian's arrival. I can imagine your feelings as you send off a second son to Tasmania – feelings, I suspect, of joy mingled with sadness too. I hope and I feel that the joy will predominate. His Grace [Archbishop Tweedy] told me where he is to go but I will leave that to him to tell you himself. I will not tell him but will let him learn it from the letter of appointment; he will have a good pastor and a variety of experience. I am still a fixture at the Deanery!

Sisters Carroll and Morse are back at Rosary House. Both much better after their holiday. We have had a good deal of sickness – or rather weariness etc. A couple of the Juniors have lost a deal of weight so that we have been concerned about them. X-rays showed negative – a good thing. The Sisters from Hobart came back on Saturday. They will have a three days' retreat beginning on Sunday night. I shall give them a few talks only.

Deloraine Monday afternoon to Sisters of Mercy. They have a little Triduum in preparation for Christmas. (I have broken off a few times. It is now afternoon.) I have arranged with Mother Patrick [Presentation Sisters] for some of the Rosary House Sisters to go to the convent at Karoola for a couple of weeks after Christmas. The change should do them good and Doctor said it is a change of air that they need more than anything else.

I got the St. Gabriel's Jubilee Number of the Annual. It is very nice. Saw Don's photo in a group. I am sure he and Charl must have enjoyed that trip very much. It is a great experience to be meeting old school companions. I was asked recently to go to the Court as an interpreter for Darcey Counsel who was involved in a car accident some time ago. The case was postponed so I expect it will now come off some time in January. Darcey is a lovely boy and I am delighted to be able to help him. I do hope he comes out of things alright. If Brian were here he would be better suited to the job than I as he is much more fluent with the sign language. The news about Portsea – Sisters of St. Dominic – is good.[8] *We are hoping to get a little lad from here to go. Bro. Cahill of St. Gabriel's is here in Tasmania at present looking for children who ought to be in the Catholic [Deaf] Schools.*

I expect that Tasmania has been in the news in your papers. The Royal Commission and its outcome have been topics of great interest here – hope Mr Cosgrove comes out of the matter quite clear. I must confess that I am not so keen about the party who brought the matter up. J. Sullivan – no relation to the J.P. Sullivans. By the way Mrs Reg Sullivan sends kind regards. She had an American Tea for Rosary House last week – worth about £2. This was a very fine response considering other appeals and counter attractions – and a cool day!

Sunday 21st:

I did not get my letter away the other night and it is now Sunday night. Brian has gone off to Hobart – will be there now (10 o'clock). I did not intend to be so late with the ring the other night but I had booked the call for 9.30. There was a long delay (2½ hours on the lines.) We wondered if you had gone to bed. He had a good trip over. I met him at the drome.

Went to Rosary House after tea and took up the Monstrance. I was very pleased with it and so were the Sisters. But they and I were disappointed that the diamonds could not be used effectively in it. I can quite appreciate the fact that they would not have been evident at all. The same was true of the rubies sent over from here and some other articles. However I am hoping to use them for something ... associated with the Blessed Sacrament.

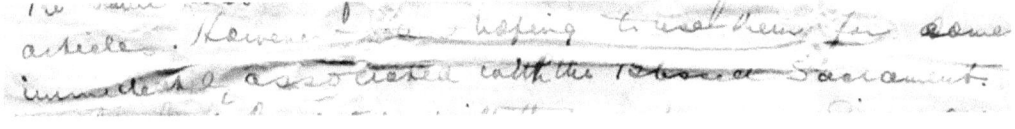

---

8   In 1948 the Dominican Sisters who had a school for Deaf children at Waratah near Newcastle established another such residential school at Portsea, Victoria.

Brian gave the first Benediction with the monstrance on Friday evening. He said Mass at Rosary House on Friday morning and on Saturday morning. This morning he said 11 o'clock Mass and preached. I did not hear it as was out in the country. On Saturday night the Sisters at Rosary House staged a concert for the two of us. It was partly for my ordination day and partly to welcome Brian. I think he enjoyed it as I certainly did.

I am very pleased with his appointment. Father Kent is a good man to begin with – there will be plenty for Brian to do. It is a country Church, with about a third of the people Catholics. They have a good school, Agricultural school etc. I think he should be very happy there and he will have experiences there that he would not have in any other parish. Bruny Island is part of the parish so he will be seeing the Dillons' over there. He will stay tonight and tomorrow night in Hobart and then on Tuesday will go to Cygnet. It is about 35 miles from Hobart. It looks as though he will have to get a car! I expect the Archbishop will discuss this matter with him. Maybe Fr Kent will be able to finance a parish car for him. In any case provisions will be made so that there is no need to worry about it. He is fairly thin and can do with a bit of building up. He will get plenty of the best of country food at Cygnet. It is good in that respect.

I expect I will see him about mid January. The retreat will be on then and then the conference of the clergy. He may come to Hobart for that. If I do not see him then I don't know when I will. Of course we are expecting further changes after Christmas and the New Year. I will be remembering you and saying Mass for you on that day and Brian will be also. If you put a call through, his number will be Cygnet 67. He told me Chester had an order in for a Ford Truck utility. I hope he can get it. Cars are hard to come by – as is petrol. I have been collecting a little here and a little there and putting it in drums – so as not to run short over the Christmas weeks.

Now Mother dear, I will close this note with love to you and all at home. I do hope you will have a happy Christmas. Brian said you have not been well. I hope it will not be so for long. I was so glad to know that you saw Mrs. Fitzgerald. I did not know till Brian told me. He told me also about the visit to Dorothy Kelleher. She wrote and told me how she appreciated your visit.

Now goodnight and God bless you.

Your loving son,
Jack

Letter 93 to Mother

The caravan idea is under discussion.
If they had their own means of transport
they would be much more independent
and able to cover a larger field of work.

In this letter six-page letter (30th December 1947) written to his mother on both sides of stationery from Rosary House, John reports on the *solid initiation* that Brian is receiving through the parish preparations for Christmas – in the confessional for eight hours indicating a big population of Catholic people in the parish. He will celebrate two Masses each Sunday and he is to be in charge of Bruny Island. Getting a car is still an issue – to find one and to negotiate a loan to buy it are the problems to be resolved.

John remarks on the centenary celebrations marking the centenary of the formal establishment of the Catholic Church in Melbourne with the appointment of the first Bishop, Dr James Goold in 1848. Archbishop Daniel Mannix has sent out invitations far and wide to attend. While the Franciscan priest, Father Patrick Bonaventure Geoghegan, arrived in Melbourne ten years earlier in 1838, John's Irish great grandparents William Dempsey and Mary Darby both came the same year, although initially William had arrived in Sydney almost ten years earlier as a convict.

Concerned about the Sisters and their health, John advises them that during the holidays they drop their daily practice of meditation, prayer, reading etc. to relax and rest. The advice to relax and rest John knows his mother would give him as well – he has been *grumpy* of late, being weary and needing a break.

Looking for mainland women who could contribute to the mission too, John wants to advertise the existence of the new Australian Tasmanian-based Sisters who would go out on the highways and byways. He plans to prepare a pamphlet to publish through the Australian Catholic Truth Society. Another thought is for the Sisters to have their own car, making them more independent – and the possibility of a caravan is up for discussion too. In this *rambling* letter as described by John, he says he encourages the Sisters to have a devotion to God's holy will and God's providence, however he knows his own weaknesses, and writes, *at times I fear that it is they who should be lecturing me!*

Housing is still an issue post-War. It is hoped in the diocese to build Nazareth House, a residential home for aged people in Launceston, but building supplies are difficult to obtain.

[30/12/1947]

My dear Mother,

I have been thinking of you all these days and wondering how your Christmas passed. It was as usual a busy time for us, but just now things are quiet and I am getting over that tiredness. Contrary to expectations Brian and I were not together for Christmas. I had a note from him this morning. He certainly would have [had] a solid initiation. He told me he had 8 hours at Confessions and three Masses on Christmas day. It will take a while to get accustomed to the two Masses etc. on Sunday.

I can see him burdened without a car. He mentioned it in his letter. Maybe he can get a second hand car to do the work on the better roads and then he may use Fr Kent's utility truck for the rougher roads – and there are some very rough ones in Cygnet parish. As for the finance for the car – if he can get one – I think his best plan is to borrow it from the Archbishop. He can pay it back in instalments. His Grace [Archbishop Tweedy] can let him have about £300 or £400. I think it better that he just battle along himself than that others' help be given. All other young priests here have been in that boat. Fr Kent is very good and will help him quite a deal.

I expect to see him about the 16th. I may even get a Sunday off to spend a few days with him. I would appreciate the break as I am afraid I have been fairly grumpy and out of sorts lately. Did not quite realise it till yesterday when I felt that the Sisters noticed it.

We have had a deal of sickness at Rosary House and it has been worrying me. Yesterday I took four – Sr Morse and three Juniors out to the Presentation Convent at Karoola. The Presentation Sisters are away. It is a nice quiet place and they should be able to have a good peaceful rest. I told them to put aside all prayers, reading, etc. etc. and to try to have a real rest. I expect you are suggesting the same medicine for myself!! Well, yes, it would be good! But if I can stay at Cygnet with Brian I will be really glad. In fact we might both go over to Bruni[9] Island for a few days. He is to be in charge of Bruni. Expects to go over there next Sunday.

We had a deal of close weather before Christmas and rain about 10.30 on Christmas Eve. The wet weather affected the Masses a good deal – especially the midnight Mass. I said Mass at Newstead at Midnight, then at 7.00 and 8 o'clock at St. Leonard's.[10] The Sisters from Rosary House went to Newstead and sang at the midnight Mass. Two of them are staying at the Convent there while the Sisters of St. Joseph are away in Hobart for their retreat. Sisters [Agnes] Ryan and [Kath] Moore came up from Hobart for Christmas. They go back next weekend and go to New Norfolk for the Summer school there. They are both looking very well, the best of the whole community. It must be the fresh bracing air of Hobart!

We go to Hobart for our Retreat on Monday Jan 12th. Brian will not be on retreat as he made his retreat before leaving College. He and Fr. [Joe] McMahon will hold the fort while the rest of us are on the Retreat. Fr. Eric Dwyer CSsR – brother of [Edmund Alfred] "Chappy" Dwyer, Australian Test Trans Selector – and the owner of E.J. Dwyer's Bookshop in Sydney is to give our Retreat.

There are a great lot of mainland people about here just now – most of them tourists who have come over by plane. On one day before Christmas there were 66 planes [that] came come across the Straits. We have got used to all sorts of aircraft about the place. There are very few people going over to the mainland just yet, but soon the flow will be that way. The weather at present is ideal – bright sunny days but with cool breezes. A lot of the folk from Launceston have moved out to holiday places.

I heard a few days ago that Fr Austin (George) Stoner is coming over for a fortnight to see his Mother. I am very pleased. She is very feeble and is not able to get about. He will stay at Bellerive. I hope to see him when in Hobart for the Retreat.

Tell Chester that I remembered his birthday – said Mass for him and his welfare. I would be glad to see him over here sometime. I think that it might be better for him not to come on the Pioneer service. I am here in the North, Brian in the South, so that between us we should be able to see that he gets set up. I would hate to be on the Pioneer runs – one has got to be at the beck and call of the drivers – and to be on the go all the time. Then too one can only go to the places they settle on. Chester would be interested in the Agricultural School at Cygnet. Of course it is still in its experimental stages – but Fr. Kent has big ideas and is out to try to do something original and constructive. Of

---

9   The original spelling of Bruny Island was Bruni. It was changed in 1918.
10   Newstead and St Leonards are suburbs of Launceston.

course I don't know where I may be at the end of next month. There are some more changes on the cards.

Brian also mentioned that you were thinking of coming and of bringing Auntie Jane. I would be delighted and will be waiting to hear more. I had a letter from Auntie Jane recently. It was in serial form. She will tell you what happened. If you thought of coming this year I think it best to try to come in the early part as it can get very cold from May on, although some of our nicest weather last year was in June and July. August and September are usually the coldest months.

I expect some of the priests will be accepting the invitation we all received from Dr. Mannix for the Centenary celebrations in May. I thought I might try to go but I have not made any decision as yet. In a way these big celebrations can be very tiring though they are very interesting and one can get a chance of meeting lots of people who have useful ideas etc. Then too I want to take any opportunity to bring the work of the Sisters to the notice of those who may be interested in it and help in one way or another.

I am hoping to write a CTS [Catholic Truth Society] pamphlet on it this year – will try to get at it early in the year. If it can be attractively got up it would have a large sale throughout Australia and would be a good publicity medium. Then too I am hoping to send a couple of Sisters to the mainland sometime during the year – [the] goal [is] to see and to be seen![11]

I have the Archbishop's permission for Sr. Carroll to go to see her nephew, Pat Carroll, ordained. This is not known in the Community as yet – though I know all the Sisters will be very pleased. I expect someone else will go with her. I would like to send Sr. Morse as she would be able to pick up ideas etc. and pass them on to the Juniors.

I had a letter from Fr. [Charlie] Mayne SJ – new Rector of Corpus Christi – in which he told me of a girl he met in South Australia who appears to be interested in our plans. The information given about her seems very satisfactory, but nothing definite has been forthcoming as yet. There are also two girls in Hobart who are interested but have not yet come to the point of decision. This new year will doubtless see developments in our scheme.

Just now I am rewriting most of our lessons for the Correspondence Course – making them more interesting in their appeal and more practical for the children. Experience is a great teacher. Then I hope to begin on a new series for the course. It would be helpful if I could be in some quiet sleepy-hollow parish with plenty of time to think things out. Of course, there is the advantage here of variety – and a break from desk work.

---

11   In other words, that the Sisters would explore ministry on the mainland as well as get known, which may attract new members and support for the mission.

Then the question of the Sisters having a car has been raised. I feel we ought to do something about it this year. If they had their own means of transport they would be much more independent and able to cover a larger field of work. The caravan idea is under also discussion. Personally I am inclined to think it should wait awhile yet.

Then too there is the question yet of beginning operations on the Hobart house. In a way I hope that we may not have to use it. I don't think it at all suitable for our purposes. I would like a place with more ground for the Sisters to use for recreation and for the children. A place on the outskirts of the city would be the most suitable.

However, all we can do is wait and pray till the good Lord lets us know his Holy Will. I often fear lest I have not the simple trusting spirit of faith that I ought to have. Again and again I speak to the Sisters about that and tell them to try to have a constant loving devotion to God's Holy Will and His Providence – but at times I fear that it is they who should be lecturing me! I know there is no need to ask you for your prayers for the work. You know I have always had great faith in your prayers – always have had it and I am confident that you will help me that way always.

Now Mother I will close this rambling letter. It is mostly full with my own interests but I know you like to hear about them. Let me know how all is going on at home. Brian told me a good deal about your visit to Mr Osborne,[12] etc. Let me know of any developments about a home in Melbourne. I don't know what things are like over there, but here the housing question is about as acute as ever. One of the problems here is to get material. There is plenty of cement for concrete but glass and household fittings are in very short supply. And then too the materials are of very inferior quality. We are anxious to go ahead with our Nazareth House for old people but it seems to be out of the question for awhile yet.

Goodbye – love to all. God bless you.
Your loving Son in Christ,
Jack

PS. *Enclosed card from Fr. P. Carmine*

---

12 Mr Osborne was the solicitor in Seymour.

Letter 94 to Mother

I often feel that my life is sadly deficient in prayer.

This is a four-page letter from John to his mother (3rd March 1948) on stationery from St Finn Barr's Parish, Invermay, Launceston, where he is stationed temporarily. It is the only surviving letter in this collection written during 1948 and two months since his last letter. John has more access with home via phone calls, so that news has already been passed on – for example, that he went to Invermay parish in January. He turns thirty-eight years old this year and this is the first parish for which he is responsible. He has a housekeeper who can cook his meals for which he is very grateful.

It is nearly four years since the first group of Sisters came together at *Rosary House* in Frederick Street. They have had intensive formation and now they are in demand for ministry in various parishes. The first missions are in little isolated towns of northeast Tasmania – Branxholm where they stayed in the sacristy of the Church, Derby where they stayed in the presbytery, Scottsdale and then back to Branxholm. For Easter week, John is to take them to Lebrina, east of the Tamar River. While he says he will stay in the sacristy of the Church, the Sisters will go to a private home. The Sisters being a very real part of his life, John writes to his mother of details regarding them – their illnesses, etc. and continually asks her to pray for their work. In September 1948 his mother and cousin Anne Douglas come to visit and are present for the profession of two of the Sisters on 8th September – Anne Murphy from Launceston and Monica (Sister Joseph) Franklin, the first one from Melbourne.

John is pleased that the Carmelite Sisters with their focus on prayer are to establish a monastery in Longford near Launceston. At the same time, he wonders if the apostolic life of the Rosary House Sisters may *danger* their spiritual life, although he impresses on them the importance of a prayer life. Then he reflectively adds: *Of course I am aware that I am the pot calling the kettle black. I often feel that my life is sadly deficient in prayer.*

Because of his own love for the bush and remote places, it is not surprising that John suggests to his mother to read a book that he has picked up, *We of the Never Never* by Jeannie Gunn, an autobiography of life and love set in the Northern Territory. First published in 1907, it is the story of a teacher from Melbourne who in 1902 settles with her new husband on the remote property Elsey cattle station near Roper River.

* * *

3/3/1948

My dear Mother,

It is now after 11 o'clock but I am at least beginning a letter though I will not be finishing it tonight. When I sent the last note I intended to write the following week but I really have not had a chance to write to anyone except on urgent business. One has few idle moments here and as time goes on they will it seems, become even fewer.

It is a large parish. There should be an assistant priest here. The Archbishop had promised one a long time ago but as yet no one is available. So far I have managed to get some help from visitors but that is just a passing help. Then they cannot help with the routine work of week days. However I am feeling very well. The housekeeper is providing well for me. It is a great relief to be able to come in and find meals ready etc. For a little while I was on my own – used to go out for meals.

There are about 2,000 Catholics in the district. Soon I hope to begin regular census of the place. It is the best way to get to know people. Then too there is the everlasting financial side of things. Personally I am well provided for, as the revenue here is really good. I hope to save up a few pounds to be used on having the car done up. But there is not a great deal in the Church account and there are lots of matters needing attention – painting, doors, windows etc. out of repair. I am waiting till after Easter before facing a meeting of the people to discuss ways and means of raising the necessary funds. I would like too to do something to the convent of the [Presentation] Sisters. It is in a bad way. I expect time will see all these things attended to.

Then of course Rosary House goes on as usual. I told you about the first Mission. I took the two Sisters out to Branxholm. They set themselves up in the little sacristy – and had a busy and solid week there. They are now at Derby; next week at Scottsdale and then back to Branxholm. I had a letter today for them from St. Marys Parish (East Coast). Father [Peter] Murphy wants them to spend some months in his parish. Then I am taking two out to Lebrina in Easter Week. I will stay at the little sacristy of the Church; they will stay in a private home. A Redemptorist [priest] will come here for a while to carry on while I am away.

As a consequence of their Missionary tours the Correspondence Course will also grow. We are at present trying to find ways of simplifying that work so that it will not take too much time. It is hard for our Juniors to pick up so much. We are looking for more recruits. I have been thinking of trying to get over to Victoria, South Australia and Sydney during the year to see if I can find any likely aspirants. Just a couple of days ago a Victorian priest wrote to ask if we could let him have two Sisters to go to some of the country districts of his parish! Not yet! is all we can say.

You will have noticed that the Carmelites are to come to Launceston! This is good news indeed. I have always hoped that they would come. Their prayers will call down blessings on our many works. I am always trying to impress on the Sisters the importance of the interior life of prayer that their Apostolate be fruitful. They have a good spirit of prayer but the busy life of the missions may at times endanger this. Of course I am aware that I am the pot calling the kettle black. I often feel that my life is sadly deficient in prayer. It is now 11.30 so I will get off to bed and finish this letter later – maybe tomorrow evening.

Thursday Night:

I have just finished a long day. Took two Sisters out to Lilydale School then on to Lebrina and towards Pipers Brook over rough roads to give Holy Communion to an old lady there. We did not get home till one o'clock. This afternoon was spent partly in cleaning out the hall which has been neglected for some while and then into Rosary House to arrange various details.

I am very worried about a couple [of Sisters] who are sick and not responding to treatment. Thanks be to God Sr [Gwen] Morse is once again in good form, though she still has to go carefully. It is all the Lord's affair. Just got word that Sr [Joyce] O'Brien's mother is not at all well. She is about 86 this year so we would not be surprised at any eventuality. Sister is at present out on the Mission. She may have to be called in, if we get any further bad report.

You will be interested to know that I am reading 'We of the Never Never'. Dip into it as I am having tea each evening. My meals are solitary affairs, so I do a little reading. Have enjoyed the book very much. Strangely I had never read it before. I thought of you when I read about the Chinese cook Cheon clearing out all sorts of things from the house – burning etc. I have had a great burn off here. Also remembered you laughing about the raisins that came instead of tea!

10.00pm Just had a phone call from Fr. Hansen in Hobart. He said Brian was up in Hobart yesterday. He is looking well and is very happy – and busy.

Has begun to put on a lot of condition. He also said that he had no news of me! I have not written. The last time I was talking to him was when I rang him about Auntie Jane. Now and then I hear of him – generally that he is always busy – there is plenty to do in that parish. Yesterday I had a letter from Father Murphy parish priest of St Marys on the East Coast asking for the Rosary House Sisters to go out there. Just noticed I had mentioned this already.

I suppose you have no idea when you might come over. Will be expecting you just the same. You will find me always on the go – but most times you will be able to come with me on trips to the country – every Thursday at least, also on Sundays. These latter are usually very very hectic and not much pleasure for anyone! The Thursday trip is quite a nice one.

Had a letter from Hobart Sisters today. On their return to the schools they asked the children about lessons done last year. Here is one answer: "What do you do after you tell the priest how long it is since your last confession?" "Roll out your sins," said one lad!

The Archbishop is due up here next week. I expect him out here for a while. May have to begin to save money for repairs to the convent. I don't like the money business but I expect it has to be. By the way, Mother, I cashed that cheque you sent me £6/10/-. It is in an account I have for special purposes that may arise. I was going to send it back but I did not think you would want me to do that. Would you tell me when you write what you would like me to do with it?

Now Mother dear, it is late and I want to post this so that you will get it on Saturday – at least so I hope. Give my love to all. Will write to Marie at the weekend – if I have a chance at all. Give my love to Chester. I do hope he comes to some finality. Also to all the rest.

Goodnight and God bless you. I am so sorry I have not written before really I am just snowed in with things to be done. I have a whole pile of papers at my side – all awaiting attention. Pray – Keep praying for the work of Rosary House. There is a great great deal to be done yet. Please God all will work out for the best.

Your loving son in Christ,
Jack

Letter 95 to Mother

I am a wandering beggar at present
... It is a strange life

This four-page letter to John's mother (6th April 1949) is the last of the surviving letters in the collection – the only one for 1949. Now a priest in Tasmania for over sixteen years, he has established himself, knowing the people, priests, religious, and the business of the Archdiocese and the Catholic schools. He has founded, formed and trained a group of women, whose work takes them into the rural areas.[13] He has become familiar with the land and the environment, the agriculture and businesses, the infrastructure and employment opportunities, as well as the politics of Tasmania. He has also come to know the people, their longings and trials, hopes and joys. All these things he has shared initially with both parents, now with his mother.

After being parish priest at Invermay for the previous year, this year John is *a wandering beggar*. He is on the appeal trail, fund-raising, visiting parishes and going to the out-of-way places, including the *wild* place, Rosebery on the west coast of Tasmania, a prosperous mining town at the time, where the people spend money freely, he says. He is setting up and arranging opportunities for the Home Missionary Sisters to work in these areas as well. He is also relieving in some parishes, one of them being Railton, where the Sisters will spend some weeks. And he wants his mother to come over then to be with him and to cook as well!

She has obviously written of the matters troubling her and asks his advice. Things have changed since her husband died and Chester has married (September 1948). John would like to discuss these matters, including the plans for selling her land or not – and whether to buy a place in Melbourne.

John is also writing brochures and more articles – for *The Annals*, a Catholic magazine published by the Missionaries of the Sacred Heart Fathers, and *The Southern Cross*, the Catholic paper in Adelaide. There are expressions of interest to join the Sisters coming in from some women as well.

To emphasise his time of wandering and his close association with the Sisters, he asks that his mail be sent to the Rosary House Sisters, Launceston till 26th April 1949. The Sisters will move to Longford south of Launceston, so his mail will go there. In August, he is finally appointed parish priest of Sandy Bay, Hobart – and more Sisters have moved to Hobart too.

* * *

---

13   They would finally become a religious order, approved by the Vatican in 1951.

HOME MISSIONARY SISTERS OF OUR LADY

Catholic Presbytery,
Burnie.   6.4.1949

My dear Mother,

I am a wandering beggar at present. I arrived here tonight at 6 o'clock and will be leaving again at shortly after 7 o'clock on my way to Rosebery on the West Coast. The Sisters (3) are there at present and finish their mission on Sunday next. I am beginning the Appeal at Rosebery on Sunday.

Since I last wrote I have been travelling a great deal. Went along to the N. West Coast – visited Smithton, Irishtown, Stanley and Forest to arrange for the Appeal and for a Mission for the Sisters. Have also been into Launceston.

The carpenters came in to dismantle Rosary House. They are in the thick of it now – also the carriers etc. I will be in Launceston again in Easter week to see to the work of dismantling the Altar, which is to be packed and sent to Hobart. The week after that I will go to Hobart to see the Novices installed and see how plans are going for additions to the House.

Then back to Railton for a week's Mission for two or three Sisters. There are about 50 children. They – and their parents are very interested. The Sisters will stay in the Presbytery – I will sleep in the Sacristy. Last Saturday eight ladies came and gave the Presbytery a good clean out. They also arranged for all the linen in the place to be washed. There is a lot of back country – very hilly and still very beautiful.

Since you wrote, plans here have been upset somewhat. Fr. O'Connor who left here to go to Ireland got to Adelaide and decided not to go any further – seasick so I heard. I am not sure if or when he may come back. I think he may come about the middle of May.

Now I would like you to come over while I am at Railton if only for a few weeks. What about being here while the Sisters are up. You could come to Launceston about April 29th (Friday). I could pick you up at the Drome and we could come on to Railton. I will be on my way home from Hobart on the Friday. The next week I would be at Railton all the time making preparations for the Sisters. If you were there and could have meals ready it would be a *great help for me and I really think you would love the country round about. The Sisters would arrive on Friday 6th. There may be two only. In that case I will have the ladies cook for them – and for the children – small cakes, scones etc. for morning and afternoon tea. You would not be any trouble to the Sisters; in fact your presence in the house might be a real help. I would really love you to see the Sisters at work. They finish up on May 16th.*

I may stay a couple of weeks more in the parish. There is no housekeeper there – and you might care to come there with me for a couple of weeks. It would fit in grand. Now, I will be expecting to hear soon from you – and I will be expecting you to say that you are coming. It is a chance I may not get again for awhile. And then we could have a talk over the matters you mentioned in your letter. It is hard to write about these things. It is often much easier to talk them over.

Certainly I do not like the idea of selling the property. All along you – and Father – had the 3 deaf children in mind. Brian and I are quite secure – there is no need to think of us. Chester has been treated fairly too. I can quite understand how the others don't feel at ease about giving up the farm. Maybe your idea of having the little cottage could help a deal. Still it is near the other place. Of course it is apart – and they can do as they like there. Yes, I think it would be a good plan. As for letting Chester have option of purchase – make improvements etc to suit his own plans – that I think would be quite in order. Still I'd rather talk it over. I really don't see any chance of getting away now for quite a while – so I would like you to come over. I have not had any letter from Chester. I have not seen Brian for sometime – nor have I heard from him. May see him when I am in Hobart later in the month.

I am at present getting a folder for Rosary House done – will send it to you when it comes off the press. The articles for the Annals of Our Lady of the Sacred Heart will appear in August and September. The editor wrote to me a few days ago. Also had a letter from the Editor of "The Southern Cross" of South Australia saying he would publish an article. I am hoping while on the appeal to pick up some vocations. I met a very nice girl at Irishtown ... She is interested. Also had a letter from a girl in Ballarat – and sent some literature to a girl in Bendigo.

Sent copy of [The] Standard to Anne [Douglas]. I may drop a line from Rosebery to you. It is a mining town – 90 Catholic children and no Convent School. Wild place ... spend money freely – so I'm hoping.

Now Mother dear, it is getting late and I'll have to be up about 5 o'clock in the morning so I think I'll turn in. Send my letters c/o Rosary House, Launceston until April 26th; after that send them to Rosary House, Longford. The Sisters move on that day. They know where I am at any particular time and send my mail on to me. It is a strange life – this appealing [for funds]. I am in a different house nearly every week. Sometimes I'm in three or four different beds each week.

Goodnight and God bless you and keep you. I know I have your prayers for me all the time. Give my love to Charl and Marie and Don when you see them – also Chester. I am sure all will work out. Mind, if you think I can help in any way, I will go over if only for a couple of days in between Sundays.

Again – goodnight.

Your loving Son in Christ,
Jack

WHAT DO WE HEAR HERE?
Tasmania 1946–1949
Letters 89 – 95

Angela Hazebroek

We hear the voice of a man of faith, hope and love

Father John Wallis' deep and abiding trust in the Providence of God shines through in his ability to place the not yet known into God's hands. He has confidence that all will be well. He does not however sit back and wait for God to provide the answers. He takes a pragmatic attitude to potential problems and initiates actions that work towards a solution. John is a man of practical action.

Compassionate love is the theme that runs through all of these letters. We hear it in his concern for his mother's health and the decisions she needs to make about the family property. We hear it in the little details in which only a mother would be interested, *"Brian has put on a lot of condition"* and *"the housekeeper is providing well for me"*. With a son's intuition he couches his invitation to her to visit him at Railton in terms of the benefit to him and the sisters.

John's deep and very personal concern for each of the women who have joined the newly established community of the Home Missionary Sisters of Our Lady is evident in his letters. While he is their mentor, educator and spiritual guide, he is interested in their whole wellbeing – their health problems, their need for rest and a change of scene, and the training to equip them for their ministry.

John's care for each of the members of his family is highlighted by the hopes he has for their happiness and his desire to be available to them.

Like a shepherd he leads his flock ...

John's pastoral vocation is directed to the poor and the excluded. There are the homeless man and his wife, the people of Flinders Island who have not had Mass for eleven months and the lonely single men of the mining towns. It is this call to reveal God present in these places that forms the Sisters' mission to go *"into the highways and byways"*.

Humility and humour

John is a man of humility and self-awareness. He does not take himself too seriously and there is often a wry sense of humour in his observations. *"Travel lightly"*, he tells the sisters setting off on holidays with everything but the kitchen sink! He recognises that it might be a case of *"the pot calling the kettle black"* when he expresses his concern that a busy apostolic life might put the Sisters' prayer life at risk.

A man of prayer

John is deeply aware of the importance of a strong prayer life and the need to sustain this through periods of recollection, spiritual reading and meditation. He knows that the apostolic life is only made fruitful through the relationship with God that prayer develops. His keen sense of the insufficiency of his prayer life and his desire to withdraw to a quiet place highlight the importance he placed on prayer.

If we accept that all of life is prayer, then we sense in John's late-night letters to his mother that God is as present in this loving encounter as he would have been if John had chosen to meditate instead.

John's connection to the land is demonstrated through his descriptions of the countryside and his awareness of farming practices. He was at heart always a *"country boy"*. He found God everywhere – in people, in relationships, in the call to service and in the natural world. He saw all that God had made and knew that it was good.

I first met John as a 17-year-old at my parents' farm house at Mount Bryan in South Australia. I had found the religious order I wanted to join and discerned this with John – so within a few months my youthful desire came to fruition, and in January 1972 I joined the Missionary Sisters of Service (MSS) in Hobart. During my four years with the MSS I learned much from John – a most compassionate spiritual director making sure that my practices supporting a prayer life were well established. I still hear his voice when connecting with God through periods of silence and solitude, spiritual reading and savouring God's presence in nature.

Angela Hazebroek is married with two adult daughters and three grandchildren. After undertaking the Spiritual Exercises of Saint Ignatius in Guelph, Canada in 2013, Angela went on to study and completed her Master of Arts in Spiritual Direction in 2016. Angela works in the urban and regional planning company she co-founded in 2003. She also relishes her time in Spiritual Direction Ministry as a team member at the Loyola Centre for Ignatian Spirituality in Norwood, South Australia.

Letters To Brian
1944 – 1947
Letters 96 – 100

Introduction

This is the period of World War II and its aftermath, the founding of the Missionary Sisters of Service, who were initially known as the Home Missionary Sisters of Our Lady, Brian's ordination in Melbourne and Emma Wallis moving to Sunday Creek near Broadford, Victoria.

This chapter reproduces five surviving letters in this collection that John wrote to his brother, Brian, from 1944–1947, one in 1944, one in 1945, two in 1946 and one in 1947.

The letters are those of an older brother by ten years wanting to share what he has learned. Or of a spiritual director encouraging this younger sibling on his journey towards priesthood and advising him how to live as a good priest and to become *a man of prayer*.

Perhaps in relation to Brian, John's heart reflects that of the future Pope Francis in the Apostolic Exhortation, *Evangelii Gaudium,* The Joy of the Gospel, Article 261:

> *How I long to find the right words*
> *to stir up enthusiasm for a new chapter of evangelisation*
> *full of fervour, joy, generosity, courage, boundless love and attraction!*
> *Yet I realise that no words of encouragement will be enough*
> *unless the fire of the Holy Spirit burns in our hearts.*

Letter 96 to Brian

In the last analysis it is the work of grace.

In this seven-page letter to Brian (23rd January 1944), John, now thirty-four years old, while writing an encouraging letter to his younger brother, is also writing for his own benefit. *I would love to have you here or to be at home to talk with you.* A momentous event has occurred prematurely for John. Archbishop Tweedy has been interested in the founding of a community to work in rural areas, but he went further and announced the new project to the Tasmanian priests when they were gathered for their retreat. He had stated that he wanted their moral and financial support. While they were indeed generous in response, John is horrified it all happened so quickly and he does not feel ready. The priests' support though was a sign to John that this project was God's will for him. Father Tim Murphy, a *saintly* person, in whom John had confided, also advised him to go ahead.

John has many ideas about the Home Missionary Sisters *project*. Two women, Gwen Morse and Kathleen Moore, have already committed themselves to it. He still needs two more women to participate before it can go ahead. John writes of the Sisters wearing secular dress and taking vows of obedience and chastity and living in the spirit of poverty. They are to have the level of commitment of diocesan priests, he thought. John takes Gwen Morse – and others – down to Cygnet for the summer camp and he sets boundaries for travelling with women: Oh! They sat in the back seat, as a precaution for purity of mind and heart! Sitting in the back seat changed in the years to come.

Further on in the letter, John writes more directly to Brian concerning matters of conscience that might be troubling him at this stage of his seminary training. He shares with Brian his own earlier scruples. With his maturing in his relationship with God and understanding of himself, he advises: *I think, relax, have a big broad spirituality and not one that constrains and worries. It is of great importance in life.* He continues with common sense spirituality: *Brightness, cheerfulness and great unselfishness are essential elements of holiness.*

In a more fatherly way, he also advises Brian to pick out a special interest or a ministry – a hobby, so that he can specialise and become an authority in that particular area. He congratulates Brian on his Hebrew studies and how well he has done generally, including with Gregorian music. (John makes fun of himself, because he was not musical and could not sing in tune.) The Hobart Catholic Bookshop has begun in a small way, perhaps initially as a hobby of John's, arising from his love for books and his belief in the importance of libraries and good Catholic reading for people.

Before he finishes the letter, John returns to the issue of doubts, anxieties and trials often prevalent before making major decisions. Similarly, he sees this in the life of the Sisters. He adds that it would be a concern if one *had not weathered serious trials and doubts and anxieties and misgivings.* He emphasises the importance of prayer, otherwise aspirants become *barren in their spiritual life.* Knowing the importance of reading for spiritual nourishment, John recommends books to Brian. He signs off by saying, *Stick at it!* John admits he has been *sermonising* and writing a book at the same time!

* * *

Hobart.
23.1.1944

My dear Brian,

It is Sunday evening and I am not on duty, so here goes for a letter to you. At this moment the Archbishop is below in the parlour talking to a prospective candidate for Our Lady's Home Missionary Sisters. Since I last wrote, the Archbishop has formally announced the project to the clergy and has asked for their financial and moral help. I think I mentioned this in a letter to Mother and Father. I feel appalled that the thing has come so suddenly and easily and I also feel certain that in all that has taken place the hand of God is evident.

I would love to have you here or be at home with you to talk it all over and tell you of other details. So far two girls have volunteered, Gwen Morse of Burnie (36) and Kathleen Moore of Hobart (33). I am sure now that I did not go to Burnie without providence guiding the step. The stay there gave me leisure to write [down] my ideas and then I sent them on to the Archbishop asking him to let me know what he thought and assuring him that his decision would be for me an indication of what was the will of God.

I also met Fr. [Tim] Murphy and from him received the advice to go ahead. Fr. Tim is a very holy and saintly person. Then, too, I saw the Sisters of Our Lady of the Sacred Heart at work. Since then the Archbishop has been interested but I did not know he intended to move so quickly.

At present I am seeking at least two more recruits for the work – we want four. Then there is the house for them to live in. His Grace, [the Archbishop] intends to give them an oratory with the Blessed Sacrament reserved! Then there is their spiritual formation and rule of life. This is a matter of vital importance and will demand much thought. Both his Grace and I think that the best thing is to let them use the de Montfort devotion to Our Lady, [1] as the basis of their spiritual life, something of the Legion spirit – but adapted to their work.

They will need a great spirit of prayer and of self sacrifice, a stability and firmness of character. I do not want them to become just like other orders with their customs etc. We propose that they wear secular dress – not a uniform, and badge – not a plaster,[2] but nice and distinctive. They will not take vows, but make a promise of obedience, of chastity and will be expected to live in the spirit of poverty – in a sense somewhat like secular or diocesan priests, living in community.

---

1   St Louis de Montfort, a French mystic and priest of the 17th century outlined a rule of life that had a devotional component to Our Lady, encouraging the Rosary to be prayed. John was influenced by Father Paddy Moloney MSC who gave the retreat referred to in this letter.
2   A Plaster brooch.

I have written to ask for the Constitution, etc. of the St Columban's Society, which has much in it that would suit our needs. I hope to have a copy of the talk His Grace gave to the women at our meeting. In a way it outlines the spirit of the Society – a kind of broad sketch of its work and methods.

I want all the prayers you can give, as in the last analysis it is a work of grace. I know you will be keenly interested and who knows but that some day you may have the service of the Home Missionary Sisters in your priestly work and you may also be called on to be a spiritual director for them. One reaction upon myself has been that it makes me want to be really holy, to be more spiritual, more deeply immersed in the supernatural to have a greater spirit of prayer, a greater devotion to God's Providence. I cannot give what I have not, therefore, I must try to get it.

So far I have talked of myself – alas too often it is so. But I did think you could be interested, so pardon my effusion. I hope you are well and that all things are going along well too. It must be hot at present in Victoria. We had a few hot days, but not a great deal of discomfort. I have been reading about the fires etc. in Victoria. I have been wondering how Mother and Father have fared in the heat. I find even the heat here knocks me out.

I was sorry indeed to hear about our friend losing her babe. She wrote me since and expressed complete resignation in the whole matter. Please God she will yet have her heart's desire.

How have the holidays been going? I am sorry I could not go over but it is not easy to get off here. One just can't say, "I am going ..." I would like to have had a yarn. I don't know any student who has not any troubles and problems. We have three or four students home at present and I have had a good deal of their company. Hope to send three lads off this year.

By the way, I must congratulate you on two feats – your success as a Hebrew scholar (78!) and your 50% for Gregorian! His Grace thinks that you must be different from me in at least one respect – that you can do something in the way of singing! That is not a strong point at all, at all[3] *with me. I hope you will get on alright this year in being promoted to Theology.*

I was talking to someone about scruples. I used to be a victim when in College – all through, but I have gone the other way now, I fear. I often wonder at the facility with which I can get out of worries about matters of conscience that once tormented me. I was talking to someone about scruples. Of course the only thing is to take a sane view of things – to give oneself the advice and act on it – that one would give to another who came asking for it and then also by being ready to accept the guidance and direction of a Confessor. I don't think I ever worry now about matters that once I would confess over and over

---

3   John often repeated something he wanted to emphasise.

again. I think, relax, have a big broad spirituality and not one that constrains and worries. It is of great importance in life.

Brightness, cheerfulness and great unselfishness are essential elements of holiness. I read only yesterday in The Ambassador of Christ that to rejoice with those who rejoice indicates and calls for greater magnanimity than to weep with those who weep. Sympathy is natural: to the cheerful to rejoice means unselfishness, often it requires effort and grace. I know of few virtues I would strive more earnestly to acquire than that of cheerfulness. The opposite is moroseness and surliness – silence and want of sociability. I notice that one is inclined to get that way unless one watches carefully.

Wed. 26.1.44

I have been busy and so your letter got put on the long finger once again. Mother will have had a letter from me re Mrs. Colraine and her child.

Fr. Moloney MSC (Paddy) gave us the retreat this year. He is very good – not high falutin' but good solid priestly matter and a great heart behind it all. Opened in rather unusual way by a talk on the De Montfort Way – or the complete consecration to Our Lady. I am convinced that there is a great deal in it and hope to make it the basis of the spiritual formation of O.L.H.M.S. [Our Lady of the Home Missionary Sisters.] It begets a deep spiritual outlook on life, fosters the spirit of zeal and also helps to relieve folk of scruples and anxieties. This is a great boon. Fr. Moloney is a born actor and a great lover of the Blacks – also of Australian outback life. He has been entertaining us ever since he came – also the [Presentation] Sisters, etc.

I think I told you I went to Cygnet a few days ago to the Summer School (Fr. Kent) for children and everything done in best style. I took Gwen Morse and two others (back seat!!) and Fr. Leo Murphy down. They were tremendously impressed at all they saw. Gwen was especially interested, as it gave her an idea of just how much is to be and can be done for the bushies. I hope the Sisters will be able to specialise in Summer Schools, viz. on the East Coast, King Island, Flinders Island. If the children could all be brought together for a fortnight, it would be better than an hour or two each day after school.

The Archbishop is very anxious to get Catholic action work under way. I fear it has fallen on evil days here. We seem to be so busy with the routine duties, that special work seems to be almost beyond us. If we had 20 priests more, we could place them easily. The situation is still desperate.

Fr. Kent is opening a Brothers' Agriculture College at Cygnet. 3 [Christian] Brothers. Besides secondary school work, special attention will be given to farming, fruit-growing, etc. etc. The idea is good. I hope it works out well. I am convinced that our whole efforts should be directed to the promotion of greater interest in Rural life. The section in Pattern for Peace that deals with Rural Reconstruction is of great value.

It is a good idea to take up a special interest – a hobby – convert-making, or converts, or rural life or some such special work. Thus, while one does all the duties of a priest, there is one special work upon which one can speak with authority. It gives interest to life and it also draws out work and qualities which otherwise might remain dormant. Generally, too, if one has a special bent he will get somewhere in that particular sphere. It helps to prevent idleness and useless drifting from one thing to another.

So far I have had no books from overseas – a time to build up the Catholic Bookshop [to make it a] paying proposition. Even now with limited supply of goods available we get a small turn over which helps to defray costs of rent etc. I pay 28/6 per week rent [for the bookshop] and £2.15.0 [for a] salary. This means that I must get about £4.0.0 a week to pay expenses. Still if I could get the goods there would be no difficulty at all.

Mrs. Howe (Joe's mother), asked me to invite you to stay with them. I would love to have you over, as I am not able to go home just now. It looks as if we will be back to the three Masses on Sunday soon. I am to take over North Hobart [section of the parish] again. New Town [area] will just get occasional visits. It is a great pity as there are 1,500 Catholics in New Town and I think it a tragedy that they are to be neglected.

I expect you are finding plenty to do during the holidays. It must be very hot at present. I am well aware that during the holidays one feels at times a strange feeling – partly a desire to be back to the regular life of the Seminary, partly a temptation to pull out. Just last night Fr. Leo Murphy who is here on loan from Sydney was talking in my room – we went on till 11.30 about our seminary days – the numbers of times we felt inclined to leave, the troubles and temptations. He missed a year and had to go back to Springwood with a class junior to him. He said the first month of that year was the hardest he ever felt in all his life. But he stuck it out and so, he learnt lessons that have stood him in good stead ever since.

I would gravely suspect a vocation, which had not weathered serious trials and doubts and anxieties and misgivings. I feel that way about the O.L.H.M.S. [Our Lady of the Home Missionary Sisters]. I only want those women, who have had to fight and endure a great deal for their religion and for their vocation. If a way of life, a vocation, a calling is worthwhile, it is worth the sacrifices and trials necessary to attain it. God knows even to this day, I have to be continually urging myself along; the flesh and all that word connotes is by no means dead – on the contrary, it is very much alive. However that fact has its compensation – it keeps one very humble and it keeps one on his knees. If it succeeds in this, then it has played its part in the spiritual formation.

More than ever, am I convinced that the great need in the priest is that he be a man of prayer. The other duties – his attention to sick, etc. etc. will be attended to – he can't neglect them, if he has a conscience at all – but it is easy to neglect the prayer. It just gets put aside, neglected, forgotten and then the fountain of grace within one's heart dries up and one is then barren, trying to give what one has not. One becomes metallic and empty and without unction. But let a man pray, let him make sure of it, even if it means leaving other duties – he must be a good priest, he must do groundwork for God.

I hope to insist on this with O.L.H.M.S. They will not have long prayers, nor many, but they will be expected to pray, to seek times and opportunities for prayer, visits to the Blessed Sacrament, evenings after work, rising early in the morning. Mental Prayer, their own prayer, a habit and atmosphere of prayer. And no scruples! More simple faith, more confidence in God's love, God's mercy.

I am sure that this year with Theology will open out a bigger broader world – one gets a big view of life and has no time to be worried about things of no moment. Fr. [Ambrose] Benneworth is letting me have Genicot's book[4] for you and may be also his dogma books. Please take care of them and keep them for him. Sometimes books so lent are destroyed or never return. However, I assured him that I would be guarantor! I shall send them on to Werribee for you – also Callan on St. Paul. I do hope you get a good knowledge of Scripture, esp. in English! If one has it in English, it is most useful for sermons etc. Unfortunately, this is something I have a lot to learn about.

Now, old man, this is a sermon and the book all in one. Please pardon the writing and the sermonising. Still I know to whom I write. Drop me a line – just a few words, as I know it is not easy to bring oneself to write when on holidays. Tell me any troubles, and Love to Mother and Father. I am afraid they are disappointed that I did not get over, but I am in a difficult spot as far as holidays go.

Cheerio and "stick at it!"
Your loving brother in Christ,
Jack

---

4   *Contours of the Middle Ages* by Leopold Genicot , regarding the medieval structure and Christian culture of Western Europe.

Letter 97 to Brian

O we are to be Christlike – Christlike in mind, in word, in deed with the poor, the sick, with women, in the confessional, at prayer, everywhere and in everything.

In this eight-page letter (14th October 1945) written post-World War II, John writes to Brian at length, intent on putting onto paper important matters he wants to convey. John and Brian have had a meaningful talk prior to this – perhaps back in Victoria and John promised to write. A month after this letter, his father died.

It is a letter calling on his young brother to step up and take more responsibility for maturing in his spiritual and life response as he prepares for the priesthood. It appears that he can talk straight with Brian because of their long-standing good relationship. Remember that it was Brian who keeps these very personal letters written to him by John and asks that they be cared for in the Missionary Sisters of Service archives. Indeed, Brian offers them in humility and openness recognising their value and being prepared, perhaps, to reveal his personal shortcomings.

John writes of the Christian way of holiness requiring sacrifice and an ascetical spirituality. *We are to be Christlike and that means the hard way, the austere way, the way of the Cross.* He believes that being called and trained for priesthood, one should strive towards the high ideals put before them and that their actions should display incomparable goodness coming from a sacrificial and prayerful life. John exhorts that this prayerful life emanates from *long and loving meditation on the Gospels*, so as to be Christ-like in mind, in word and in deed in all pastoral situations – with the poor, the sick, with women, everywhere and in everything. He adds that no books can take the place of the Gospels.

The idealistic young man of thirty-five years expects that the five priests in Hobart should each be *homo Dei* par excellence, reflecting the mind and heart of Christ *more than any other person in the city*, if they are meant to be leaders in faith. Though understanding the failings of his own spiritual journey, he also warns of the potential danger for priests of becoming *dry of the sources of affection,* so as to be *off hand*, ambitious, self-centred, thinking of their own interests and plans, considering themselves to be better than others and becoming *indifferent to the demands of filial love and affection and charity.*

Perhaps there has been some lapse on Brian's part towards his parents. In referring to *how we must respect, love and have affection for Mother and Father*, John points out the need for gratitude and the spirit of poverty, recognising the danger for priests who are comfortable having everything they need and despising those who have less. Then he gives an example with the comment of *good parishes*, the parishes that have status and are better off financially, rather than offering *to spend and to be spent* in ministry. That is what the priesthood was for, he points out. Otherwise, is this something of what a clericalised church looks like?

Lastly, he advises Brian to work out *a rule of life* that is of his own volition, because, as John reminds him, he will be on his own once he leaves the seminary. It is his responsibility. John outlines three main segments to place into the routine of his life: mental prayer, spiritual reading and living and working in a Christ-like way. He adds that these spiritual exercises need to be carried out with sincerity and generosity rather than superficially for the sake of getting them done. In reality, John outlines a way of life not only for priests. All are called to respond to the universal call to holiness about which subsequently both Vatican II and Pope Francis speak explicitly.

To note is that John is now responsible for the Pontifical Mission Aid Societies, which included the Propagation of the Faith, the Holy Childhood Society[5], and the Society of St Peter, Apostle.[6] He is also in charge of the Catholic Library in Hobart, as well as Vicar for Religious for both men and women in the Archdiocese. His role as a spiritual director or companioning people in their spiritual life was developing. Many people come to speak to him in confidence.

With the sensitive nature of this letter, which could seem to be another sermonising encounter, John signs off purposefully and with a filial love, *Your most loving brother in Christ. Jack.*

* * *

---

[5] A missionary organisation for the awareness and benefit of children in the world and originally involving children donating to children in disadvantaged countries.
[6] This organisation is the Catholic Church's official fundraising organisation for training priests and religious in mission countries.

The Deanery,
Launceston.
14/10/1945

My dear Brian,

Last night I sat down and wrote a lengthy letter along the lines I mentioned when I was over recently. It was well after midnight when I finished – but when I did go to bed I decided I would not send the letter. I was not satisfied that I had said what I wanted to say and in the manner I wanted to say it. It is now Sunday morning and I am on the late Masses 10.00 and 11.00, so I want to get this letter on the way before I go out. I expect I should be making my meditation, but I have a good deal of time yet. It is no rest for me to sleep in, so I generally get up early even when on late Masses.

I said that I had somewhat to say to you, and I feel that I can say it. The fact is that you are in my thoughts always, day by day. I pray that you will be a priest after God's own heart – a priest who has no less an ideal or standard than sanctity – priestly sanctity. That means very high sanctity – the highest. There are in this city some 35,000 people. There are many good people; there are some very good people; there are some really holy people. But actually none of them – should be holier than the five priests in the city. These five men are to be each a homo Dei par excellence, each should reflect the mind and life of Christ more than any other person in the city.

I often feel that we are inclined to leave Sanctity to the Sisters! No, we are to be Christ-like and that means the hard way, the austere way, the way of the Cross. Each of us must be holy in a way the Master wishes – the Sanctity of St. Peter was different from that of St. John; that of St. Vincent de Paul, different from that of St. Ignatius Loyola – but there is one thing that should be distinctive – that is the priestly character.

There is firstly prayer, priestly self-sacrifice, priestly charity, zeal, etc. And that can be reduced to the ideal of being Christ-like. No man should be more Christ-like than the priest – Christ-like in mind, in word, in deed – with the poor, the sick, with women, in the confessional, at prayer, everywhere and in everything. This in turn can only come from long and loving meditation on the Gospels. We do not I fear love the Gospels as we should. Other spiritual books are good but none can ever take the place of the Gospels.

Now that is the ideal and here are a few things to which I draw attention as not being Christlike. As a matter of fact Mother spoke to me about these things while I was home, I said little. I think I understand the student mind as only a student or a priest can. Even Mother cannot quite see the outlook of the priest on many issues. Yet on the other hand a Mother has a strange intuition as to what is truly priestly and what is not, and mind you, our Mother is a hidden Saint. How we must respect, love and have affection for Mother and

Father! It is possible for priests to become dry of the sources of affection, and become a bit off hand, a bit above others and become almost indifferent even to the demands of filial love and affection and charity. The fact is that we can be very selfish, self-centred, thinking only of our own interests, plans and ambitions. This is dangerous for us priests.

God alone knows all that Mother has done for each of us, the sacrifices she has made, the prayers she has prayed, the longing loving interest she has had for each of us She is grateful to God that the grace of vocation should have come to two of her sons – I know she thanks God every day for that fact and I know how she prays for us both. I noticed this more this last visit home. She seems to have much in her mind, including some lapses of priests. Indeed, I myself grow more and more distrustful of myself and feel I must pray more, be more stern with self – "lest perhaps when I have preached ..."

Let's let Mother know and feel how we appreciate all she has done. I am sure you do. – but showing of it means so much. Our vocation demands renunciation, it demands separation, it demands leaving kith and kin; it does not and cannot demand that we crush our true nature. I hope you will understand my feelings as I write and that you will pardon me if I seem to be over direct.

Gratitude. "Were not ten made clean and where are the nine". Our Lord looked for gratitude. He was but human in that: So too do others. They do not ask for effusive thanks. A warm expression of gratitude is always appreciated. It is so easy to take things for granted, especially if they come to us without much effort on our part. You and I owe more in gratitude to Mother and Father than all the rest of the family put together. Often we have to sacrifice ourselves to show gratitude. Writing a letter or doing some little thing speaks volumes.

How good a father our Father has been to us. In the last twelve or thirteen years, I have come to "know" my own Father as I never knew him when younger. I feel that he has the Faith. I have enjoyed his visits here immensely; he has often written to me – long and interesting letters and I have returned the favour. I don't think he will be with us very much longer. I would like to think that we did make his closing years happy. I feel he is sometimes just silent. He would deeply appreciate our kindness.

We need to learn to be content with our lot, with what we have in the way of goods etc. We must be on our guard against finding fault. (*Medice aura teipsum!*) There may be much that is not to our way of thinking – old fashioned, etc. etc. We need not worry too much over these things.

Have you read "*Luke Delmege*" by Patrick Augustine Sheehan? For priests – there is the danger of looking down on those who have not all we are used to. That is a definite danger for priests. They usually have a comfortable home – everything just so – and sometimes they are inclined to despise those with whom they once were as equals – or even as less than they. Especially read the chapter "Disenchantment".

I may be allowed here to put in a word for an outlook which I deem to be essentially priestly – and which, I think is not as common amongst priests – or students – as it might well be – and that is the attitude towards material comfort, conveniences in work, etc. We are called to be disciples of a Master who chose poverty as his portion; so we too should love poverty – not only from afar or love for the poor people – but we should practice poverty in our own lives. We make no vow, we may not do so, but we must learn to be detached and even more than that to actually do without things that are not really necessary or useful for us in our priestly life and work. I have always felt that I am bound to the spirit of poverty every bit as much as any religious is because of his vow. All I may have to use – car, books, clothes are simply lent to me by God to be used in so far as they help – no more, no less – in my work.

It is the fundamental exercise of St. Ignatius. We must want to be saintly – not theoretically but in actual fact and the saints were utter realists. Above all we should have before our minds priests who were great saints – Vincent de Paul, Francis de Sales, John Vianney – men who lived lives much along the lines of men who became generous and self sacrificing in all things.

I hate to hear priests speak of "good parishes". What did we choose the priesthood for? Our Lord's standard was different, "Having joy set before Him, He endured the Cross". He came not to be ministered to, but to minister and to give His life as redemption for many. St. Paul's ideal was "to spend and be spent myself for your souls".

I hope you will bear this sermonising. I was delighted at the prospect of your making the long retreat. It is an experience and I hope you can manage it. I am sending on the questionnaire I mentioned. It may not be typed for a few days but will be sent as soon as it is done. It was given me by Fr. McGlynn. I would, if I were you, begin even now to think out a rule of life – certain ideals, certain practices that must be clung to at all costs. Of these, I could mention just a few:

i) Mental prayer:

It is the most important thing of all and yet strange to say it is the first thing that goes. Don't let it go. And if it is to be done there must be preparation. Hence I would say that the first resolution of all should be to prepare your Meditation every night.

Give 10 minutes to it; even now get into that habit. Get down on your knees in your room, read the Gospel passage – or the spiritual book, pull it to pieces, see something of its application – compare parallel passages, look up a commentary or a Life – Howard, Meschler, Goodier, Fillion (The Life of

Christ: a Historical, Critical and Apologetic Exposition) – and even if you find it helps, jot down a few ideas – just a skeleton or outline of the prayer – select a phrase that will sum up the whole idea. Of course, this is all familiar to you, but the thing is to make it personal, part of your own life, independent of whether someone helps you do it or not. I have had a very good chance to watch the whole matter during the past 12 months. For the love of God, and as you hope to be a good priest, set your heart on becoming a man of prayer – a contemplative and the rest will take care of itself.

    ii) Spiritual reading:

Good solid matter especially on the Life of Our Lord, on Prayer and the Interior Life. I would make it a point to read for one full ¼ hour each day and not as a mere pawn following the customary practice of the house – but as if you were a priest all on your own deliberately doing this independently of any bell or custom or rule of the Seminary.

    iii) Christlike gentleness, kindness, charity – and this necessitates a great deal of genuine humility and self effacement. God resists the proud ...

Often one notices that one's spiritual exercises are very superficial. I have seen priests and religious who for years have done all these things – who did make their meditation and did say the Rosary and did appear most exact and correct – and yet there was something wanting, they have not got down to the great underlying principle that Sanctity is love gone mad. Until you find yourself longing for the higher things, looking wistfully at the heights to which the great souls have scaled – until this happens, you will never be holy – you may be moderately good; decent, no-one may point a finger of reproach at you, but you will not be a saint of God. The saints were generous. So too must we be generous: To give and not to count the cost, (the self probing, the painful truth about ourselves, the humiliation which alone seems to teach us humility). To fight and not heed the wounds (the sarcasm of others, may be ridicule or ill suppressed contempt of the worldly wise and those of common sense. "Ut quid perditio haec?" (Why this waste? Mt. 26:8). It was a candidate for the priesthood who spoke thus, cf. St John XII.

My dear, dear Brian, I have poured out my feelings in this letter. Maybe you will wonder what has come over me. Only this – I do have love for you and my one great desire is to see you the priest I feel you can be. I shall not write more just now. Maybe you will drop me a line soon. Please be very frank with me. You can say to me what you may not say to anyone else. Pray for me too "lest perhaps"... And pray for Rosary House. I am so hopelessly inadequate.

    Your most loving brother in Christ,

Jack

Letter 98 to Brian

*If we do the reading, we will do the Prayer,
but let the reading go and the prayer will go too –
simply because of spiritual and mental starvation.*

In this four-page letter (26th November 1946), preserved by Brian, John corresponds with his brother from Rosary House in Launceston. On 8th December, Brian will receive his Diaconate, the last stage before ordination to the priesthood. His mother cannot be there and it is just over twelve months since his father has died. John is also unable to be present. This letter, another letter of advice for Brian to consider during the seminarian holidays from December till March, is written in haste with John's thoughts flowing easily onto the paper. Anticipate each day; take time for prayer and spiritual reading and remember that *our duty in the circumstances makes our line of conduct clear.* John is saying the same things to the Sisters.

Interestingly, the Sisters have made a decision to wear a uniform, similar to that of nurses, and a veil. John takes on the administrative task of writing letters to firms to find fabric dyed grey for the veils that will have a white head-piece. A firm in Melbourne is chosen to provide the fabric. How amusing that John becomes so involved telling Brian, *I hope it will go alright!* He signs off this time in a more clerical mode, *Yours in great haste and in Domino.*
Fr Brian Wallis ordained by Archbishop Daniel Mannix in Melbourne 1947.

Launceston.
26.11.1946

My dear Brian,

I am actually writing this at Rosary House where I am waiting for a phone call to Melbourne. We have been searching Australia for material for veils – recently sent out some 30 circular letters to firms that might be interested. So far we have had 16 answers. One firm in Melbourne, Snows Gunning & Evans have 100 yds. We are ringing through to ask that it be kept for us – dyed grey – and sent on. The Sisters have decided to have grey with white head piece. I hope it will go alright.

I hope you got the Breviary I sent on. It [has a] supplementary for new feasts – St. John Bosco, St. Gabriel C.P., St. Bernadette.[7] Otherwise I think it should be satisfactory until you can get the new ones. Are they on order? I expect you are in the thick of exams just now. They are the order of the day everywhere. When do you go on retreat for Orders? I shall be giving you a memento day by day that every grace and blessing will be yours on Dec. 8th – and that your own oblation will be a very complete and generous one. In a way I think Sub-diaconate means more ask than priesthood in the sense that you cross the Rubicon. The dye [die] is cast for life. I hope the Retreat will be a good one – not a kind of entertainment affair – but a very definite and solid work setting forth the highest ideals of sacerdotal sanctity.

Father Joe Howe is in the Deanery at present. I have been very pleased with his general way of doing things. He is a splendid lad – full of fun and wit but on the job always. I notice he is always about at half five – a sign that the meditation is done. I also noted he had the Gospel of St. Matthew with his Breviary.

I would try to settle on one or two definite rules for the holidays – and for that matter for all times.

---

7   St John Bosco, died 1888 in Turin, Italy, aged 72. Born in Italy, St Gabriel of Our Lady of Sorrows, a Passionist priest, died 1862, aged 23. St Bernadette of Lourdes, died 1879 in Nevers, France, aged 34.

i) *I would definitely advise you to get into the habit of anticipating. There are those who argue against it but my experience is that the methodical men and the men who are most careful about the spirituals[8] are also the ones who are most regular about anticipation. Fr. McGlynn often mentioned it to me. I try to have all my office said by 9 o'clock. This means Matins and Lauds in the afternoon – generally before tea or soon as possible after tea. Then Small Hours before Mass. Vespers and Compline immediately after breakfast. Arguments re liturgical times etc. don't cut a great deal of ice; in any case they don't allow for sick calls, visits, etc. etc. And I wonder if "Aferi Domine" for today's Matins at 8 or 9 pm is very liturgical!*

ii) *I would make a hard and fast rule to do at least a quarter of an hour of Spiritual Reading each day. I put this before Mental Prayer. If we do the reading, we will do the Prayer, but let the reading go and the prayer will go too – simply because of spiritual and mental starvation. Begin the Reading with [an] Act of Presence of God and Prayer to [the] Holy Ghost. This makes it a definite spiritual exercise. A good solid book – read steadily – not in fits and starts.*

iii) *Aim at least a full half hour of Mental Prayer each morning before Mass. This I know sounds very common place. It is not quite so common as one could wish. This means foresight – settling on the hour of rising, time for Small Hours or for Prime at least – and then ½ hour. You will hear men poo-hoo the half hour idea; suggest that it can be done later, etc. "Manyana"[9] is the devil's great watch word. The first exercise we drop – I know from experience is the full half hour of Mental Prayer. I would rather omit the Office, Rosary and other prayers than let the Mental Prayer get put out of the first hour of the day.*

Other rules – there are any number of them – but keep those three and I guarantee your real sacerdotal sanctity. Of course in the Mental Prayer I include a deliberate and careful preparation of the subject matter the night before. I am a bit afraid that my letter has turned into a homily. But if the cap will fit, so much the better. I expect I am harping on these points with the Sisters so much that it becomes second nature.

Two new girls arrived. The two older postulants shaping very well – have caught on to the spirit of place – more silence than at first.

---

8   Liturgy of the Hours, meditation and spiritual reading.
9   'Mayana' is Spanish for tomorrow.

I am sorry Mother cannot be there for the Sub-diaconate. She had been looking forward to my coming over but my last visit hit that on the head. I feel worried about Mother being on her own. After all, she has had a lot to think of and do. I would be glad if she could get a place in Melbourne. I hope you can spend a good deal of the holidays with her. You will not be able to get to Mass, etc. but I think that has to be accepted. Our duty in the circumstances makes our line of conduct clear.

Kind regards to Joe. Rex Donohue gets sub-diaconate on Sunday Dec. 6th, Mass for you on 8th. Don't forget to include me in the daily office. If possible drop a line before the day.

Cheerio. Yours in great haste and in Domino,
Jack

Letter 99 to Brian

*The Lord forgive me
but I cannot get terribly enthusiastic about a deal of the formality.*

Brian was ordained in Melbourne on 17th July, two weeks prior to this two-page letter from John (28th July 1947), who is quite effusive following the ordination ceremony. He has been a priest for nearly fifteen years, and now Brian, his brother, is finally a priest too. He states that they now have a *double fraternal relationship*, as brothers and priests. This is very important to John. Soon Brian will receive notification re coming to Tasmania in December. It seems that John has some notion of a move to Hobart for himself in the near future.

While in Melbourne, John takes the opportunity to go to Sorrento on the beautiful Mornington Peninsula for a private retreat for two days at the Missionary Oblates Fathers' community. He withdraws from any social involvement – time out for which he seems grateful and would have liked to extend.

John adds his thoughts telling Brian about the *worth getting* scriptural book, *Harmony of the Gospels.* Not only did he get one copy but six copies so that he could enthuse others about it, and give them a copy, the practice he continued throughout his life. Presumably a copy would also go to the Sisters.

Already the Home Missionary Sisters have about 100 children in the religious correspondence lessons and they are considering restricting the number to include only those who cannot receive regular religious instruction. Also the time has come to have a dedicated Sister for the work, rather than Sisters doing it part-time along with other mission duties. John continues a close involvement with the Sisters – driving them to Hobart and other places, through his interactions in regular classes and listening to them in relation to their medical conditions.

John continues his aversion to pomp and ceremony as is evident in his comment about all the Church formality that would take place for the Tasmanian visit of Sydney-based Cardinal Norman Gilroy, who is due to arrive in Hobart on 4th October 1947.

* * *

HOME MISSIONARY SISTERS OF OUR LADY

Phone L'ton 552

Rosary House,
1 Frederick Street,
Launceston.
28.7.1947

Dear Father Brian,

How happy I am to address you so! There is no need for me to say it. You know it all. May the years as they go by find us only more closely united than ever in our double fraternal relationship – brothers in the flesh and brothers in the priesthood of Our Blessed Lord. Now I am not going to sermonise in this letter – just a line to ask how you are and to let you know how things are here.

Have been very busy since I came back. Retreat by Fr Glover was good so I was told. Incidentally, I had two delightful days at Sorrento.[10] *Arrived about 6 o'clock. Retreat began at 9.00. Night prayers and a book to read! No conductor of retreat. Had meals with Fathers – eight in all. Could attend exercises if I so wished. Did go to Benediction. Otherwise kept to myself. Did not have visitors nor did I visit. Mass at 8.30. Would have liked to have stayed longer there. They have an interesting custom of having full recreation for an hour to an hour and a half one night of their retreat. It struck me as strange but somehow it did seem to work quite well. Not exactly Ignatian and by no means Alphonsian!*[11]

Have resumed classes at Rosary House. Took two Sisters to Hobart a couple of weeks ago. One had a slight operation. Another in St Vincent's Hospital in a few days. It looks as if one will have to have a major operation ... She should be in good form in about six or seven weeks. Otherwise things are going along fairly well. Preparing in one way, or another for the Missions work. Correspondence Course is growing every day. We have to restrict ourselves to children who cannot otherwise receive regular instruction. I think we must be

---

10   The Missionary Oblate priests care for the parish of Sorrento in the Archdiocese of Melbourne.
11   Ignatian spirituality (Jesuits) according to the Spanish founder of the Jesuits, St Ignatius Loyola. Alphonsian *spirituality* (Redemptorists) according to the Italian founder, St Alphonsus of Ligori.

in the vicinity of 100 now. Later we will have to have Sisters given full time to this work alone. At present it is "inter alia". (Ed: 'Among other things.')[12]

Preparations are in full force for the Cardinal's visit. The Lord forgive me but I cannot get terribly enthusiastic about a deal of the formality connected with it.

Forgive the writing, the smudges etc. My pen has not been in good form. I don't seem to be able to get to write without scratching and dropping ink.

Are you using that Pars Autumnalis of the Breviary that I sent you? If not I would be glad to have it as it is handy to leave at Rosary House so that I can use it if I have a little time while there. No news yet of the new Breviaries from Europe? By the way I got a good Harmony of the Gospels from St Anthony Guild Press £2.50 – 15/- less 40%. Got six copies – all told. Uses the new American Translation – parallel columns and good index etc. Worth getting.

[The] Bishop[is] likely to call for you about mid-December. Rex [is] to be ordained in December, as far as I know. My move [is] still 'in camera', but some steps [are being] taken just quietly.

Goodnight. Dominus tecum.[13]

Your loving brother in Christ,

Jack

PS. Please give my very kind regards to Matron and thank her for kindness to me when at Corpus Christi College. J

---

12   Inter alia translated, 'Among other things.'
13   Dominus tecum translated, 'The Lord be with thee.'

Letter 100 to Brian

*I am sure you appreciate
the opportunity of getting to know the Mass well.*

This two-page letter (28th September 1947) is the last in the collection. From Launceston John writes to Brian in his last months at the seminary, perhaps to encourage him to use his time well in these first months after ordination – *time to find your feet before being thrust into a parish*. Archbishop Tweedy, unwell in Hobart Calvary Hospital, will let Brian know that he is to come to Tasmania to begin his priestly ministry before Christmas – about 18th December. It seems that Brian has doubts; he has been in touch indicating that he does not seem ready or know enough yet for priestly ministry. *You did your best and you tried*, writes John most compassionately. John is aware that Brian may struggle financially in this period and offers *mass stipends* to assist him.

John asks Brian for some of his ordination cards to give to his good and generous friends, who have contributed to the purchase of religious items for the Sisters' chapel, namely a stole, book on rituals, and a monstrance. John has been busily writing articles for various Catholic magazines looking for possible candidates to join the Sisters. He updates Brian on a few things that are happening with the formation and training of the Sisters, reminding him to remember the Sisters on the feast of the Rosary, 7th October.

While John is to go to Hobart and join in the functions for Cardinal Gilroy, he states that his priorities are to visit the two Sisters living at North Hobart and to have time with them – he is their spiritual guide and surely, now, friend.

* * *

Phone L'ton 552

Rosary House
1 Frederick Street,
Launceston.
28.9.1947

Dear Brian,

I am not in letter writing form tonight but if I don't write now I may not write for quite a while. The Cardinal comes to Hobart on Saturday; here on Wednesday. I am going to Hobart next Sunday after early Masses – not so much for the Cardinal's functions as to see the two Sisters there and to arrange a few other details that are long overdue.

How are things going? I suspect that you are busy enough. There seem to be so many things that you want to know at the end of your Course. Never mind – you did do your best and at least you tried and that is all we can look for. A few questions:

How are you off for Mass stipends?[14] Just let me know if you want any. I can always let you have all you want. Of course if you are supplied already don't worry.

Could you let me have a few extra ordination Cards?[15] You sent 1 to Presentation Convent. Actually they really needed 25 so I gave them all I had. I have in mind Mr & Mrs Charlie Ward. You might send them direct. Address: 3 Wellesley St. South Hobart. Charlie is one of the very best – and so is his wife. Also Mr and Mrs A. Hunt of Abbott St., Newstead. They gave me £2.2.0 for the Ritual, Stole etc. Balance to go to Monstrance for Rosary House. As yet have no word of the design – but am waiting patiently!

Archbishop is in Calvary still. Expect he will be up for [the] Cardinal's visit. Had a letter from Mother – also had talk on phone. Anne [Douglas] put us through. I must write to Mother this week.

Have been busy with October sheets, special lesson on Rosary, etc. Also article for "Catholic Missions." May not be in till next year. Thinking of doing one for A.C.R. [Australasian Catholic Record] – also Messenger and Rural Life. Articles in papers help to bring the work to the notice of possible candidates. Two have now begun second year of Novitiate and four are in [their] Spiritual Year. The former two are now going out to schools. Tomorrow night we will be having a Speech night – four are to deliver talks on matters outside "shop". Very nervous about it – so much so that I thought I might have to call it off, but I think we will get through. Just a private affair but for all that they dread

---

14   Mass stipends refers to the financial offering given to a priest for services, e.g. weddings, baptisms, funerals or a Mass said for deceased family members. Often these supported the priest in his daily living.

15   Ordination cards were given out to family, friends and parishioners, so the priest would be remembered in prayer.

standing up to address anyone. I am the only visitor. May give marks etc. Hope to have it as a regular feature in training courses.

The Archbishop said he would let you know about coming over. May be about December 18th.

Now Brian I will not write any more. I feel "done in" and in no form for letters. Regards to lads at C.C.C. [Corpus Chrisi College]. I know I need not ask you [for] a memento in the Mass day by day. I am sure you appreciate the opportunity you have of getting to know the Mass well. I think the first six months spent in the Seminary after Ordination are a great blessing. One has time to find his feet before being thrust out into the life of a parish. Remember the Sisters on Rosary Feast day.

Goodnight and God bless you,
    Your loving Brother in Christ,
       Jack

Breviary came to hand. Any news of the new Psalter Breviary?

DEFINING GENUINE SANCTITY
Letters to Brian 1944–1947
Letters 96–100

David Ranson

It is fitting that the final five letters in this superb and significant collection bring us to John's priestly heart and spirit which were central to his identity and contribution. John's contributions to the Church in Australia through the 20th century, and especially to the Church in Tasmania, are well documented. They cannot be interpreted, however, without appreciating his priestly character, which finds its expression especially in this correspondence to this brother, Brian.

Through these concluding letters, we are presented with an understanding of priesthood that will be echoed nearly 80 years later in Pope Francis' metaphor of mercy as the key to priestly life, understood as passionate involvement with those who find themselves on the margins. This imperative to view the world, not from the centre, but from the peripheries has now found itself in the language of the Magisterium itself. John lived this evangelical demand prophetically. For him, it was critical for one involved in ministry to identity that *"special work upon which one can speak with authority"* – in other words, to know with clarity to which margin the Spirit calls, and to whom one's ministry is uniquely at the service. For him, the specific margin was to be discovered in the isolation of rural communities. *"I am convinced that our whole efforts should be directed to the promotion of greater interest in Rural life"* – to *'the bushies'*, as he affectionately calls those living in such communities.

Because of this, John's priesthood was never reduced to cult. It was a manifestation of how he defined genuine sanctity – *"love gone mad."* And because it need be first and foremost an expression of love, ministry must be engaged always with humanity and warmth. John is remembered for this quality and for which I, too, fondly remember him as a young boy growing up in Tasmania in the 1960s and 1970s. This affective ministry was forged for John between, on the one hand, never relinquishing his ideal of Christ-like imitation, but on the other hand, never being forgetful of his own fragility and struggle to be faithful. Indeed, the latter became for him *the* mark of vocational discernment: *"I would greatly suspect a vocation which had not weathered serious trials and doubts and anxieties and misgivings."* Again, the intimation of Pope Francis' contemporary evaluation of an authentic call to ministry as the capacity to *"touch the wounds of another"* is unmistakable. Reading the letters, one hears a beautiful integration of the classic spiritualities of a De Sales and a Chrysostom. Though most likely unaware of doing so, John gave life to these at the very margin of the world in the small society of mid-twentieth century Tasmania.

As Pope Francis is clear to expound, sacred ministry is never mere social activism. Through these final letters sanctity's provenance is clear. It is sacrificial love animated by prayer. As John understands ministry from a double perspective, so too he understands prayer as both meditation and reading, never one without the other. *"Let the reading go and the prayer will go too."* The heart is nourished by silence; the mind is nurtured by text, above all by the texts of the Gospels themselves. Without this daily exercise, ministers become *"dry of the sources of affection . . . indifferent to the demands of filial love and affection and charity."*

Generosity is the fruit of such a ministry – a ministry known for its largesse, its hospitality, its grand vision. *"Brightness, cheerfulness, and great unselfishness are essential elements of holiness . . . I know of few virtues I would strive more earnestly to acquire than that of cheerfulness."* In his gentle demeanor, John was graced with such magnanimity. He leaves the Australian Church a legacy of unmistakable holiness. More importantly, his memory extends an invitation to everyone who follows in his steps.

Father David Ranson, a priest of the Diocese of Broken Bay, was born in Launceston, Tasmania in 1959. A sixth-generation Tasmanian, his mother's family were influential in the growth of the Church in Devonport and his grandfather donated the Missionary Sisters of Service their first caravan in the 1940s. In 1980, David joined the Cistercian community of Tarrawarra Abbey where he was ordained in 1992. Discerning a more active ministry, he served as Chaplain to St Vincent's Hospital, Melbourne (1998-2000), before lecturing in Christian Spirituality at the Catholic Institute of Sydney from 2001-2015. From 2012, he has had leadership of the Parish of Holy Name Wahroonga. In 2015, he was appointed Vicar General of the Diocese of Broken Bay, and in 2018 he was elected as Diocesan Administrator.

Epilogue

Letters are among the most significant memorial a person can leave behind them."

Johann Wolfgang von Goethe

Stancea Vichie

Johann Wolfgang von Goethe's words are indeed true when reaching the end of this unique collection of letters written by John Wallis to his mother, father and brother Brian from 1927 through to 1949. They span a twenty-two year period where John went from being a 16-year-old boy to a man heading towards 40 years of age. They offer significant insights into John's maturing into adulthood and the development in his thinking and in his spirituality, as he responded to the life experience in which he found himself. It is a story of the young student who follows his dream to serve the people as priest, and more.

It was a turbulent 22 years in which John lived through two world wars, interspersed with the Great Depression, a time of great political, social and economic change. The Church in Australia was experiencing some change in that John became a priest just when there were more Australian-born priests than Irish born.

However, this story does not stop in 1949. What of the next 52 years until John's death in 2001? To do justice to that long period of time, another book is needed! A summation of these years could be encapsulated in the quote from Luke's gospel, *"He grew in wisdom and stature and favour with God and people"*. Luke 2:52. Flowing out of his passionate commitment to deepening his inner life, he continued to simply give himself wholeheartedly to the people of Tasmania, the Archdiocese, and the Australian Church. To honour his presence as a servant priest for close to 70 years, the Hobart Archdiocesan archives centre was named the Wallis Centre.

After 1949, John's love of good reading continually nurtured him through the great scholars of theology, scripture and ecclesiology. Change was in the wings. When the Vatican Council and its vision burst upon the scene in 1962, it became the central force in John's life. It impacted upon him so deeply that he felt compelled to share this vision, this challenging expression of the gospel for the church to be on mission in the world and not separated from the world.

We MSS women were very fortunate recipients of John's passion for change, prior to and after the Council. His copy of *The Documents of Vatican II* became well-worn very soon after its publication! My first meeting with John was in January 1968 when I arrived at the Hobart airport with three other young women from Queensland to join the Missionary Sisters of Service. John hardly spoke a word on the way to Lindisfarne and left soon after our arrival. During the next week, he came to lead a class on the Vatican Council with us new recruits. It was here that I saw a very different John. He came alive in a way, which sent me into reading my copy of *The Documents of Vatican II* with great enthusiasm and a desire to live this vision.

However, during the couple of years that I was in the formation program, we did not see him as regularly for classes as previous formation groups had. This was for a very good reason as he was on his great missionary journeys around Australia bringing the vision of the Vatican Council, particularly to the religious congregations. Many talks and retreats took him away from Tasmania during the years after the Council.

As has been said previously, John was continually *"About the Master's business"*, so much so that he gave little time to other things outside his overwhelming commitment to the work of the day. In the late 1970s he participated in a Jesuit group program at what is now known as the Canisius Centre of Ignatian Spirituality at Pymble in Sydney. The three months was a wonderful opportunity for John to stop his hectic daily work schedule and do what he desired so much, to have time for prayer and reading, to nurture his inner life, and be in a place where he could share with a trusted spiritual director. On his return to Hobart, he had obviously been through a transformative experience. He was very open about the sense of freedom he felt. The obvious difference in him really set the stage for the next phase of his life.

He now gave himself licence to take time for enjoying something he had put aside from student days. Not long after the Pymble experience, at the age of 70, he took up bush walking! In his usual spirit of determination (and some would say stubbornness!), he tackled numbers of long and difficult walks with a small group of priests and religious into some of the most spectacular parts of Tasmania. He revelled in the beauty and majesty of the landscape. In the midst of these opportunities, he wanted to capture something of this beauty so then took up photography. For those who knew John and saw that his handwriting became harder to read as each year went by, we treasure the photos he took after that and sent to us with a message on the back of the photo. When I once asked him to tell me what he wrote because I could only pick a few words here and there, he simply laughed! The warmth of his presence and humour only increased.

As the years went by, John experienced a time of inner pain and shared freely about his vulnerability, his sinfulness, and regrets. He shed tears sometimes as he spoke of his sinfulness. He struggled with growing deafness, which in latter years made communication very difficult. It was as if his experience of deafness in his immediate family, and his great love of people who were deaf was now visiting him in a profound experience of deafness. The inner journey of these years was for him an experience of *"the dark night of the soul"*.

In time, *"the dark night"* passed and he peacefully lived his last years at Mary's Grange Aged Care facility in Hobart. His room was resplendent with favourite books, the scriptures, and a small number of precious possessions. Visitors were a special part of his day when stories of all the people he knew in Tasmania would be remembered. (It seemed he had celebrated baptisms, marriages and other sacraments with a number of generations of most of the Catholics in Tasmania.) Then gradually his life ebbed away. He achieved his life's vision in death on 3rd August 2001. The God whose mercy he craved took him into the next life.

And now what of the new life that came from his death, his vision, which continues on still in to the 21st century?

Perhaps a story can illustrate very simply something of this legacy, a story which goes right to the heart of John's passion for those people who were so vulnerable and unable to have opportunities for education, employment, housing and acceptance in the wider society. In his letters, his spirit of compassion for the forgotten ones was palpable. His compassion and vision still lives on through the unfolding legacy, which the Missionary Sisters of Service continue to live. In the last ten years, we have created structures, which enable this to happen as we themselves move into the days of their completion and fulfilment.

A year or two ago, a small group of women from rural areas, and who had been released from prison, came together for a weekend with their daughters to renew the bonds, which had been fractured at times. A woman, who leads writing workshops, facilitated the weekend. The women and their daughters were in a peaceful bush camp setting, surrounded by the sounds and sights of nature. It was such a calming experience for them. They spent time alone, mother and daughter time, and time as a group. As they sat and wrote, they touched into the deep pain, joys and hopes in their lives. As they shared this with one another, their lives were transformed. They wrote in glowing terms of the new start, which they felt they were beginning with one another.

There are many parts of John Wallis in this recent happening – his love for those who have been in prison, and their families, his strong desire to bring about reconciliation, his capacity to write in such depth, particularly to his mother, pouring out his vulnerability, pain, his hopes and dreams, his love of the bush and its people, and the beauty found there. It is as if John was sitting around the campfire with the women and their daughters. He would have relished that experience. It would have been for him yet another experience of the mercy of God.

This is just one story of many which has seen John's vision carried on by us women of the Missionary Sisters of Service community, which celebrated its 75th anniversary on 8th July 2019. The experience of the women related above was made possible by a grant from the foundation, which was set up by the Missionary Sisters of Service in 2010, and named the John Wallis Foundation. After eight years, the mission of the Foundation has now been absorbed into one with a broader scope through the setting up of an entity, which is called *Highways and Byways: A Community of Service*. This entity will allow for greater opportunities for partnerships and expansion of the mission, especially into the rural and isolated areas in Australia, places so dear to John's heart.

To mark the beginning of the 75th Anniversary celebrations of the Missionary Sisters of Service, a pilgrimage to John's beloved Bruny Island took place in November 2018. MSS sisters, friends and colleagues began the pilgrimage at 1 Frederick Street, Launceston, the home of the first women who came together in 1944 to step out into the deep with John to begin the life and mission of the Home Missionary Sisters of Our Lady, which in 1971 became known as the Missionary Sisters of Service. The pilgrimage went from there to some of the significant places in Tasmania where sisters worked in the earlier years. It reached the little church at Alonnah, Bruny Island a few days later for the blessing and dedication of a memorial to John, the Missionary Sisters of Service and the mission and vision being continued on through *Highways and Byways: A Community of Service*. The last of the anniversary celebrations will be a Walking Pilgrimage on Bruny Island in November 2019. John used many ways of getting around to search out the people on Bruny Island. Walking was one of them so the pilgrimage gives the opportunity to take time to reflect on John's vision and all that has come from it and the initial conversation he had with Kit Hawkins on Bruny Island in 1933.

Since 2009, John Wallis Memorial Lectures have been held on and off in Hobart, Melbourne, Toowoomba and Whyalla. These events seek to continue the yearning of John for openness to the new, to the big maps, to the need for peoples' spirits to be nurtured by enlivening and challenging thinking, especially in those parts of Australia which do not always have the opportunities afforded to people in the cities.

What has been written of John thus far is all part of the big story, but nevertheless, a story, which is not always a very well known story. His influence on religious life and other aspects of a pastoral vision in Australia is still being played out. He belonged to a great band of visionaries who wanted to see the essence of Vatican II embedded in the lives of all the people, a church of the people on mission in the world, rather than a great fortress pitted against the world. He maintained a determined spirit of freedom where the law serves the people rather than oppresses them.

The question could be asked of him, *"What good could come out of Yea, or of Tasmania"?* In the minds of some, not a lot of good could possibly come from a small rural community or a little island at the bottom of the world. A 22-year-old priest began to turn that notion on its head in 1933. We are invited to reflect on Philip's response to Nathanael in John's gospel.

Philip found Nathanael and said to him, *"We have found him of whom Moses in the Torah and also the prophets wrote, Jesus of Nazareth, the son of Joseph."* Nathanael said to him, *"Can anything good come out of Nazareth?"*

Philip said to him, **"COME AND SEE."** John 1:43-46

Stancea Vichie
Missionary Sisters of Service
Congregational Leader

Acknowledgments

First of all, I acknowledge my uncle, Brian Wallis, who rescued John's letters and put them into safe keeping for us to ponder now. Secondly, thank you to the Missionary Sisters of Service archivist, Carmel Hall, for your attentiveness to the preservation of the letters. John's writing was often difficult to read. Thank you, Carmel and Gemma O'Callaghan, for assisting in translating and transcribing the letters in this collection. You previously typed many of John's manuscripts when he was alive so could understand his writing.

I am ever grateful to Stancea Vichie and others members of the Stewardship Council of the Missionary Sisters of Service, Deirdre O'Donnell, Gabrielle McMullen and Doug Sumner for recognising the importance and value of John's letters as well as their constant encouragement, as I embarked on the task of publishing the private collection of personal letters.

Thank you to the advisory committee who guided me in the structure of how to present the letters, the initial editors, and supporters with various aspects of the book – Gabrielle McMullen and Moira White. Thank you, Corrie van den Bosch, Bernadette Madden, Gerard Wallis, Mary Fran Coonan and Ray Kent, for different sections of some research and work on the illustrations and photos. It made it easier for me at the end stages. Thank you to other researchers in various centres, including Assumption College, Kilmore and the Hobart Archdiocesan Archives.

Thank you, Kate Fogarty, Austin Cooper, Edmund Campion, Corrie van den Bosch, Graeme Howard, Bobby Court, Gabrielle McMullen, Adrian Doyle, Angela Hazebroek and David Ranson, for writing the rich reflections to the particular chapters. Thank you, Stancea Vichie for concluding the book with the epilogue, a great overview.

Thank you to all my companions in the Missionary Sisters of Service – I have valued your interest. Thank you, too, to the John Wallis Foundation and now Highways & Byways – a Community of Service, especially Joan Donohoe, who was chair till the end of 2018 and Liz McAloon, the executor officer who offered encouraging comments from the other side of our shared office.

To Hugh McGinlay and team at Coventry Press – a big thank you for reassurance and advice – and for taking on the task of publishing this work.

Let's celebrate the book concluding the celebrations of the Missionary Sisters of Service 75th Anniversary of foundation.

Chart of John Corcoran Wallis' Letters

Letter	Chapter	Age	Year	Date	Pages	From	To
1.	1. Springwood 1927	16	1927	2 May	2	Springwood	Mother
2.		16	1927	May	4	Springwood	Father
3.		16	1927	Late May	2	Springwood	Father
4.		16	1927	Late May	5	Springwood	Mother
5.		17	1927	25 June	2	Springwood	Mother
6.		17	1927	June	2	Springwood	Mother
7.		17	1927	June	3	Springwood	Mother
8.		17	1927	July	2	Springwood	Father
9.		17	1927	July	2	Springwood	Mother
10.		17	1927	August	6	Springwood	Father
11.	2. Springwood 1927–1928	17	1927	September	3	Springwood	Mother
12.		17	1927	September	4	Springwood	Father
13.		17	1927	October	2	Springwood	Father & Mother
14.		17	1927	October	3	Springwood	Mother
15.		17	1928	11 March	4	Springwood	Mother
16.		17	1928	25 March	6	Springwood	Mother
17.		17	1928	2 May	2	Springwood	Mother
18.		18	1928	19 August	4	Springwood	Mother
19.		18	1928	28 September	8	Springwood	Father
20.		18	1928	18 November	2	Springwood	Mother
21.	3. Manly 1929–1931	18	1929	17 March	3	Manly	Father
22.		19	1929	September	5	Manly	Mother
23.		19	1930	5 March	4	Manly	Mother
24.		19	1930	16 March	3	Manly	Father
25.		20	1930	12 October	2	Manly	Mother
26.		20	1930	26 October	4	Manly	Mother
27.		20	1930	6 November	2	Manly	Mother
28.		20	1930	20 November	1	Manly	Mother

Letter	Chapter	Age	Year	Date	Pages	From	To
29.		20	1930	1 December	4	Manly	Mother
30.		21	1931	29 June	3	Manly	Brian
31.	4. Ordination	21	1932	2 May	2	Manly	Mother
32.		21	1932	16 May	4	Manly	Mother
33.		21	1932	June	1	Manly	Mother
34.		22	1932	June	2	Manly	Mother
35.		22	1932	16 September	2	Manly	Mother
36.		22	1932	3 October	2	Manly	Mother
37.		22	1932	3 October	3	Manly	Father
38.		22	1932	6 November	4	Manly	Mother
39.		22	1932	18 November	2	Manly	Mother
40.		22	1932	November	1	Manly	Marie
41.		22	1932	20 November	2	Manly	Mother
42.		22	1932	30 November	3	Manly	Mother
43.	5. Launceston & Hobart 1933	22	1933	14 February	4	The Deanery, Launceston	Mother
44.		22	1933	23 February	3	The Deanery, Launceston	Father
45.		22	1933	26 March	4	The Deanery, Launceston	Mother
46.		22	1933	17 April	6	The Deanery, Launceston	Mother
47.		22	1933	1 May	3	Archbishop's House, Hobart	Mother
48.		23	1933	June/July	3	Archbishop's House, Hobart	Mother
49.		23	1933	15 August	2	Archbishop's House, Hobart	Mother
50.		23	1933	30 August	3	Archbishop's House, Hobart	Mother
51.		23	1933	10 September	3	Archbishop's House, Hobart	Father
52.		23	1933	22 September	10	S.S. Mangana	Mother
53.		23	1933	11 November	7	Archbishop's House, Hobart	Mother
54.	6. Tasmania 1934	23	1934	23 April	2	Hobart	Mother
55.		23	1934	May	4	Archbishop's House, Hobart	Mother
56.		24	1934	11 or 23 June	4	Archbishop's House, Hobart	Mother
57.		24	1934	15 July	3	Hobart	Mother
58.		24	1934	11 August	4	Archbishop's House, Hobart	Mother
59.		24	1934	15 October	2	Archbishop's House, Hobart	Mother
60.		24	1934	5 November	3	Hobart	Mother
61.		24	1934	November	2	Hobart	Mother
62.		24	1934	Late November	4	Archbishop's House	Mother
63.		24	1934	11 December	4	Hobart	Mother
64.		24	1934	25 December	4	Archbishop's House	Mother

Letter	Chapter	Age	Year	Date	Pages	From	To
65.	7. Priesthood & Columbans 1935	24	1935	17 January	4	S.S. Dover	Mother
66.		24	1935	1 April	2	St Columban's Seminary, Essendon, Victoria	Mother
67.		24	1935	4 June	2	Archbishop's House, Hobart	Mother
68.		25	1935	23 June	3	Archbishop's House, Hobart	Father
69.		25	1935	12 July	4	Presentation Sisters, Blackman's Bay, Tas.	Mother
70.		25	1935	10 August	1	Archbishop's House, Hobart	Mother
71.		25	1935	22 September	5	Archbishop's House, Hobart	Mother
72.		25	1935	16 October	1	Hobart	Mother
73.		25	1935	16 October	3	Hobart	Father
74.		25	1935	4 November	4	Hobart	Mother
75.		25	1935	18 November	4	Stowell Hospital, Hobart	Mother
76.		25	1935	Late November	2	Stowell Hospital, Hobart	Mother
77.		25	1935	December	1	Orford. Tas.	Mother
78.		25	1935	11 December	4	Mt St Canice Presbytery, Sandy Bay. Tas.	Father
79.		25	1935	December	2	Mt St Canice Presbytery, Sandy Bay. Tas	Mother
80.	8. Tasmania 1936–1937	25	1936	14 January	4	Archbishop's House, Hobart	Mother
81.		25	1936	25 February	5	Hobart	Mother
82.		25	1936	15 April	6	Hobart	Mother
83.		25	1936	5 May	5	Hobart	Mother
84.		26	1936	3 September	1	Hobart	Mother
85.		26	1936	3 September	4	Hobart	Father
86.		26	1936	22 December	3	Hobart	Father
87.		26	1936	22 December	1	Hobart	Mother
88.		26	1937	6 March	4	Hobart	Mother
89.	9. Tasmania 1946–1949	35	1946	5 February	3	The Deanery, Launceston	Mother
90.		36	1947	23 January	2	The Deanery, Launceston	Mother
91.		37	1947	29 November	6	Presbytery, Derby. Tas. & The Deanery, Launceston	Mother
92.		37	1947	18 December	4	Rosary House, 1 Frederick St, Launceston	Mother
93.		37	1947	30 December	6	Rosary House, Launceston	Mother
94.		37	1948	3 March	4	St Finn Barr's, Invermay Road, Launceston	Mother
95.		38	1949	6 April	4	Catholic Presbytery, Burnie	Mother

Chart of John Corcoran Wallis' Letters

Letter	Chapter	Age	Year	Date	Pages	From	To
96.	10. Letters to Brian 1944–1947	33	1944	23 January	7	Hobart	Brian
97.		35	1945	14 October	8	The Deanery, Launceston	Brian
98.		36	1946	26 November	4	Launceston	Brian
99.		37	1947	28 July	2	Rosary House, Launceston	Brian
100.		37	1947	28 September	2	Rosary House, Launceston	Brian

Time Line of Events

Pre 1860	Abraham's parents, Henry Wallis & Mary Dempsey, and maternal grandparents arrive in Australia from Ireland. (Abe's father, Henry, came from London.)
Pre 1860	Emily's parents, John Corcoran & Maria McAsey arrive in Australia from Ireland
1865	Abraham Knight Wallis was born
1882	Emily (Emma) Corcoran was born
22 January 1908	Abraham & Emma Wallis married in Sacred Heart Church, Carlton, Victoria. They go to Hobart for their honeymoon
1909	St Columba's College, Springwood, opens
8 August 1909	Death of St Mary MacKillop, Sydney
11 June 1910	John Corcoran Wallis is born in Yea and baptised four days later by Fr Gerald Byrne at Sacred Heart Church, Yea, Victoria. (His sister Marie was born 18 months before him, Don his brother 18 months after him. Both were deaf.)
1915	John's sister, Marie, from the age of six, boards at the Waratah School for Deaf Children near Newcastle, N.S.W.
1916 – 1918	World War I
1916	John attends the Homewood State School. His brother Chester is born
1919	Co-founder of the Columbans, Fr Edward Galvin makes a lasting impression on John and the world of the overseas missions was introduced to him.
1920	John's brother Brian was born
1922	St Gabriel's School for Deaf Boys, Castle Hill, N.S.W. conducted by Irish Christian Brothers opens. Don Wallis attends from 1923–1931. Charles Wallis attends from 1930 – 1939
1923	John attends the new Sisters of St Joseph school in Yea
1924 – 1926	John studies at Assumption College Kilmore. His brother Charles was born. He is also deaf
1925	John decided to become a priest during an annual school retreat
1927	Archbishop William Barry accepts John for the Archdiocese of Hobart
1927 – 1928	John studies at St Columba's College, the minor seminary in Springwood N.S.W.
1927	John's mother, Emma, sets up her business, Wallis' Café, The Motorist Tearooms on the old Hume Highway, Seymour
1928	Eucharistic Congress, Sydney
1929 – 1932	John studies at the seminary, St Patrick's College, Manly, N.S.W.
1929 – 1939	Great Depression
1929	Death of Archbishop William Barry
1929	William Hayden is appointed as Archdiocese of Hobart
1932	John is ordained at St Patrick's Church, Kilmore, Victoria
1933 Feb – March	John begins priestly ministry in Launceston, Tasmania
1933 April	John is transferred to the Bishop's House, St Mary's Cathedral under the administration of Fr Vincent Green
1933 June	John's first visit to Bruny Island, south of Hobart, meeting Mrs Kit Hawkins, who asks the question, 'But have not our children souls as well as those in the towns and cities?'

1934 Jan – Feb	John's parents visit John in Hobart. They brought Brian Wallis, who studies for one year at St Virgil's College, Hobart
1935 April – June	John joins the Columban Fathers. He makes a 30-day long retreat. Because of reports on his health, he was not accepted and returns to Hobart
1934	John sends experimental correspondence lessons in religion to children on Bruny Island
1936	Death of Archbishop William Hayden in Hobart
1937	Archbishop Justin Simonds appointed to Hobart. Encouraged diocesan priests to give retreats. John was appointed Diocesan Director of the Propagation of Faith
1938	John did relief work in Westbury parish. First-hand work with country children over a length of time. Appointed director of Catholic Action
1938	A group of young women in the parish start a small lending library at the back of St Columba's Hall at St Mary's College, Hobart.
1939 – 1945	World War II.
1939	John hears about the Sisters of Service and their work in Canada's isolated prairie country. He writes a paper on the need for Sisters who would reach out to rural families
1941	John goes to Broken Hill, west NSW and visited Fr Pat Carmine. Officiated at his brother Don's wedding at Barooga NSW on his return journey.
1941	The Catholic lending library transferred to Commercial Bank, Hobart. First manager was Miss Neroli Goodey
	John published a paper 'Why not Peregrinating Sisters?' in 'Emmaus', editor was Bishop E Gleeson CSsR, Maitland and whose secretary was Dr Ernest Victor Tweedy
1942	Brian Wallis enters Corpus Christi seminary at Werribee
1943	Archbishop Justin Simonds transferred to Melbourne
1943	Dr EV Tweedy appointed to Hobart as Archbishop
1943	First meeting with women interested in forming a religious community, Hobart
1944 January	At the Clergy Conference, Archbishop Tweedy announced the establishment of the community for the rural outreach in the Archdiocese
1944 8 July	John moves to Launceston. Beginning of the new community known as The Home Missionary Sisters of Our Lady
1945	World War II ended
	Death of John's father, Abraham Wallis
	First correspondence lessons sent to Flinders Island
1946	End of year two Sisters move to North Hobart, visit families in nearby country areas and give catechetical instruction
1947	Approval from Rome for the new society to live in community without vows
	John's brother, Brian, was ordained to priesthood in Melbourne, arrives in Cygnet parish prior to Christmas to serve in the Hobart Archdiocese
1948	John's mother Emma and cousin Anne Douglas visit Tasmania. The Sisters accept the first invitation for mission in Derby parish, north-east Tasmania
1949	The Sisters used the caravan for the first time for a mission in Stanley north-west Tasmania
1950	John went overseas, including Rome, with Archbishop E.V. Tweedy. Obtained approval of Constitutions of Home Missionary Sisters of Our Lady. Visited Sisters of Service in Canada and other religious orders overseas
15 August 1951	Establishment of the Home Missionary Sisters of Our Lady as religious institute of Diocesan Right
1955	Death of John's mother Emma Wallis

Index of Names

Name	Letter
Ahearn (Auntie Kit)	64, 72, 89
Ahearns paddock	3
Allen, Bro Damian	26, 27, 45
Allen, Fr	80
Allen, Mrs	52
Alf	64, 67, 69, 80
Assumption College	4, 5, 7-12, 14, 16, 18, 19, 28-33, 34, 37, 45, 59, 63, 65, 71, 82, 85
Auntie Clare	See Keating
Auntie Jane	See Douglas
Auntie May	See Lovelock
Auntie Kate	See Neville
Auntie Kit	See Ahearn
Baker, Fr	22
Bainbridge, Arthur	27
Barry, Archbishop (Hobart)	1, 16
Barwick, Bill	51
Benneworth, Fr Ambrose	96
Bett, Grace (Yea)	3
Blackheath	2, 10
Boland, Fr	40
Bonny (horse)	4, 52
Booker, Arthur	11
Bottomley, Mrs	52
Bowers, Fr	4, 15
Bowman, Frank	38, 39, 42, 60, 64, 65
Boyara, Maurice	29
Brannigan, Martin CSSR	6, 41, 42, 46
Bratt, Mrs., Mabel & Thelma	56, 62, 64, 58, 68, 69, 71, 75, 80
Brauer, Monsignor	2, 4, 15, 16
Brennan, Joe	30
Brown, Lil and Flo	1
Brown, Fr Roy	16, 40
Bruce, Mr (in politics)	4
Bruny Island/ (See also Dillons)	48-53, 55, 56, 61, 64, 65, 67, 69, 72, 73, 81-83, 92, 93
Bugden, Joe	14
Bush, Keith	16
Cafferey, Mr	22, 25
Cahill, Bro Dunstan	92
Callahan, Vin	19
Carmelite Sisters	69, 94

Carmine, Pat/ Fr	12, 23, 29, 32, 33, 39, 42, 46, 47, 53, 58, 63, 71, 78, 79, 82, 93
Carrigan, Sr Martina OP	10, 13, 38
Carroll, Fr Pat	93
Carroll, Sr Monica MSS	89, 91, 92, 93
Casey, Sr Valerie/ Venard MSS	89
Clarke, Dr Ned	44
Cochrane, Cyril	4, 9, 25, 29
Cochrane, Vin	2
Coleraine, Mrs	96
Columban Fathers SSC	55, 61, 62, 63, 64, 65, 66, 69, 82, 83, 96
Concannon, Fr	40
Conlan, Fr	75
Conley, Mrs Albert & Doreen (Bruny Is)	81
Conroy, Misses	56, 79, 81
Conway, Jim	25, 28
Coonan, Michael (Mick) (Homewood)	2, 3, 4, 23, 29, 78
Copeley, Reg	32, 40
Corcoran, Fanny (Auntie)	71
Corcoran, Charles (Uncle)	71
Corcoran, Fr Jack SJ	39, 41, 42
Corcoran, Maria (Grandma)	4, 32, 71
Costigan, Dr (Medical)	66
Counsel, Darcey	92
Crowe, Fr	34
Cullen, Fr J.H.	60, 67
Cullen, Fr Joe	69, 85
Cunningham, Charlie	27, 32, 33
Dando, Fr Rene	49
Dalton, Fr MSC	57, 75
Deane, Fr Pat CSSR	41, 42, 46, 82
Delaney, Fr	14
Devlin, Fr SSC	69, 71
Dillons	48, 73, 81, 92
Dillon, Lily	72
Dillon, Mrs	56, 57, 65, 72, 73
Dillon, Mrs Frank	52
Dillon, Pat	52
Dillon, Patricia	81
Dillon, Mr & Mrs Stan	72, 81
Dillon, Terence	52, 81, 83
Dillon, Mrs Ted	52
Dillon, Violet	55, 56, 72
Doctor (Medical)	75, 76, 78, 82, 92
Doherty, Brian	11, 32, 34
Doherty, Fr Pat	34

Dominican Sisters, Waratah (School for Deaf Children)	13, 39, 42, 47, 49, 50, 52, 89, 92
Donaldson, Jack/ McDonald	4, 9, 15
Donohue, Rex	91, 98, 99
Douglas, Anne (Cousin)	60, 62, 64, 71, 86, 90, 95, 100
Douglas, Auntie Jane	9, 10, 12, 14, 45, 46, 50, 65, 79, 82, 86, 90, 93, 94
Downey Fr	4
Doyle, Fr	36
Doyle, Dr (Medical)	66
Drysdale, Alex (Homewood)	3
Drysdale, Bill (Homewood)	78
Dunn, Oswald	82
Dunne, Fr	19
Dutton, Mary	46, 55
Dwyer, Dr Joseph (Bishop of Wagga Wagga)	19, 27
Dwyer, Fr Eric CSSR	93
Dwyer, Kathleen/ Sr Columba OP (See Waratah)	47
Dwyers	57
Egan, Fr	1, 10, 38
Elliott, Frank	16
Ellis, Fr	35, 38
Elsie	66
Esmonde, Br cfc	65
Evans, Jim	19
Fiscalini, Charlie (Fr)	14, 82
Fiscalini, Bro	42
Fitzgerald, Jim (Fr)	16, 19, 67, 82, 83
Fitzgerald, Mrs	92
Fitzpatrick, Fr	55
Flarty, Pat	4
Flood, Bro CFC	57
Flynn, Fr	91
Foley, Fr	22
Forrest, Fr MSC	53
Ford, Steve	16, 39, 40
Franklin, Sr Monica/ Sr Joseph MSS	81, 89
French Ladies – Mademoiselle	67, 68
Friar, Mr & Mrs	52
Fulton, John (nephew)	90
Galvin, Bishop Edward SSC	59, 60, 62, 63
Gard, Tom	11, 16
Garvey, Bro CFC	54, 55, 62
Garvey, Jack	16, 19
Giani, Mary (nee McAsey)	47

Index of Names

Gilby, Bill	25, 26, 27, 28
Gillie, Miss	91
Gilroy, Cardinal Norman	100
Glover, Fr	99
Gonzales, Bro SM	59
Good Shepherd Sisters/ Mt St Canice	55, 57, 74, 75, 76, 78, 80, 81, 83
Grandma	See Maria Corcoran
Green, Fr Vincent	44, 46, 47, 49, 53, 56-60, 62-65, 67-69, 76, 78, 82, 85, 88
Green, Peter	63
Gregory, Bro SM	56
Hack, Fr	13
Hackett, Fr SJ	65
Hall, Fr CM	26, 41
Hall, Fr SSC	57, 58, 60, 70, 76
Hamilton, Chas (Yea)	85
Hanohoe, Fr	80
Hanlon, L & Win	38, 42
Hanlon, Fr Pat	80, 82
Hansen, Fr	94
Harris, Mr	78
Hatswell, Leo	23, 28, 32
Hatswell, Tony	25
Hayden, Archbishop William	28, 32, 33, 35, 43, 44, 46, 50, 51, 55-57, 60, 62-65, 68, 69, 78, 82, 83, 85
Hayes, Fr	16, 26, 40, 62, 64
Haywood, Hubert	80
Healy, Fr SJ	23
Healy, Mr	41
Hegney, Fr	16
Hehir, Fr SJ	60, 64, 65, 80
Hennessey, Dean	43, 44, 45, 46, 65, 83
Henley, Fr	58
Henry, Fr Jim	11, 38, 39, 40
Hepworth, Mr	80
Herring, Fr SM	28, 29
Hogan, Sr Gabriel OP (See Waratah)	47
Honner, Corey	19
Home Missionary Sisters of Our Lady/ Rosary House/ Rosary House Sisters Our Lady's Home Missionary Sisters, Home Missionary Sisters	89-100
Hood, Bro	69
Howe, Fr Joe	97
Howe, Mrs	96
Hudson, Cyril	25
Hunt, Mr & Mrs A	100

Hurley, Fr	13
Jones, Miss	62
Joyce, Bro CFC	60
Joyce, Eileen	83
Keating, Auntie Clare	65, 66, 71, 79
Keenan, Mr	68
Kelliher, Dorothy	92
Kelliher, Fr	80
Kelly, Archbishop Michael	18, 19, 24, 25, 26, 28, 29, 38
Kelly, Fr CSSR	6
Kelly, Fr Patrick CSSR	46
Kelly, Jim	38, 42
Keneally, Dennis	19
Kennedy, Bill	23, 24
Kennedy, Fr Bob	16, 19, 58, 67, 68, 69, 70, 78, 80, 82, 85
Kent, Fr	52, 56, 60, 68, 69, 85, 92, 93, 96
Kerr, Tom	12
Kilmartin, (Nurse)	55
Kincella, Fr	6, 7, 11
Lacey, Gus	2, 4, 9, 25, 29, 38
Lane, Fr	22
Lang, Premier John (Jack)	32
Lanke, Fr	33
Leahy, Helen	76
Leonard, Dr	22, 25, 32
Leonard, Fr Timothy SSC	22
Lola	71
Long, Mick	82
Long, Ross	59
Lovelock, Auntie May	45, 50, 65, 66, 71, 75, 79, 82
Lynch, Fr	34, 37, 38, 46, 47, 55, 56, 59, 67, 68, 71, 80
Lyons, Sheila	76
McCarthy, Mr & Mrs	64
McCarthy, Mr & Mrs Neil	45, 46, 67
McCarthy, Nell (Yea)	78
McDermott, Mons	25
McDonald, Jack	See Donaldson
McGlynn, Fr	70, 83, 89, 97, 98
McGoldrick, Fr SSC	76
McGrath Mr & Mrs (See also Reilly)	49, 50
McHugh, Fr	35, 38
McKay	52
McKenna, Miss/Mrs	50, 60, 62, 68
McMahon, Bill	11, 13, 20
McMahon, Fr Joe	91, 93
McPoland, Fr	88

Index of Names

McRae, Mrs H (Homewood)	56
McRae, Sr (Medical)	75
Madden, Dr	22
Maher (Homewood)	35
Maloney, Miss	27
Manion Family	91
Mannix, Dr	33, 43, 93
Marist Sisters	71
Marsh, Fr	34
Massey, Fr Bernie	43
Massey, Fr Frank	4, 10, 40
Mayne, Fr Charlie SJ	93
Michael, Bro SM	7, 12, 14, 18, 57, 59, 60, 62
Mitchell, Miss	62
Molloy, Bro William SM	1, 3, 5-7, 11, 15, 18-19, 29-30, 38, 46, 49, 52, 56, 58, 60, 62, 64, 68, 82-83, 85
Moloney, Fr Paddy MSC	96
Moran, Cardinal Patrick	18
Morgans	80
Morgan, Mary	80
Morgan, Virgil	38, 39, 42, 45, 46
Morganti, Eddie	12, 14, 24
Morrissey, Nick	12
Mother Alphonsus PBVM	55
Moore, Kathleen/ Sr Vianney MSS	89, 93, 96
Morse, Gwen/ Sr Teresa MSS	89, 91-94, 96
Mother Joseph PBVM	79, 80
Mother Margaret Mary RGS	81
Mother Patrick PBVM	92
Mother Paul PBVM	54, 56-58, 62, 79
Mother Teresa PBVM	55
Mullaney, Fr Luke SSC	55, 59, 60, 65, 66, 82, 83, 88
Murphy, Sr Anne	89
Murphy, Fr Leo	96
Murphy, Mick	23
Murphy, Fr Peter	64, 94
Murphy, Fr Tim	75, 96
Murtagh, Dr	34
MSC Fathers	48, 52
Nazareth Sisters	83, 93
Nelson, Fr	39 40
Neville, Auntie Kate & Uncle Harry	4, 7, 8, 16, 49, 50, 51, 62, 63, 79
Neville, Honora (Cousin)	8, 63
Nevin, J. J. Dr	25, 26, 28, 29, 30, 32, 39, 45
Newman, Frank	18
Nolan, Fr	4

Noonan, Jim (Yea)	71
O'Brien, Fr Eris	4, 12
O'Brien, Joyce/ Sr	89, 94
O'Bryan Fr Eddie (Ted)	13, 14, 29, 30, 32, 35, 39, 45
O'Callaghan, Fr Des	43
O'Connor, Fr P.B. (Seymour)	16, 32, 38, 40, 44
O'Connor, Fr James (Tasmania)	43
O'Doherty, Dr, (Ireland)	19
O'Donnell, Fr T.J.	54, 58, 68, 85
O'Flynn, Dr	24, 36, 38, 40
O'Leary, Fr SJ	37, 39
O'Loughlin, Martin Fr	59
O'Loughlin, Fr MSC	53, 57, 73, 81
O'Loughlin, Sr Dolores PBVM	57
O'Meara, Fr SSC	80, 82
O'Neill, Bro CFC	89
O'Shea, Bro CFC	43,
Osborne, Mr	93
Our Lady's Home Missionary Sisters	See Home Missionary Sisters of Our Lady
Patterson, Cyril	71
Pearce, Mrs	81
Perrott, Fr SJ	65
Pollington, Frank	45
Power Fr (Vincentian)	19
Power Fr Albert SJ	60, 64, 65
Presentation Sisters (See also Sr)	43, 45-48, 64, 65, 69, 71, 81, 85, 88, 89, 92-94, 96, 100
Purcell, Joe	25
Quinn, Joe	29
Quinn, Bill	11
Quinlan & Nance Quinlan (Yea)	1, 19
Rector/ Monsignor Brauer	6, 10, 18, 20
Redemptorists	53, 55, 60
Reed, Bernie (Tasmania)	89
Reilly, Fred	1, 4
Riley, Jane/ Kate Also McGrath	47, 49, 50
Roberts, Dr	33
Roberts Mr (Tasmania)	76
Rod (Homewood)	4, 7
Rogers, Dr (medical)	74
Rogers, Fr Bernard (Tasmania)	91
Rosary House	See Home Missionary Sisters of Our Lady
Ross, Jordan	10
Rouget, Robert	26
Rumble, Dr MSC	44
Rush, Ormond	29
Russell, Jack	32

Index of Names

Ryan, Winifred/ Sr Magdalen/ Agnes MSS	89, 93
Ryan, Fr Bill, Fr John, & Mrs Ryan (Tasmania)	43, 44, 46, 82
Ryder, Alex	20
Scarfe, Fr (Tasmania)	43, 44, 45, 46
Schmude, Alf	3, 11, 12, 13, 19
Scullin, Mr (Prime Minister)	26
Shanley, Pat	3, 30
Sheehan, AB	21, 47
Sherry, Fr (Tasmania)	46, 75, 76, 77, 82
Siers (Homewood)	1, 53, 78
Simonds, Fr, Dr, Archbishop	4, 9, 15, 16, 88
Simpson, Chris	49
Sisters of Mercy	38, 43, 92
Sisters of Our Lady of the Sacred Heart	96
Slattery, Fr	7, 16, 18, 39, 40
Slavin, Mrs (Homewood)	13
Smart, Mary	45
Smith, Bluey/ Smith, Reg	43
Smith, Mr (Bruny Is)	73
Smyth, Roley	20
Sr Antoinette RGS	78
Sr de Sales PBVM	81
Sr Ignatius PBVM	46
Sr Stanislaus PBVM	45, 46
Staffords (Yea)	78,
Stoner, George Fr (also misspelled Stonor)/ also Fr Austin	60, 69, 80, 82, 89, 93
St Columba's School Hobart	50, 55, 62, 63, 64, 76
St Columban's College Essendon	12, 23, 24, 55, 58, 65, 66, 71
St Gabriel's School for Deaf Boys/ Castle Hill	13, 26, 27, 37, 52, 89, 92
St Mary's College	47, 48, 56 58, 62, 63, 76, 85
St Patrick's College Manly	28, 78
St Virgil's College – CFC	47-49, 51, 53, 55-57, 62, 63, 64, 65, 67, 83, 85
St Virgil's, CFC Community/ Brothers	56, 64, 68, 69, 76, 77, 80, 96
Sullivan, Mrs Reg	90, 92
Tehan, Rosie	79, 80, 82
Thomas, Mr	12
Tierney, Jack	18
Toall, Fr	16
Toohey, Mr, Mrs, & Frank Fr	32, 38, 43, 46, 64, 82
Traynor, Mr & Mrs John (Jack)	50, 55, 81
Traynor, Miss	46, 47, 49, 50, 55, 58, 67, 69, 71
Tratford, Miss Win (Yea)	35

Tullins, Allen	16, 19
Tweedy, Archbishop Ernest	89, 90, 92, 93, 94, 96, 99, 100
Tye, Harry (Seymour)	76
Upton, Dean (Tasmania)	90
Vaughan, Cardinal	11,
Wallace, Fr	1, 2, 4, 10, 14
Wallace, Fr CSSR	60
Wallis boys	46, 50, 60
Wallis, Brian	5, 7, 10, 11, 13, 20, 30, 32, 33, 38, 41, 43, 45-47, 49, 50, 54-60, 62-64, 67-69, 75, 81-83, 85, 88-95, 96-100
Wallis, Charlie	5, 10, 11, 30, 42, 58, 60, 63, 66, 69, 75, 78, 79, 83, 89, 92, 95
Wallis, Chester	4, 5, 7, 9-11, 13, 14, 18, 20, 30, 32, 38, 41, 44, 54, 56, 64, 71, 72, 75, 83, 90-95
Wallis, Don	1, 4, 9, 10, 12, 13, 22, 23, 27, 29, 30, 41, 43, 45, 50, 58, 64, 71-73, 75, 76, 78, 83, 92, 95
Wallis, Marie (Fulton)	1, 4, 7, 9, 10, 14, 15, 18, 20, 22, 29-34, 36, 38-42, 44-53, 55, 57-60, 62-64, 66, 67, 69-72, 75, 78, 79, 81-83, 91, 94, 95
Walters, Charlie	68
Waratah/ Castle Hill/ Deaf	See St Gabriel's School/ Christian Brothers/ Dominican Sisters
Ward, Mr & Mrs Charlie	100
Wentworth Paddock	1
Whyte, Bishop James, N.Z.	13
William, Bro SM	See Molloy, Bro William
Willis, Fr	1, 2, 35, 38
Wilson, Mrs	44

Index of Topics

Topic	Letter
Assumption College, Kilmore including Marist Brothers	3-7, 11, 12, 14, 16, 18, 29, 30, 34, 37, 38, 44-46, 52, 56-60, 62-65, 68, 71, 81-83, 85,
Benediction	See Devotions
Blue Mountains / Bush Picnics	3, 7, 9, 10-12, 14-16, 18-20, 22, 30,
Bruny Island including Dillon family	48-53, 55-57, 60, 62-65, 67, 69, 72, 73, 81, 83, 92, 93
Carmelites	36, 94
Castle Hill	See Deaf
Catechesis – religious instructions/ converts / marriage preparation	43-46, 52, 53, 55-57, 67, 71, 73, 80-83, 88, 91, 92, 96
– Children/ Summer School camps/Vocational Holiday School	89, 93, 94, 96, 99
– Correspondence Lessons/ sending instructions	43, 47, 49-52, 55, 67, 68, 93, 94, 99
Catholic Action	96
Catholic Bookshop – See also Library	96
Church Associations – The Hibernian Australian Catholic Benefit Society, Children of Mary/ Legion of Mary/ Sacred Heart Sodality/ St Vincent de Paul/ Altar Boys/ Crusaders of the Blessed Sacrament	18, 45-47, 50, 52-54, 58, 64, 69, 82, 83, 85
Columban Fathers	22-24, 26, 52, 55, 57-67, 69, 71, 76, 80, 82, 83, 88, 96
• China Mission	12, 22, 23, 24, 26, 58, 59, 60, 62, 64
Corpus Christi College/ Seminary, Werribee	89, 91, 93, 99, 100
Death/ After life/ Funerals	4, 11, 13, 18, 22, 26, 27, 32-33, 44, 50, 53, 54, 58, 59, 61-63, 69, 74, 89, 90
Debates/ Manuscripts/ Papers e.g. Conversion of Australia, Evolution, Capital Punishment, Remaining in the British Empire, A Plea for Australian Literature, Fostering Vocations, Australian Freedom in Government, Irish Pioneers	3, 11, 12, 14-16, 18, 19, 32
Deaf – Also Rosary School for Deaf Girls, Waratah/ St Gabriel's School for Deaf Boys, Castle Hill/ Dominican Sisters and Christian Brothers in relation to Deaf education	13, 20, 22, 25-27, 29, 30, 37-39, 42-45, 47, 49, 50, 52, 65, 78, 80, 89, 92, 95
Devotions / Benediction / Exposition/ Novenas/ Parish Mission/ Rosary/ Visits to Chapel/ Forty Hours/ Bless House	4-6, 9, 11, 14-19, 22-24, 26, 27, 29, 30, 32, 43, 44, 46, 47, 51-53, 55-58, 60, 62-64, 66, 71, 75, 76, 80, 83, 88, 89, 91, 92, 97, 98
Eucharistic Congress	6, 13, 18, 19, 24, 59, 60, 62-64,
Finance/Money	
• Family/personal	1-5, 8, 15, 16, 20, 22, 28, 33, 34, 36, 38, 41, 45, 49, 54, 56, 57, 58-60, 62-64, 82, 83, 86

- Diocesan/ Parish finances including fund-raising — 52, 58-60, 64, 68, 71, 73, 82, 83, 85, 88, 92-95

Health/ Accident — 1, 2, 12, 15, 16, 66, 68, 70, 74, 75, 76-79, 82, 83, 86-88

Home Missionary Sisters of Our Lady/ Rosary House[1] — 89, 90, 91, 92, 93, 94, 95, 96, 97, 98, 99, 100

- Accommodation — 94
- Articles/pamphlet — 93, 95, 100
- Formation/classes — 90, 91, 96, 97, 98, 100
- Mission work — 89, 94, 95, 99
- Transport/Car — 93
- Hobart — 93, 94, 95
- Spirituality/prayer — 96
- Chapel/monstrance — 91, 92, 96, 100
- Retreat — 89, 92

Irish Catholics/priests, Language/ Culture — 4, 9, 12, 14, 16, 19, 21, 24, 26, 45, 55, 59, 60-65, 70, 71, 82, 91, 95

Library/ Books/ Reading — 1, 4, 10-12, 14, 15, 21-23, 33, 38, 39, 42, 46, 55-57, 61, 65, 68, 94, 97-99

Liturgy

- Liturgy of the Hours/ Breviary/ Office — 11, 16, 33, 34, 36, 40, 42, 49, 63, 76, 88, 89, 98-100
- High Mass/ Solemn Mass/ Sung Mass/ Missa Cantata — 5, 11, 12, 14, 15, 16, 18, 23, 24, 38, 46, 56, 82

Manly Seminary — See St Patrick's College, Manly

Marion devotion/ Feasts of Our Lady/ Mary/ Rosary — 4, 9, 10-14, 16-19, 22, 26, 27, 30, 36, 42, 45, 49, 52, 55, 56, 58, 72, 83, 96, 97

Melbourne Centenary of Appointment of First Bishop — 93

Missions – parishes including Hobart — 26, 31, 45, 53, 62, 75, 82, 81, 84

Mt St Canice/ Good Shepherd Sisters — 55, 57, 72, 75, 76, 78, 80, 81, 83

Nazareth House Sisters — 93

Ordination

- Ordination /Sacrament/ others/ — 12, 25, 26, 29, 36, 53, 57, 60, 89, 98-100
- John's Ordination, Kilmore — 27, 28, 32-35, 37-39, 41, 58, 63, 66, 78

Outreach – country / rural/ outlying places/ Mass Centres — 43-46, 52-54, 64, 67-69, 71, 78, 81, 91, 92, 94, 96

Parishes in Tasmania including Derby, Cygnet, Rosebery, Burnie, Invermay, Zeehan — 43, 44, 45, 67, 68, 69, 80, 83, 89, 91, 92, 93, 94, 95, 96

Pastoral duties – Confessions/ visitation including hospitals, gaols, census — 43-47, 50, 52, 53, 55, 56, 60, 63, 64, 67, 71, 73, 80, 83, 85, 90, 94

Poor/ Poverty/ homeless/ housing/ unemployed/ ill health — 26, 43, 49, 50, 51, 53, 57, 64, 68, 69, 70, 71, 73, 85, 88, 89, 92, 93, 97

Prayer/ meditation/ particular examen/ spiritual reading — 12, 13, 14, 17, 18, 29, 32, 33, 36, 42, 45, 47, 82, 84, 94, 96-100

Presentation Sisters Tasmania – Hobart / Launceston/ Karoola — 43, 45-47, 48, 54-57, 60, 62, 64, 65, 69, 73, 79, 81, 82, 85, 88, 89, 92-94, 96

---

1   Later re-named Missionary Sisters of Service

Index of Topics

Priesthood/ rule of life	4, 5, 6, 17, 29, 31, 36, 37, 38, 43, 44, 46, 55, 57, 62, 66, 69, 80, 81, 82, 89, 91, 96, 97, 98, 99
Retreats/ spiritual direction	11, 16, 23, 26, 28, 29, 38, 39, 41, 42, 46, 48, 50, 52, 53-58, 60, 62, 64, 65-69, 75, 80, 83, 84, 92, 93, 96, 97, 98, 99
• Personal	2, 6, 11, 18, 23, 26-29, 39, 40, 42, 48, 52, 55, 64, 65, 66, 67, 80, 83, 92, 93, 96, 99
Rosary	See Devotions
Redemptorists	6, 11, 41, 42, 46, 53, 55, 60, 67, 82, 93, 94, 99
Saint/ saintly/ 'hidden' saint/ called to be 'something of a saint'	14, 16, 29, 36, 46, 48, 55, 57, 59, 61, 62, 65, 75, 81, 96, 97
Saints – including Don Bosco/ Ignatius Loyola/ John Berchmans/ • Francis de Sales/ Peter & Paul/ Joseph/ Stanislaus/ Teresa of Avila/ John Vianney & others	1, 5, 7, 11, 13, 14, 16, 19, 21, 24, 26, 27, 30, 38, 39, 41, 42, 45, 47, 67, 69, 70, 96, 97, 98,
• Sts Monica and Augustine	16, 41, 42, 45, 47
• St Therese of Lisieux	26, 36, 38, 41, 61
Sermons/ Preaching	30-32, 34, 38, 39, 43-47, 50, 52, 53, 57, 63, 64, 66, 71, 76, 78, 80, 96
Sisters of St Joseph	69, 80
Sisters of the Good Shepherd	See Mt St Canice
Sport, including football, fishing, boxing, billiards	2, 3, 7, 8, 10, 13, 15, 16, 18, 19, 21, 22, 24, 30, 37, 49, 51, 54, 55, 58, 63, 66, 88,
St Columba's School, Hobart	50, 62, 63, 64, 76,
St Columba's Seminary, Springwood	1, 14, 16, 21, 30, 82, 96
St Gabriel's School, Castle Hill	See Deaf
St Joseph's Church, Hobart	60, 80
St Marys Cathedral, Sydney	21, 30, 32,
St Mary's Cathedral, Hobart/ Bishop's House Hobart/ Palace	46, 50, 53, 55-57, 60, 62, 64, 67, 68, 71, 78, 83, 85,
St Mary's College, Hobart	47, 48, 53, 56, 62, 63, 85
St Patrick's College/ Seminary/ Manly	2, 3, 7, 9, 13, 16, 19, 21, 37, 40, 43, 53, 67, 68
St Virgil's College, Hobart/ Christians Brothers Tasmania	47, 48, 49, 51, 53, 55, 56, 57, 60, 62, 63, 64, 65, 67, 68, 76, 80, 83, 85, 96
Studies – Seminary/ Theology, Philosophy, etc.	1, 2, 4, 5, 7, 8, 10, 11, 14-16, 18, 19-23, 27, 29, 31, 32, 36-39, 51, 53, 66,
Telephone/ wireless	82, 86, 87, 92, 94, 98, 100
The Standard (Tasmania)	46, 52, 56, 60, 65, 67, 68, 71, 83, 85, 95
Transport for pastoral work – bicycle/ horse/ walking/ car/ Tram/ motor bike	43, 44, 47, 49, 51, 52, 67, 69, 73, 77, 78, 80-83, 85, 86, 91-93
Vocation to priesthood/ Diocesan or Religious Life – See also Columban Fathers	3, 6, 11, 12, 15, 16, 28, 29, 38, 52, 53, 55, 58-60, 62, 64, 65, 69, 97
Waratah, School for Deaf Girls	See Deaf
Yea/ Homewood/ Seymour/ Local people	1, 2, 4, 10, 33-35, 37, 46, 53, 62, 68, 71, 73, 78, 79, 81, 85, 88, 92, 93

John Corcoran Wallis 1910 to 2001

A Man of Vision

Fay Woodhouse

John Corcoran Wallis (1910-2001), Catholic priest, missionary and founder of the Missionary Sisters of Service, was born on 11 June 1910 in Yea, the second of six children born to Abraham Knight and Emma Kathleen (née Corcoran). John Wallis was educated locally and at the Marist Brothers' Assumption College, Kilmore (1924–1926), where attendance at spiritual retreats helped crystallise his decision to become a priest.[2]

In 1927, the tall, gangly and 'somewhat weedy 16-year-old' began training for the priesthood at St Columba's Seminary, Springwood, NSW and later St Patrick's, Manly, NSW.[3] With a special dispensation for his young age, Wallis was ordained a priest at Kilmore on 18th December 1932. Throughout most of his life, Wallis was a priest who went about doing what he referred to as 'the Master's business'.[4] His daily readings of the scriptures and the liturgy were the core of his theological development and nourished his life. He was a man whose efforts contributed to change in the Australian Catholic Church.

During the 1930s the Catholic Church was renewing its attention to a theological framework for the devotional and intellectual practices of Catholics. Papal Encyclicals refocused the way Catholic men and women should live their lives and ranged from issues such as contraception and abortion to children's education. Two encyclicals were issued in 1931 while John Wallis was training for the priesthood. *Quadragesimo Anno* (On Reconstructing the Social Order) and *Non Abbiamo Bisogno* (Concerning Catholic Action)

---

[2] 'Early history of the Home Missionary Sisters of Our Lady', MSS Beginnings, Missionary Sisters of Service Archives.
[3] Monsignor Brauer at St Patrick's College, Manly recalled that he 'welcomed "Mr Wallis"... a somewhat weedy 16-year-old to the seminary.', Penelope E. Edman, *One Man's Yes to God*, Missionary Sisters of Service, Forest Hill, Victoria, 1992, p. 20.
[4] *One Man's Yes to God*, Missionary Sisters of Service, Forest Hill, Victoria, 1992, p. 6.

were particularly significant in influencing Catholic intellectual thought and activity.[5] His interest in the work of the laity through Catholic Action, and his desire to teach disadvantaged Catholics living in the Australian outback, may be traced back to his understanding and interpretation of these two encyclicals. Wallis was involved in the work of Catholic Action and the development of a mature understanding of the proper place of the lay vocation in the life of the Church, which became 'the cornerstone' of the Second Vatican Council's understanding of the Church and its engagement with the world.[6]

In 1937, Wallis arrived in Launceston, Tasmania, where, in 1938, he was appointed Diocesan Director for Catholic Action. This appointment allowed him to explore the possibilities of working toward changing the Catholic Church's attitude to ecclesiastical teaching. On his first visit to the small Catholic congregation on Bruny Island in 1933, Wallis met Mrs Kit Hawkins, an anxious and concerned mother who asked: 'Has the Church no responsibility for souls of people in the country – out of sight, out of mind?'[7] This cry for help was an S.O.S. to the Church; it had a lasting impact on Wallis.

Six years after his visit to Bruny Island, Wallis heard of the work of the Sisters of Service (S.O.S) in Canada, founded by Catherine Donnelly. He immediately investigated the possibility of having a 'convent that runs on wheels' operating in outback Australia and began corresponding with Redemptorist Father George Daly, spiritual director of the Sisters of Service.[8] Wallis instinctively knew that Australian Catholics in remote areas needed an equivalent of the Sisters of Service. In the 1930s, he first approached Justin Daniel Simonds, Archbishop of Tasmania, with his vision of women religious seeking out Catholics in isolated areas. He was told 'it would never be approved' because the moral and physical danger would be too much for women.[9] Yet he persisted with his ideas of a mobile service for Catholics in the outback. While obedience was very important to Wallis, he was known as one who found it difficult to accept 'no' for an answer.[10] Rather, Wallis was happy to argue his point with his Bishop, but if the Bishop insisted, he would offer 'tacit resistance' then go and do what he was told. As he often said: 'Some

---

5 A Fremantle, *The Papal Encyclicals in their Historical Context*, New American Library, New York, 1956, pp. 228-235.
6 Max Vodola, 'In the Vanguard and ahead of their times: John XXIII, John Wallis, Guildford Young and Vatican II', John Wallis Memorial Lecture, Launceston, 22 October 2012, p. 4.
7 Rev. J C Wallis, 'Home Missionary Sisters: An Australian Need', *Emmaus*, 1942.
8 http://www.catherinedonnellyfoundation.org/cath.html
9 *One Man's Yes to God*, p. 7.
10 Interview with Sr Bernadette Wallis, June 2013.

regulations call for passive resistance.'[11] In 1941, the development of his ideas were portrayed in his seminal article 'Why Not Peregrinating Sisters?' published as 'Home Missionary Sisters: An Australian Need', in *Emmaus* in 1942.[12]

From September to November 1943, meetings of priests and the laity to discuss the possibility of forming an association of women with a passion to reach out to Catholics in remote locations were held in Hobart and Launceston. Money was raised for the venture and on 8 July 1944, four women committed to serving the church, came together as the Home Missionary Sisters of Our Lady in Launceston. Directly modelled on the Sisters of Service in Toronto, Canada, the community was officially inaugurated on 15 August 1944. On 3 November 1944, they made promises of Poverty, Chastity and Obedience for a period of twelve months.

In 1947, the Holy See gave permission for the Sisters to live as a Society of Religious Women in Community without public vows. Their first full-scale mission to north-east Tasmania began in 1948 and in 1949 the first mission house was established in Longford, near Launceston.[13] The name of the Congregation was changed to the Missionary Sisters of Service in 1971.[14]

In 1950, on his first overseas trip, Wallis accompanied Archbishop of Hobart, Dr Ernest Tweedy to Rome. At a private audience with His Holiness, Pope Pius XII in November 1950, they requested and received the Pope's blessing for the new religious community. The status of the community was also raised to a Religious Congregation with public vows. Less than one year later, in August 1951, twelve Sisters took public vows and the Home Missionary Sisters of Our Lady was formally constituted as a religious congregation. On this occasion, Wallis wrote:

In some real sense the Home Missionary Sisters of Our Lady are a modern Congregation – modern in point of time, modern in dress and modern, too, in the ways and means of carrying on their apostolate.[15]

Wallis' method and approach to the pastoral outreach of the Church into the community was ahead of its time; new and modern, it embraced some of the social justice ideals of Catholic Action. His group of 'peregrinating sisters' first operated in Tasmania then extended into New South Wales, Queensland, Victoria and South Australia. They soon became fondly known, especially in

---

11 *Inspirations from Father John*, Mementos of John put together on the occasion of the 70th anniversary of his Ordination to the Priesthood on 18th December 1932, Missionary Sisters of Service, 2002.
12 *One Man's Yes to God*, p. 7 and 23, and Penelope E. Edman, *Around the Kitchen Table*, Missionary Sisters of Service, Rangeview, 2008, p. 42.
13 *Around the Kitchen Table*, p. 3.
14 *Around the Kitchen Table*, p. 4.
15 *One Man's Yes to God*, p. 39.

Victoria, as the 'Caravan Sisters' for the miles they travelled in the spirit of the Gospels, seeking out people in small remote communities and isolated properties.

Once the congregation was securely established, Wallis ceased to have direct involvement with the order yet he remained their spiritual guide. Notwithstanding his lack of direct involvement, his spiritual teachings remained pivotal to the work of the Order. As Catholic historian, Max Vodola has written:

The vision of John Wallis in founding the Congregation ...very much paved the way for a new style of religious life here in Australia, a style of religious life and pastoral ministry very much adapted to the needs of this country, as opposed to importing a 'stock standard' European model. A new style of pastoral ministry and adaptation to new and changing conditions were the hallmarks of the Second Vatican Council...'.[16]

Wallis and his vision of nuns living their lives outside convent walls was a radical, effective and eminently successful idea for the times. In a small way, his attitude progressed the changing role of women – especially women religious. His enlightened thinking is one example of his belief that one must 'read the signs of the times!'[17]

In 1956, Wallis was appointed parish priest to the new parish of Glenorchy, in Tasmania, a position he held for seven years. Initially, the parish had only one church; Wallis soon changed this situation. During his term at Glenorchy, he built the St John's complex, St Monica's church, Chigwell, and planned and built Holy Rosary School. To do this, he had to convince an order of nuns to establish a congregation in Tasmania. After approaching eleven orders of nuns and receiving nine rejections to his request, the tenth response propelled him into action. He flew to Sydney where he 'persuaded the Dominican Sisters that "No" was not the answer the Lord expected them to give to his request that they should come to Tasmania'. So convincing was his appeal to the Dominicans that they agreed to his request and arrived in Tasmania in January 1959.[18]

The next major phase of Wallis's life began with the Second Vatican Council which opened in October 1962. Wallis followed all developments enthusiastically. As the Council's documents came off the press, 'he

---

16 Max Vodola, 'In the Vanguard and ahead of their times: John XXIII, John Wallis, Guildford Young and Vatican II', John Wallis Memorial Lecture, 22nd October 2012, p. 1.
17 *Inspirations from Father John*, Mementos of John put together on the occasion of the 70th anniversary of his Ordination to the Priesthood on 18 December 1932, Missionary Sisters of Service, 2002.
18 *One Man's Yes to God*, p. 27.

"devoured" them and spoke about them regularly, frequently and often!' His informative and insightful commentaries of Vatican decisions and their anticipated outcomes for the church, the laity and the congregation were widely distributed. He 'fed the Sisters on a diet of sixteen conciliar documents' and not only introduced them to the documents, 'but lured us inside them, walked us around them, in them, climbed up and down through them. His enthusiasm knew no bounds. He wanted everyone to see, feel and taste what he saw and felt and tasted.'[19] Vodola draws illuminating parallels between the work of John Wallis and that of Pope John XXIII. He believes they were both men who intuited change; they 'discerned changing conditions in the Church and in the world'. Furthermore, he sees them as men who 'were able to return to the biblical imperative given by Jesus in the Gospel to "read the signs of the times"'.[20] Wallis always described Vatican II as the 'biggest event in his life'.[21] The Catholic Church's relationship to the world formed one of the themes of Vatican II. Wallis's enlightened attitudes to pastoral teaching began in the 1930s. His early promotion of nuns moving wherever their presence was required and allowing them to journey freely in the community is illustrative of his significance as a Catholic intellectual.

In 1964, Wallis was appointed Vicar for Religious with oversight of all male and female religious orders, a position he retained into the 1990s. In December 1982, he celebrated the golden jubilee of his ordination to the priesthood. By the time of his retirement, he had also become well known for leading retreats, something he valued and practised as part of his own spiritual development. He served under six Archbishops, served in ten different parishes, some for more than one period; had been Missions Director, Founder of the then Schools Provident Fund (now the Catholic Development Fund), Founder of the Catholic Bookshop in Hobart, Vicar for Religious, retreat director, hospital chaplain, and founder of a religious congregation.[22]

After sixty years as a priest, in 1992, his very important work was recognised by the Australian Government. Father John Wallis was awarded the Member of the Order of Australia in the General Division 'For Service To Religion'.[23]

Wallis is described as 'a man of God and a true pastor for his people,

---

19   Maria Kavanagh mss, *Reflections on Father John Wallis*, Memorial Mass celebrated at St Francis Xavier's Church, Prahran, Vic. 31st August 2001, MSS Archives
20   Vodola, p. 4
21   *One Man's Yes to God*, p. 6.
22   Archbishop Adrian Doyle, *Homily for the Mass of Christian Burial for Father John C. Wallis*, St Mary's Cathedral, Hobart, 8 August, p. 1, MSS Archives.
23   http://www.itsanhonour.gov.au/honours/honour_roll/search.cfm?aus_award_id=885808&search_type=quick&showInd=true

seeking them out in their homes, in hospitals and prisons'.[24] Two of his most constantly used phrases and tools for teaching were *'humano modo'* or 'in a human way', and *'suprema lex caritas'*, that is 'the supreme law is love'.[25] Fundamental to his belief was his view that the Sisters of Service were 'called to be a "journeying" community, going into the highways, byways and skyways of the outback'.

The young John Wallis often displayed tendencies to resistance, a trait that remained with him throughout life. He is also described as a man who was 'not a stranger to pranks', and his sense of fun and delight in the ridiculous, 'saw him through many sticky situations'. In later life, while still enjoying a strong sense of joy and wonder, people experienced him as a man of deep humanity, understanding, compassion and wisdom, as well as a keen sense of humour.[26] Wallis's passion and ability to embrace the ideals of the 1931 Encyclical on Catholic Action and later effectively communicate the radical changes instigated by the edicts of Vatican II, his teachings and spiritual guidance from the 1930s to the 1990s, cannot be underestimated.

John Corcoran Wallis was a priest for sixty-nine years. The once shy, tall and gangly teenager who, against the odds, entered the seminary at the very young age of sixteen, grew into a man of solid stature both physically and spiritually. He was a man sometimes underestimated by his peers and at times very much on the periphery of Church life, 'going about his work' with little fuss and fanfare.

He died on 3 August 2001, aged 91, and was buried at Cornelian Bay Hobart. The John Wallis Foundation was established in 2010 by the Missionary Sisters of Service to continue the vision and mission of Father John and the Sisters. It honours the memory of this enlightened Australian priest.

Fay Woodhouse
29.09.2014

---

24 http://www.highwaysandbyways.org.au/about-john-wallis/
25 Bernadette Wallis, *Eulogy for the Vigil Liturgy for Father John C Wallis*, St Mary's Cathedral, Hobart, 7th August, 2001, p. 2, MSS Archives.
26 *Inspirations from Father John*, Mementos of John put together on the occasion of the 70th anniversary of his Ordination to the Priesthood on 18th December 1932, Missionary Sisters of Service, 2002.

Bernadette Therese Wallis was born to Don and Kathleen Wallis and is a niece of John Corcoran Wallis and granddaughter of Abraham and Emma Wallis. Born in Melbourne, Bernadette then grew up with her family on the land in the rural town of Berrigan in the Riverina, NSW.

Educated by the Presentation Sisters in Berrigan and at Mt Erin High School, Wagga Wagga, she later joined the Missionary Sisters of Service in 1965. Having worked pastorally in rural and outback parish settings of Tasmania and far-flung parishes in western NSW, she then worked with the Catholic Deaf organisation, The John Pierce Centre in Melbourne, and provided advocacy, counselling and community involvement in the Deaf community throughout Victoria. Self-published in 2016 she is the author of *The Silent Book – a Deaf Family and the Disappearing Australian-Irish Sign Language.* (Available through the Missionary Sisters of Service.)

Besides being in leadership positions and presently a director on the Stewardship Council of the Missionary Sisters of Service, Bernadette was a director of *The John Wallis Foundation* and is presently a director of *Highways and Byways – A Community of Service,* both entities having been established to work in today's world in the spirit of the Missionary Sisters of Service and Father John Wallis, the founder.

www.ingramcontent.com/pod-product-compliance
Lightning Source LLC
Chambersburg PA
CBHW080344300426
44110CB00019B/2500